Top row, from left: Baptism in Lake Maranatha; Campfires add meaningful times for singing and reflection on the day. Here, Rocky Schultz leads in a chorus.

Second row, from left: This camp sign greeted campers for years as they drove in going south of the Platte River and long before I-80; The dining hall was such an important place for visiting and enjoying meals together. The same clock that told campers it was time to line up for lunch is still operating today.

Third row, from left: A group performing on center stage; Skit time in Needham Hall; Campers on Sioux Lookout. The Indian statue was relocated to the North Platte court house lawn in the 1990s and the hill is now closed to the public.

Maranatha

The Miracle Camp
on the Plains

MARANATHA BIBLE CAMP

TURNER PUBLISHING COMPANY
NASHVILLE, TENNESSEE

Turner®
PUBLISHING COMPANY
Publishers of America's History

www.turnerpublishing.com

Turner Publishing Company Staff:
Keith R. Steele, Publishing Consultant
C.T.L. Spear, Project Consultant
Charlotte Harris, Project Coordinator
Frene Melton, Designer

Maranatha Staff:
George W. Cheek, MBC Book Editor
Tad Stryker, MBC Managing Editor

Library of Congress Control No.: 2003107325

ISBN: 978-1-68162-585-0

10 9 8 7 6 5 4 3 2 1

Table of Contents

Acknowledgements

I am very aware that in spite of our best efforts to solicit testimonials, when this book comes back from the printer, there will be those whom we discover we have overlooked. Please accept my apology in advance. Thankfully God is keeping the real and final records of service and accomplishment. In fact, the sum of your personal effort (either publicly or behind the scenes) is known only to Him.

It is said that most people during the course of life have contact with five generations — their parents and grandparents, and then the younger children and grandchildren, or nieces and nephews. A key responsibility of the middle generation is to pass on to the younger generation stories learned from the older people. Should the middle generation fail, the record of a whole generation's experiences with God and people is lost.

Part of my desire in pulling this book together is to preserve the eyewitness accounts of God at work in and through the ministry of Maranatha Camp and those who served sacrificially here.

As far as historical accuracy is concerned, we have taken a considerable amount of time and effort to research this book, which was compiled from a variety of sources, including previous interviews with Ivan & Alice Olsen, Hugh Clark and other people who have been involved with Maranatha for decades. We perused the minutes of Official Camp Board meetings, as well as letters, memos, Camp scrapbooks, written testimonies by campers and other eyewitnesses, original Camp brochures and other promotional material. We cannot verify the accuracy of all testimonies, which often are based on memories of events that occurred decades ago.

We recognize that our listings of summer staff, fulltime staff and other Camp residents in the Appendix are not complete, and we welcome written updates from readers who have information that could be used in a possible reprint of this book. Something else that would be included in a reprint is an item that has eluded me for years — a photograph of Lake Maranatha while it was under construction during 1964. I would be grateful for such a photograph, if any exist.

God has used many people to do His work at Maranatha over the years. He also has used a variety of people to produce this book, which would not be a reality if it had not been for the efforts of the following:

- Tad Stryker, director of marketing at Maranatha Camp and a fulltime staff member since 1989, did the bulk of the research, organization and writing of this book, including the main text of each chapter. Tad, who has a degree in journalism and history from the University of Nebraska-Lincoln, spent much of March, April and May 2004 in a conference room at Camp while working on this project. As you can appreciate, there were boxes of files to go through, piles of testimonies to edit and hundreds of photos to sort, as well as electronic media to utilize.

- C.T. "Lloyd" Spear is an associate of Turner Publishing, Paducah, Kentucky. He really got this project off the ground by showing me his company's ability to facilitate the production of a quality coffee table-style history book. The sample that touched me most was the New York City Fire Department history book completed just months before September 11, 2001. FDNY is now working with Turner Publishing on a new edition in an attempt to document these national heroes. Lloyd is one of Maranatha's alumni, a childhood camper who returned to Maranatha as a youth speaker for seven years. He and his wife, Sharon, are long-time friends of Maranatha. Lloyd is currently working as national church planting coordinator for Baptist Missions to Forgotten Peoples, Inc., and as his schedule allows continues to do evangelistic or revival meetings in churches.

- Faye Ward, personal secretary to Rev. Ivan E. Olsen until his death, preserved many things in the files that others might have thrown away. Estelle Hocquell, a friend and neighbor of Faye's, kept scrapbooks filled with information related to Maranatha Bible Camp and the Berean Fundamental Church in North Platte from 1932-1979. These women's efforts provided us a wealth of information to work with.

- Russ Johnston, the man who introduced me to Maranatha Bible Camp, traveled to Florida in 1989 and visited the Olsens for the express purpose of interviewing them. Together they recorded several tapes of interviews and had planned to write a book at that time. As a result, we had more than 100 pages of large print double-spaced material to work with.

- Jo Ann Beetem and Ruth Ann Rodgers (each Maranatha fulltime staff veterans of more than 20 years) worked the databases, did mailings, took phone messages and handled book orders. Pauline Tallman also did some research for the book, and in 1990, typed a transcript of Russ Johnston's tape recorded interview with the Olsens.

As his life began to draw to a close, Rev. Olsen often remarked that a book needed to be written to preserve the history of Maranatha for future generations. At one point, he decided to write it himself. He started producing handwritten outlines and ideas, but was never able to take it past that stage. He planned to call it *The Miracle Camp*, and wanted it to be "evangelistic and emotional."

"This book is not a writing, it is a telling what God did," Rev. Olsen said. When he died, some of the stories that would have been told died with him, although many stories in this book are taken directly from his sermons, church newsletter and "Pastor's Hour" teaching times at Maranatha. Thankfully, much of Maranatha's past — preserved in boxfuls of photos, letters and the memories of people who invested a portion of their lives as campers and workers — has found its way into this book, which is a narrative of how God has used a camp in an unlikely location for His purposes. May He continue to do so until Jesus Christ returns.

– George W. Cheek,
CEO, Maranatha Ministries
June 2004

The Olsens

Ever since November 1, 1936, when he first stepped into the pulpit as pastor of the fledgling Berean Fundamental Church in North Platte, Nebraska, Ivan Edwin Olsen had proven that he was not one to waste time.

The athletic young man with close-cropped hair and horn-rimmed spectacles kept up a tremendous pace, organizing the ministry, preaching on prophecy, overseeing a church building project, organizing a revival that lasted three weeks and volunteering his church to host the State of Nebraska Fundamentalist Convention.

His church's board of elders was becoming concerned. The men decided that the young pastor had been working too hard and needed a two-week vacation, to commence soon after the convention ended on July 9, 1937. They were right; Ivan had pushed himself in the suffocating heat until he was so sick he could not get out of bed. After several days of rest, he boarded a train, heading for his parents' home in Michigan's Upper Peninsula. It would be a new location for him to get used to; his parents, Harry & Dagmar Olsen, had left his boyhood home of Bergland and moved about 30 miles west to Bessemer, a small rural community near Ironwood, along the Wisconsin border.

Never a slacker, Olsen used his idle time to develop a plan. He knew that he would never be as effective as he should in ministering to the women of his church be if he remained a bachelor. As the train clacked its way north, the 23-year-old pastor decided that he would use his time off to find a wife.

It was not his first opportunity to look for a mate. Many of his parishioners had tried to play matchmaker, perhaps inviting him home for dinner after one of his long sermons on Bible prophecy. Some would mention that they had a daughter of marriageable age. Sometimes the girl was present at the table, listening to the conversation.

"I was 22 years old, and probably at least average in good looks, and when they would invite me for a meal, they would always have the one that they would imagine would make a good wife for me," he recalled. But Olsen had determined while in Bible college not to date a girl from his church, and he had been careful not to "lead anyone along at all."

As Ivan's train rolled northward, Alice Gustafson also was returning to the Upper Peninsula. Alice had finished her freshman year at Moody Bible Institute and was doing domestic work for a Chicago-area family for the summer. When the family left for a trip to Florida, Alice decided to drive back to Ironwood and see to her own family. On July 17, she and her sister Dorothy Mae took a walk from their home to the rural community of Bessemer to visit Dagmar Olsen, who by that time attended the Ironwood Swedish Baptist Church with the Gustafsons.

When the Gustafson sisters, reached the Olsen house, Alice knocked on the door. Ivan, who had arrived earlier that day, opened the door and invited them in.

This was the girl, and Ivan knew it. And Alice knew that he knew.

"He said right under his breath, 'Thank you, Lord, for showing me my wife,'" Alice recalled.

Later that evening, Ivan asked his father for permission to borrow his car and take Alice back to her house. It was the start of a two-week courtship.

"We actually became engaged before he went back to North Platte and I went back to Moody," said Alice more than 60 years later. "He said he would be sending me an engagement gift. I was telling my girlfriends at Moody that I was looking for this package. I thought it was going to be a little tiny, dainty box, but it was a big box. I opened it, and it was the biggest Scofield Reference Bible that you can get.

"We looked at one another, and one of the girls said, 'Well, what better for a future pastor's wife than to have the sword of the Lord, carrying the word of God?'"

When they parted earlier that summer, Ivan gave her an escape hatch; if she fell in love with anyone at Moody, their engagement would end. If receiving a Scofield Bible as an engagement gift had tempted her to look for other options, she never showed it. Many young men at Moody asked her for dates, but she turned them all down. She and Ivan wrote to each other every day. After originally planning a Christmas wedding, they moved up the date, and were married in Chicago on November 11, 1937, which was also Ivan's parents' wedding anniversary.

"Now sometimes you'd say that was a quick wedding," Alice recalled, "but we both felt that this was God's leading and direction, and it proved to be."

Having taken the plunge, Ivan realized he had a loose end to tie up. About two years later, he had saved enough money to buy his wife a diamond. By then, the Olsens were totally immersed in the ministries that would define most of the rest of their lives.

A decade earlier, a career in ministry was a longshot at best for Ivan, whose father, Harry, worked as a sawyer at a lumber mill in Bergland. Ivan started earning some money by carrying water for a local pool hall. Soon, he moved up to shaking dice and at age 13, started working behind the bar. By age 16, he was well established in a double life: he tended bar at dances on Saturday nights and went to the Lutheran Church on Sunday mornings at the insistence of his mother, Dagmar.

In 1931, the Olsens welcomed a new next-door neighbor. Dick Zoet was a former alcoholic who had been saved under the ministry of Dr. M.R. DeHahn in Grand Rapids. A businessman, Zoet decided to sell his real estate holdings in Grand Rapids. He donated the money to the church, moved to Bergland and became an itinerant evangelist, preaching daily in small communities around the Upper Peninsula.

Almost immediately, Zoet struck up a friendship with the 16-year-old Ivan. Three weeks later, on a Thursday night in a little school auditorium in Bergland, Ivan listened to Dick Zoet preach about the reality of hell. "I was afraid of falling into it that very night," said Ivan, "and when he asked how many wanted to be saved, I raised my hand and I was saved the very first time I heard the gospel."

Shortly afterward, Ivan got lost in a swamp while going on a fishing trip with his brothers. After wandering for some time, becoming more lonely and frightened by the minute, he prayed, telling God, "If you'll get me out of this place, I'll give my life to you."

"And you know, when I got through praying that prayer by a tree in the swamp, God told me, 'Your brothers who are fishing with you, they can't be far.'" He shouted for them, they answered, and Ivan was on his way to serving God with his life.

Almost immediately, Ivan felt God calling him to be a pastor. He briefly resisted the call, but soon "gave in" and began helping Zoet with his heavy workload. He started reading the Bible, and Zoet gave him commentaries on Daniel and Revelation, which he eagerly consumed.

At a street meeting, 16-year-old Ivan preached his first sermon on Daniel 5 ("You are weighed in the balances and found wanting"). One day he led his old employer, the proprietor of the hotel where the pool hall was located, to Jesus Christ.

"That," said Olsen, "was one of the most gratifying experiences of my life."

He wanted a Bible school education, and chose Denver Bible Institute. He cut and sold firewood to earn money for school. Before he left for Denver, he led his brothers to saving faith in Christ and encouraged his father — who had been saved at a Billy Sunday "sawdust trail" revival campaign — to rededicate his life to Jesus.

An energetic man with a hard-driving personality, Ivan eagerly sought God's will for his life. At DBI, he was encouraged to look outside the school for hands-on training. Ivan procured a free pass on the Burlington Northern Railroad, and each weekend he traveled to northwestern Colorado, where he rode on horseback to more than a dozen unchurched towns to spread the good news about Jesus. He also joined a gospel team that visited towns in the Rocky Mountains and Midwest, and one day in 1934, he and his friends found themselves stranded in a small prairie town that was locked in the dismal clutches of the Dust Bowl.

As the wind whipped over the plains and fine particles of sand and dirt stung his eyes, Ivan gritted his teeth and said, "I'm willing to go anywhere the Lord wants me to go, but with all the 48 states to serve in, I'm sure He won't call me to Nebraska!"

But when the dust cleared, Olsen had settled in North Platte. Although he eventually spent winters in Florida for health reasons, Olsen served God in Nebraska for the rest of his life. "One of my strongest convictions has been that God calls to a job and God calls to a place," he explained.

Soon almost everyone in North Platte knew that Olsen had been called. That was because he seemingly called on everyone in North Platte. He hit the road like a highly motivated salesman for Jesus Christ.

Olsen's name quickly became known in the area. He was the one who was always pushing — pushing new ideas, pushing new programs, pushing people. To those who saw the need for a revival in North Platte and the surrounding region, he was a godsend. To those who liked the status quo, he was a major source of irritation. He wasn't bashful about laying out his vision, and he recruited people to help make it happen. Once workers were enlisted, he wasn't afraid to ask them to sacrifice for the kingdom of God. One pastor refused to cooperate with Olsen, calling him a "slave driver."

An itinerant evangelist whom Olsen had called to North Platte soon found that Olsen was used to thinking big. "I've ridden more miles, spoken to more people and slept in more different beds than on any other campaign," he said.

Whatever Olsen had on his mind became the most important thing in the world for that particular day. He was impulsive, he stirred things up and he got things done.

Olsen pushed himself harder than he pushed anyone else. Within a few years, his daily schedule included running both Maranatha Camp and the Berean Church in North Platte; he often spent half the day on each ministry, usually making the 40-mile round trip in his little 1931 Chevy (which Alice wrecked quite early in their marriage as Ivan was teaching her to drive). But there were days that his other ministries demanded his attention. He started other Berean churches in Nebraska and beyond, eventually organizing them into the Berean Fundamental Church Council. Later, he learned to fly an airplane so he could visit them more efficiently, and he had a crude landing strip built on the grounds of Maranatha Bible Camp. He visited pre-Castro Cuba and spoke at gospel rallies there. He organized and led tours to the Holy Land. He founded Christian bookstores. He started a children's home in North Platte that housed orphans.

He was personally involved in all the summer Camp programs for many years, and presided at almost every evening meeting. "He was a marvelous director," recalled Hazel Johnson, the Camp nurse and dean of women in the early days of Maranatha. "I've seen him making decisions with God's help, settling disputes between campers, doing the most menial task, or taking charge of the large evening meetings with God's help so wonderfully well that I praise the Lord for leading him into this work."

Olsen was the driving force behind Maranatha Bible Camp. He was not a tall man, but he could be intimidating as he rattled off a series of orders with his raspy, high-pitched voice. He was infamous for his 5 a.m. phone calls to enlist workers for projects that had come to mind during the night. At Maranatha, no one doubted that he was the boss, but Olsen saw himself as a "young, impoverished nondescript," a "young sapling, an upstart kid," wholly unprepared for the great tasks that God had laid out for him. He pressed ahead anyway.

Fundraising was one of his greatest gifts. Olsen split his time with his various ministries, but seemingly always was involved in raising money for Maranatha, and he continued to do so after his retirement. The fundraising letter he was working on at the time of his death spoke of his desire to raise $80,000 for the Camp as "a goal I would like to accomplish in my 80th year."

Alice was always a vital part of Ivan's ministry, both at the Berean Church (where she regularly gave "sermonettes" during the morning worship service and blended her alto voice with Inez Maline's soprano) and at Camp (where she prayed with individual campers throughout her life). Alice's prayer ministry and her quiet, purposeful work were honored and respected among the churches.

Alice was pregnant with their first child during the first week of Maranatha Bible Camp in 1938. Ivan and Alice had five children — Ivan Daniel, Joy, Faith, Dwight and Precious. For much of their lives, they lived at a parsonage a few blocks west of the church in North Platte, although the family spent most of its summers at the Camp. They attended school in North Platte. In 1967, with only the youngest daughter, Pre-

cious, still left at home, Ivan and Alice moved into a house along the north shore of Lake Maranatha.

Olsen took his calling and position very seriously, and so did his contemporaries. From the beginning of his ministry, the pastor used his middle initial when referring to himself. Perhaps to account for the amazing amount of things he was involved in, Olsen sometimes referred to himself in the plural ("We feel better today than we have felt for many months" … "At 10 o'clock, we had another counseling session for 45 minutes. At 11, we conducted the morning church service and brought the message.") Even his closest friends usually called him "Rev. Olsen" or "Dr. Olsen" (in 1976 in Denver, he was awarded an honorary doctorate by his alma mater). Although he surrounded himself with men of excellent reputation and ability, he was the unquestioned leader throughout his 51-year tenure as general director.

His brothers died of heart failure, and the family history of heart trouble caught up with Ivan as well. In December 1981, he underwent quadruple bypass surgery in Kansas City and had a pacemaker installed, but characteristically, he bounced back quickly. "A complete new life was given to me," he said. Soon, he was hard at work again, although he had reduced his schedule by that time. He no longer was president of the Berean Fundamental Church Council, and he had resigned as pastor at the Berean Church in North Platte. He promoted the Camp, as well as the activities of his children. He and Alice enjoyed living in Boca Raton, Florida, during the winters, where they frequently attended and spoke at Bible conferences. It was especially convenient for them to be near their son Dwight, who had a substantial music ministry in the region.

Ivan & Alice always came north with the return of summer and lived at their home at Maranatha, but the house was only a base of operations. Even after his retirement, Olsen spent summers preaching — and usually, the topic was prophecy. He drove hundreds of miles (by then, he preferred full-size Buicks and Oldsmobiles) to fill pulpits all over the country.

Their lives took a sudden turn in 1989, when Dwight had a series of strokes. Ivan & Alice assumed guardianship of their son until he died September 14, 1991, at 50 years of age.

Although Ivan had a bout with prostate cancer in his later years, he battled through it. He had developed a nagging dry, hacking cough, but he ignored it. During the summer of 1992, he spent every Sunday preaching at churches in Nebraska, Kansas, Colorado, Wyoming and Michigan. It was as though he hadn't aged in years.

But by 1993, Ivan's pace was slowing, although he still preached many Sundays at various locations, including Bergland and Ironwood, Michigan on his annual trip to the Upper Peninsula. At age 79, he had learned to enjoy the chattering of the blackbirds outside his home. Early one June morning, he tape recorded more than 60 seconds' worth of the cacophonous chorus and played it for the entire Maranatha Summer Missions staff at its daily meeting. Although he still preached from the Scofield Reference Bible (King James Version), Ivan enjoyed reading the Living Bible together with Alice for their morning devotions. But his health was deteriorating. By the end of the summer, his kidneys were failing, and he had to take dialysis three times a week, three hours each day. He began working on a fundraising letter, saying he was determined to use that time in prayer.

Monday, September 20, 1993, was a characteristic day for Ivan Olsen. Over the weekend, he had sent some handwritten copy to his longtime secretary, 87-year-old Faye Ward, to be typed. Rising at about 5 a.m. on Monday, he drove to North Platte and stopped at her house, located a block west of the Berean Fundamental Church, to pick up her work. "He seemed so well and so urgent, in quite a hurry," Faye remembered.

Olsen hurried from appointment to appointment. One of his greatest desires at that point in his life was to help publicize a book that his daughter, Precious Atchison, had recently written. He still stirred the waters when he passed through town.

He returned home and ate dinner that evening, then began feeling worse. He spent a difficult night, and finally, about 5 a.m., he had to be taken by ambulance to the hospital in North Platte, where he died a few hours later of complications brought on by kidney failure.

His funeral was held Friday, September 24, at the Berean Fundamental Church in North Platte. Fittingly enough, it was a long service, as friends, family members and fellow pastors shared testimonies, personal stories, poems, songs and eulogies. At the close of the service, the procession went on to the North Platte Cemetery, where the remains of the visionary pastor, camp director and church planter finally were committed to the ground.

He had earned that rest.

VOICES OF MARANATHA

Growing Up At Camp

I had the privilege of spending every summer of my growing-up years at camp. I absolutely loved it. Camp was open space to explore, create, play and meet new people. From an early childhood spent in enjoying Camp as a big playground, to seasons spent serving as Camp staff member, Maranatha has always been about building and nurturing relationships.

What a honor it was for me to hear the passionate voices of people who came to stir a deeper love for Jesus. In my younger years, I remember being captivated by the storytelling of my uncle, Cliff Gustafson, that made me want to be part of God's bigger story. There was the gentle prodding of Pastor Glenn Adams with his stirring and humorous ways that communicated to my young heart. Adrian House's gracious teaching with his comfortable southern drawl made me want to live differently. I remember Russ Johnston's stories that highlighted his compelling belief in the God of the impossible. All of these colorful servants of Christ challenged me to share my faith, and to grow in a community of people who wanted to make a difference.

My father's teaching in Pastor's Hour invited me to go deeper in my study of God's word. I remember sitting in the wooden pews of the Tabernacle being so proud of him and wanting to know more about the big, generous God who my dad knew.

In that same old building where most of the meetings were held, I also remember the music. Songs like "All Hail The Power of Jesus' Name" and "Like A River Glorious" echoed beautifully off the wood-planked walls of the Tabernacle. What a taste of the heavenly choir we all experienced!

Eventually, I left home for college and marriage, but the familiar faces I looked forward to seeing year after year at Maranatha made me look forward to the beginning of camping season with great anticipation. One of my most treasured Camp relationships was with Reuben Hasenauer. He was a kind servant of God who had a beautifully simple faith. Every spring he planted flowers in the flower boxes of my family home at Camp. He was a gardener and handled the plants with gentle care. Often I would visit with him, hear his stories, and enjoy his laughter. I remember talking to Reuben the day after he found out that he had cancer. We were outside my parents' home making small talk. Then he paused and looked up at the birds in the cedars and remarked about their beautiful singing. He told me that he thought their song was so beautiful because they were so close to heaven. Reuben truly lived a sermon before all who knew him, he was a good and faithful man.

I am who I am today because my father had a dream he believed in and a wife who prayed. The people who I met and experiences I had at Camp helped to shape my passion and purpose in life today. It would be the place I would take my children to build into their hearts as well. It is a place they remember fondly and they, too, have their stories of relationships built and nurtured.

We all need rest stops along the way that refuel and refresh us on our journey of faith. I am grateful to God that Maranatha continues to be such a place.

— Precious Olsen Atchison,
Manhattan, Kansas

First Came the Vision, Then the Rolling up of Sleeves

Alice Olsen, who worked alongside her husband to found the ministry of Maranatha Bible Camp, wrote this in 2004.

It was probably the fact that my husband, Ivan Olsen, was reached for Christ at a critical stage in his own youth that gave him such a burning passion to have a camp with the mission of reaching young people.

Determined not to be discouraged by the overwhelming challenges, expenses and potential criticism connected to starting a new work of this kind, he forged ahead to find a place and the backing to help make his vision become a reality. God provided a team of people who were willing to roll up their sleeves and make the dream happen.

The fact that many people made decisions for Christ at that first Camp confirmed that God was behind my husband's vision. Maranatha Camp was finally launched, but then, more than ever, Ivan wanted to make whatever preparations were needed to provide a place that was set apart. He envisioned a place where folks could get away from the distractions of the everyday world and hear the wonderful plan that God had for their lives.

Camps were held at two other locations. After that, God provided land to be developed at Maranatha's present location. When Ivan first saw this new property that was so far off the beaten path and populated with thick groves of cedar trees, he felt that this land was sacred ground. This was a place where God would do mighty things in the hearts of people. So Maranatha Camp was built and sustained through the gifts and labor of people who wanted to be part of what God was doing there.

This vision was realized through the hands of volunteers who were willing to work in the hot Nebraska summers before air conditioning.

My husband's desire was to bring in respected speakers to challenge people to consider what God wanted in their lives. In large tents and later, in the Old Tabernacle building, surrounded by those fragrant cedar trees, folks with hungry hearts would come and respond to the offer of the free gift of salvation, and were stirred to give their hearts fully to God's service.

One of the highlights for my husband was the "Pastor's Hour" that he taught. His audience was college students brought to Camp each summer (from 1958-71) by the Navigators for training and growth. My husband loved teaching Bible doctrine and speaking to them about what he was most passionate about. It energized him even more! The students came to serve, had teachable hearts and so were eager students of the Bible. Ivan loved sharing the joys of serving the Savior and the stories of God's provision.

I remember one time when my husband led the Navigator students in prayer that God would provide beef for them all to enjoy. The kitchen seemed to have plenty of potatoes, but little meat to go with it. Beef was expensive. During one Pastor's Hour, Frank Shimmin and his sister, Jessie, drove into the Camp. They were farmers and came to tell him that, because God had so blessed them, they wanted to donate money so that all those hard-working students and Camp staff could enjoy a steak dinner. Now I'm not talking about itty-bitty steaks; these were huge!

A steak dinner may seem like a small part of what God is doing in the world, but I can tell you that there were a couple of hundred students and Camp staff who were changed by encountering the same God who transformed the lunch of a young boy into a feast that would feed the multitudes.

I was part of those Navigator camps, too. A highlight for me was to be able to spend time in individual prayer for anyone who wanted someone with whom to pray. I had open hours in the afternoons and my schedule was soon filled with meeting staff and students for prayer time. Some of the precious relationships formed in those days have continued to the present.

Ivan and I were grateful for the seasons the Navigators shared with us. We were so blessed by them, and in more ways than one. It would be through contact with one of the Navigator staff members that God would bring the person my husband would train to take over the leadership of the Camp. Russ Johnston had met a student who was interested in making camp work his career. Russ told him he needed to meet Ivan Olsen of Maranatha Bible Camp. So in 1973, that student, George Cheek, came to be trained by my husband. Ivan saw that George had an unusual passion and giftedness for camp work. After several years of working at the Camp, it became obvious to my husband that God wanted Ivan to pass the baton of leadership for the Camp to George. George's abilities made it possible for Camp to make the needed improvements that met the challenges of a changing culture without compromising the original mission of the Camp.

Camp became even more than Ivan originally envisioned it could be. It was, and is, a place where God will do a mighty work in lives of people. It is a meeting place for people to reconnect with one another and to be encouraged in their faith year after year. It is a haven of rest for people who need to get away. It is a place where men and women can meet and fall in love with Jesus (and one another). It is a place where souls are delivered from a dark eternity. It is a place where people catch the vision for God's worldwide work and want to be a part of what He is doing. Maranatha was indeed, and continues to be, holy ground, just as Ivan said it was. God shows up there and meets with people hungering and thirsting for a relationship with our soon-coming Lord.

Maranatha

Dedicated to Dr. Ivan Olsen, Founder of Maranatha Bible Camp

In the heartland of Nebraska
Near where two Platte Rivers meet;
Lies a spot of hallowed ground there;
Touched by many pilgrim feet;
For God gave a man a vision
Who would not accept defeat
And God is worshipped here.
Maranatha, Maranatha,
Heavens corner of Nebraska;
For God called and one man answered.
Now God is worshipped here.

It was way back in the thirties
When the call from God came through;
And the Olsens met the challenge;
For they knew what God could do.
May their faith inspire others;
For we've learned much from these two;
At Maranatha Camp.
Maranatha, you're a beauty;
Symbol of response to duty;
Of a dream fulfilled ne'er ending;
At Maranatha Camp.

'Neath the pines at Maranatha;
Oft decisions here were made;
That would shape a life forever;
As we studied and we prayed.
Old and Young have made commitments
As they knelt here in the shade
At Maranatha Camp.
Maranatha, you're a winner;
Gave a choice to many a sinner.
Joy and peace and love you offered;
For God is worshipped here.

Memories of Maranatha
Fill our mind, our soul, our heart;
And the treasured precious times here
That will always be a part
Of our life, though we may stray far;
Many of us got our start
At Maranatha Camp.
Maranatha, there is joy here;
Family, Friends and much we hold dear.
Love has conquered, cast out all fear;
For God is worshipped here.

— Samuel Heinrich,
Scottsbluff, Nebraska

Bless This Man

In 1971 Eugene Clark wrote a song, "Bless This Man," in tribute to Rev. Ivan E. Olsen.

Bless this man, Oh Lord, we pray!
Guide his footsteps night and day.
Grant him courage, joy and peace.
Let Thy blessings never cease,
Thank You Lord that through the years,
In the midst of toil and tears,
Thou hast kept him strong and true,
Seeking out Thy will to do,
Holding forth the Word of Life,
Standing firm in times of strife,
Trusting in Thy mighty hand,
Pressing on at Thy command.

Thank You Lord that through his days,
Thou hast filled his heart with praise,
Thou hast kept him faithfully
Pointing other men to Thee,
Helping others in their need
By a kindly word or deed;
Sharing every anxious care,
Giving of himself in prayer.
Bless this man, Oh Lord, we plead!
In the past Thou hast indeed!
Make his future life to be
Like incense rising up to Thee.

— Eugene L. Clark

They Took Me Into Their Home

I have so many memories of Maranatha, as that was where I gave my life to the Lord and was baptized when I was 14.

Rev. and Mrs. Olsen took me into their home and family when I was 16.

During the summer, I worked in the snack shop. In fact the money from the snack shop helped to pay my way to Moody Bible Institute where I met my husband, Millard, who was ordained at Maranatha.

Our three sons and I spent many weeks during the summer at Maranatha.

So many great men of God spoke at Maranatha, such as Dr. Harry Ironside, Kenneth Wuest, and many missionaries.

I feel so blessed to have spent part of my life there at Maranatha.
— Love in Christ,
Marie Hudnall Sall,
Temecula, California

Marie Hudnall (left)
with Judy Clark in 1950.

Being Raised as One of the Founder's Daughters

Camp meant many things to me. I have fond memories of my dad and mom letting me have slumber parties and bringing my girlfriends out to camp on a Friday night in the winter and to be campers for a week during the summer. I thank the Lord that early my dad and mom gave me the vision to win lost souls by reaching out to my friends at school and exposing them to Jesus Christ by ways such as coming to church and Camp.

My dad was one of the trailblazers of "cross training," what many huge companies today have found great success in doing in the workplace with their employees.

Just to name a few jobs I worked at through my growing up years on into my married life was: in the sweet shop, the bookstore, as the lifeguard at the pool after I came back from college and had gotten my Red Cross lifesaving certificate, did town run, assigning the Camp staff their job assignments and following up with them until the job got completed, working on setting up the menus, getting food and supplies ordered, etc. I have a distinct memory of myself and my dad driving through the Campgrounds; he would see the big picture and give me the job assignments of things that needed to be done and I would assign them to the Camp staff. My husband and I worked on staff the first two summers after our marriage while going to Calvary Bible College and Western Bible Institute (now Colorado Christian University) in Denver.

One summer I went through the Navigator Training Program, which was a five-week intensive program. I learned a great deal about the importance of consistent quiet time with the Lord, memorizing God's word, knowing how to witness to unbelievers and of a good work ethic. I so loved going out onto the Campgrounds and sitting on a picnic table or a log and spending time alone with the Lord. The Camp provided an excellent haven for getting to know the Lord better. Those five weeks I worked on the dish crew in the dining hall. We also learned how to use the 4 Spiritual Laws tool in our witnessing.

I have two classmates in particular from school who have come back to me and thanked me so much for my reaching out to them and inviting them to Camp, where they heard the gospel. Camp was just one of the many seeds planted in their lives that brought them to a saving knowledge of Christ. In fact my mother, the co-founder of Maranatha, was able to lead one of them to the Lord on a sleepover I had one Friday night.

I remember many services in the Old Tabernacle and decisions for Christ that I made there. I count it a privilege to have been exposed to many guest speakers. I remember my Uncle Cliff Gustafson and how he preached what we used to call "hellfire and brimstone" type of sermons. Its concept of "scaring people straight" that is used today to try to connect prisoners to juvenile delinquents to get them to turn around and stop breaking the law. They tell them just what prison is like. Well my uncle told us just what hell would be like and many of us kids knew we did not want to go there after hearing the vivid descriptions he would tell us in his sermons. My Uncle Cliff led many children to the Lord at Camp.

I remember my dad's prophetic sermons that he preached during the training hour each day in the Old Tabernacle during the Navigator training programs and how so many of the college students from all around the United States were for the first time given the meat of God's word that would mature them in Christ.

My dad saw the vision of using the Camp grounds to the fullest by renting them out to other Christian organizations and churches, a vision which George Cheek has carried on and expanded to this day. One of my job responsibilities on summer staff was to walk around the grounds with one of the rental group's leaders prior to the week beginning and assess the condition of the dorms and then walk around at the end of their rental week and assess any damage that had been done that the rental group needed to pay to have fixed.

After I got married and had my two sons, one week my family volunteered to do dishes during a Hmong Camp week when they would have so many hundreds of campers that they would even have to get large Army tents to house them in. We worked on the dish crew in the new Dining Hall that week. The Hmongs cook with a hot spice that creates very strong fumes when the pots are washed with hot water. The fumes got into our eyes and made them burn. That is a memory our family will not soon forget! We are able to laugh about it today as a memory to put into our scrapbook of ways in which we were able to help out the camp as a volunteer. I am excited to see the way the volunteer program has developed with seniors sharing their gifts with the younger generation. I have memories of many people sacrificially volunteering their time to, for example, build a cabin like my Uncle Eldon Sandin did.

Our two sons loved coming to camp and experiencing what their Grandpa and Grandma had allowed the Lord to use them to do for Him at Camp Maranatha. Truly a godly heritage was passed from one generation to the next. I praise the Lord that it truly was and is God's work because when you take the founder and first director out of the picture and it still continues and grows by reaching the next generations where they are at with what excites them to come for a week at Camp to hear the gospel and see that Christians can have fun too, that can only be a work of God and not of a single man.

I know as a little girl the lifeguards had their hands full with myself, my sisters and my cousins wanting to swim all of the time. We hated when it was the boys' turn to swim. (SMILE) I remember one time when my cousins were at Camp when Uncle Cliff was the speaker and we had a mock wedding while we were playing. So Camp Maranatha provided lots of fond memories throughout my childhood on into my adult life and still today. My husband and I had the privilege to attend one of the Couples' Conferences a couple of years ago, so the ministry continues to affect our lives today.

My husband, Steve, was able to lend a helping hand for two weeks one fall and volunteer to do the drywall in the current director, George Cheek's new home on the lake. He was richly blessed by the opportunity to serve the Lord in this way. To show you that you cannot out give God by giving of two weeks out of your life, when he came home, the Lord exploded his drywall business and gave him so much work he needed to hire one of our sons to come and work with him. My family praises the Lord for what God is continuing to do at Maranatha Bible Camp.

– Faith Eppler,
Gardner, Kansas

Nature provides beautiful settings around the lake. At left is a blue heron, and at right are geese.

Top row, from left: Ivan and Alice Olsen in the early 1960s; Alice Olsen speaks during the 1995 Ladies' Retreat.

Second row, from left: Ivan Olsen at Denver Bible Institute, where often on weekends, he would travel by rail and horseback to preach at churches in 13 rural Colorado communities; Ivan and Alice Olsen sent this greeting card to many of their friends shortly after being married in November 1937.

Third row, from left: Alice Olsen with Joy, Ivan Daniel, Faith and Precious after Rev. Olsen's death in September 1993; Pastor Ivan Olsen often had a Scofield Reference Bible in his hand; Dwight Olsen became well-known for his musical skills, especially as an organist.

Fourth row, from left: Alice Olsen leads in prayer during a banquet held in the Maranatha gymnasium October 1994; One of the last times Ivan Olsen and Hugh Clark saw each other (this side of Heaven) was a banquet at Maranatha in 1990; Ivan and Alice Olsen in 1992; Ivan Olsen's parents, Harry and Dagmar Olsen of Bergland, Michigan.

Greetings in Christ Jesus
Rev. and Mrs. Ivan E. Olsen

Top row, from left: Letter of congratulations; From left: Dr. Olsen, Paul Whaley, Leonard Leigh, Hazel Leigh, Georgianna Lindquist, Hilda Visser Hall, Clyde Shaffstall. All but Georgianna and Clyde were 1936 graduates of Denver Bible Institute. (Photo taken early 1980s)

Second row, from left: A family photo at the 50th wedding anniversary celebration, summer 1987. From left: Dwight Olsen, Ivan Daniel Olsen, Ivan E. and Alice Olsen, Marie Hudnall Sall, Joy Lucht, Faith Eppler and Precious Atchison; The "Olsen tribe" gathered at Camp to celebrate Ivan and Alice Olsen's 50th wedding anniversary.

Third row, from left: Alice Olsen's sister, Marian, married Eldon Sandin at Maranatha in 1949. It was the first wedding ever held at the Camp; Fifty years later, they celebrated their anniversary along with their children, Eugene (at right) and Beth Ann and husband, Richard Rodriguez.

15

Beginnings: The First Six Years

Ivan E. Olsen had a lot on his mind during the autumn of 1937. Having been hired a year earlier as pastor of the newly-formed Berean Fundamental Church of North Platte, Nebraska, he already had established a vigorous routine. Even though his church had fewer than 50 members and North Platte had fewer than 15,000 inhabitants, Olsen had big ideas. He had revival meetings to organize, sermons to prepare, people to visit, workers to recruit and a hundred other things to do, including preparing for his own wedding.

Even with all that on his agenda, something else kept burning in his heart. He wanted to start a Bible camp. It kept perking in his mind, keeping him restless, even after he married Alice Gustafson in November.

Rev. Olsen had grown up on the Upper Peninsula of Michigan where he worked in a pool hall before accepting Jesus Christ as his savior as a teenager. He attended Bible college in Denver, where he began to discover methods of reaching people for Christ. He was impressed by what he had read about the Winona Lake, Indiana, and Gull Lake, Michigan, conference grounds and was convinced that God wanted him to start something similar in west central Nebraska.

"My husband was burdened all winter," recalled Alice. "He said 'We need a Bible camp.' I don't know if there were any Bible camps in Nebraska; we didn't know of any at the time."

Finally, "when I couldn't carry the burden alone any longer," Ivan decided to share it with some trusted friends. He mailed one of the elders of his church, Hugh Clark, and asked him to pray. Neither had ever seen a Bible camp, but both believed that the young people of Nebraska and the surrounding region needed the opportunity.

Precisely who made Olsen's "inner circle" at first is unclear. It is almost certain that Olsen called Clark and another friend, Nick Janzen, a Mennonite wheat farmer who pastored churches in the small communities of Madrid and Roscoe, to join him and Alice for a prayer meeting on Tuesday, March 15, 1938. There are written references by Ivan Olsen that at least one more man (possibly John Goodmanson, an elder in the Berean Fundamental Church at North Platte) may have been in the original prayer meeting, but Alice Olsen, in a March 1997 interview, said that it was only four people — herself, Rev. Olsen, Clark and Janzen. Their meeting place also is uncertain. It was likely at 309 W. 7th Street in North Platte, but possibly in Olsen's small office at the Berean Church at 202 W. 8th St. The uncertainty is due to the fact that apparently no one bothered to write down anything at the time. No written record of the March 15 meeting is known to exist, but the Olsens referred to that date verbally and in writing so often throughout their lives that its accuracy is almost certain.

Alice Olsen placed the original prayer meeting in the former location, the home of Nellie Lantz, a widow who lived with her grandson. Nellie was convinced of the need for a solid Bible-preaching church in the community. She let the Olsens live rent-free for nine years at her house, located about a block from the church building.

"We met for this prayer meeting and asked God to direct us, in first of all, getting a place to have the camp, and a date to have the camp," said Alice. "The prayer meeting was very significant, because there were specific things that Rev. Olsen said: 'We want a place where young folks can hear the gospel and respond to the gospel, and a place where they can be taught the word of God and be challenged to give their lives to serve the Lord.'"

The next month, on April 26, 1938, the group met again, with several new members attending, and began acting as a board of directors. At that meeting, Hugh

Clark began keeping handwritten notes, a practice he would continue for all meetings of the board and its various committees until 1949, when the secretary job fell to others.

The first thing on the agenda was naming the camp. Clark moved for the use of "Maranatha Bible Camp." Janzen seconded the motion, and it was approved. (No one knew at the time that a camp using the Maranatha name had been launched in Michigan the previous year.) They moved right into the election of officers and the setting of fees.

It was obvious that the Olsens and their inner circle, plus friends from other area churches, were of one heart and mind in this matter. And so, with a Holy Spirit-sized burr under his saddle, and with encouragement from his wife and a group of friends from several area churches, a 23-year-old pastor started Maranatha Bible Camp. He had no clear idea of how it would work; he just knew it needed to be done. The details could be worked out later. Doing what God wanted him to do — that was the main thing.

Once Olsen reached a decision about almost any topic, any course of action, it typically became a consuming passion in his life, at least for a short amount of time. But this passion was bigger than any other that would come along for Rev. Ivan E. Olsen, and it would never die out.

"More than ever, Ivan wanted to make whatever preparations were needed to provide a place that was set apart," said his wife. "He envisioned a place where folks could get away from the distractions of the everyday world and hear the wonderful plan that God had for their lives."

The first campsite was a cottonwood grove along the Platte River on the property of Ralph Talbot, about six miles southeast of North Platte. At least 33 campers (30 of them were registered fulltime) and 13 adult leaders gathered from Monday, June 6, through Monday, June 13, 1938.

"Devotions, Bible study, music, lectures and sports will fill the campers' days," said a story in the June 7, 1938, North Platte Daily Bulletin. "A nurse will be on the camp grounds to render first aid if necessary." Even so, two campers had to go home due to illness before the week was out.

The first session was a campfire service the night of Monday, June 6. At least 50 people gathered around the large fire. Hazel Johnson, the Camp nurse and superintendent of women, was so impressed that she decided to keep a record of what God would accomplish during the week. "On the opening evening of camp many guests from North Platte and neighboring towns were present," she wrote. "A huge camp fire lighted up the scene, revealing the camp with its tents, cook shack, trees, benches, etc. Rev. Ivan E. Olsen led in the opening meeting. As the fading twilight in the west lent beauty to the scene, we believe that God in heaven was pleased as He looked down upon the happy hearts bowed in reverence to Him.

"Choruses were sung, testimonies given, and camp officers introduced: the get-acquainted-service will long be remembered. The closing chorus expressed the thought of every heart:

Just one day nearer home, when shadows of the night descend.

Just one day less to roam, when fading twilight colors blend.

Beneath that starry dome, I rest beside my Guide and Friend.

With each day's tramping, nightly camping; one day nearer home."

The campers (they were teenagers for the most part, although a few were in their 20s) stayed in a variety of borrowed tents and sang along every morning as Ivan's younger brother, Lloyd Olsen, led music to the accompaniment of an old upright piano that had been loaded onto Janzen's flatbed truck. Speakers also used the truck bed as a platform. Campers heard Rev. Merle Lefever of the First Baptist Church in Maxwell challenge them about getting involved in missions work worldwide. They took classes on prophecy (taught by Janzen) and on errors in religious systems (taught by Lloyd Olsen).

When the weather was clear, they enjoyed meals and teaching sessions on picnic tables under the cottonwoods. The meals were cooked in a shack framed with 2x4s and covered with canvas and cardboard. The campers endured rain at least once every day that week. When it rained, they had their meals and meetings in a funeral tent borrowed from Maloney, Cox & Kuhns Morticians, who said they would be out to get it if they needed it, but it was a slow week for deaths in North Platte; Maloney, Cox & Kuhns had no customers to bury while Maranatha was using the tent.

It was a good week for eternal life. Olsen and his team envisioned a weeklong revival service in the wilderness, and to that end, they recruited speakers, including Rev. W.C. Anderson of the Free Mission Church in Gothenburg, and Rev. Clifton L. Fowler, president of Denver Bible Institute, a mentor of Rev. Olsen. It was Fowler who originally suggested that Olsen use the name "Maranatha," based on 1 Corinthians 16:22.

On Saturday, many campers and adults rode into town on Janzen's truck and held a street meeting, attracting a large crowd with trumpet and organ music. "Several were saved then and there on the street corner," reads the account of the First Annual Session.

There were many salvation decisions among the campers as well, and the Camp leadership gave thanks to God for the encouraging results. On Sunday, Rev. Olsen held a baptismal service in the Platte River for 20 candidates (including his brother Lloyd, whose name was omitted from the original roll of campers and staff, but was immortalized in Hazel Johnson's recap as the best flapjack eater in the Camp). Janzen and Lefever assisted with the baptismal service.

Swimming was a popular pastime during the first week of Camp (the campers were driven to a sandpit a short distance away where Ivan Olsen served as lifeguard), but baseball proved to be the biggest hit. The married men defeated the unmarried men 2-1 and the married women bested the unmarried women 18-6. The losers demanded rematches the next summer, and a longstanding Camp tradition was born.

It didn't take long for the first Camp pranks to occur. "Ask Charlie (Smith) if it pays to run away from doing dishes!" reads an entry in Hazel Johnson's recap, which also chronicles Wyatt Beauchamp's embarrassing pratfall when he was caught trying to snitch some food.

Lyle Carper, an elder in the North Platte Berean Church, had installed crude water pumps and outhouses at the site. Determined to keep things in order, he prowled to "rid the camp ground of nightly disturbances."

Despite sunburns, windstorms and piles of soggy bedding, the First Annual Encampment was judged a resounding success, and the leaders eagerly made plans for the following year. Feeling a bit crowded on the Talbot place, they decided to move the whole enterprise a few miles east to a lovely grove of elm trees along the Platte River. The site, owned by Harold Bockus, was just north of the U.S. Post Office at the now-defunct settlement of Bignell.

Attendance increased to 44 campers in 1939 and to 76 in 1941 at the Bignell site. By now, it was time to stop borrowing equipment each year, so Olsen organized his first Maranatha fundraiser and Hugh Clark used the proceeds to buy canvas and lumber for long, narrow dormitory tents. Eventually, volunteers built other outbuildings (on skids, since they were using borrowed land). Much of the work was done in the spring of 1940, when men from North Platte and Maxwell took Janzen's flatbed truck on two trips to Colorado to obtain cheap "slab" lumber to build a 14-by-72-foot dining room and kitchen.

"Inclement weather does not interfere," claimed the 1941 brochure. Generally, that was true, although heavy thunderstorms sometimes sent unwelcome streams of water inside the tents.

Theodore Epp, director of the Back to the Bible Broadcast in Lincoln, was introduced to Maranatha in May 1940 and was a speaker at Camp that summer. He became a board member and a 35-year relationship was launched. In 1941, Maranatha offered two programs (one for children and one for teens) and attendance jumped dramatically to 276 as "The Musical Family" — Rev. Sam Becker, along with his wife Ella and preschool-age daughter Darlene — played the guitar and marimba, gave object lessons and told stories. The Beckers would direct the Children's Camp for 15 years. Ernest Lott, who would be closely involved with Maranatha until his death more than 50 years later, began serving as director of music in 1943.

Maranatha Bible Camp was expanding, both in numbers and influence. During the early 1940s, more than 25 different church denominations were represented at Maranatha. The economy was starting to recover from the iron grip of the Great Depression, farmers in the area were feeling optimistic; many were providing chickens and garden vegetables for the Camp. More and more people were volunteering to work during the summer encampments. The work was hard, but Maranatha seemed to be settling into a happy routine. Still, Olsen was restless. He knew that things couldn't go on much longer as they were.

VOICES OF MARANATHA

Riding Lester Kittle's Pickup to Camp

The following was submitted by an early camper and longtime Maxwell resident, whose children and grandchildren also attended Maranatha:

I remember riding in the back of Lester Kittle's pickup to Camp, where we attended services and played games. People from Kansas also arrived in farm trucks using straw bales as their seats. Later on, beds were made from planks with straw between them and with canvas stretched across them. Everything was held in tents.

The first building was the dining hall. Then they built the tabernacle. The most popular building was the Sweet Shop. Camp ran from Monday noon till Saturday noon. They had Sunday afternoon services before World War II with big name speakers such as John R. Rice and Bill Rice.

Mrs. Krause and Mrs. Hugh Clark would call churches to supply the staff and food for one day during the week for each camp. After the War, they furnished the dormitories with beds and cots from World War II prison camps.

Rev. Olsen came to Lester Kittle and my father-in-law, Frank Christensen, concerning financing. They mortgaged their own property to get Dr. Olsen the money needed to purchase the land where Camp is presently located.

– Enid Christensen

Prayer Meetings, Not 'Pair' Meetings

Although Maranatha Bible Camp strove to provide recreational activities that were "second to none," from the very beginning, the founders were determined to emphasize Bible teaching and the worship of Jesus Christ.

Their main goal was to train young men and women who would serve Christ with their lives. The first promotional flyer included an excerpt from Ecclesiastes 12:1 — "Remember now thy Creator in the days of thy youth." The stakes were high. "Modernism," a collection of loosely related humanistic philosophies which held that the Bible was not necessarily the literal word of God, had sprung up in Europe in the 19th century and was spreading throughout the United States, making its presence felt even in churches that had been considered "fundamental." Rev. Olsen and the other families who started Maranatha strongly believed that no compromise with the enemies of Jesus Christ was to be tolerated. If it were to err, the Camp would err on the side of caution (some called it legalism).

By the 1939 camping year, Maranatha had published its "constitution" as follows:

I. DOCTRINE
We believe in:
The triune God: Father, Son and Holy Spirit
The plenary inspiration of the Bible
The Depravity of man
Salvation by faith through the Blood of Christ
The literalness of heaven and hell
The premillenial second-coming of Christ
The world-wide obligation to missions
A closed door to all forms of modernism and fanaticism

II. CONDUCT
Ladies: The camp shall ever require the girls to wear no modern interpretations of men's clothing; no exceptions to this considered. Deut. 22:5
Men: The use of tobacco, intoxicants or profanity will be strictly prohibited. Violations must be disciplined.
General: Mixed bathing will not be tolerated. Prayer meetings will be encouraged, pair-meetings discouraged.
If at any time the above doctrines and principles be no longer maintained, the properties and possessions of this fellowship are to be sold and given to Faith Institutions which hold to the same views which are advanced in this constitution.
In 1941, the slogan, "In Essentials — Unity. In Non-Essentials — Liberty. In All Things — Charity," was added to the Camp literature.

"The Bible is given pre-eminence, vacationing and recreation are secondary," read a Camp folder a few years later.

Emphasis on Bible teaching, its application to daily life and Christian service has been the hallmark of Maranatha since its inception. Over the years, Camp leadership took care to keep the focus on those issues, but distractions were inevitable. The kids who came to Maranatha were every bit as human as those who attended other camps.

Defining which clothing styles were appropriate was a controversial issue throughout the 20th century. Christian organizations in general and Maranatha Bible Camp in particular were no exception. Maranatha board meeting minutes over the years reveal a gradual change in policy regarding the dress of campers. In 1946, a proposal to allow women and girls to wear slacks during recreation was not approved by the Maranatha executive board; it was not allowed until the early 1960s. As late as 1967, the Camp brochure specified that boys and girls would not be allowed to swim together ("mixed bathing"). Campers could not wear shorts or cutoffs until the late 1960s. Maranatha policy changed as social norms changed and as the Camp's board decided that they were non-essentials of the faith. Some wondered if Maranatha had been locked in a time warp; others were dismayed at how "liberal" the Camp was becoming.

By the end of the 20th century, Maranatha had changed significantly in how it regulated camper conduct. Pets, fireworks, alcoholic beverages and weapons were banned for everyone, and smoking was prohibited in Camp buildings. Youth and children were forbidden to bring electronic music devices to Camp. "Clothing shall be neat, clean, non-revealing, free of obscene or offensive printing and appropriate for the activity in which the camper is participating," a policy passed by the Camp board in 1981, was the standard for campers of either gender.

In the early 1990s, there was debate at Maranatha as to whether the Summer Missions staff should be allowed to wear shorts while on the job. The debate later focused on whether male Summer Missionaries should be allowed to wear earrings while on duty. Maranatha leaders chose to emphasize the inner life, not the outer appearance, of their staff, mandating that Camp staff should help create an atmosphere that draws attention to Jesus Christ, not themselves, and dealt with questionable cases on an individual basis.

– Tad Stryker

The People of Maranatha: Hugh Clark

If Ivan Olsen was the propulsion behind Maranatha Bible Camp, Hugh Clark was the transmission, channeling Olsen's vision into reality. God used Clark's mind and hands to build the Camp's tangible assets, including many of the major buildings.

A tall, lean man with a soft, low-pitched voice and a seemingly endless capacity for hard work, Clark was a hallmark of stability and durability, a strong base of operations for the emerging parachurch organization.

Hugh Clark was born in a sod house in 1905, midway through the Theodore Roosevelt administration. His parents were Christian farmers who took Hugh to church and Sunday school regularly. He was educated in a country school. He lived on the site of the abandoned Ft. McPherson (formerly a U.S. Army outpost located about a mile southeast of present-day Ft. McPherson National Cemetery) and recalled playing at the military dumping ground, where he found discarded items like horseshoes and whiskey bottles.

At age 11, Hugh went to an evangelistic meeting and accepted Jesus Christ as his Savior. He graduated from Maxwell High School and stayed in the North Platte area. He married Lela Beauchamp, and they started a family. Early in his marriage, Clark showed that Jesus Christ occupied first place in his life.

By the early 1930s, he perceived the Baptist church that the Clark family attended was "drifting away from the early doctrines of the church." He was at a crisis point in his life.

After much prayer, Hugh Clark decided that he would "stay true to the God of the Bible," and he backed his decision with a lifetime of prayer, giving and work.

The Clarks and four other families decided to start another church, which they called the Church of the Open Bible (because it was being confused with a charismatic ministry of a similar name, they soon changed it to Berean Fundamental Church). Hugh and the other men took turns preaching. Hugh also served as Sunday school superintendent at the church until 1956.

The church members soon decided that they needed a fulltime pastor. They selected Ivan E. Olsen, a graduate of Denver Bible Institute, who also proved to have a seemingly unending supply of administrative energy.

Olsen had a tremendous desire to start a Bible camp, and Clark was quick to jump onboard. He was there during the prayer meeting on March 15, 1938, when Maranatha Bible Camp was born (he served as secretary of the Maranatha board for more than a decade). Over the next three months, Clark and a small group of committed Christians from several denominations worked out the logistics of setting up the first week of camp. The properties consisted mainly of borrowed tents and equipment set up at the Ralph Talbot farm southeast of North Platte.

The group puzzled over how to prepare three meals a day for several dozen campers over a week's time.

"We didn't have any place to do our cooking, so we took a stove out there and built a cardboard shack for it, to keep it clean. That's the way we did the cooking for the first camp," said Clark. His wife was head cook in the "cardboard kitchen" during the First Annual Encampment.

In 1939, Maranatha Bible Camp was held on the Harold Bockus farm. After that summer, the Camp leadership agreed that borrowing equipment for the growing ministry was not practical anymore, so in the spring of 1940, Hugh built dormitory tents (10-by-64-foot creations of dimension lumber, covered with canvas). He made double-size beds from lumber and stretched woven hog wire across each frame to support a straw tick. The campers were impressed.

"They were pretty rough beds, but they liked them anyway," Clark said.

The demands of the new ministry were growing. Back in North Platte, Clark was a machinist at the Union Pacific Railroad. In that, he was no different than many other residents of the blue-collar town, but soon Clark's 40-hour-a-week job started to seem like a sideline. His supervisors and co-workers started to wonder about Clark when he passed up promotions so he could put in more time volunteering for the Camp and the Berean Church.

"After awhile, I was putting in more unpaid hours than paid hours," Hugh said. "Somebody had to take ahold of the work and get it done, and that was my job. If I could get somebody to help me, I did."

Clark's work was vital at Maranatha. Olsen usually recognized his own shortcomings when it came to anything dealing with building construction or machinery. He trusted Clark completely and depended upon him to carry out much of the physical work of the ministry. A sensible, practical man, Clark saw Maranatha as an instrument to help bring boys and girls to Jesus Christ and train them for service. He was grateful to be part of what he perceived could be an effective ministry team.

The team leader, Olsen, had strong opinions about nearly every topic, including where buildings should be located and how it should be done. Clark respected Olsen from the beginning, but it wasn't simply a matter of Olsen giving the orders and Clark carrying them out. The lanky farmer-turned-railroader sometimes disagreed with his younger friend's strategies and pointed out a better plan — especially when it involved how to build something.

"Pastor Olsen was a great man and a good minister," said Clark. "I worked with him for years. We never had any problems between us. If I wanted to do something, why he just backed off, because he didn't want to get in the way. So, I think that's one of the reasons we did so well working together, because he knew where he had his limit, and he'd depend on me to finish the job."

His building skills were put to the test after the purchase of the permanent site in 1944. From then on, the projects were many. Clark was involved in constructing many of the permanent buildings, and he planned and built the swimming pool in 1954.

Clark was a builder who often had to press forward under financial limitations with a skeleton work force, using the most basic of tools and materials. It didn't seem to bother him in the least.

"It was a good thing we did it when we had a chance," the Maranatha patriarch said in a 1995 interview. "So many times, we don't have jobs that God gives us to do that was so specific as this one was, but I was very happy that God chose me to work with Pastor Olsen.

"I can't understand why God used me in his work. I was just a farm boy, really, and I didn't have too much on the ball, so to speak, so I thought so many times, 'Why did God pick me out and use me on these jobs?' I'm glad that He did, of course, but I don't understand yet why. I think the Lord kept me alive so I could serve Him in different areas."

Hugh moved on to another area of service in 1956, when he left North Platte and moved to Lincoln to work in the accounting office at Back to the Bible. He began attending the newly-formed Lincoln Berean Church, and helped it grow into a flourishing ministry while serving as treasurer. He remained on the Maranatha Camp board until his retirement in 1988, having served 50 years. One of his last meetings with Olsen came at a banquet at Maranatha in October 1990.

As his physical condition began to deteriorate, Clark's ministry continued as he prayed for Maranatha, along with many churches, missionaries and family members who were never away from his thoughts for long.

Hugh Clark died in Lincoln on January 10, 1998. He was buried in Plainview Cemetery, just southwest of Maranatha Bible Camp's present location.

"Hugh Clark was a very humble, quiet-mannered man, gentle in spirit, strong in the Lord, faithful in prayer and to the service of his Savior," wrote Hugh's grandson Bryan, who became pastor of Lincoln Berean Church and officiated at his grandfather's funeral. "He leaves a rich legacy."

– Tad Stryker

Hugh and Lela Clark were instrumental in the founding and development of Maranatha. Hugh built many of the Camp buildings and was on the board. Lela served in the Camp kitchen for many years.

The People of Maranatha: Hazel Johnson

Hazel Johnson loved working with children and helping build the foundations for spiritual growth in their lives, so when the opportunity arose for her to take part in the first year of a new camp ministry, she eagerly accepted.

A teacher at Denver Bible Institute, Hazel was one of several people from Ivan Olsen's alma mater who helped launch the ministry of Maranatha Bible Camp. Lloyd Olsen, Ivan's brother and himself a D.B.I. student in 1938, alerted Hazel to the plans for a new

Camp in Nebraska and sharing the broad vision for bringing young people to Christ. Delighted, Hazel wrote Ivan Olsen to get more details. She soon secured the position of dean of women, taking responsibility for the oversight of the female counselors and discipline of the girls at Camp. She would also serve as Camp nurse.

Hazel Johnson was someone who wanted to make things a little nicer than she found them. Wouldn't the Camp be more meaningful if it had its own song? She pursued the idea, consulting Florence E. Jones, a musical arranger and instructor who also accompanied the choir at D.B.I. Hazel wrote the lyrics and Florence composed the music with some help from her husband, Jesse, a professor at D.B.I. The result was the "Maranatha Camp Song," which was finished more than a month before the First Annual Encampment.

At least three other songs were written for Maranatha Bible Camp, including "Maranatha (Our Lord Cometh)" by James E. Spong for the Camp's 25th anniversary in 1963 and a pair of choruses by Ronald Winstanley: "Maranatha March" and "Maranatha Melody." (Winstanley wrote "Maranatha Melody" in 1964 while serving as a missionary in Bolivia.) Ultimately, the "Maranatha Camp Song" by Johnson and Jones was the most widely used at Camp.

As Hazel and the contingent from D.B.I. drove into the Talbot farm in June 1938, the beauty of the scene enchanted her, although she was surprised at its starkness.

"I love this!" she thought as she looked at the cottonwoods and the Platte River flowing by the clearing, which already had its own crude baseball diamond. However, she was puzzled.

"The only building I saw was a small shed constructed of rough boards and even cardboard," Hazel recalled 50 years later. "There were tents scattered around, but no dining room, no place in which to meet … and no dispensary. How could we get along without them?! We did get along, and after a day or two of Camp, we didn't even miss them.

"The tent space where I slept became the dispensary. We ate outdoors on constructed tables and sat on benches. We thoroughly enjoyed the luscious food served from that little shed, near which the tables were placed."

While the young people were in a missionary class, Hazel taught another class (on teacher training and child study) to the adults.

Her written account of the First Annual Encampment, including a humorous poem, " 'Twas the First Night of Camp," is a valuable source of information about the Camp's beginnings.

Hazel Johnson was an important member of the Maranatha leadership team and was the only woman listed as such on the Camp literature in the early years. She took part in several board meetings in the 1940s and was appointed associate editor of "Maranatha Camp Echoes," a mimeographed newsletter published every few months throughout the year, and daily during certain summer Camp weeks. Eventually, she and her husband, Harry, moved to Seattle. After their move, Hazel taught in other Bible camps in Washington, but she stayed involved with Maranatha for some time.

"I praise the Lord for the influence this Camp has had on the lives of young people all through the Midwest," she wrote in 1988. "As it continues its ministry, I will continue to pray for Maranatha Bible Camp."

THE DENVER BIBLE INSTITUTE

CLIFTON L. FOWLER
PRESIDENT EMERITUS
ARVEL S. PAYNE
VICE PRESIDENT

WM. J. GIRVIN
SECRETARY
JESSE R. JONES
TREASURER
C. REUBEN LINDQUIST
DEAN—BUS. MGR.

TWENTY · FORTY · SEVEN · GLENARM · PLACE · DENVER · COLORADO

May 3, 1938

Dear Ivan:

Happy indeed am I to be able to be with you in the work of the Maranatha Bible Camp. Children's and Young People's work has always interested me intensely and even more so this year since I have been teaching a class in children's work.

My delay in writing you has been because there has been a possibility that I might have to return home to care for my mother while my sister is in the hospital. It now looks, however, as though I will not be needed.

I would like to know more about the morning class work. How many classes and what subjects you would want me to teach. Would you want any hand-work?

I appreciate your invitation to ride to North Platte with you and Alice and am glad to accept it.

How would you like a Maranatha Camp Song? Thinking that perhaps you would be favorable, I wrote the words to a song and Mrs. Jones wrote the music. I am sending you a copy for you to accept or reject as you deem best. Lloyd suggests that if you use it, you do not let anyone around there hear it but keep it new for the Bible camp.

Last evening Lloyd and I discussed the rules of the camp but we hardly know enough details of your plans to formulate any, so we thought that you and Mr. Goodmanson would have to draw them up or else wait until we get together at commencement time.

I am looking forward with happy anticipation to a week chuck full of work for the Lord with the blessing which always follows labor enthusiastically given.

Remember me to Alice.

In His Precious Name,

Hazel M Johnson

(Mrs. H. J. Johnson)

Rev. Ivan E. Olsen
309 West Seventh Street
North Platte, Nebraska

Mornings could be chilly at Camp. Hazel Johnson, the dean of women and author of the "Maranatha Camp Song" is standing at the far left. Bethel Armstrong is the young girl seated, third from left.

First Annual Session of the Maranatha Bible Camp
North Platte, Nebraska
June 6-13, 1938

Camp Directors:
Rev. Ivan E. Olsen, Chairman
Rev. N.P. Jansen, Assistant Chairman
Mr. Hugh Clark, Secretary and Treasurer

Camp Roll Call:

Mr. Herbert Sivits, North Platte
Miss Vera Hendricks, Wellfleet
Miss Alma Suller, Paxton
Miss Marilyn Hunt, North Platte
Miss Alberta Craven, Roscoe
Mrs. Harry Most, Roscoe
Miss P. Combe, North Platte
Mr. Charles Smith, North Platte
Mr. Daniel Lefever, Maxwell
Mr. Clarence Clark, North Platte
Miss Ethel Johnson, Maxwell
Miss Irene Burton, North Platte
Mr. Wyatt Beauchamp, North Platte
Miss Vada Schimmel, North Platte
Miss Nettie Jennings, North Platte
Mr. Eugene Clark, North Platte
Mr. Clarence Hendricks, North Platte

Miss B. Andreus, North Platte
Mr. H. Crawford, Maxwell
Mr. V. Harder, Roscoe
Mr. W. Harder, Roscoe
Mr. H. Harder, Roscoe
Mr. G. Schoolcraft, North Platte
Miss Beulah Hendricks, North Platte
Mr. H. Hall, Brady
Mr. J. Law, Curtis
Mr. Davis Law, Curtis
Miss J. Kelly, North Platte
Mr. Albert Buyer, Maxwell
Miss A. Schimmel, North Platte
Mr. D. Combe, North Platte
Miss D. Foster, North Platte
Miss Dila Grandy, North Platte
Miss Thelma Most

Camp Helpers:

Mr. and Mrs. Lyle Carper
Mr. and Mrs. Hugh Clark
Mrs. R. Grandy

Mrs. N. Lentz
Mr. Clarence Hendricks

Space forbids recognizing everyone that assisted in making the camp a success; indeed it went far beyond our expectation. We cannot express in words our appreciation for the splendid cooperation, may God be your rewarder.

On the opening evening of camp many guests from North Platte and neighboring towns were present. A huge camp fire lighted up the scene, revealing the camp with its tents, cook shack, trees, benches, etc. Rev. Ivan E. Olsen led in the opening meeting. As the fading twilight in the west lent beauty to the scene, we believe that God in heaven was pleased as He looked down upon the happy hearts bowed in reverence to Him.

Choruses were sung, testimonies given, and camp officers introduced: the get-acquainted-service will long be remembered. The closing chorus expressed the thought of every heart:

"Just one day nearer home, when shadows of the night descend,
Just one day less to roam, when fading twilight colors blend.
Beneath that starry dome, I rest beside my guide and Friend.
One day nearer home."

Daily Program

MONDAY
8 P.M.   Public Campfire Service

TUESDAY   "A—Day—At—Camp"
6:00   Trumpet "Get-up"
7:00   Breakfast and devotions
8:45   Evangelistic service - Pres. Clifton L. Fowler, speaker
9:45   Bible Study - Rev. Ivan E. Olsen, teacher (Tues.-Thur.)
               Topic: "Salvation"
                   It's start—the new birth (Tuesday)
                   It's growth—victory (Wednesday)
                   It's consumption—the rapture (Thursday)
10:15   Recess
10:25   Music—Mr. Lloyd Olsen, Instructor.
                   Orchestra, choir singing, and chorus learning.
11:00   Missions—Rev. Lefever, teacher
                   Teacher's training (child study), Mrs. H.J. Johnson
11:25-11:55   Prophecy—Rev. N.P. Jansen, teacher
                   Errors in religious systems, Mr. L.L. Olsen, teacher
12:20   Dinner
1:00   Baseball, swimming, games, tennis, etc. or rest and Bible study.
5:30   Supper
7:00   Street-meeting (voluntary) Tuesday and Thursday evening
8:00   Preaching service in North Platte, Pres. C.L. Fowler, speaker.

WEDNESDAY

               Pres. Clifton L. Fowler, special speaker 8:45 a.m.—8 p.m.

THURSDAY

               Rev. W.C. Anderson, special speaker 8:45 a.m.—8 p.m.

FRIDAY

               Rev. H.G. Rodine, special speaker 8:45 a.m.—8 p.m.

SATURDAY

               Rev. R.J. Molzahn, special speaker 8:45 a.m.—8 p.m. Campfire

SUNDAY

               Rev. N.P. Jansen, speaker 11:00 in North Platte
               Rev. Ivan E. Olsen, speaker 8:00 in North Platte

MONDAY

               Camp dismissed after morning devotions.

Speakers on above program subject to change.
There will be a nurse on the camp grounds to render first aid.
Cheerful obedience and regard for all camp rules is expected.
Exceptions for young people under 14 years of age will be considered.
Entire camp program schedule will be run on Central standard time.
Girls asked not to wear modern interpretations of men's clothing (Deuteronomy 22:5)
Do not wear your Sunday best for camp, there will be lots of fun and recreation.
Bring horse-shoe sets, indoor baseballs, etc.

"COME PRAYING YOU'LL LEAVE REJOICING"

The Inside Scoop on the First Week of Camp

I attended the first Maranatha Bible Camp held in the summer of 1938. I was 13. They must have really hurried to set up, as every tent they could find was put into use, holes and all. We found the holes quickly as it rained nearly every night. The wind blew every day, and this caused our picnic breakfast, lunch and supper to be liberally sprinkled with sand.

The beds in the girls' tents were old bedsteads with mattresses on top. We had no indoor plumbing or electricity. I remember that some of the gals got dysentery. The rest of us were in class, which meant we were under a tent with the flap up, for our air conditioning. One morning we kids kept grinning from ear to ear, and the teacher, with his back to the outdoors, kept wondering what was going on. The outhouse and girls' quarters were in our view, so we could see the Russian and Finish process.

We were a congenial bunch, all participating in KP duty, setting tables or doing dishes for every meal. Many people brought in food and farmers donated beef and pork.

I recall a Mr. Jensen (Nick Janzen) who was a wheat farmer from around Madrid. He was very involved helping Pastor Olsen direct every phase of the camp, making sure there was enough help in every department and that food was always on the tables. J.C. Brumfield and wife, Betty, were at several early camps, with their small daughter.

That first year Lloyd Olsen, brother to Ivan, was there from DBI. He and Pastor Olsen were good runners. We played games like "Run Sheep Run" where speed was important. Of course, we gals could only wear dresses so we weren't speedy at all. When was that policy deleted? The Olsen brothers played softball, volleyball and headed up most the games we enjoyed.

We went to a sandpit to swim. The policy of no mixed swimming was in force. One day a girl accidentally got out over her head, which was easy as it got deep quickly. I was close by, so kept pushing her up and toward the bank, while I went down to the bottom. I think I gave her about three big pushes before Pastor Olsen was able to reach out and grab her. My four older brothers had taken us to sandpits or to the river from an early age, so I wasn't overly afraid, but wasn't in any hurry to help save anybody else.

My brother Darrell joined me the next year at a new site. Mom made it possible for our cousin, Marian Jackson, to join us from Benkelman. Darrell's best memories of Maranatha were the times he joined Hugh Clark and Eugene at camp to work. Neither boy was old enough to drive, but this was the time he learned some carpentry.

Darrell, Virginia and I were all three there the third year. We don't remember showers or bathhouses, but we did have a few electric lights. They were turned on and off by a switch in another building, as I remember.

The second year they set up long rows of bunkers, with wood framing overlaid with canvas. We could walk down the middle and each side had a bunk for two. We must have put our suitcases under the bunks. Not sure how the girls put on makeup ...

The wildest the girls got my second year happened the last night. Marjorie, Irene and others I didn't know, decided to go to bed with their clothes on and then get up when all was quiet. They went down to the main building to throw rocks. The next thing I remember was the light shining overhead and Mrs. Roberts giving everyone a scorcher of a scolding. I had slept through party-time!

Virginia remembers a fad somebody started, by writing on each other's white blouses. We went home and embroidered the signatures so they would withstand washing. We were proud of them and wore them a lot. It was a good way to remember our friends. How much easier this would be today, 66 years later, with permanent inks.

Virginia also remembers a year or two later when she and some friends met some boys at the river. The fireflies were out and mesmerized her. She says she doesn't remember watching them before or since on summer nights.

Last day of camp meant going over and climbing Sioux Lookout. Most of us were transported in the back of a big truck. Usually one evening during the week a bunch would go into town for a street meeting. Virginia remembers going to Maxwell once.

My eight kids went to camp at least once. Barbi spent a summer at camp in 1974. She looks back on it as a good learning experience and has fond memories of the kids she met and worked with. She spent most of her days off in North Platte with her Grandmother Hunt.

My mother was physically busy working those years. She also had her father with her at the time, who was about 90. Once in awhile, she would take Grandpa Jackson and drive out for the evening service. They went home rested and ready for another day.

— Marilyn Hunt Maseberg,
North Platte, Nebraska

Camping at the Bignell Site

My memory of Camp the first time I went (possibly in 1940) was a place very primitive. We slept in dormitory tents set up on the grass or weeds. The mattresses were stuffed with possibly corn shucks or something like that. One night it rained and we had water under our beds. There was an outside pump from a well for water. We washed our faces and brushed our teeth with water at the pump. There was no building.

The chapel was a large tent. One evening a hard wind blew the tent down but the men put it back up again. This tent was also used as our dining room.

Of course, not having any of the modern conveniences there did not hinder our learning or having fun, since most of us were not accustomed to having a lot more at home because these were very hard, lean years.

That week we were privileged to hear many renowned speakers. To name some — Rev. Theodore Epp from the "Back to the Bible" radio program, the "Back to the Bible" quartet including the Rev. Melvin Jones, Ernest Lott and a couple of others. Also Rev. J.C. Brumfield from California; Rev. Carl Tanis, an outstanding missionary; the Rev. L.E. Maxwell from Prairie Bible Institute in Canada; Rev. Melvin Nordin and his wife, Alice, who had a radio program from Grand Island called "Haven of Rest"; and several others.

Though I had been raised in a very strong and solid Christian home, these men's messages greatly impacted my life for eternity. They reaffirmed the teachings that we had been taught at home. Also, these men's messages helped me to have full assurance of my salvation, whereas before, I did have doubts of some things.

Since then I have attended Camp many times down through the years, including Ladies' Retreats, Family Camps and other times, but my first experiences of the Camp are treasured memories. I thank the Lord for making it possible for us to go — way back then.

The cost of Camp one of those first years was $5.00 a week. It may have been $3.00 the first couple of years.

I remember our parents gave us 25 cents for spending money.

— Eleanor Johnson,
Broken Bow,
Nebraska

Eleanor (Bratten) Johnson is baptized in the Platte River near the Bignell campsite. Rev. Melvin Nordin from the "Haven of Rest" radio ministry baptized her. Photo taken approximately 1940.

Digging the Baptismal Pond

I remember attending Camp in the early days. I had a special friendship with Eugene Clark. Eugene always accompanied the sing-spirations.

Eugene and I helped dig out sand (in the edge of the river) for the baptismal pond and also worked on tennis courts. We had baseball games with staff.

The last night of Camp was always a hike to Sioux Lookout and roasting marshmallows over a campfire.

— Darrell Hunt,
Loveland, Colorado

Almost Like Outdoor Evangelism

Our praise to God for the beginning ministry of the Maranatha Bible Camp in 1938. Many godly men and women helped Rev. and Mrs. Ivan E. Olsen see their vision become a reality. At first it was almost like outdoor evangelism. When I attended Camp in 1939, 1940 and 1942, there began to be real progress, but most of all, young people like myself made serious commitments to serve the Lord. The inspiring ministry and great fellowship was like a taste of heaven on earth and still has an impact in my life today. Later, our two children also had the opportunity to attend Camp as well. I pray it will be there for generations to come.

Hebrews 6:10—I think of many people who gave so much of their time and support, and have gone on to glory, but God will not forget their labor of love.

May God bless the leadership of George W. Cheek and Jan, and the many godly men and women who are involved in carrying on the great commission of Maranatha Bible Camp.

— Emma W. Darnel,
North Platte

First Camp at the Talbot Farm

The first Camp was in a corner of the Talbot farm meadow, down by the river. We used baled hay to build walls for hay cabins and tarps for roofs. Each unit was for girls and the boys had their section; and each unit had a kerosene lantern hung on a pole laid across the hay bale walls.

Then others built long wooden tables and benches and with all the church families and a few others, Maranatha was born.

I might also mention we dredged out a swimming hole on the edge of the river.

When the present location became available Vernon Weeks and I were appointed camp electricians and we began to set poles for street lights and distribution centers.

The electric company set us a pole with a 100-amp switch and it wasn't long before we outgrew that and the present system was installed.

There were a lot of tents and temporary structures and the main meeting place was a tent with wooden benches and speaker's platform.

Those who are presently at Camp probably wouldn't believe how the Camp started. And only the Lord knows how many souls have been saved by such a humble beginning.

And I, at 91, saw the start and progress that has been made through the years and glorify God.

It is no secret what God can do.

– Yours in Christ
J.C. McCullough

My Testimony of Maranatha

The summer of 1942 I was 10 years old when Mr. and Mrs. Sam Becker came to our little one-room school house in the Sandhills and gave a beautiful felt-o-graph lesson from the Bible ... I realized for the first time that I needed a Savior, but I didn't acknowledge it that night. Mrs. Becker talked to my parents about Maranatha Bible Camp and they decided that they would make arrangements for me to attend. I had time to think about the gospel that I had heard and decided that as soon as I got to camp I wanted to invite the Lord Jesus into my life. At Maranatha the story was told again and Mrs. Becker prayed with me and Jesus came into my heart and life and became my Savior!

That week of camp was a wonderful time for me. We slept in the tent dorm. As I remember we had a big roundish (hot) tent for chapel and classes. I think the kitchen area may have been built of rough slab lumber, but I do remember that the cooks were such kind and happy ladies even though they worked very hard under far less than ideal conditions. The long hot hike up to Sioux Lookout was a special event! As I remember it, my mother was baptized in the Platte River on Sunday when they came to pick me up, and the following year Rev. Olsen baptized me in the same river. I remember that the large company of believers sang as we all walked to the river. As we stood in the river, I told that I loved the Lord and I really desired to live my life in obedience to the Lord. As an adult one of the privileges I had as a deaconess in our church was helping ladies prepare for baptism and witnessing their dedication and love for the Lord

and their willingness to be obedient to His commands.

Camp Maranatha played a vital role in my spiritual growth as I attended for four consecutive years, helping me to learn the scriptures and strengthening my walk with the Lord. Some workers I remember were Mr. and Mrs. Ivan Olsen, Mr. and Mrs. Sam Becker, Mr. and Mrs. Theodore Epp, Mr. and Mrs. Melvin Jones, Mr. Brumfield, Mr. and Mrs. Hugh Clark and Eugene, the Glenn Krause family, a Mrs. Nolte and of course there were many many I don't recall, but I'm so thankful for their love for the Lord and willingness to spend long hours of hard work to make it all happen.

In 1946 my dad and mother joined the ranks of the American Sunday School Union and we as a family ministered for the next 25+ years through that channel in Sunday schools, VBS, Bible camps, etc. In 1995 the Howard Childerston family (49 of us) returned to Maranatha for a memorable reunion and fellowship in the Lord. During that time my husband, Wallace Goff, and I celebrated our 40th wedding anniversary. In 2002 and 2003, Wally and I have enjoyed and appreciated the Biblical Concepts in Counseling Family Camps. The Lord has been so good to me. He indeed is my Light, my Song, my Savior and Lord, and Maranatha has had a part in my spiritual birth, growth and maturity. I praise the Lord for the vision He has given to His obedient children down through the years. May The Lord Jesus continue to be the focus at Maranatha!

– Leora (Childerston) Goff,
Crawford, Nebraska

Beckers Were "The Musical Family"

It is with very fond memories that I look back on our years at Maranatha Bible Camp. Sam and I were in our last year at Moody Bible Institute when we received a letter from Dr. Ivan Olsen containing a call to come to western Nebraska for children's work. We came to Nebraska in time to set up for the first camp for boys and girls on June 12, 1941. We helped set up tent dormitories and stuff mattresses with straw to provide beds for the kids to sleep on.

Our services were held in a large tent with the floor covered with sawdust and the kids sitting on planks. Sam would teach the kids choruses and provide object lessons that taught scriptural truths. I would tell Bible stories illustrated with flannelgraph and also character building stories. Our daughter, Darlene, was 6 years old at that time and sang in trios with us, so we also provided the special music, using our marimba, guitar, and trumpet. The highlight of the week was the Sunday afternoon musical program. Campers were asked to bring their instruments and the program consisted of vocal and instrumental numbers.

During the first week of camp at Maranatha, we became thoroughly convinced of the value of the Camp. It provided an environment so conducive to acceptance of spiritual values, that regardless of the camper's background, he would respond to accept Christ as Savior and continue spiritual instruction.

Sam and I organized and led the children's weeks at Maranatha for many years.

God has blessed us with great joy in hearing testimonies of those who accepted Christ as their Savior during our years of ministry there. One of our greatest blessings has been to keep in touch with the camp over the years and see that it has remained true to its vision of sharing the gospel and helping believers grow in their walk of faith.

– In Christ,
Ella Becker

Ella Becker

Sam and Ella Becker, and their daughter, Darlene, provided music and object lessons for campers, 1941.

Sam Becker baptized his daughter, Darlene, in the Platte River during a week of Camp.

Helping Pay for an Early Meeting Tent

In the '40s Ivan Olsen contacted my father, Henshaw H. Flaming, then a farmer in the Grainton, Nebraska, area about a large tent he needed for the Camp. Dr. Olsen's plan to purchase this tent was to sell squares for donations. He knew my father did not have much money, but that he was very missionary-minded and that his actions were emulated by others, so Dad was asked to purchase the first square. With Dad's endorsement, Dr. Olsen was confident he could get his tent. Dad purchased the square and Maranatha got a large tent.

A very few years later, in 1945, my mother, Margaret, became seriously ill. Dr. and Mrs. Olsen were close counselors to Dad when Mom died. Their friendship was very, very much appreciated by Dad in the aftermath of her death. Mom's death left Dad with three boys ages 5, 7 and 9.

In approximately 1948/49 my younger brother and I attended Maranatha Camp. The two of us and our older brother were known for our three-part a cappella singing. When the two of us attended Camp, Dr. Olsen knew who we were and we were introduced to Eugene Clark, the Camp musician. He teamed us up with another boy and we sang at every service during that week. On the Sunday that concluded the week, we had to get up early, travel to North Platte with Eugene and sing on the morning radio show. At the time, all of this was quite an inconvenience to the two of us, because singing was not the reason we wanted to go to Camp.

– Paul Flaming,
Reedley, California

"T'was the First Night at Camp"

T'was the first night out,
And all thru the camp;
Not a creature was stirring,
And all things were damp.

When from the girl's tents,
There rose such a clatter;
That every one wondered,
Just what was the matter.

The squeals and the giggles;
The yells and the shouts;
Soon gave us the clue,
We could no more doubt.

For in the far tent,
Upon the right hand,
In an old squeaky cot,
We found Miss Joan.

Her deep alto voice,
Rang out in the night;
And the girls all giggled;
With peals of delight.

Then Marjorie yelled out,
In a high frightened tone;
"Needles in my bed,
Do let me alone."

The boy's in their tents,
Were all just as bad;
They just couldn't sleep,
For no sleep could be had.

The bumps in their beds,
The cold chilly breeze,
Made them keep laughing,
So they wouldn't freeze.

Till about two o'clock,
Not a single one slept,
Then over the camp,
A dull stillness crept.

But soon at four-thirty,
It was just getting light;
When Marilyn awakened,
No more sleep that night,

Lloyd blew his bugle,
At six A.M. with might,
But every one was up;
Oh my! what a night.

— *Mrs. H. Johnson*

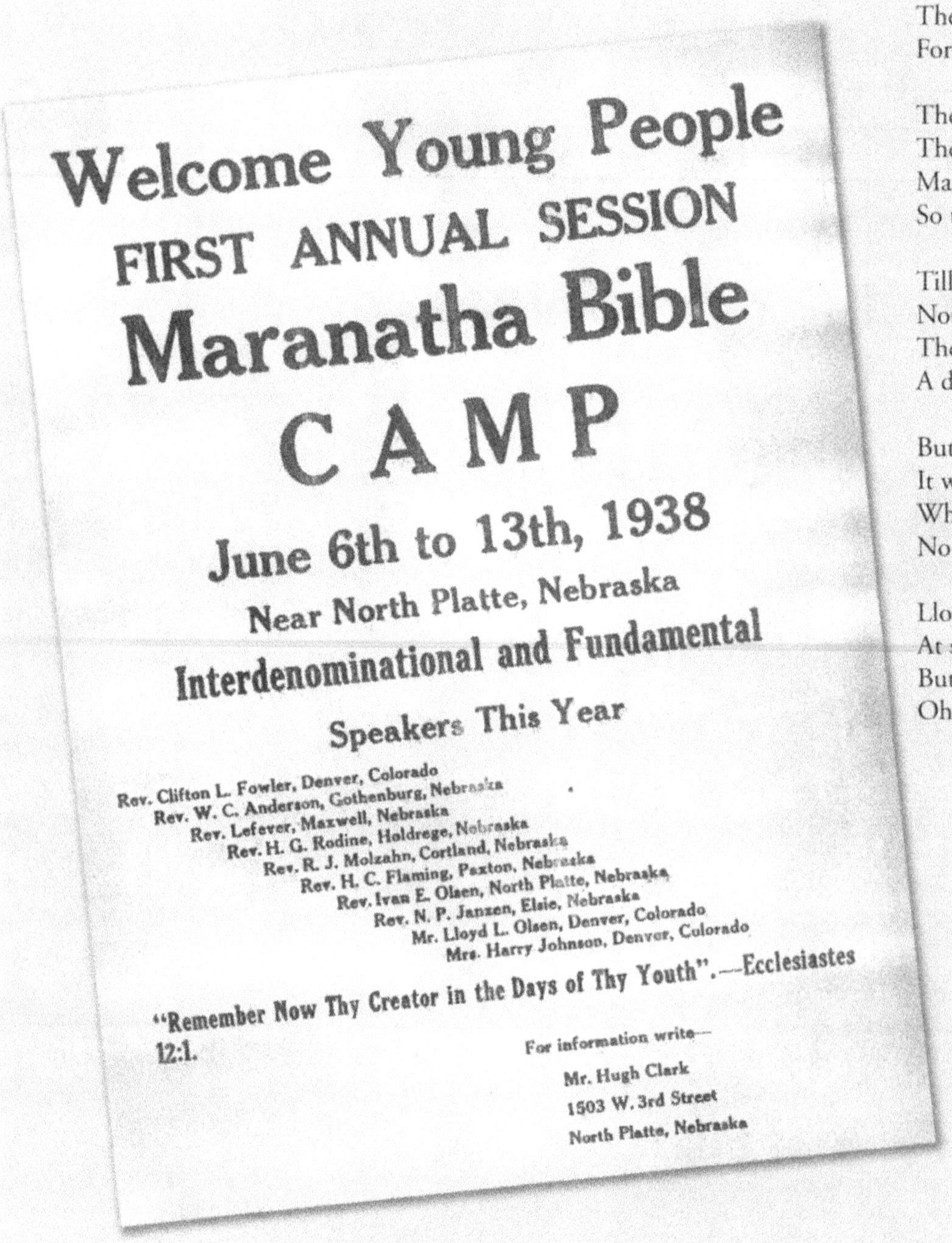

Welcome Young People
FIRST ANNUAL SESSION
Maranatha Bible
CAMP
June 6th to 13th, 1938
Near North Platte, Nebraska
Interdenominational and Fundamental
Speakers This Year

Rev. Clifton L. Fowler, Denver, Colorado
Rev. W. C. Anderson, Gothenburg, Nebraska
Rev. Lefever, Maxwell, Nebraska
Rev. H. G. Rodine, Holdrege, Nebraska
Rev. R. J. Molzahn, Cortland, Nebraska
Rev. H. C. Flaming, Paxton, Nebraska
Rev. Ivan E. Olsen, North Platte, Nebraska
Rev. N. P. Janzen, Elsie, Nebraska
Mr. Lloyd L. Olsen, Denver, Colorado
Mrs. Harry Johnson, Denver, Colorado

"Remember Now Thy Creator in the Days of Thy Youth".—Ecclesiastes 12:1.

For information write—
Mr. Hugh Clark
1503 W. 3rd Street
North Platte, Nebraska

Vera Hendricks Remembers the First Week of Camp

Our aunt, Vera Hendricks Hasenauer, was among the young people who attended that first Camp. Recently we interviewed her regarding memories she has of that week, and since you may only want to use a few of these, we decided to put them in the form of bullet points ... use as you wish.

• Her brother, Clarence, had to talk their dad into letting Vera and their sister, Beulah, go since no one had ever heard of "Bible camp" before. Mr. Hendricks had to be assured that the girls would be "looked after." She was 20 years old at the time.

• She thought that there were approximately 35-40 campers of all ages. Some of the smaller children would cry for their mamas at night, and their cries could be heard throughout the camp.

• They slept in tents on blanket rolls and/or camp cots, and, since it rained a lot, whoever slept near the tent flaps got rained on! She got tickled at that memory!

• The food was good, and the camp cooks prepared "normal food" such as eggs, toast, fried chicken - "not a lot of meat but lots of taters and gravy!" Don Hunt brought food and supplies out from North Platte each day, and since there was no refrigeration, the food had to be used that day.

• They ate their meals under a canvas tarp, and wind blew the rain in sideways so they would get soaked as they ate. We wondered if that was miserable for them, but she laughed ... "It was fun!" she said! They ate on dishes that "didn't break when dropped."

• They saw some snakes.

• "It was fun" and "It was interesting" were her general summaries. They had a lot of fun she recounted. They played ball games and croquet, had Bible studies, listened to speakers ("The speakers were good"!), did lots of singing in the evenings, and also had prayer meetings in the evenings.

• Any cute boys there? "No! I didn't see any there." Maybe that was because Julius Hasenauer, her future husband, came out to visit her frequently! She did say that there were more girls than boys there because the boys had to work.

• Maranatha Bible Camp remained an important part of Jay and Vera Hasenauer's lives in many ways throughout the years. Their involvement continued through the 1960s, 70s, and 80s as they prayed, gave, worked, and supplied onions and vegetables from their truck garden. They exemplify the fact that God uses "that which every joint supplies" (Eph. 4:16) to cause the growth of the Body of Christ!

– Priscilla Hendricks Millsap and
Sharon Hendricks Jost,
Kearney, Nebraska

The First Annual Encampment was held at a cottonwood grove along the Platte River on land owned by Ralph Talbot. There were 33 campers listed on the roll (30 of them attended full-time during the week of June 6-13, 1938). There are a few campers missing and a few extra workers in this photo when compared with the original roll call. The Camp workers are toward the front of the photo. Front row (crouching), from left: Lloyd Olsen, Nick Janzen and Hugh Clark. Second row (seated), from left: Merle Lefever, Ivan E. Olsen, Alice Olsen, Hazel Johnson, Myrtle Grandy, Mrs. Monroe, Nellie Lantz, Viola Carper and Lela Clark. Third row, from left: unidentified, Eugene Clark, Ethel Johnson, unidentified, unidentified, Margi Coombs, unidentified, MaryBelle Most, Harry Most. Fourth row, from left: Clarence Hendricks, unidentified, unidentified, unidentified, unidentified, Vera Hendricks, unidentified, unidentified, unidentified. Fifth row, from left: unidentified, unidentified, Vada Schimmel, Irene Burton, Beulah Hendricks, Maxine Pace, unidentified, Arlene Schimmel, Dorothy Foster, Marilyn Hunt, unidentified, unidentified, unidentified.

What Would You Do at a Bible Camp?

As we think about the significant part so many have played in Maranatha from the beginning, it truly is amazing and serves as an example of how God uses "the whole body, joined and knit together by what every joint supplies, according to the effective working by which every part does its share," causing the growth of the body. (Ephesians 4:16, NKJV). We are thankful for the multitude of believers who have been willing to use their gifts on behalf of Maranatha from its inception because we are a part of God's forever family whose lives were impacted through its ministry.

Our parents, Clarence and Bessie Hendricks, were two such believers who used their gifts of service to benefit the Camp for several decades, and who had a heart to see young people come to know Christ and grow in their faith, often personally inviting and taking kids to Camp. It all began for us when Dad began attending a Bible study in North Platte. When they called Rev. Olsen to become their pastor, he and our dad spent a great deal of time together in those beginning years of the Berean Church since they had known each other at Denver Bible Institute, and since both were single at the time. He relayed to us that Ivan "always had a lot of ideas" and would often "bounce them off of him." As Rev. Olsen was processing one such idea, he asked, "Clarence, what would you think about (our church) start-ing a Bible camp for young people?" Confused at such a foreign concept, our dad responded "A *Bible* camp? What's a Bible camp? What would you *do* at a Bible camp?" He, nor anyone he knew, had heard of such a thing but, after an explanation that young people would hear the Gospel and have a chance to study the Word of God, he was excited about the idea and volunteered to help with anything that needed to be done.

As Rev. Olsen's vision began to unfold, Dad talked his folks into letting his sisters, Vera and Beulah, attend the Camp, assuring them that they would be "looked after." He helped with preparations, and moved out of the camper-trailer he was living in at the time so that it could serve as a place to safely house the office equipment, a shelter for the sick, and a study room for the speakers. He also stayed that first week to help with anything that needed to be done including putting up tents, fixing many leaks in the tents, and construction of a kitchen...out of cardboard and canvas. He expressed to us that there was a *tremendous* amount of work to be done by many to make the dream come true - a vision which would affect and influence countless young people for eternity!

– Priscilla Hendricks Millsap and
Sharon Hendricks Jost,
Kearney, Nebraska

Sleeping in the Girls' Dorm

As one of the first campers to attend the boys and girls camp at Maranatha Bible Camp, I remember how excited I was, at age 6, to sleep in the tent dormitory with my mother, Ella Becker, just across the aisle from me. She served as the girls' counselor that year. Sleeping on a sack of straw was a fun experience for me, however, I'm not sure it was all that comfortable for my mother.

Maranatha Camp holds a special place in my heart because it was at Camp that I was baptized by my father, Sam Becker. Maranatha Camp provided a wonderful environment for growing spiritually and forming Christian friendships that have lasted over the years.

– In Christian love,
Darlene (Becker) Franz

Left: In June 1938, a local mortuary allowed Pastor Olsen to borrow its funeral tent as long as it was not needed for a service at a cemetery. Campers were able to use it as a dining hall all week long. Center: Standing in the back of Nick Janzen's flatbed truck, Lloyd Olsen leads campers and guests in singing during the first Maranatha Bible Camp session in 1938. Behind Lloyd are Ivan Olsen (left) and Janzen. The pianist is unidentified. Right: Plenty of eating and teaching was done at open-air tables in 1938. Notice the water pump installed for the week.

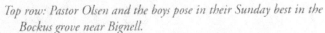

Top row: *Pastor Olsen and the boys pose in their Sunday best in the Bockus grove near Bignell.*

Second row: *Parents and other visitors came to hear the word of God taught in 1938.*

Third row, from left: *The "cardboard kitchen" was the center of cooking operations during the First Annual Encampment in 1938 and was run by many volunteers, including (from left) Mertle Grandy, Nellie Lantz, Viola Carper and head cook Lela Clark; Nick Janzen participated in the original prayer meeting that started Maranatha Bible Camp. A wheat farmer, Janzen also pastored small churches at Madrid and Roscoe, Nebraska. He was affectionately known as "Nickodemus, Ruler of the Jews." This photo is from the First Annual Encampment, where he was assistant chairman.*

Fourth row, from left: *Lyle Carper (right) was in charge of the grounds and maintenance during the early days of Maranatha Bible Camp. He is shown with his wife, Viola; son, Dickie; and daughter, Joyce; "Home sweet home" for a week at the First Annual Encampment, 1938; Pastor Ivan Olsen led the first-ever Maranatha Camp baptismal service at the south bank of the Platte River on Sunday, June 12, 1938. There were 20 people baptized that day.*

Fifth row, from left: *Counselor with her girls. Dormitories were tents with dirt floors. The beds were made of short 4 x 4 posts for legs, framed with 2 x 4s and hogwire stretched between them for the "springs." The mattresses were ticks stuffed with straw. There were "daddy longlegs" spiders everywhere. If anyone touched the canvas top when it rained, the tents would leak. There was no electricity or plumbing. Toilets were tiny log two-seater huts and sometimes the lineups were pretty long. Water was available at hand pumps throughout the area; A group of campers at the Bockus grove; In 1939, John Goodmanson (front row, on the right), shown with his young men's Sunday school class, was appointed Maranatha's Registration Committee to recruit campers. Eugene Clark is in the front row, third from left.*

God Provides a Site

In 1941, as the United States tried to stay out of the Second World War, Maranatha Bible Camp was wrestling with a smaller issue of its own. Although Harold Bockus had been agreeable to work with, there were problems with the Bignell site (not the least of which was the unmistakable odor from the Bockuses' nearby pigpen). As the U.S. mobilized for battle, Maranatha renewed its agreement to borrow the Bockus grove for the summers of '42 and '43, but there were doubts about the future.

The Maranatha board wrestled with the need to acquire a permanent site for its camping programs. There were differing opinions about where to move. Denver-area businessmen nearly convinced the Maranatha leadership that the most appropriate place to build a Bible camp was in the Rocky Mountains near Denver. Maranatha even held a camping program in the Rockies in 1941, as it occasionally would in future years. But, as Ivan E. Olsen wrote years later, "the God of the 'cloud by day' & the 'pillar of fire by night' made it so clear the plains of Nebraska was His plan."

Olsen had second-guessed himself after viewing the beauty of the Black Hills to the north and the Rockies to the west. "I thought, 'My! How typical of my stupidity, starting a Bible camp out in the Sandhills of Nebraska, out in the dry, hot, hot place,'" said Olsen, "but the Holy Spirit so dealt with me that He had shown us where He wanted Maranatha Camp. He opened my eyes; He anointed my eyes with divine eye salve like the Book of Revelation says. I was able to see one of the most desperately needy areas. 'Take off the shoes from your feet, for the ground that you are walking on is holy ground.'"

The Camp would not move to Colorado. God would carve out a stronghold along the Platte River, as it slowly meandered through Nebraska's sparsely-populated countryside. He would use a small army of volunteers led by Olsen, a straight-ahead preacher who rarely took no for an answer from anyone, and Hugh Clark, a practical builder who did anything that needed doing — "whether I knew how or not." The Maranatha leaders were in the middle of a faith walk — one that they hoped would lead to some real estate.

After the Fifth Annual Encampment closed in August 1943 and the equipment was stowed for the winter, the Camp hit its crisis point. Harold Bockus died, and the Bockus grove would no longer be available. Now, in the spring of 1944, Maranatha Bible Camp began in earnest to search for a permanent site.

Olsen and Hugh Clark, accompanied by Lyle Carper, an elder of the Berean Church in North Platte, and Lester Kittle, who owned a grocery store in nearby Maxwell, went out looking for a piece of ground to build the Camp's future on. They found a good prospect on a large "island" of land surrounded by the unpredictable channels of the Platte River just southwest of Maxwell. Like the two previous sites, it was located in Lincoln County. It was a tract of "accretion" — a thin layer of topsoil over sand, built up over many years by the flooding of the Platte (a near-annual occurrence until a system of dams was installed on the North Platte River earlier in the 20th century). It was just a few miles northeast of the Bignell site.

"Four of us made our way, sometimes almost on our hands and knees, crawling through impenetrable brush," Olsen recalled.

They arrived at the approximate site where the "Old Tabernacle" would be built four years later.

"It was so amazing; I was so immediately convinced that, because of the layout and the availability of this land, that it was the land God wanted us to have," Olsen wrote. "At that time, we thanked God for giving it to us."

Half a century later, Clark reminisced about the discovery of the original site:

"We started out looking. We came up the island, right there where the Camp is now, and we saw this campground, and we thought it would make a good one, a lot of trees, and a lot of good things. We got out of the car, walked in and looked around, and we knelt down and asked God for it, because it was about what we were looking for."

The four men went to see North Platte realtor J.E. Sebastian, who was handling the sale of the property. The land that caught the eye of Olsen and his friends turned out to be part of a tract called the "old Louis Rayome place" which was owned by Richard & Josephine Kern. Much of it was farmland. For six months, no one had been interested in that particular piece of property, so an overjoyed Sebastian spontaneously agreed to sell it to the Maranatha contingent without asking for a down payment. (Unbeknown to Sebastian, the four men had agreed among themselves that this would be the sign from God that it was the right piece of land, since they had no money to put down at that moment.)

Quickly, on D-Day, June 6, 1944, Olsen put together a fundraising letter, one of many he would write during his tenure as general director. He had his secretary, Faye Ward, prepare a 1,500-piece mailing (in this case, a postcard) which went to the database that the Camp had compiled in only six years. Within days, even though wartime rationing was in full swing, donations were arriving for the purchase of the new site.

A short time later, Sebastian received an offer from a farmer was willing to pay cash on the barrelhead for the entire tract of land, so he tried to renege on his verbal agreement with Maranatha. When he left a phone message for Olsen telling him he had sold the land to the farmer, the ambitious young pastor became irate. He rushed to Sebastian's office, along with Clark, Kittle and Carper. While Sebastian tried to wriggle off the hook, Olsen, never one to waste time on diplomacy, wondered out loud if he would have to tell his constituency that "North Platte's principal realtor" had turned out to be a dishonest one. "You wouldn't do that; that would destroy me!" exclaimed Sebastian. "Well, I'm certainly not going to destroy myself," retorted Olsen.

At that moment, a freely perspiring Sebastian came up with a compromise plan to sell the land to the Maranatha contingent (which really wanted only about 80 acres of river bottomland) if the Camp would pledge to sell the remainder (the tillable land) to the farmer, John Charles Hupfer. After some vigorous negotiation, all parties agreed, and Kittle immediately wrote out a $1,000 check on his grocery store account for a down payment.

By the end of July, using the money that had come in from Olsen's appeal, the Camp reimbursed Kittle and bought the entire tract of land for $6,800 in the names of Clark, Kittle and Carper. The Camp then sold Hupfer the tillable land for $5,800, keeping approximately 80 acres of accretion for a net output of $1,000, and had money to spare for obtaining electrical service and other necessary improvements.

The purchase was made, but much remained to be done to get ready for Young People's Camp and Boys' and Girls' Camp in August. Maranatha, which already had announced in its brochure that the 1944 program would again be held at Bignell, quickly moved three dormitories and 12 cabins several miles by road from the Bockus grove to the new site. On July 21 — 10 days before Clark, Kittle and Carper finalized the deeds — the Camp ran a full-page ad in the North Platte Telegraph announcing the new location.

Once the buildings were placed, volunteers unloaded 75 new mattresses that already had been purchased, and declared the new site ready to go. The two weeks of Camp went well, and optimism reigned supreme.

The Camp board started discussions about how to improve the grounds. By the end of 1944, the Rural Electrification Administration had provided electrical service to Maranatha. In August 1945, Ernest Lott suggested that a permanent dormitory be built. That, however, would take some serious money.

The new site had a place for recreation; workers dug a sandpit, about 50 by 50 feet, for campers to go swimming in. Much of Olsen's time each afternoon while Camp was in session was devoted to serving as lifeguard there.

Even at the new site, "Camp" still meant nothing more than tent meetings and tent dormitories for five years. Maranatha had borrowed, then purchased, a big tent from a mainline denominational church that had "gotten away from their revival efforts." The tent had sat unused for years in a barn and was no longer waterproof. Olsen heard that a mixture of melted wax and either kerosene or gasoline (he couldn't remember which) was a "crude but inexpensive" way to waterproof the tent, and he periodically did it himself.

"It was such a dangerous operation that I wouldn't allow anyone else but myself to put it on, and with my tennis shoes on, I sprinkled the whole top of that tent with a water sprinkling can," said Olsen.

LaVerna (Krause) Wescoat recalls that during one especially bad thunderstorm, the meeting tent collapsed.

"Rev. Olsen instructed us to march out under a large canvas, two by two, to the tent dorms," she said. "We proceeded walking in water and mud past our ankles in the complete blackness of night … and then, there was no place to wash up before going to our soaked beds."

To reduce weather-related incidents, the Camp decided to build permanent buildings. In the January 1, 1947, board meeting, a $10,000 fundraiser was launched to bankroll the building program.

A meeting house, (or "Tabernacle," as Olsen referred to it), boys' and girls' dormitories and a dining facility were the top priorities. By the end of the decade, they all had been built. A new state-approved well for drinking water had been dug and tested.

A new question arose. Until the purchase of the permanent site, "Maranatha Bible Camp" had merely referred to a program that existed for a couple of weeks every summer, then folded its tents until next year. Should the new property, growing more valuable every year, have its own unique name? There were differing opinions. For a short time, the property was referred to as "Camp O' Cedars" and the schedule of programs continued to be known as Maranatha Bible Camp, but soon, the name of the site itself reverted to "Maranatha Bible Camp."

As the decade ended, the Soviet Union seized control over much of Eastern Europe, erecting an invisible dividing wall that Winston Churchill called "the Iron Curtain." The United States unveiled its Marshall Plan to rebuild Europe from the devastation of World War II, developed a fascination with Big Band music and witnessed the birth of the National Basketball Association.

At Maranatha, Ivan Olsen had a sense of great accomplishment. Looking back at the birth and growth of the young ministry, its founder drew a deep breath as Thanksgiving 1949 approached.

"The past 12 years have been struggling years — years full of manual labor, prayer, tears, sacrifice, endurance," wrote Olsen in his November 19 fundraising letter. "Someone has had to bear the heat of the day to get Maranatha started. We thank God for every one of you who have done this."

The beachhead was secured, but more fundraising, promotion and manual labor lay ahead to develop the "holy ground" that had been carved out of the wilderness.

VOICES OF MARANATHA

Bible Verses, Sioux Lookout and a 1947 Chev

My first recollection of Camp as a boy of 7 years old was at Bignell, where a large tent was set up and Ray Ransom and his oldest son, Ira, ministered to us by singing choruses and teaching from the Word of God. Then Maranatha Bible Camp moved to its present location and I remember hiking to Sioux Lookout hill and back with a group of boys and our leader. That was a lot of fun to do.

Our North Platte Berean Fundamental Church encouraged us to memorize scripture so we could go to Camp. If we memorized, I believe it was 200 verses, we could go free. I didn't go free but I still remember a lot of those verses that I memorized then.

During chapel time in the evening at Camp, I remember Rev. Olsen talking to us about Jesus coming back and if Jesus did come back that night, he would give us his car because he wouldn't need it. He would go to be with Jesus.

I believe that the teaching and memorization of God's Word at Camp helped me make the decision to accept Christ as my Savior when I was 9 years old at the Berean Church.

The spring of 1950, I was asked by Rev. Olsen to go out to Maranatha to help carry mattresses to the cabins and do odd jobs. When we arrived at Maxwell, we stopped at Mr. Kittle's hardware store. Rev. Olsen said he would drive the truck out to Camp and I was to drive his car. Boy, what a thrill that was at the age of 14 driving a 1947 Chev all the way from Maxwell to Camp by myself!

– Harry J. Most,
Hershey, Nebraska

Robinsons Have Good Memories

I attended Maranatha in 1944, '45 and '46. I was saved in the Old Tabernacle, married a Christian boy, and we give God the glory for our children who are in turn raising their families in Christian homes.

Our desire is to see our family grow in His love. Thanks to Maranatha's faithful servants.

– Betty Robinson,
Beaver City, Nebraska

The People of Maranatha: Theodore Epp

Ivan Olsen met Theodore Epp in May 1940, at a gathering of Moody Bible Institute graduates in Loup City, Nebraska. Ironically, neither was a Moody graduate (Olsen received his degrees from Denver Bible Institute and Epp, from Southwestern Theological Seminary in Fort Worth, Texas), but few moments in the history of Maranatha Bible Camp were more significant.

"It was a case of respect at first sight," said Olsen, who became a close friend of Epp, the founder and director of the Lincoln-based Back to the Bible Broadcast.

Epp was a pastor in Goltry, Oklahoma, where he preached on the radio before moving to Nebraska to start Back to the Bible.

Epp first's speaking assignment at Maranatha came in June 1940, and later that year, he was invited to join the Camp board. He soon started promoting the Camp on the Back to the Bible radio network.

The announcements over the Back to the Bible radio network in the 1940s and 1950s helped make MBC a credible and attractive option, especially on the fateful day when the storyline in the beloved "Danny Orlis" series had Danny deciding to attend a week of camp at Maranatha.

"A near riot developed when hundreds wanted to come to meet Danny Orlis," recalled Rev. Olsen in notes he wrote in 1988 for the Camp's 50th anniversary celebration. "Author Bernard Palmer and Bro. Epp ... learned how real characters such as this become to children listeners."

"It was all in the providence of God," wrote Olsen in 1975. "Probably the largest single contribution made by anyone was by Rev. Epp and Back to the Bible Broadcast in their promotion of MBC." During Maranatha's 50th anniversary celebration, Olsen said that Epp was one of the "upper three" men who most influenced him. (As for the other two, Alice Olsen said that they probably were missionary Dick Zoet, who led Ivan to saving faith in Jesus Christ in 1931 and served as an early Christian example, and Clifton Fowler, president of Denver Bible Institute and mentor for Ivan when he attended there, although Dr. M.R. DeHahn, who spoke at Maranatha in the 1950s and whose church sent Zoet as a missionary, may have been among that group.)

Olsen marveled that Epp never missed a Maranatha board meeting in 35 years, including at least 12 years (1950-62) as president. He spent much of every summer at Maranatha speaking and helping organize the programs. One summer, Epp originated most of his Back to the Bible Broadcasts from North Platte so he could be closer to Camp.

Epp provided valuable administrative advice to Olsen, admonishing him to use camper fees to pay for food and other overhead expenses and raise offerings to cover the cost of his building projects. Their confidence and trust in each other grew throughout the years.

Their families grew quite close as well — literally, during several summers in the mid- to late 1950s, when the Epps and Olsens lived across the hall from each other in the east end of the Prophet's Chamber. Each family had a modest-sized room with a double bed and bunk beds to accommodate their five children. There was a sink in each family's room, but they walked down the hall to use the dormitory-style bathrooms.

Olsen's friendship with Epp led him to a post on the Back to the Bible board of directors. Olsen resigned that position after Epp died in 1985.

Some people claimed that Epp and Olsen began to look more and more alike as they aged. "Many times down at the Boca Raton (Florida) Bible Conference," said Olsen, "there were several who would come up to me and say, 'Well, Brother Epp, I never thought I would meet you here.' I always felt it was a compliment."

It was more than a case of physical similarities between Epp, a burly German Mennonite whose parents were missionaries to Indians in the Southwest, and Olsen, who was of Norwegian descent and attended the Lutheran Church as a child. Both were bastions of orthodoxy. Both delighted in teaching the Bible and both launched interdenominational ministries.

Epp received Christ as a youth while attending a Bible camp for American Indians in Arizona. Epp's children grew up at Maranatha Camp during the summers and he often said they made many important spiritual decisions there, especially involving giving through the Maranatha faith promise program.

"I feel that having known you and served the Lord together for the big part of our lives, we thank God for you," wrote Epp's wife, Matilda, to the Olsens in 1987. "Yes indeed, you are a part with so much I remember. Now we have reached the time of change. Not inactive and I trust not at all unfruitful, but different. Being autumn and almost winter reminds me that autumn years are upon us — winter just around the corner. But then comes resurrection springtime. But I also know each season has its beauty. May this season prepare us for that glorious resurrection!"

– Tad Stryker

Theodore Epp and his wife are flanked by members of the Back to the Bible board of directors in this 1960s photo. From left: Ord Morrow, Ivan E. Olsen, Melvin Jones, Matilda Epp, Theodore Epp, Ernest Lott, J. Darrel Handel, G. Christian Weiss.

The People of Maranatha: Eugene Clark

If a movie were produced about the early days of Maranatha Bible Camp, Eugene Clark's music would be its soundtrack. The bespectacled Clark emerged from one of Maranatha's founding families and imprinted the Camp forever in the minds of many with his musical accompaniments.

Eugene was an original Maranatha camper, attending the First Annual Encampment at the Talbot farm in 1938. He recalled playing baseball in the pasture, swimming in a sandpit and riding in a flatbed truck to North Platte each night for worship services. He gave many days of his boyhood as a carpenter's helper for his father, Hugh, who supervised the construction of many early Camp buildings. Eugene spent 12 years working where needed at Camp.

As a preteen, Eugene earned a bicycle by mastering 25 hymns on the piano. He demonstrated his considerable musical talent at North Platte High School. By age 16, he had compiled a songbook of his own original material. Eugene was a 1948 graduate of Moody Bible Institute and also studied at Wheaton College. For a short time, he was minister of music and organist at the Berean Church in North Platte.

Soon he took over directing the music at Maranatha, then moved up to organizing and directing music camps. After Rev. Theodore Epp heard him play at Maranatha, he was invited to join the staff at the Back to the Bible Broadcast, where he served for many years. He wrote more than 100 songs and three cantatas, but he may be best known for his chorus, "Nothing is Impossible." He also wrote numerous articles and devotionals for various publications.

Few campers from the 1940s through the 60s will forget the image of Eugene wearing his thick glasses while playing the organ or piano at Maranatha. He also played many other instruments, including the trombone, vibraharp and solovox.

"I recall a fine young man always at the piano playing excellently," wrote Fern Roszhart, a camper in the 1940s. "One time I remember singing in their choir and I happened to be standing next to the piano, where I could watch

Eugene play. His variations were ever so intriguing. He didn't always play the same, but added new notes. This particular time, he even surprised himself. As I looked over to him quickly, Eugene was grinning a great big smile!"

So were hundreds of Maranatha campers over the years.

"It did not take long to realize that this was a very important part of his life," said Ferne (Vincent) Clark, Eugene's wife. "He had many stories of his summers there and the profound effect it had. Pastor Olsen was also a big influence on him and gave him much direction in his life.

"My second trip to Maranatha was quite a few months later. Eugene and I had gone to North Platte to

Teenage musical wonder Eugene Clark posed with Ivan Olsen for this promotional photo, approximately 1940.

have Thanksgiving with his parents, and during this long weekend, we drove out to the Camp, and it was there Eugene asked me to share his life.

"We spent many happy times at Camp during the next few years when Eugene played the piano for Back to the Bible Week, Family Week and many others. While there, we stayed in the little cabin Eugene and his dad had built. It was one of the few buildings with indoor plumbing, and we enjoyed the luxury of such modern facilities."

Without warning, Eugene's life changed dramatically. He became increasingly incapacitated during the prime of life by a deadly combination of iritis and rheumatoid arthritis, but Eugene continued to write music with the aid of specialized equipment. Although mainly confined to his home in Lincoln, he never complained about his plight — in fact, his selfless attitude was a source of encouragement to all who knew him. Still, the Clarks missed Maranatha Bible Camp.

"After Eugene became bedfast, we only reminisced about those years and did not dream we would ever be able to go back," said Ferne. "Pastor Olsen continually urged us to think about going, and with many fears and worries on my part, we rented a van, put Eugene's bed in it and headed for Camp. The first three years, we spent two weeks in one of the little summer homes on the lake, and then a mobile home was purchased and we spent many happy summers at Camp. I will always remember those early mornings as Eugene and I would have coffee and I would try to describe the beauty of the lake with the fog lifting. Then, as nighttime closed in, the peaceful sunset reflecting on the quiet lake. Those were wonderful years.

"Our children, Bruce, Bryan and Diane, also spent many happy times at Camp, first as campers and then as members of the staff. Some of their most important decisions for Christ were made there, and it made a deep and lasting impression on their lives." Bryan went on to become a pastor of Lincoln Berean Church, which sent more campers to Maranatha in the 1990s than any other church. He has served as a program director and speaker at Maranatha, and became a member of the Camp board.

Despite being bedfast the last years of his life, Eugene never lost his desire to serve God through music. Once, when a woman told Eugene how she used much of his music for church work, he thanked her and said, "That's like saying 'Sic 'em' to a dog. It gives me enthusiasm for my work."

In the 1970s, his health continued to decline. After visiting him near the end of his life, Ivan Olsen was convinced that "though taken aside from public eye, Eugene has been actually dwelling in the secret presence of the Most High, and the divine fragrance seems to fill the very room." It was often said that those who went to encourage Eugene would themselves leave refreshed.

Eugene Clark died June 29, 1982, at age 57.

– Tad Stryker

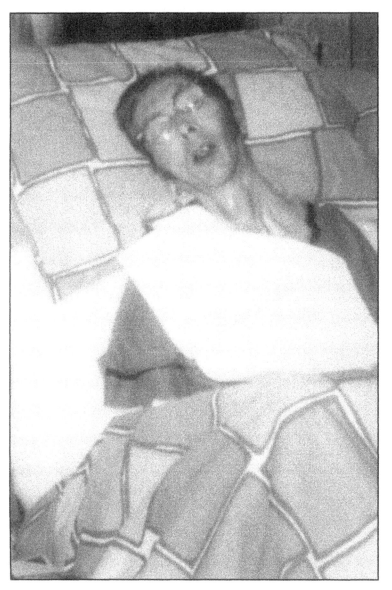

Eugene in Clark trailer, mid-1970s.

The Original 80 Acres

This account was taken from a "Pastor's Hour" message given by Rev. Olsen to the Navigator trainees in 1969.

Many of you have not heard how God gave us the campgrounds. The grounds on which the Tabernacle is built (approximately where Goltz Cabin is now located) is part of the original 80 acres that Maranatha received. In 1943, four of the board members were forced to look for a place where we could start building the conference grounds.

Maranatha started in 1938, across the river on borrowed land. One year later, we decided to move to a different place, and a kindly-dispositioned man, Mr. Harold Bockus, let us have our Maranatha Camp on his land. It was in the midst of a grove of trees. Joining us was a large hog pen, and the fragrance was none too pleasant, but we appreciated the kindness of this man. We held our conference there for five years (1939-43). When this man died unexpectedly, we took that as God's marching orders that we should not build a conference ground on somebody's land. At first, we tried to buy the land, but they would not sell it.

Then we learned that this piece of ground was for sale – 320 acres (the farmland to the north and this property, which they call river bed or accretion land). Four of us made our way, sometimes almost on our hands and knees, crawling through impenetrable brush. When we arrived near the (place where the Tabernacle would be built), the four of us got on our knees. We were convinced, because of the layout and the availability of this land, that it was the land God wanted us to have. At that time, we thanked God for giving it to us.

We went to a North Platte realtor who had it for sale. He was thrilled! He had it on the market for six months and hardly had an inquiry. This was in 1944. He unwisely did what we four previously agreed would be God's indication that He wanted us to have this land. No realtor would ever do it! He gave us first option to buy for 30 days without a down payment! If he had asked for a down payment, we had no money.

A week after he gave us the first option, we sent a letter to our Maranatha constituency of about 1,500. We told them that we had a chance to buy this land (320 acres) and we asked them to help us get it.

The telephone rang one day. I was at Vacation Bible School, and the realtor left a message. "Tell the Reverend when he gets back that I sold the land he was interested in." I cannot possibly describe my emotions — probably it is best not to describe them, anyway! In minutes, we four were at the office of the realtor. He began to apologize in every way he could. But remember, we did not make any down payment. He said, "I must be true to the man that I am selling it for. When this other man came with a check in hand to buy it, I felt I had to sell it."

The Spirit of God led us to tell him of our embarrassment. There was no time to plan what we would say – no time to plan an attack. We told him that we sent 1,500 letters to our constituency, telling them that we had first option to buy. We asked him what he would do if he were in our place. We told him that we had to write these people (living in this area where he was doing business), and tell them that we had dealt with a dishonest realtor!

He immediately said, "You wouldn't do that!" I said, "Well, surely we aren't going to be blamed of having been ignorant adults who would do a stupid thing like you brought us into." He said, "I realize I am totally at fault. The man will probably be here before we finish this discussion, to finalize the deal. We have not put our names on the deed. If you can buy this property right now, I will still honor my word." We asked him how much we would have to pay down in order to take the first step. He immediately said, "Six thousand or seven thousand dollars, something like that."

He wanted almost all of the money because he was in a tight spot! Well, the other men knew far more than I did. They said, "Well, surely only $1,000 would hold it." He agreed. So we put $1,000 down.

Just about that time, the other man came in and the realtor apologized to him. He said, "Why can't I keep both of you as friends? The Bible camp, this religious group, only wanted the riverbed — the accretion — and you mainly want the farmland. Why can't I sell the part to each of you that you are interested in?" We both nodded. We did not want the farmland, and he did not particularly want all of this riverbed. This is how God gave us the original 80 acres.

As far as we are able to tell, we do not see how the Indians used this land. As far as the white man is concerned, we negotiated at the beginning with the homesteader who was the first owner of this land.

We like to feel that prior to our having cleaned and fixed this ground, it never had anything done to it or with it since the creation of the world. The only thing it has ever been used for since the creation of the world is to sing praises to God as a meeting place with Him.

We thank God that He has manifested His leadership in giving us these grounds. This is God's camp. It is a tender tree of God's planting and for its existence, God has maintained it.

– Ivan E. Olsen

Maranatha – The First Wedding

Maranatha Bible means much to me for many reasons. I was a part of the beginning years. I was a counselor while they had canvas on top and dirt floors. Those were exciting days. I also remember dedicating my life to the Lord for full-time service, desiring to be either a missionary or a pastor's wife. I said I wanted to be a good pastor's wife like my sister, Alice.

I thank the Lord for the many blessings at Camp. I thank God for Ivan Olsen's influence in my life, strongly urging me to go to Bible School. I went to Omaha Bible Institute and there I met my husband-to-be, Eldon Sandin. We also dated some at Camps.

Olsen saw the potential in my husband-to-be, so Eldon did some early building at Camps. Olsen asked if we'd like to get married at Camp, so we were the first to get married at Camp. Eldon felt called to the ministry and we served 50 years.

My brother, Cliff Gustafson, and Ivan Olsen performed our wedding ceremony. There were over 400 young people at Camp that week.

Our two children, Eugene and Beth Ann, have also been blessed at Camp. Our grandchildren have loved Maranatha. Thereafter comes blessings in the generations to follow.

Then in June of 1999 we celebrated our 50th at MBC. Where else?

God bless Maranatha Bible Camp. Ivan Olsen would be delighted to see things progressing so well under George Cheek.

Maranatha is certainly Holy Ground!

– Marian Sandin,
Cheyenne, Wyoming

Eldon and Marian Sandin were married August 19, 1949. From left: Chuck Smith, Dick DiStefano, Eldon Sandin, Marian Sandin, Alice Olsen, Lorraine Booth. The flower girl at left is Colleen Booth. At right are ringbearers Joy Olsen and David Gustafson. The Sandins were the first to be married at Maranatha.

A Change in Direction

A week at Maranatha Bible Camp literally changed the entire direction of my life. I grew up on a ranch in the beautiful rolling prairie Sandhills about 15 miles south of North Platte. In 1942, when I was 11 years of age, Rev. Ivan Olsen came to the Echo schoolhouse near our community to hold a three-night revival meeting. The American Sunday School Union held Sunday School there each week. During those meetings, as Inez Maline and Mrs. Olsen sang "Pass Me Not, Oh Gentle Savior," I went forward and knelt at the stage. Rev. Olsen prayed with me and I received Christ as my Savior. I never doubted my salvation from that moment on.

I attended Maranatha several summers as a young person. The summer of 1946 was a turning point in my life. The wooden tabernacle had not been built as yet and we were meeting in a large circus-type tent. G. Christian Weiss, at one time the director of missions at Back to the Bible Broadcast, was the speaker and his message was entitled "Not I, But Christ." At the invitation time, he asked all those who wanted to surrender their lives for full-time Christian service to stand. Now, I was a very bashful country boy - but all of a sudden I found myself standing. That discovery made my heart beat so hard I thought it would jump out of my chest. I did not think it through rationally and logically and then decide to stand. It just seemed that something or someone (perhaps an angel from heaven?) made me stand up - and when I discovered I was standing I was petrified. However, after the service Rev. Olsen took nine of us out under the cedars where we knelt down and had a round of prayer of dedication. I had never prayed audibly before, so you can be sure I had in my mind what I was going to say before my turn came. I looked upon this experience as God's special call and throughout life I have attempted to remain true to that calling.

I had in my young mind that I wanted to fly airplanes. I grew up during World War II when many warplanes flew over Nebraska. I had all kinds of plastic model airplanes which came in cereal boxes and could tell anyone the kind of plane flying overhead by looking up underneath it. But my vocational aspirations changed completely that day at Maranatha Bible Camp. When my parents came to pick me up at the end of the week I announced to them that I was going to be a preacher. This delighted them, of course, since they were loving, ardent Christians.

After my junior year in high school at a Christian Academy in South Carolina, I preached my first sermon in 1948 at age 16 at the Block Schoolhouse located a few miles north of North Platte. I was ordained at 20 years of age in July 1952 under the auspices of the Berean Church after meeting with an examining council at Maranatha. Between my junior and senior year in college, I stayed out a year in 1952-53 and was assistant pastor to Rev. Olsen at the Berean Church in North Platte. During the summer, I helped at Maranatha and often Rev. Olsen had me give my testimony in camp meetings about my surrendering to preach while at Maranatha. During this time, I also worked as a public relations representative for the Camp and showed a slide presentation in many area churches.

After pastoring churches in Nebraska, Texas, South Carolina and Minnesota and serving at Christian radio stations in Nebraska and Wisconsin, I retired in 1996. We are now living near Green Bay, where our final assignment from the Lord was as general manager of Christian radio station WRVM which reaches northeast Wisconsin and south central Upper Michigan. We are members of Wycliffe Associates, the volunteer support arm of Wycliffe Bible Translators, and serve short terms whenever possible.

I thank God for the ministry of Maranatha Bible Camp and for the turning point and new direction its influence gave my life back in the late 1940s. It resulted in a lifetime of service for Christ.

– Wendell Baxter,
Suring, Wisconsin

Wendell Baxter (at left) surrendered his life to God for full-time Christian service while at Maranatha. Bill Combs of North Platte is in the other swing. The third man is unidentified.

A Rescue in the Old Swimming Hole

In 1948 to 1949 I was pastoring a circuit of two United Brethren churches. One was in the country, the other in a little town of Angus, Nebraska. Which today the town is dissolved and the churches torn down. Not satisfied with E.U.B.C., we happened to hear an announcement over the radio. Rev. Epp of Back to the Bible program announced there would be a free week of camp at Maranatha for all Christian workers. So very low on finances, we went and got acquainted with Pastor Olsen. He gave us a recommendation to the Congregation Church of Venango which was in need of a pastor. We were accepted and moved that fall. We pastored there in the early 50s. Every summer we would take our young people to Maranatha Young People's Camp. Maranatha didn't have a swimming pool, but used a sand pit in the far western part of Camp property. I was the lifeguard for three years during Young People's Camp. This and pit later became part of the big Lake Maranatha. We used the buddy system—everybody who swam had to have a buddy. When the whistle was blown, they all had to account for each other. If they disobeyed they had to sit on the bank for five minutes. One time, two girls got into a spat in deep water and soon were dunking one another until they began to cough and sputter and they being in danger to drown, I had to grab them both and flutter like mad with my legs to bring them both in. It ended up without incident but it was a drastic moment. They were then both in shallow water after the tow.

Another time, I made a contraption with a jug and tubing to smoke a cigarette and to deposit the nicotine in a vial to show the dangers of smoking. I put the nicotine in the mouth of a lizard or mouse (whatever I could get) and it would die on the spot. Some of the kids said "I'm never going to smoke again." After this I would pass the jug around which held the water to siphon air to smoke the cigarette. Letting them smell it they almost passed out. I told them that is how your lungs are after you smoke.

You know when you work with Ivan Olsen, you really get involved. If he discovered you had certain talents, he put you to work using them. Bless his heart, I got to use a lot of talents I didn't know I had. Ha Ha.

Hope you will forgive my writing. I'm getting a little shaky. In April 2003 I was 90 years old and still counting. If Jesus beckons I'm going, if comes in the clouds I'm soaring.

— Your brother in Christ,
Bob Wieduwilt,
Kansas City, Missouri

Helping Build the Swimming Pool

My memoirs are many, but the building of the swimming pool was a real highlight. Hugh Clark was the designer and builder.

Getting the site ready was a challenge in itself, such as putting the forms on a somewhat unstable ground. Bert Needham would let enough air out of his tires to where he would drive back and forth on the fill to pack it, so we could put in the forms. I would ride down many mornings with Don Shonkwiler and Roy Hoover to work on it, both missionaries serving at the church.

We got the cement from North Platte in open beds because in those days it had to be mixed at the plant. Hugh would always wonder what condition it would be in when we got it, but it was usually about right. We had to use a farm tractor front end loader to get the cement up and into the forms.

The pool was a real blessing because the campers were having to swim in the lake and that was a real concern for Hugh and Rev. Olsen.

I'm thankful I got to have a part in the project, and many more down through the years.

— Leon Buttermore,
North Platte

So This is 'Fellowship'?

I was pastoring the Brady Berean Church. One Saturday morning, as I was preparing for Sunday and "minding my own business," I was rudely interrupted by a group from Camp—Rev. Olsen, Earnest Skoog, Glenn Adams and several others.

That morning, I learned what "Berean fellowship" meant. Rev. Olsen said, "Come with us for some fellowship." The term is misleading, to say the least!

We drove to Maxwell and found ourselves driving along the tracks, picking up old railroad ties that were used at Camp for the septic system.

Later that afternoon, they brought me back, tired, but glad I could help. Truly, you get to know a lot about others when you work with them.

— Oliver Gustafson,
Elgin, Illinois

Peeling Potatoes, Pouring Cement

We have been married over 60 years and during those early years we saw God's blessings upon Maranatha Bible Camp expanding to what it has become today.

I remember the early days when the Berean ladies went together to work at camp, getting it ready for the camping season. How energetic those ladies were. We swept down spider webs, floors and scrubbed.

During camp weeks, we helped in the kitchen. It was so small that we had to peel our potatoes outside, prepare cabbage for slaw and do whatever was necessary. A lot of garden produce was brought in and it never went to waste. Mrs. Krause was our chief cook and what a dear lady she

Harold and Lilus George

was. We were always at her beck and call.

Tables and benches were used in the dining hall. Food was served from bowls and volunteer campers waited tables and kept the bowls filled with delicious home-cooked food. No one left the table hungry. Volunteer campers helped wash the dishes and there was always singing as they went about their work.

My husband, Harold, helped pour cement for the Tabernacle in those early years. I served as camp treasurer from 1966 to 1969. This was during the Navigator Program, directed by Dr. Olsen. What a blessed spiritual time it was for the young people.

We had the privilege of sending our children: Timothy, Thomas and Rebecca, to Camp and also our grandchildren: Kevin and Bradley George, Jonathan and Jason Niehus, Carrie Ann and Trevor George. Each one has unforgettable memories that made an impact on their lives.

God Bless Maranatha Bible Camp.

– Harold and Lilus George,
North Platte

The ladies (and some men) from the surrounding churches selected a day to help with kitchen duties. They would peel hundreds of pounds of potatoes while sitting at tables under the shade trees.

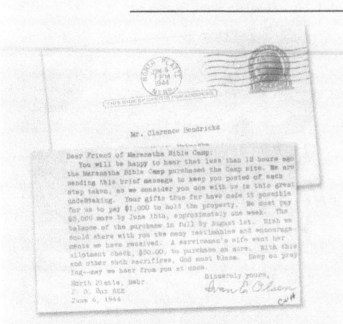

Clarence Hendricks of Wellfleet received this postcard from Pastor Olsen asking for a donation to help pay for the newly-purchased site.

Young Peoples Camp, 1945.

Beauchamp Family Memories

We were happy to know a history of Maranatha is being planned. We have felt quite close to Maranatha from its beginning. Though we lived 50 miles west of North Platte near Keystone, Nebraska, through our relationship with the Hugh Clark family, we were aware of what was taking place. Mrs. Clark was my husband's, sister.

In 1944 our oldest son, Dale, attended Camp. At that time they were sleeping in tents. He was 9 years old, and accepted the Lord as his Saviour at that time. I am happy to say he has served the Lord all these years. He and his wife, Darlene, attended Bible school. Throughout their married life they have both taught Sunday school classes. Dale taught adult Sunday school class and often filled in when the pastor was away. He serves as a board member and they are both active in every area of the church. Our two daughters also attended Camp in later years.

Harold and I helped out at Camp at various times for many years. One summer in the late 1950s Harold worked at maintenance all summer and I had charge of the kitchen. Other years we were counselors along with other activities for a week. One time at a Junior Camp I was impressed with what happened. During the evening service we had a thunderstorm and the lights went out. Cliff Gustafson was in charge and he told the Campers to stay in their seats and he started them singing choruses. Ruth Gustafson played the piano and we sang until the lights came on. All was well and no panic. Praise the Lord for the ministry of Cliff and Ruth all the many years they served at Maranatha.

During the 1950s, ladies from the Ogallala Church would go to camp once a month and serve the meals that day. We enjoyed it very much.

We moved to Denver County in 1962 and continued our service there for 25 years.

While in Denver we were not able to get to Camp very often. The Lord took Harold home in 1989.

In 1991 I was visiting relatives in North Platte and Hugh happened to be in North Platte at the same time visiting his brother, Ward. He took me on a tour of Maranatha. I was amazed at the progress since I had last been there. I could not help but look back through the years and marvel at all God had done. He has used so many people and so many thousands—no, maybe millions—of people and children have been blessed and many came to know the Lord. All this because Dr. Olsen and Hugh Clark had a burden for the need of a Camp and did something about it. I am sure they had no idea of what the Lord was going to do through Maranatha in the years to come. It has been awesome!

I have many memories of Camp. We attended family week many times and other special sessions. I'll never forget some of the wonderful speakers and workers.

– Floy Beauchamp,
Butte, Montana

Traveling Volunteers Enjoy Their Septembers

My wife and I are proud to have been able to serve at Maranatha Camp since 1995. I am a mechanic and Elaine does a variety of jobs, but her favorite is to help out in the office with the girls. We travel the year round helping different Christian organizations but the folks here at Maranatha are the best to work for. They not only care about us, they always put God before any of their own needs. God certainly knew what He was doing when He sent us here to help out. We appreciate their hospitality and friendship. They certainly carried us through a storm.

The staff has become almost like a family to us, and we are pleased to call Nebraska "home" for the month of September. We look forward to working together with them for as many years as the Lord allows. We serve an awesome Lord and the people here are just an added bonus. May God continue to bless this Camp and His workers.

– Roger and Elaine Ford,
On the open road

Top row: The old sandpit was the only swimming option at Camp until the cement pool was built in 1954.

Second row: The swimming pool fence had been installed by the time this 1957 photo was taken.

Third row, from left: The dining hall was ready for use in the summer of 1948; The swimming pool fence had not yet been built in 1955.

Fourth row, from left: A day at Camp always began with flag salute to both the American and Christian flags. Then at eight o'clock, everyone lined up for breakfast. This photo was taken during Children's Week in 1946. Note the slab building with the tin roof - this was the dining hall; The Tabernacle was first used in 1948. Eventually, it would become known as the "Old Tabernacle." It stood 46 years before major structural problems led to its demolition.

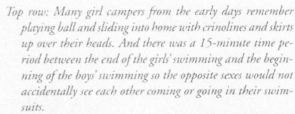

Top row: Many girl campers from the early days remember playing ball and sliding into home with crinolines and skirts up over their heads. And there was a 15-minute time period between the end of the girls' swimming and the beginning of the boys' swimming so the opposite sexes would not accidentally see each other coming or going in their swimsuits.

Second row: Slab cabins blended into the cedars at Maranatha, offering a rustic sort of privacy to Camp speakers and pastors.

Third row, from left: This was the Family Week in 1946. Electrical lines had been added in 1944. The slab dining hall is in the background; Meals in the new Dining Hall were served family-style by counselors and kitchen volunteers.

Fourth row, from left: By the early 1960s, women were allowed to wear slacks during recreation times at Camp; All meetings were held under a large tent until 1948. The seats in this tent tabernacle were wood planks with no backs. Campers survived the hot afternoons by fanning themselves with cardboard (with pictures of the Dionne quintuplets on them) on sticks, donated by a funeral home.

Volunteers

Without volunteer workers to organize the programs, build the dormitories, prepare the food and maintain the facilities, there would never have been a Maranatha Bible Camp.

For more than 20 years, no one outside of Ivan Olsen and an on-site caretaker was paid for any work related to Maranatha. No expenses were reimbursed; no honorariums were given.

"Never have I seen a camp operated on as little cash as Maranatha," said Theodore Epp in a 1954 fundraiser letter.

When Ivan Olsen, Hugh Clark, Nick Janzen and several of their friends started preparing for the First Annual Encampment in the spring of 1938, there was no one else to do the work but themselves and no way to pay anyone for his time. Everyone worked for free, and no one thought anything about it. People traveled to Maranatha at their own expense to make an investment in the lives of youth and children.

Armed with few other options, Olsen began to raise money and recruit workers. He quickly developed a reputation as a man who could get other people to do what was needed — regardless of whether they had training in the job they were being recruited to do.

The properties of Maranatha expanded, and it took a massive amount of work to carve a park-like campground out of the sandy soil and scrubby cedar trees. Olsen appreciated what had been accomplished, but every day, he saw more that needed to be done. Obtaining workers became almost as necessary as eating and breathing. As he neared the end of his life, Olsen occasionally spoke about how fundraising had become exhausting, but he never said that about recruiting volunteers.

"(Olsen) only sleeps about two hours a day, and even when he's sleeping, he's thinking of work for somebody else to do," said Richard Crocker at Maranatha's 50th anniversary celebration in 1988.

The person Olsen called on first and foremost was Hugh Clark. It's likely that no one put in more volunteer hours at Maranatha than the lanky railroader (with the possible exception of Reuben Hasenauer), but many came close.

There never will be an accurate estimate of all the man-hours that volunteers have expended at Maranatha, and the names will never be properly recorded until heaven, but several should be mentioned.

Ward Clark worked on various projects at Maranatha with his brother, Hugh, in the 1940s, including the construction of the Tabernacle. Ward and his wife, Maxine, built a cabin at Camp and stayed for weeks at a time while he was working on projects. Their daughter, Virginia, helped in the dining hall and kitchen when she was not a camper. Ward collects used golf balls at courses around the area and donates them to Maranatha's mini-golf course.

Don Hunt, a conductor with the Union Pacific Railroad at North Platte, volunteered at Maranatha for decades after he came back from World War II. Hunt worked on a variety of jobs over 40 years. Clyde West was a regular volunteer at Camp during the 1960s. Bert Needham helped with everything from carpentry to installing septic systems. After donating their ranch to Camp, Bert and his wife, Anna, lived at Maranatha (Anna worked in the Camp kitchen) until her death in 1970, and Bert continued until his death in 1985.

Reuben Hasenauer was a farm worker who had fallen on hard times in 1974. Ivan Olsen visited him in the hospital and discovered that until he fully recovered from surgery, the farmer he worked for would not be able to pay him. So it was that Reuben began helping as able on the Maranatha grounds during his recovery. After he had fully recovered, his former employer came looking for him when the farm work began, but Reuben told him, "No thanks; I'm going to spend the rest of my days in ministry at Maranatha."

Many campers young and old recognized this quiet man as a saint with a servant's heart. He worked at his own pace to trim trees, mow lawns, trap mice and gophers and enjoy the company of others in the dining hall and Sweet Shop. In his later years, some would chide him to go home and rest after supper in the summertime. "What is there to do at my house besides watching TV?" he would ask. Over the years, college-age young men stayed at Reuben's house while at Camp for a few months to work on projects. They found him to be a genuine Christian in bib overalls and a seed corn cap, a man who faithfully prayed, read his Bible daily and could discuss spiritual truths with unusual understanding and an infectious burst of laughter. Reuben faithfully worked throughout his sunset years, until late in the afternoon of November 27, 1998, when he lay down for a nap after putting in a day of work and died peacefully in his sleep.

George Cheek made strides at recruiting people to serve as retired resident volunteers at Maranatha. He started in 1980 with a couple from northeast Colorado.

Hank & Evelyn Wambolt had been serving the Lord as lay ministers in western Nebraska and eastern Colorado for many years. When they grew close to being able to retire, they contacted a radio ministry that had been an encouragement to them with its Bible teaching. Back to the Bible suggested the Wambolts contact Maranatha as a place for volunteer missionary service. George & Jan Cheek drove to meet them in their home in Julesburg, Colorado, and struck up an immediate friendship. Upon acceptance as resident retired volunteers, they made financial arrangements for a life estate in a mobile home owned by Camp and began work in 1980. Evelyn was the health care person. Hank was able to fix almost anything as a carpenter. He organized "Hank's Hardware" as efficiently as any camp storage can be. Many volunteers over the years have expressed their amazement about the near-photographic memory Hank had when it came to locating a needed part or material for the job at hand.

Hank gave plenty of notice that when he turned 90, he no longer wanted to be responsible for the upkeep of the shop. As of this writing, he still comes in several days a week to help as able. Evelyn took up painting after age 65 and has become prolific. Her works are in many of the guest rooms and on sale in the Gift Shop to benefit the Camp.

George's own parents, Merle & Stella Cheek, soon got involved as retired resident volunteers. The Cheeks arrived at Camp in 1987 after selling their home in Steamboat Springs, Colorado. They had an interest in Maranatha, since all four of their children had worked there on summer staff. They had come to visit and helped with painting and other projects several times. After moving to Maranatha, Merle worked in maintenance and took care of raising and lowering the American and Christian flags for many years. He gets the Camp mail

and does landscaping work. Stella managed the Gift Shop for more than 10 years and still works there.

Dick & Bonnie Feay arrived at Camp in 1988. Dick was getting ready to retire from Williams Pipe Line and he and Bonnie wanted to do something to serve the Lord. They were fascinated by the work of Maranatha and thought it would be a good place to start. After installing a new mobile home in the name of the Camp, they settled down to help in many areas of the ministry. Bonnie helped in the office and Gift Shop. Dick, with his electrical and phone technology skills, has done projects all over the Camp. The winter of 1992-93, they stayed at Camp while Dick helped with all of the wiring that went into building the gymnasium/multipurpose building. Their winters in later years have been spent in Apache Junction, Arizona.

Jack & Virginia Ashcraft have served at Maranatha since 1989. They had children who attended as campers and then served on summer staff. Their son Dan also had attended the Navigators Training Program. After retiring from the Air Force, they worked at Back to the Bible until retiring again. It was at that time they decided to come be resident retirees at Maranatha during the summers and winter at Bibleville near McAllen, Texas. A mobile home on Camp was available; they took over its stewardship and soon had it in good shape. Their family visits each summer as able. Virginia soon took on the responsibility of managing the Sweet Shop with the help of her good friend, Eleanor Fasse. Many improvements were made during their watch. Virginia stepped down as manager after the summer of 2002, but continues to work in the Sweet Shop.

Neil & Pauline Tallman, former missionaries to Ecuador, moved to Maranatha in 1990. Neil, a former pastor, served in the cassette tape ministry. Neil passed away in 1994, but Pauline continues to volunteer in the office.

Most volunteers are not able to spend their retirement years living at Camp, but have given of their time and ability for days, weeks, or even a month at a time. Again, many cannot be mentioned for lack of space, but these people have been among the most frequent volunteers in the last decade.

Jim Van Mark of Lexington, Nebraska, was the major designer and builder of the Camp's 100-ft. waterslide and the Blob tower on the Waterfront, and his wife, Jean, has helped in the laundry facility during the 1990s and 2000s. Roger & Elaine Ford of Iowa have volunteered the entire month of September during about that same period of time. Roger fixes automobiles and Elaine helps in the office. Eleanor Fasse spends her summers volunteering in the Sweet Shop. She hosts a family reunion at her cabin each summer during one of Maranatha's family camps.

Maranatha Bible Camp is about a 20-minute drive from North Platte, and in order to save time and gasoline, staff members have tried to find ways to reduce their number of trips to town. In the early 1970s, Ed & Alice Felgate and various summer staff members obtained a list of supplies needed and made a "town run" to North Platte. In the 1980s, Don &

Marguerite Hunt expanded the ministry of "town run," to five days a week. The Hunts were succeeded by George & "Mac" Welsh, Russ & Stevie Taylor and Everett & Darlene Small, among others, and it has proven to be a blessing to the Maranatha staff.

Often, churches have sent groups of various sizes to work on a project at Maranatha. In these cases, the Camp usually buys materials and provides meals and housing for the workers, but some volunteer groups have bought materials and cooked their own meals as well as giving a cash offering to Maranatha Camp. One of the most noteworthy recent groups has been a confederation of several churches from Pennsylvania and Maryland led by Frank Jones who make a nearly 3,000-mile round trip to Camp in a school bus for a weeklong missions adventure. They have remodeled the dish lobby, painted buildings, installed air conditioners and built floating docks for the Waterfront.

Another notable group from a Christian school in Aurora, Illinois, called itself "Mission Impossible." In April 2000, more than 100 youth and sponsors helped build the director's house on the south shore of Lake Maranatha, helped build a bathhouse in the RV park and cleared several areas of the woods of dead branches, sawing them into firewood.

A host of churches within a three-hour drive of Maranatha have helped build new buildings, remodel old buildings, paint rooms and upgrade recreation areas.

On Saturday night, June 13, 1998, Cheek put out an appeal on radio and television for volunteers to report to Maranatha the next day to help clean up after a tornado ripped through Camp and destroyed approximately 150 trees. More than 100 volunteers showed up the next afternoon and spent several hours hauling limbs and helping the staff reduce them to wood chips.

Perhaps the biggest outpouring of volunteer help, however, has come in the Camp kitchen. From 1938 until the 1960s, Maranatha depended daily upon volunteers from area churches to prepare and serve three meals a day. Many women, and a few men, cooked and cleaned for countless meals throughout those years. To a lesser degree, that tradition continues today in the Camp kitchen, dining hall and Sweet Shop when the fulltime staff puts out an appeal for help during the busiest Camp weeks.

VOICES OF MARANATHA

We Knew That We Were Loved

I have so many good memories of Maranatha that I couldn't begin to enumerate them all, but one thing stands out above everything else ... we knew as kids, whether we were working there or were campers, *that we were loved* - by the staff, speakers, counselors, and most of all by God!! A deep passion for God and a love for kids permeated the Camp, greatly influencing my concept of God as a child. It was there that I dedicated my life to the Lord to be used in any way He would choose, and it was also there that one friend whom I took to Camp accepted Jesus!

One of the other memories I have of Maranatha is of the many women and men of our church (North Platte Berean) who faithfully worked year after year to clean and help maintain cabins, buildings, and the grounds ... and then there were the *mountains* of potatoes to be peeled and endless dishes to be washed! Of course our mom felt that work and service were important lessons for us to learn, so we did our fair share of cleaning and kitchen duties as kids ... and it blew my mind that they would so *joyfully* chatter and sing while they worked (gr-r-r-r! I had a really hard time singing while doing dishes in that sweltering kitchen! How did they do it?!).

The provision of food for the camp was another significant way in which many farmers in the area served God. As did other farmers, our folks would plant rows of vegetables to be used at camp each year and would donate as much meat as they could afford. Rev. Olsen believed in keeping the cost affordable and prayed for God to provide food accordingly. It was often miraculous how God did just that - sometimes on the very day it was needed! He would call or come out to our farm (and other farms also) and ask, "Clarence, do you have any _____ ? They need it for (a certain) week", or "Clarence, what do you have that you would be able to donate to Camp?" Sometimes he would need to locate additional food for the meal that night, and then it would be more urgent. God faithfully provided so that the campers always had plenty to eat and blessed many with the joy of giving in the process! He's eternally caring and good!!

– *Sharon Hendricks Jost,*
Omaha, Nebraska

Felgates Ministered to Teens at Camp

In July 1973, Ed and Alice Felgate moved to Maranatha Bible Camp. We felt the Lord leading us to serve him there, so we brought a mobile home and moved in. We were so lovingly greeted by all who were there at the time. It was so beautiful a place, so well kept.

I think one of the couples serving there at the time, Rex and Patsy Shaver, had everything under control. Rex was in charge of outside fixing and many other things and Patsy was in charge of the kitchen, all the cooking and serving, which was a great work and I must say she cooked such delicious food, well in charge, the bigger the crowd, the better she did. I'm sure none other surpassed her position. She is now rejoicing in Glory with our blessed Lord.

Ed right away started with many duties during the camping time in summer, he made the town runs.

Ed so enjoyed working with the young teens as he supervised their duties. Warren Cheek, who became director of United Indian Ministries, said Ed taught him how to drive a stick shift pickup. He also enjoyed working with Bryan Clark, Bruce Clark and Tom Walker.

As an R.N., I did the caring for any camper who had a physical need for awhile, then Cheri Geise, an R.N. from Iowa, came and took over for a few summers. She has served in Cote d'Ivoire, West Africa, as a missionary nurse.

What a blessing to have young teens that were helpers to come and solve any problem and we could talk, then quote scripture and pray with them.

I must say the six years we were at Maranatha were such a blessing and now we have all those precious memories that we'll always cherish. God bless all those who serve the Lord at MBC, and our prayers are for them daily.

– Ed and Alice Felgate,
Norfolk, Nebraska

Ed and Alice Felgate spent six years as retired volunteers at Maranatha.

Left: The old slab dining hall and kitchen was a popular place, as might be expected. Women from many area churches made sure that campers were well fed. Sundays were especially planned to bless the parents and friends who visited. Visitors could have dinner at the camp for 25 cents a plate. (Often over 1,000 were served on a Sunday noon in two or three sittings. Two favorite menus were meatloaf and chicken and noodles.) Since there were services morning, afternoon and evening, many drive-ins came to hear the special Camp speakers. Center: Sorting through donated potatoes in the 1970s are, from left: Reuben Hasenauer, Bert Needham and Floyd McCall Sr. Right: The Roving Volunteers in Christ's Service have provided work crews many times over the years.

North Platte Berean Church and Maranatha

There has always been a close connection between Maranatha Bible Camp and the nearby North Platte Berean Church. Rev. Ivan Olsen was the first pastor of the church and served there for 40 years, beginning in 1936. He was also was recognized as founder of the Camp along with other individuals who worked right along with him and his wife, Alice, from day one. Many of the earliest Camp workers, including Hugh & Lela Clark, Lyle & Viola Carper, John Goodmanson, Nellie Lantz, Faye Ward, John Maline and Ralph Talbot, attended North Platte Berean.

As time went on, many more people from North Platte Berean were called upon for volunteer work. The men of North Platte Berean built many of the Camp buildings, and countless meals have been cooked by women of that church. That tradition continues to this day.

Though our fulltime missionary staff are free to attend various area churches, many of them attend North Platte Berean and are involved in a variety of ministries there, including the music ministry, drama, the nursery, and teaching Sunday school and midweek children's clubs.

Over the years, the church made available several associate pastors or interns and their wives to assist at Maranatha for various programs. They include Eugene Clark, the Wieduwilts, Ward & Yvonne Childerson, Ken & Sophi Blood, Denny & Ruth Norris, Don & Deb Larreau and Tim & Katie Brown. In 1982, Rev. Carl Goltz of Scottsbluff, Nebraska, who already served as the Camp board chairman, was called to be senior pastor of North Platte Berean, so he and his wife, Doris, continued to serve at Maranatha from a much shorter distance.

Pastor Tom Walker and his wife, Janet, began serving North Platte Berean during the 1990s and have been a source of encouragement to our fulltime and Summer Missions staff team. The Walkers led a Maranatha-sponsored short-term missions trip to an Indian reservation in Canada in 1992, and their advice and availability has been a real asset, coming as it does from the perspective of non-board members who are quite knowledgeable of the Camp operation.

Over the Camp's more than 65 years of existence, general directors Ivan Olsen and George Cheek have acknowledged the members of North Platte Berean and their many different contributions. Part of the reward, both now and in eternity, goes to this forward-looking church, not forgetting those who have "gone on before."

– *George W. Cheek*

George and Jan Cheek, 2002.

Top row, from left: Oliver Gustafson, the brother of Alice Olsen, repainted this sign in 1985; Becker Hall addition.

Second row, from left: Retired resident volunteers enjoy a relaxing moment in the dining hall during the summer of 1997. From left: Jack Ashcraft, Virginia Ashcraft, Eleanor Fasse, Pauline Tallman, Shirley Gayman, Fred Gayman, Stella Cheek and Merle Cheek; Don Hunt, a Union Pacific Railroad employee and Camp board member, arranged in 1986 for the donation and delivery of a refrigerated boxcar to use for food storage. From left, Mark Swesey, David Jones, Don Hunt, George Cheek and Joe Dapra.

Cold Nights in the Cabin Were Worth It

When my family moved to Skellytown, Texas, my folks had bought a dry goods store with the living quarters in the back. We started attending the Community Church at Skellytown faithfully. I don't remember exactly when I became a Christian. But it was at the church at Skellytown. I don't know how our pastor, Albert Stroh, found out about Maranatha. But some of the girls from there went to Camp in 1951.

I do remember the nice warm days in late summer and nearly freezing every night. Some of the girls had heavy enough blankets and some of us didn't. We were in a long, cinder block barracks with old bunk beds. It had been divided in small rooms and had fairly large windows in it. Anyhow, we tried to keep our side cleaned up. The girls in the other side were messy and one of our girls could hardly handle that. We had an outside bath house. It seems that we were on the left side cabins as we faced the bath house. When we went the next year, 1952, we were on the right side of the bath house. I got the top bunk again and it wasn't so cold then. The first year, I was out exploring, it seems. The girls remarked that I was never there. The second year I stayed in the cabin most of the time, reading or sleeping.

I have good memories of the "Old Tabernacle," a square, cement block building with its book store in the back, the pulpit in the front, the old benches. Eugene Clark was there at the organ and his thick glasses. Outside was the snack building and the mess hall across the way. There were lots of tall trees. I never did go swimming, but it seems that it was some sort of sandpit. There was no mixed swimming and you had to be covered well going and coming. I helped out sometime in the small mess hall with its benches. Now, as I play or hear Eugene Clark's beautiful music, especially, *"Nothing Is Impossible,"* I think of him at Maranatha. Paul (Levine) and Bob (Findlay) were at one camp. The blind Bob sang beautifully and the kids loved to be around him.

My future husband, Earlin, and I met on a Saturday afternoon, while he was playing table tennis. I was watching him play. When they quit, he and I stood and talked. He sat back of our group that night at chapel. We walked around some and ate dinner together on Sunday, then we left for home on our separate ways.

Earlin remembered the cold showers at camp and not much else, except meeting me and who some of the kids from Orienta were.

I also remembered when we first went to Camp that some of the kids would come up to us and say, "talk Texan," because of the way that we said "y'all." We married at Skellytown in my parents' home November 21, 1953. The Lord has been so very good and answered so many prayers for us through the years. We were at Maranatha in the 1980s and stayed in a trailer house for a short time. So much had changed since we were there. We couldn't find anything that we remembered, except our good memories. But for an Okie guy and a Texas gal to meet at Maranatha Bible Camp in Nebraska is only with our gracious Lord's guiding hand!

– Bette (Foster) and Earlin Penner,
Fairview, Oklahoma

It Changed the Direction of Our Lives

The year was 1953. We came to know the Lord through the death of our 9-month-old niece, who was killed in a household accident. The Lord used that incident to bring the two of us to faith in Christ. The news of our conversion spread around the neighborhood and our pastor challenged us to visit the Maranatha Bible Camp at Maxwell, Nebraska. Little did we realize how that one week would change the direction of our entire lifetime. It was our first experience of meeting Christians from many different backgrounds, which we found rather exhilarating and encouraging. Then too, we were challenged every day and evening by the late Dr. J. Oswald Smith of the People's Church in Canada. On a given evening, Dr. Smith challenged us to take our hands off our life and just let the Lord lead us, which sounded very reasonable to us and so we took our two little sons and went down to the altar and surrendered our lives to the Lord for that purpose.

That decision led us to follow the Lord for training to Grace Bible Institute, Fresno Pacific College, The California Graduate School of Theology and an honors degree from the Briercrest Biblical Seminary in Saskatchewan, Canada. Well, here we are now 50 years later having spent those years in the Lord's service as a pastor, evangelist, Bible teacher, counselor and friend to many for Jesus' sake.

We have also had the joy of serving with the Billy Graham Evangelistic ministries in encouraging others to become involved in City Wide Evangelistic Campaigns and served in Amsterdam 2000 as a staff person. We also served as chairman for the Franklin Graham services in Saskatoon, Saskatchewan with 140 churches involved. Presently, we are serving with the Haggai Institute in training national leaders from the developing nations of the world in evangelism and discipleship and fund raising in their own countries.

Yes, we are deeply grateful for the founders of the Maranatha Bible Camp and pray God's richest blessing upon your continued ministry and may the Lord always have the liberty to work at Camp even as He did with us.

– Dr. Robert and Ione Radtke,
Fresno, California

"Uncle Cliff and Aunt Ruth" Made Their Mark

The date was May 8, 1945, the Peace Treaty signed, closing World War II, in Europe. It was also the day set for the wedding of Ruth Clasper to Rev. Clifford L. Gustafson. Ruth was living in Ohio; Cliff had just resigned his pastorate in Marshall, Michigan, and Grabill, Indiana had been chosen for the wedding because, due to gas and tire rationing, it was easier for folk in Ohio and Michigan to meet there for the big wedding. No one knew that it would also be the big holiday for closing restaurants, gas stations, etc. so folk doubled up in their cars to come to the wedding. It was held in a lovely red brick church, built by Ruth's grandfather, one of the early pastors there, who also gave Ruth in marriage, since her father, Rev. John Clasper, was the officiating minister. Cliff's brother-in-law, Rev. Ivan E. Olsen, was his best man, and his sister, Alice Olsen, was one of Ruth's attendants.

Soon after the wedding they were to conduct the children's camp at Maranatha Bible Camp, near North Platte, Nebraska. Cliff had been there before, but this was Ruth's first time to be at Maranatha. They shared a two-room cabin with the camp nurse, Beulah Hasenauer, and worked diligently at the Camp, resolving to possibly return again the following summer.

After the children's camp ended, Cliff and Ruth were to summer in western Colorado, to conduct an extensive ministry of children's meetings, and to observe places where some Gospel churches could be established. Rev. Theodore Epp, director of the Back to the Bible Broadcast, himself personally supported Cliff and Ruth in their outreach that summer. They ministered in many out-of-the-way places, with Scene-o-felt pictures, vibraharp music and Gospel messages, locating many places in need of a church ministry. At the close of the summer work they knew they would return at the Autumn season to begin with a radio ministry in Grand Junction, Colorado.

The months of October and November found them holding children's services in Lexington, Nebraska (the beginning of the Berean Church there) and in Ogallala, Nebraska, where they left with their home attached to their car—a 24-foot Cozy Coach trailer, bound for Grand Junction, Colorado. They invested the next 10 years there, planting churches, and a Bible Camp, named Twin Peaks.

Cliff and Ivan Olsen worked together for so many years, in church planting, and raising funds for Maranatha Bible Camp. Cliff and Ruth came every summer to help. Junior camps grew and Cliff became convinced there needed to be a division of those camps, and by the late 1950s, Junior High camps were soon part of the schedule.

During those years, they had the help of teams from Prairie Bible Institute, Three Hills, Alberta, Canada. These young people worked tirelessly and served so faithfully in music, counseling, baking, cleaning, whatever needed to be done. Mrs. Krause and Mrs. Clark gave numerous hours of effort in the kitchen, and NO air-conditioning, and not much equipment either! Remember the aluminum plates and cups, and the first kitchen on the grounds? How well I recall the efforts and love these folk put into making Camp grow and become so meaningful to children, young people, and adults! The Lord keeps all the records! He sees all the faithful women and men from many places who willingly gave of their time and strength to serve the Lord at Maranatha.

In 1955 it was determined that Gustafsons would leave the Calvary Bible Church in Grand Junction, and moved to North Platte where Cliff would become more involved in the Camp ministry. Rev. Theodore Epp was then president of the Camp board. It was an exciting time for Cliff and Ruth, and their children: David, Anna and Christine. In 1957 the youngest Gustafson (Dan) was born ... right in the middle of the nine weeks of Maranatha Camp! *What a busy time!!*

In 1960, the Gustafsons moved to California to start a church there. The most memorable thing about the first year the Gustafsons returned from California to come back to Maranatha for Junior Camps, was the fact that son, David, came to Nebraska with cut-off jeans ... unheard of! But it was decided he could wear them. The Training Program had al-

Cliff and Ruth Gustafson and son, David, 1947.

ready been started earlier, and the Gustafson older children were part of that, and profited spiritually from those years ... LeRoy Eims, Russ Johnston, Walt Hendriksen and other godly men and women were of great help to the young people! Eternity alone will reveal all that implanted in the lives of those who were there.

Cliff and Ruth returned to Maranatha every year that they possibly could. Adults today will remember Uncle Cliff and Aunt Ruth, and their love for children, and teaching them God's Word.

In the 1970s, Cliff and Ruth moved to Oregon, then to Minnesota. Cliff and Ruth came to Maranatha those summers, also. In 1982 the Gustafsons moved to Ogallala, Nebraska. This put them much nearer the work of Maranatha Bible Camp. Their six-year ministry there culminated in 1988. About that time Maranatha was considering adding a Senior Adults' Ministry to the Camp schedule to the lists of Camp. Cliff was chosen for that new venture. As Cliff set up the agenda, subject: DEPRESSION, Cliff was very ill, hospitalized for surgery, etc. and told me to go ahead with the program ... it was set for May 1989. April 1, 1989, Cliff was called home to Heaven. I carried on the Senior Adult Retreat the next month, finding others who came who had the same kind of needs, and the Lord gave them a good camp. The Senior Retreats were carried on for several years by me, with faithful helpers. I am still corresponding with many of the folk who attended the Senior Retreats.

Later, in 1994 I married Walter Gibson, a retired Baptist minister who lived in Michigan. For the next two years we came back to Maranatha to do the Senior Retreats. Those were special occasions, and I have happy memories of the times at Maranatha! Walter had a serious heart condition, and that limited our travels. He passed away in October 1999. I moved back to California, to be near family, in August 2000.

I have a quiet ministry of correspondence and prayer. I count it a privilege to be near my family. I pray often for the outreach and faithful staff at Maranatha.

I do not cease to give thanks for the spiritual blessings on thousands of lives through the ministry of Maranatha Bible Camp! Blessings on each of you!

— *Ruth Gustafson Gibson,*
Claremont, California

Overseas Christian Servicemen's Center/Cadence

Overseas Christian Servicemen's Center/Cadence held its first three annual Bible and Missionary Conferences at Maranatha in 1956, 1957 and 1959. Tom and I "were" the home office in 1956, since OCSC had only been in existence two years. Dates: August 25 to September 1, 1956, Speakers: Ed Spahr, Ken Engle; Cost: $1.75 per adult per day, half price for half pints 2-12, no charge under 2; Mom Miller (Jesse's mother) and Mammy Hamilton were the cooks.

This is an excerpt from page 52 of my book *"Fill These Rooms"* published in 1998:

"We had a strong desire to have a Bible conference in the U.S. like the ones the GIs had experienced in the Millers' home in Manila. So when Pastor Ivan Olsen from our Berean Fundamental Church in North Platte, Nebraska offered the facilities at Maranatha Bible Camp for the Labor Day weekend in 1956, we jumped at the opportunity. Invitations were sent to all of the people on the mailing list.

Dr. Ed Spahr, a missionary on furlough from the Philippines, agreed to be our speaker. Jesse Miller's mother volunteered to do the cooking. It was a grand reunion of many from the Manila home as well as relatives and friends. Sid Hendry brought a group of airmen from the Denver Servicemen's Center. The Bible teaching was deeply challenging, the fellowship warm and uniting. Most of us were poor in this world's goods, but all were rich in God's blessings. Before leaving, someone handed Chuck Hall, then a student at Moody, a 10-dollar bill. But Chuck felt Sid needed it more so placed it into his hand. Thrilled to have money to give, Sid felt burdened for our needs to get back to California so gave it to us. But Tark and Alma were heading for the Philippines soon and needed funds, so we passed it on to them. I'm not sure who finally kept it, but it didn't matter for that 10-dollar bill gave all of us the joy of both giving and receiving."

— *Tom and Dotty Hash,*
Lakewood, Colorado

Just the Kind of Family We Hope Will Come

Back in the summer of 1948; the Kenneth Blood family received a letter from Rev. Theodore Epp, informing us of the Maranatha Bible Camp near Maxwell, Nebraska. He told us they were offering pastors and their wives a week of Family Camp free. We, as a family with five little children, had never been to a Bible Camp, so it sounded like a wonderful opportunity. It sounded too good to be true! We were asked to respond to the invitation by writing to Rev. Ivan Olsen in North Platte, Nebraska.

So a letter was sent to Rev. Olsen, the founder and director of Maranatha, thanking him for the wonderful opportunity he was offering us. However we had five small children and would not be able to leave them at home in Guthrie Center, Iowa. Thus our attending seemed impossible. A reply to our letter came within days, saying "You are just the kind of family we hope will come! Most pastors with children cannot afford a week of Camp." Of course we could say Amen to that. The letter finished with: "So please plan on coming and bring the children. We have a dormitory room with six bunk beds set up for you." What excitement in the Blood home as we prepared to drive to Maxwell and attend the Family Week for pastors and their families.

What a wonderful time we had. Things were a bit primitive in those days, but we didn't suffer a bit. We could even take hot baths if daddy Ken could run fast enough with a pail of water from the kitchen area. In spite of the lack of things we all now take for granted, that week was like a taste of heaven. Good food, great Christian fellowship and best of all wonderful teaching from some great men of God.

Rev. Olsen arranged for Ken and Sophia to meet Mrs. Barbara Rice, Mrs. Nellie Wolcott and Mrs. Maria Rawson, who represented the Berean Fundamental Church of Lexington, Nebraska. However at that time we were comfortable in the Baptist Church of Guthrie Center and didn't even know there was a Lexington. We found out that the church was looking for and praying for God's choice for a pastor. We enjoyed our visit with them and promised to pray for their need.

The short version of the story is that it was Maranatha that God used to get the Bloods acquainted with the Berean Fundamental Church of Lexington. We were called to be pastor in late September of 1948 until February of 1962.

Thus began our real relationship with Maranatha which extended from 1948 to 1976. As the church attendance grew, our group of ladies volunteered to drive to Maranatha every Thursday, during the summer camp season. There they would relieve Mrs. Krause and her faithful workers from North Platte. We cooked dinner for as many as 200 people, then baked cakes in the afternoon, fixed and served the evening meal. Then we would drive the 50 miles back to Lexington, happy that we had been able to help in the ministry to Children, Youth and Adults.

We spent 28 years in a blessed relationship with Maranatha and with Rev. and Mrs. Olsen and family as well as many co-workers. The ministry of the Camp program was a real testimony to our five children.

In 1955 Ken was asked by the Camp Board to serve as recording and legal secretary. He accepted the position and served consistently until May of 1976 when we moved to Michigan.

In May of 1969, Ken took the position of assistant manager of Maranatha and we moved there for 15 months. Then we moved back to Colorado in September 1970. However we continued our relationship on the Camp board. What a wonderful privilege to be associated with these wonderful men like Ivan Olsen, Theodore Epp, Ernest Lott, Hugh Clark, Carl Goltz, Curt Lehman and others who were on the board for a time.

— *Ken and Sophia Blood,*
Jenison, Michigan

Ken and Sophia Blood in 1999.

Memories From the Thompsons

How well I remember the times in the early days of the Camp, when Mrs. Glenn Krause was the Camp cook, and the women of the Berean Church took turns every day to go to Camp to help prepare the meals. What fun we had, but we did work!

What a difference in what Camp is today compared to ones then. How we praise God for the lives saved by Christ through the years at Camp.

— *John and Laurine Thompson,*
North Platte

Wambolts Got Things Organized During Retirement Years

Having retired from 32 years in church planting, and because of Hank's hearing loss, and he was 65 years old, we began seeking God's direction for us to be of service in God's work somewhere.

Hank and I (Evelyn) were both saved under the ministry of Theodore Epp's, Back to the Bible broadcast.

One morning, Hank suggested we contact Back to the Bible concerning a place to serve God. In no time a reply came to contact George Cheek at Maranatha Bible Camp. He invited us to visit, and on our second visit we were invited to come as retired volunteers in the autumn of 1980.

The job George had in mind for Hank was to organize the Old Tabernacle, which was being used for storage and supplies. That building was full from side to side and almost from top to bottom.

Hank took one look at it and said, as Caleb did, "Lord give me this mountain!"

(Later on when comparing notes and dates, at the time we were writing Back to the Bible, George Cheek and John Meschke were at the Old Tab looking for something. John said, "I wish someone would come and make some order of all this stuff." So George said, "Let's pray about it." It's so utterly awesome how God answered all our prayers before we even met one another. What a great and wonderful God He is!)

Jan took us to look at housing. The first mobile home we looked at I (Evelyn) fell through the bathroom floor. That night a little pack rat made off with one of Hank's hearing aids. In spite of all this it didn't dampen our spirits. Hank likes to kid, saying "If anyone sees a mouse with a hearing aid in its ear, that's mine!"

We were shown the nice mobile home where we have lived for 23 years now. Our agreement is when room is needed to put up guests they could stay with us.

We have had many, many lovely people stay with us. Some for as long as two weeks at a time. I would like to name them all, but for fear of leaving some out, and space as well, I will only mention The Cross Road quartet. Two lovely couples. They made their stay with us special in that they came into our living room and sang just for us.

One other special time was when Mrs. T. Epp came to our home to visit us. She was a very sweet, lovely Christian lady.

Hank and I are both organizers. Hank worked all that first winter and organized the Old Tab. He did get the job done.

I worked at the office with Ruth Ann Rodgers and George and JoAnn Beetem. JoAnn came to Camp that same fall.

They kept me very busy. I organized all of George's filing cabinets and his missionary files.

George had an unusual filing system in that he kept every note, letter, and all business papers to be filed. I found notes on envelopes, paper napkins, etc. It's all filed away. I think I could go to those files even yet today and find what George needed. Well as time went by, the computers came in and the filing system has been less and less.

Many summers I took care of the flower beds and was Camp nurse for the first seven years. Then my health slowed me down. I still do numerous jobs such as making aprons for the kitchen help, Camp mending, repairing chairs, go for stamps or whatever comes my way. I also enjoy fishing in Lake Maranatha when the weather is nice.

There have been so many improvements and repairs in the 23 years we have been here. There isn't a building on the place that Hank hasn't worked on inside and out. He checks all the windows and screens after each group of campers leave. Just to name a few things.

One of the earlier jobs Hank did, came about after George had had about all he could take of the stacked water glasses on the counter being bumped and they would come down with a crash. After one such occasion George said, "I wish someone could come up with a better way of making the glasses available." Because of that, Hank's inventive mind went to work and he came up with the glass dispenser, which holds several hundred glasses. It has been in use for over 20 years.

Another job, which seemed impossible, was that Hank built a stairway up to the attic in George's and Jan's home. It is the Summerville house. The stairway is right in the center of the house. Tad and Jean Stryker and their family live in that house now. This attic is used for bedrooms and is quite cozy.

We remember George singing "The Lighthouse." Certainly Maranatha Bible Camp is God's lighthouse.

Both Hank and I rejoice every year at the number of people being saved, lives changed and dedicated to our Lord Jesus Christ.

Hank and I have retired as of October 24, 2003. This is Hank's second retirement.

The Camp presented us with a beautiful plaque, which we treasure. And while we retired from responsibility, we haven't quit working, just slowed down a bit.

— Hank and Evelyn Wambolt,
Maranatha Bible Camp

Longtime resident volunteers Hank and Evelyn Wambolt celebrated their 60th wedding anniversary at Maranatha.

Summer Weeks Revolved Around Camp

Maranatha Camp will long remember the Glenn Krause family for its many contributions and long years of service spanning over three decades: 1940s, 1950s and the 1960s.

Glenn Krause was a board member of Maranatha Bible Camp and served as the treasurer for many years. He brought supplies to camp daily in his old Studebaker pulling a trailer, both loaded to the maximum. He helped with building of the Tabernacle, the Dining Hall, the tables and cupboards and later built the two-room "Camp cabin" (Krause Memorial). Glenn also managed the Camp bookstore for a number of years.

Matilda Krause was the chief cook during those years. She made out the menus and gave the shopping list to her husband, who brought out supplies. She organized the crews of women who came in to help with the cooking. We especially remember the long linoleum topped tables with circles of noodle dough covered with tea towels, drying and waiting to be cut for chicken and noodles.

LaVerna Krause Wescoat worked as a counselor and dining room helper for several years. The annual trip in the back of a truck to Sioux Lookout and then climbing up to the top (rain or shine) was another memory ... of course the girls wore dresses! She also enjoyed being part of the Maranatha Gospel Team (which included several Bible school students). She recalls these journeys during the hot summers in an old vehicle, windows all open, over dusty gravel roads to various churches for the services. The car got hot, the radiator boiled over and had flat tires, but the team made every scheduled meeting.

LaVonne Krause Childerston also served as counselor and assisted in the dining room. "Vonnie" remembered that as a pre-schooler, there wasn't always money for her to put in the offering plate, so she, along with other children (of speakers and workers) scrounged the camp grounds for empty gum and candy bar wrappers, filled them with sand to make them look full. Then they set up their own stand next to the sweet shop and sold them to campers. Others must have felt compassion for them as they always had money for the offering. Even after she and Ward were married, they still spent some summers helping at Maranatha, and some of their boys were privileged to attend as campers and to help on work crews.

Phyllis Krause Wiebe remembers working in the dining hall under the supervision of Mrs. Clark, setting tables, serving, and then clearing and cleaning tables. This meant she could stay free for that week. She said she never knew what it was to "get paid." We remember her as the Camp's champion ping-pong player. She remembers memorizing pages of Bible verses each week so that her team would win. (Of course, the girls were always anxious to see which boys were on the same team.) Funny, she says, she can't remember what they won, but still remembers many of those verses. Sunday afternoons were spent in the Krause cabin helping Dad count offerings, writing receipts, and recording pledges. She remembers the trips from home to camp each week, loaded down with all their clean clothes and freshly ironed dresses wrapped in a housecoat across their laps. The car's trunk and trailer were filled to more than capacity. Because of the concern for tires blowing, they drove very slowly.

Mary Ellen Krause Miller literally grew up at Maranatha. Every summer she joined the "camp kids" (those whose parents were working or speaking at Maranatha). It was here that she learned to swim, and much to the surprise of her mother, dive off the diving board. She made many childhood friends and has many vivid memories of waiting for the truck loads (yes, cattle and grain trucks) of kids arriving, mainly from Kansas. She remembers in later years, the services on Sunday afternoons when they had a special financial appeal ... it was so hot in the tabernacle (even with two large fans in the front facing the audience). After the service, she would help her dad adding up the pledges. She remembers trying

Left: Glenn and Matilda Krause. Glenn became the Camp treasurer in 1945. His wife, Matilda, served as head cook for many years. Right: Photo taken in front of the building built by Glenn Krause as Donald Dean Memorial, later part of the Kiddie Park. Left to right, Phyllis Krause Wiebe, Mrs. Glenn (Matilda) Krause, LaVonne Krause Childerston, LaVerna Krause Wescoat and Mary Ellen Krause Miller.

to figure out the handwriting on forms or checks. Of course, all receipts were handwritten. She also helped in the camp bookstore.

Before camp season every year, the girls helped clean the old wooden slab cabins. About all that would fit into the cabin was a bed and the suitcases. It was a dreadful task, cleaning out the spider webs, mice messes and the bird nests. The kitchen and the dining room were scrubbed spotless. Who could forget the snipe hunts, the big ice cream cones served up by Dwight Olsen at the Sweet Shop, or the anticipation of seeing friends each week! We will never forget the musicians (Paul and Bob, Eugene Clark, the Joneses, the quartet from Prairie Bible Institute), the speakers (Darrel Handel, Dr. Walter Wilson, Theodore Epp, L.E. Maxwell, the Beckers, the Brumfields, etc.) or the challenging messages. All four Krause girls went to Bible college. Two of their husbands were saved at Maranatha — Ward was led to the Lord by Rev. Payne when he was 11, and Howard went forward after a message by Dr. Walter Wilson, and was saved when he was 16.

Camp was summer and summer was Camp! Yes, the Krause Family played an important role in Maranatha's history, but Maranatha also played a very important role in the lives of the Krause Family.

– LaVerna Krause Wescoat,
North Platte

Crossing the Jordan from 'Port Maranatha'

We came to Nebraska in 1982 when Neil accepted a call to pastor the Brady Berean Church. We had seen the Maranatha Bible Camp cross occasionally while traveling across Nebraska, but now we became acquainted with the Camp firsthand.

In those days, audio tapes of the speakers who ministered at Maranatha each year were much in demand, and Neil was asked to do the duplication and mailing of the tapes. Whenever friends or family members visited us, Neil proudly took them to the Camp as one of the area's special sites.

After a short time in a Kansas church, we came to Maranatha in 1990 and helped in a number of ways while deciding what to do next. We soon recognized that we had found our spot right here; we became retired volunteers, the beginning of a new and very satisfying period in our sunset years.

When Neil was diagnosed with malignant melanoma in 1995, we felt the comfort and support of all the staff. The disease invaded his brain and advanced relentlessly. The friends and family members who came to see us were warmly received by our larger Maranatha family. As Neil grew weaker and it was obvious that his days were numbered, our daughter and her family came to help in his care. Then our oldest son and his family joined us during the last 10 days of his life. The Camp kitchen and dining room were made available to us for meat preparation, and housing was also provided, as our numbers increased and the rest of our family arrived.

Maranatha Bible Camp has been the gate into the Christian life for many. Here children, young people, and many adults have met the Savior and began their walk with God. For Neil this was the sally port through which he passed to enter the Lord's presence and begin that higher life which is the Christian's true goal.

– Pauline Tallman,
Maranatha Bible Camp

Transparent Miscalculation

Back in the days before the swimming pool at Maranatha, Rev. Olsen held a baptismal service one Sunday afternoon in the old sandpit. He wore a white shirt and white pants which made it look like an idyllic setting - like pictures from the mission field. The only problem was he evidently had forgotten that when white cotton gets wet it becomes somewhat transparent. When he came up out of the water it could be plainly seen that he was wearing red, white and blue wide striped boxer shorts. I have never forgotten the look of helplessness and chagrin on his face. I presume that combination was not worn again.

– Wendell Baxter,
Surling, Wisconsin

'Trophy Cup' Didn't Tarnish the Victory

While a counselor at Maranatha in the early 50s I won the horseshoe tournament during the week. A big promotion and commotion was made about the presentation of the trophy cup. Eugene Clark, later a songwriter and musician with Back to the Bible Broadcast, and at that time also a camp counselor, was to present the trophy. A white cloth covered the trophy cup and a string ran from the center of the cloth up over a rafter in the old slab dining hall and down to the hand of Eugene. I could picture in my mind a bright, shining silver cup with beautiful engraving. After much ostentatious oratory, the string was pulled, the cloth lifted and the cup was unveiled. On the table was a forlorn looking old tin cup from the dining hall with words written on the side with typewriter whiteout. There followed abundant laughter. I treasured that cup and experience for many years.

— Wendell Baxter,
Surling, Wisconsin

Top row: This Christian school group from Illinois helped build the director's cabin on the south shore of Lake Maranatha, plus many other projects, 2000.

Second row, from left: These well-dressed servers, many of them volunteers, did their duty at a banquet during Ladies' Retreat 1995. Back row, from left: JoAnn Beetem, Jeanette Andrew, Jan Cheek, Louise Crooks, Jean Stryker. Second row, from left: Kris Cheek, Michelle Crooks, unidentified, Tara Cheek, Beth Christensen, Colleen Babcock, George Cheek. Front row, from left: Andy Feeney, Kirk Feeney, Gregg Madsen, Jeff Miller, unidentified, Harald Bjerga, Bill Crooks, Dave Burbach, Lance Gerry and Rachel Stucky; Bert Needham did maintenance work at Maranatha during the 1970s; Serving as resident retired volunteers at Maranatha in the spring of 1990 were, Back row from left: Dick Feay, Hank Wambolt, Merle Cheek, Reuben Hasenauer, Jack Ashcraft and Neil Tallman. Front row, from left: Bonnie Feay, Evelyn Wambolt, Stella Cheek, Virginia Ashcraft and Pauline Tallman.

Third row, from left: Kitchen volunteers prepared fried chicken for hundreds of people on Sundays at Camp; Stella Cheek managed the Gift Shop for more than 10 years; Faye Ward (left) and Estelle Hocquelle were prayer warriors for Maranatha. Faye also served as secretary for Pastor Olsen.

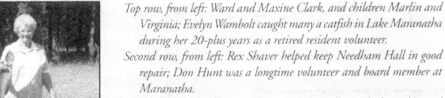
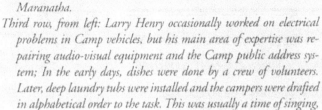

Top row, from left: Ward and Maxine Clark, and children Marlin and Virginia; Evelyn Wambolt caught many a catfish in Lake Maranatha during her 20-plus years as a retired resident volunteer.

Second row, from left: Rex Shaver helped keep Needham Hall in good repair; Don Hunt was a longtime volunteer and board member at Maranatha.

Third row, from left: Larry Henry occasionally worked on electrical problems in Camp vehicles, but his main area of expertise was repairing audio-visual equipment and the Camp public address system; In the early days, dishes were done by a crew of volunteers. Later, deep laundry tubs were installed and the campers were drafted in alphabetical order to the task. This was usually a time of singing, laughing, and fun; Virginia Ashcraft (left) managed the Sweet Shop during the 1990s, assisted by Eleanor Fasse.

Fourth row, from left: Volunteers from Trinity Bible Fellowship and other churches in eastern Pennsylvania and Maryland took several missions trips to do work projects at Maranatha Bible Camp. This is the 2001 group; Jean Van Mark washed, dried and folded mountains of laundry in the 1990s and 2000s; Many staff and volunteers enjoy a reception at Needham Hall, December 1980.

Fifth row, from left: It's time to prepare meatballs in the old Dining Hall kitchen; Drying silverware by hand was a time consuming task; Ursula Geary (left) and Karen Kramer of North Platte volunteered in the Sweet Shop during a busy week in 2003.

The 1950s

"We offer praise to Almighty God for the successful conclusion of nine weeks of summer camp," said Ivan Olsen in his director's report to the board following the 1952 camping season. "From the beginning of Camp this season, throughout the entire period, we were surrounded in this area with threatening epidemics, such as polio and diphtheria. Realizing from the opening hour of Camp to its close, that should any one of these diseases break out at Maranatha, the summer's Camp season would come to a sudden close, almost daily your director, and others, claimed the promises of Psalm 91 as our protection. 'Thou shalt not be afraid for the terror by night; nor for the arrow that flieth by day. Nor the pestilence that walketh in darkness; nor for the destruction that wasteth at noonday. A thousand shall fall at thy side, and ten thousand at thy right hand; but it shall not come nigh thee. THERE SHALL NO EVIL BEFALL THEE? NEITHER SHALL ANY PLAGUE COME NIGH THY DWELLING (punctuation and caps are Olsen's; he typed many of his own reports). For he shall give his angels charge over thee, to keep thee in all thy ways.'

"Now we believe it is only fitting to pause and give praise to God, who is able to work as our God has worked. It was not until the entire summer was over that we fully realized that claiming the promises of this Psalm not only protected us from any of the epidemics, but we completed our biggest summer at Maranatha (1,788 people attended), and did not have as much as a minor injury among our campers. The promises of Psalm 91 reached farther than we even dared ask or imagine. For all of this, we praise God."

Even after Jonas Salk discovered a vaccine for polio in 1953, God's protection of the Camp was never far from Olsen's mind. No significant tragedy had befallen Maranatha during the early years, for which he was thankful. Quick action on the part of lifeguards prevented several potential drownings over the years (Olsen himself pulled at least one young woman out of the old sandpit swimming hole), but no other close calls involving life and limb are recorded.

In 1953, Hugh Clark went to work on a project he had been pondering for some time. He began laying the groundwork for a new cement swimming pool. That fall and during the spring of 1954, as the U.S. Supreme Court decided that the segregated public school system in Topeka, Kansas, was unconstitutional, Clark masterminded the construction of the pool, hauling in fill dirt and raising up a hill to build the pool into. Leon Buttermore and Bert Needham helped Clark with the project. "I remember Bert taking his old Cadillac, letting some air out of his tires and driving back and forth on that hill, packing that dirt until his car overheated," said Buttermore. "He'd let it cool off, then start over again."

The pool opened for use in summer 1954 and proved to be very enjoyable — "far beyond our fondest expectations," said Olsen. It was much easier for lifeguards to keep track of swimmers in the clear, 55-degree water that filled the pool. (The pool stayed cold all summer long; there was no filtration system until the early 1970s, so it had to be drained and refilled on a weekly basis.) Within three years, there was another safety feature: volunteers built a chain link fence around the pool. In 1962, Maranatha added a bathhouse.

Before 1950, most of the Camp's energy and resources were spent on programming and promotion. Now, with several major buildings on site, the Camp began to allocate resources toward their maintenance and protection.

The first people to live on site at Maranatha for longer than a few weeks at a time were Rev. & Mrs. Joseph Switzer. In 1947, the Camp board had chosen Switzer to work at Camp at $50 per week during June, July and August. In 1949, the Switzers stayed on as caretakers throughout the fall and winter, steadily making improvements in the facilities. By 1956, Mr. & Mrs. Kenneth Martin had become caretakers. A few years later, Mr. & Mrs. Wendell Williams took over that task. Bill Broeder, a retired man who lived nearby, spent many days volunteering at Camp, often using his own equipment, well into the 1960s.

By the end of the 1957 camping season, the Prophet's Chamber (Rawson Hall) and newly-built Yeutter Hall had heating systems installed. The Martins had overseen wiring and plastering projects, the addition of a new stove in the kitchen, the removal of some of the old slab cabins, the removal of many trees and the gravelling of the Camp roads.

The property on which the caretakers so faithfully toiled had been transferred to a new owner. The action occurred at the Camp board's first Labor Day weekend meeting, on September 5, 1949. Seeking to bring more clarity to the governance of the Camp, the board dissolved itself as an entity and then created a new Official Board, which would be hereafter separate from the Advisory Council. The board members would be required to sign the Camp's doctrinal statement every year or be dropped from membership.

The newly-created board took an even bigger step a few minutes later, when Ivan Olsen read a prepared statement: "Having been chosen by God to begin the Maranatha Bible Camp in March of 1938, having labored ceaselessly during all of the years since then as director — I find an increasing burden on my heart to safeguard the property of Maranatha against any attempts by modernism, denominationalism, or fanaticism to succeed in taking this property from those who through sacrifice, sweat, tears and prayer, have these 12 years made Maranatha what it is."

Anxious to protect the Camp not only from medical but spiritual misfortune as well, Olsen proposed transferring ownership of the Camp property to the Berean Fundamental Church Council, an organization he had founded a few years earlier to govern the several Berean churches he had founded throughout Nebraska. Many of the Camp board members also were members of the BFCC.

"In this hour in which so many independent groups are seeking protection of their properties against denominational thievery, the Berean Fundamental Church Council has become an incorporated body to offer protection to any religious or charitable group so wishing to safeguard their investments so as to continue their original intentions as an organization," Olsen continued.

The motion was unanimously carried. For the next 45 years, the title deed to the Maranatha property said, "Berean Fundamental Church Council /dba/ Maranatha Bible Camp."

Theodore Epp, a Mennonite, was a major force behind the move. He had observed dangerous trends forming in other Christian camps throughout postwar America.

"Rev. Epp said his heart was broken throughout 1947 for the lack of standards in Bible Conferences throughout the land," said Hugh Clark's board meeting notes for January 1, 1948. "In one large evangelical conference, he rebuked them for their lack of standards. It is because of our Camp standards that he has been friendly toward Maranatha." A longtime opponent of liberalism in every form, Epp became president of the Camp board in 1950.

Unwavering from its evangelical roots, Maranatha Camp continued to see souls saved throughout the 1950s. One of the most memorable moments occurred early in the decade, as recounted by minor league baseball player-turned-evangelist Paul Levin. One night during the Young People's Camp, many campers came forward while Levine was giving the invitation to receive Christ as savior. Among them was a young woman whom most thought was one of the older campers.

"She knelt, weeping in front of the pulpit," wrote Levin in 1988. "After a few minutes, she arose, came up to the platform, walked over to Dr. Olsen, asked if she might say something to the congregation."

The singing stopped, and the young people became quiet. The woman stood before the microphone and made an announcement that profoundly affected the rest of the Camp week.

"I am a preacher's wife," she said. "We are camping nearby and have been attending the services. Yesterday morning when the evangelist preached on how you can **know** you are saved, I realized I'd never been saved at all.

"Tonight I decided to settle it," she said. "I have just now definitely received Christ, and this is the first time in my life that I have confessed Jesus Christ publicly as my Lord."

Young People's Camps, which had been directed by Rev. Olsen since 1938, grew tremendously during the 1950s. There were as many as three of these Maranatha-sponsored teen camps per summer throughout much of the decade, and more than 600 teens attended each summer from 1952-56. There were stories of youth returning from Camp to their home churches and starting revivals among the youth of their communities, most notably in Aurora, Nebraska.

Carl Goltz, who had done youth work in eastern Wyoming and western Nebraska for a decade, took over as program director for Young People's Camp in 1956.

Sam & Ella Becker served 15 years (1942-56) as program directors for Children's and Intermediate Age Camps. Cliff & Ruth Gustafson took over directing that age group in 1957 and served through 1963. In 1959, Maranatha's Children's and Intermediate Camp (which had included grades 3-8) divided into separate Junior Camps (grades 4-6) and Junior High Camps (grades 7-9) under the leadership of the Gustafsons. Carlo Pietropaulo, an evangelist from Italy, was one of the most memorable speakers at Maranatha's children's camps in the late 1950s.

Winter programming premiered at Maranatha when a "Snow Camp," which became known as Winter Retreat, was held January 2-3, 1958. Eventually, it was moved to the week between Christmas and New Year's Day.

The Camp developed a bookstore called the "Maranatha Book Room," which was located in the back of the Old Tabernacle. Glenn & Matilda Krause ran the Book Room, which sold "good evangelical Bibles, books, mottoes, music, and greeting cards." Maranatha brochures said the Book Room included "one of the largest and most complete stocks of evangelical material in this part of the country." The Book Room was an outgrowth of the Bible Supplies Christian bookstore in North Platte, which in 1949 began in the basement of the Berean Fundamental Church and moved downtown. The Maranatha Book Room operated independently of the bookstore in North Platte.

Matilda Krause also served as head cook for much of this decade. Ernest Lott was advertising director and Mr. & Mrs. John Paton were deans of men and women.

Those laboring behind the scenes saw evidence that their work was paying dividends. One of the original purposes of the Camp, training young people to be fulltime Christian workers, was being fulfilled. Some were beginning to go to Bible school to train as missionaries. Others were supporting missions work financially.

During a Young People's Camp in the mid-1940s, Carl Tanis, director of Sudan Interior Missions, received a year's worth of financial support to send Dick Brandt to be a missionary to Sudan, North Africa. In subsequent years, campers gave offerings for the Brandts' support.

"Every time I come, I'll bring a missionary for you to raise the support for," Tanis told Olsen.

On a Sunday afternoon at Maranatha in the late 1940s, Rev. Olsen and Oswald J. Smith of Toronto raised $33,000 in faith promises from adults and children alike to support missionaries. In 1951, the Camp raised $12,000 to build a Maranatha medical clinic in Africa. The momentum continued throughout the 1950s, as Maranatha Bible Camp took a leadership role in the growing faith missions movement throughout the world.

Growing tensions between the United States and the Soviet Union signaled a deepening of the Cold War, but as the two nations deployed nuclear weapons and raced to put the first man into outer space, Maranatha Bible Camp grew from adolescence into vigorous young adulthood, becoming established as a robust ministry whose influence was growing throughout the world.

In 1956, a young rockabilly singer and guitarist named Elvis Presley teamed up with his new band, the Jordanaires, and released "Heartbreak Hotel," which quickly rose to the top of the charts and became his first Gold Record. Later that year, President Dwight D. Eisenhower signed the Federal-Aid Highway Act, legislation that established the nation's Interstate highway system. As the Eisenhower administration drew to a close, it became apparent that the popular general-turned-president had unleashed something that would radically change the physical and social landscape of America. Besides tying a vast continent together with a superhighway system modeled after the German Autobahn, it would have profound implications for many landowners, including a Christian camp in west central Nebraska.

VOICES OF MARANATHA

LeBars Appreciated Missions Emphasis

In early 1948, we were in the Berean Church in Curtis, Nebraska. We came to Camp for the dedication of the first chapel. Dick sang a dedication song. Years later at Back to the Bible week with J. Oswald Smith the speaker, funds were raised for us to take a printing press to the Philippines under FEGC.

In 1958, the Ken Martins lived at camp and opened their home for our son, Stephen, to live with them while we returned to the Philippines. He played the trumpet at many services.

In 1965, Pastor Dan Johnson from LaGrange, Wyoming and Dick from Hastings, met at camp and shared the burden of the need for a Bible school in the west. They prayed and left it in God's hands and he brought it to pass in the founding of Frontier School of the Bible in LaGrange, Wyoming. The school was organized in 1967 and continues to this day.

–Edith LeBar,
Hot Springs, South Dakota

She Married the Second Tenor

A week at Maranatha's Children's camp, and later attending Youth People's Camp was a highlight for my sisters and me when I was about 9 to 17 years old. Although I was already a believer, Sam and Ella Becker's Bible stories and evangelistic lessons cemented my faith. The many missionaries who presented their works over those years were inspirational as well.

Then in 1956 a men's quartet from Prairie Bible Institute was part of the staff for the youth weeks. I had a crush on the second tenor, Joel Bardwell. The next summer, the quartet returned. Two of the guys, Joel and Bob Jones, became good friends of my family. Joel began corresponding with my sister, Precious. That year, she began going steady with a local boy, and I took over the letter writing.

A few years later, when Joel was attending Trinity College in Chicago, and I was a nursing student in Hastings, Nebraska, my parents invited Joel to come to our farm for Thanksgiving. Finally, Joel became interested in me. We were married two years later, and will celebrate our 42nd anniversary in December.

Now when I go past that big white cross on the roadside four to five times a year driving from Colorado to relatives in Nebraska and further east, many pleasant memories are revived. I thank God for the ministry of Maranatha Bible Camp.

– Wanda Hofrichter Bardwell,
Centennial, Colorado

Left: The Prairie Bible Institute quartette that performed at Maranatha in 1956, from left: Loyd Linstrom, Joel Bardwell, Phil Doud, Bob Jones. Right: At the 1953 Children's Camp, from left: Wanda Hofrichter, Elvira Becker, Charlann Botts, unidentified.

The People of Maranatha: Lester Kittle

I n the early 1940s, a Maxwell grocer, Lester Kittle, was concerned that a permanent location be found for Maranatha Bible Camp, and he got actively involved.

Lester joined Hugh Clark, Lyle Carper and Ivan Olsen in searching for a new location, and prayed with them near the future site of the Tabernacle building. When they spoke with the realtor about the tract of land, Lester asked who would have the first opportunity to purchase it. The response was, "whoever is the first one to come up with the money." Immediately Lester wrote out a check to secure the land for the Camp.

After the Camp was organized, Lester served on its board for many years before he passed away in 1979.

Lester served on the original Camp advertising committee. In later years, he helped obtain government surplus items and recruited volunteers. Lester's grocery sold food to Maranatha for years and he helped with their transport to Camp. His grocery store, which sold on credit, also supplied the Maxwell Public School.

Lester and his two sons, Dean and Donn, spent many hours doing projects at Camp, including planting and hand-watering cedar trees along with the caretaker, Rev. Joseph Switzer. Some of these trees later were torn out to make way for the construction of Interstate 80.

Lester was a board member at First Baptist Church in Maxwell, many of whose members helped with the acquisition of lumber slabs and the construction of the slab cabins in the early years.

A frame cabin at Camp carries the Kittle name in memory of Lester's leadership in the early years of Maranatha.

– Donn Kittle,
The son of Lester Kittle

Lester and Bernice Kittle of Maxwell were early supporters and promoters of Maranatha. Lester, a grocer, played a key role in the acquisition of the current Camp site.

Left: The sound of the old Camp dinner bell is still a pleasant memory for many. Center: Dorothy Wieduwilt and her son, Aaron, pose in slab cabin #3 at Maranatha. Right: Dr. Clate Risley, president of the National Sunday School Association, spoke at Maranatha in the 1950s and 60s.

Governance

The Official Board of Maranatha Camp had its begin nings in the small group of interested people who started the Camp. The first organized meeting was April 26, 1938, in the pastor's study of the Berean Fundamental Church in North Platte. Those present were Ivan Olsen, Nick Janzen, Hugh Clark, Lyle Carper, John Goodmanson and Harry J. Most of Roscoe. Carper and Goodmanson, along with Clark, were members of the North Platte Berean Church's board of elders. Olsen was elected chairman. Janzen was named assistant chairman. Clark became secretary/treasurer. Immediately, this group started acting as a board of directors and began to create various advisory committees, appointing other people not present at the meeting to participate on those committees.

From the beginning, the governance of Maranatha was never very formal. People were invited to join a committee, and some of them started meeting with the board. Eventually, it was hard to tell where the main governing body (usually referred to as the Camp board) ended and the advisory committees began, because many of the same people served on more than one entity. There was a spiritual committee, a constitution committee, an advertising committee, a programming committee and a rules committee. Camp officers sometimes met separately; eventually that group evolved into the executive committee. The official board agreed to meet at least annually, on or about New Year's Day. In January 1949, the board changed its annual meeting to the Labor Day weekend.

That same year, on September 5, 1949, the board dissolved itself as an entity and then created a new Official Board, which would be separate from all advisory committees. The board members were required to sign the Camp's doctrinal statement every year or be dropped from membership. Board members who reached age 65 also were to be automatically dropped from membership unless invited by the board to remain on an annual basis.

The meetings themselves were round table-style discussions. Olsen, who did not use a bulletin in his church on Sunday morning and freely departed from his order of service on many occasions, was not inclined toward formality in running meetings. Precise parliamentary procedure appears never to have been a major concern, although important issues were presented in the form of motions, and were voted upon.

Fittingly enough for an organization that was born in a prayer meeting, Maranatha Camp board meetings usually started with a Bible devotional given by one of the members, and often included prayer meetings that lasted half an hour. Although there have been disagreements, a spirit of unity has prevailed among those who have served on boards and committees throughout the history of Maranatha Bible Camp.

There was a female voice in the leadership of Maranatha from almost the very beginning. Hazel Johnson, the Camp nurse and dean of women during the first few years of Maranatha's existence, was on the Advisory Council. In 1953, Olsen recommended that a woman be appointed to the Official Board. Although no woman was appointed for another 43 years, a women's associate board was created in the 1950s and Wilma Markham and Mrs. Herbert Roszhart were elected. The only female member of the Official Camp Board has been Joy Lucht, a daughter of Rev. Olsen, who was appointed to the board in 1996.

In 1970, the board mandated that members would automatically leave the board upon reaching 65 years of age unless given an one-year extension by vote of the board. Several received extensions year after year.

Many have served long tenures on the Camp board, but only three have served at least 50 years. Hugh Clark, who was present at the first Maranatha board meeting and whose motion gave Maranatha Bible Camp its name, served 50 years (1938-88). Founder Ivan E. Olsen presided at the first board meeting; he served 51 years as general director (1938-89) and 52 years, 5 months as a board member (April 26, 1938-October 11, 1990). However, no one served longer than Ernest Lott, whose 52-year, 9-month tenure as a board member began January 1, 1945, and ended with his retirement after the October 24-25, 1997, board meeting.

Other board members and their tenures include: Carl Goltz, 37 years (1957-1994) Theodore Epp, 35 years (1940-75); Lester Kittle, 32 years (1938-70); Curt Lehman, 29 years (1965-1994) and George Cheek (1976-2004 and still active as of this publication).

"Maranatha's success relates to so many sticking to the job so long," said Olsen in 1985. The longevity, continuity and dedication among Maranatha's board members, staff and volunteers have been exceptional.

In 1950, Theodore Epp was chosen as president of the board, having already served as a board member for 10 years. Previously, Olsen had served as chairman (the two terms appear to have been used interchangeably.) Epp served as president until 1962, when he resigned that position while retaining his board membership. Goltz became president in 1962, serving in that capacity for 32 years, until 1994, when he resigned from the board. Elton Streyle served as president of the board from 1994-2001, then stepped down as president while staying on as a board member. Richard Crocker took over the presidency in 2001.

Hugh Clark served as secretary of the board from 1938 until the late 1940s, when it appears that several men shared the responsibility, ending with Lester Kittle in the early 1950s. In 1953, Kenneth Blood became secretary and continued to keep minutes of the meetings for a Camp-record 24 years until he resigned from the board in 1977. Ernest Lott, who already had served on the board for more than 30 years, replaced Blood as secretary in 1978 and served in that office until his retirement from the board at age 90 in 1997. Royce Norman was secretary from 1997-2002, and Mark Geist has served as secretary since then.

Hugh Clark was chosen both secretary and treasurer in 1938. By 1949, Glenn Krause had taken over as treasurer and served until 1963, when the board chose to hire a bookkeeper to do the work previously done by the board's treasurer. Lilus George did the bookkeeping work in the 1960s (she was referred to as the treasurer in the Camp board minutes). Louise Merriman served as Camp bookkeeper/treasurer well into the 1970s, when she was succeeded by Brenda Harder. Ruth Ann Rodgers became bookkeeper/treasurer in the mid-1980s. In 1989, Terry Jensen joined the board and soon was selected as treasurer, ending approximately a quarter-century of the board's operating without its own financial officer. Jensen began working with George Cheek and Ruth Ann Rodgers, who continued as the head bookkeeper, to oversee the Camp's finances.

For the first 30 to 40 years of the Camp's history, Olsen was the main driving force, the initiator of much of the action

that was taken. By the mid-1970s, Olsen was approaching age 65 and George Cheek had joined the staff. Olsen delegated a large amount of responsibility to Cheek and the board started becoming more active in dealing with the day-to-day management of the Camp. In 1983, the board formed a board of management to oversee the administrative details of the expanding ministry and appointed board president Carl Goltz, plus Curt Lehman, Cliff Gustafson, Ernest Lott and Cheek as members.

However, by the mid-1990s, after Cheek had become established as general director, the Camp board began to rethink its theory of governing. The board of management still existed, but it became much less active. Several members recommended that the Official Board scale back its role and serve primarily as a policy-making board, leaving most administrative decisions to Cheek and the management team that he was assembling. Throughout the end of the 1990s and into the 2000s, the board pursued that direction. In 1997, it authorized the creation of director-level positions for properties, programming, marketing, operations and conference center, all of whom were accountable to Cheek as general director.

In March 1996, board authorized the creation of the Maranatha Camp Foundation with its own governing board (the members were all on the Official Camp board). Jim Davidson was elected as president of the Foundation board and Mark Geist was selected as executive director.

In 2001, Maranatha added SportReach as a sports/adventure arm of the ministry with Kris Cheek, the son of George Cheek, as executive director. In 2003, the entire organization was reworked into Maranatha Ministries, consisting of Maranatha Bible Camp, SportReach and the Maranatha Camp Foundation.

– *Tad Stryker*

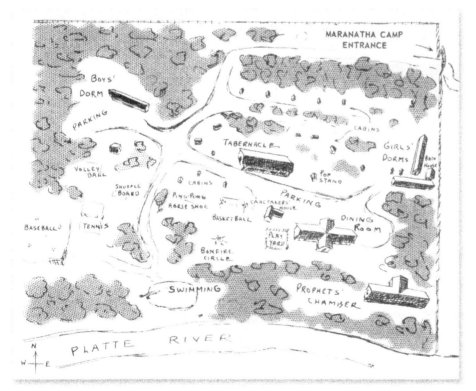

This map was included in the 1953 Maranatha brochure. A sandpit served as the swimming area (the cement pool would be built in 1954). Within 15 years, Interstate 80 would cut through the northern edge of the grounds. Within 40 years, the boys' and girls' dorms would be made into adult housing (Lott, Clark and Becker halls) and the Camp's size had quadrupled.

Time at Maranatha Gave Direction for Life

It was the summer of 1955. I had just completed my first year at Kansas Wesleyan University in Salina. God had graciously brought me to the place of commitment to Christ during my first year of college. But I had yet to make a most important decision, and God used Maranatha in my life to help me at that strategic time.

A friend of mind and I decided we wanted to go to camp the summer of 1955. I had known about Maranatha only from literature we had received. Somehow we were on Dr. Olsen's mailing list. The camp in Colorado we had been to in the past had become so expensive ($25.00 a week) that were attracted by the $6.50 per week cost of Maranatha.

The camp we attended at Maranatha that summer of 1955 was very well attended. Dr. L. E. Maxwell, then President of Prairie Bible Institute, and Dr. Joseph Schmidt, then President of Grace Bible Institute in Omaha, were the main speakers. My how God blessed those men as they preached, and God brought conviction to my heart as I sat on those hard benches made out of 2-by-6 boards in the Old Tabernacle. I also remember Dr. Olsen directing the meetings and giving invitations. I had never heard such preaching in all my life. God mightily spoke to me through the messages and the times of personal counsel with those men of God.

I also remember the lines of bunk beds in Olsen Hall (now Lott Hall), where I bunked next to Pastor Ken Blood, then pastor of the Lexington Berean Church. I also remember the early-morning project where some of us helped pull out a tree stump so they could build on the west wing of the old dining hall, now the Sweet Shop. I also remember that we all took turns doing the dishes after meals.

After returning home from camp, still not having nailed down the decision God wanted me to make, Dr. Schmidt sent me a letter. He did not tell me what to do in the letter, just shared a word of encouragement to me, but God used that letter to bring me to the immediate decision that I needed to transfer to Grace Bible Institute the next fall.

So God used the ministry of Maranatha Bible Camp to prepare me for that decision. Apart from salvation, dedication to Christ and the call to the ministry, this is one of the most important decisions I have made. At Grace I was grounded in the Word of God and it was there I met the wonderful girl, Joan Nussbaum, who would become my wife.

Little did I realize during those days in 1955 when I was at Maranatha, l that I would become a Berean pastor and have the privilege of being involved in the ministry of Maranatha for 28 years. Since retiring from helping at Junior Camp, I have attended many meetings and retreats there and continued to promote Maranatha in our church. In August of 2002 my wife, our two sons and their wives, and nine grandchildren had a two-day family reunion at Maranatha.

I praise God for Maranatha Bible Camp, not only for what its ministry has meant in my life, my family, and also for the spiritual help is has been to many who have come to Maranatha from our church.

– Fran Harwerth,
Colby, Kansas

Fran Harwerth helps at crafts time.

Fran Harwerth, 1955.

VOICES OF MARANATHA

A Life-Changing Truck Ride to Camp

I began attending Maranatha as an 8-year-old camper back in the 1950s. I remember riding to Camp from western Nebraska in the back of a farm truck. The sides were up and a canvas tarp was stretched over the top of the rack. I had saved $1.50 for spending money from mowing lawns, and I lost that same amount right after arriving on the grounds. This was the rather inauspicious beginning of a relationship spanning almost 60 years.

It was in the old Tabernacle, with Dr. Olsen leading the service, that as a 12-year-old I responded to the call for full-time Christian ministry. It was during a Navigator Training Program as a 16-year-old that I met my future (and present) wife. I eventually served as program director of Youth Week for more than a decade. My children all attended camps.

I have been a pastor for almost 30 years, and Maranatha has always figured prominently in my ministry, and I often recall that night when I knelt in the Old Tab and answered God's call.

– Frank Van Campen,
Malcolm, Nebraska

Adrian, Where's the Parakeet?

My husband, Pastor Carl Goltz, directed two weeks of Young People's Camp for several years. One year, I was in charge of the Rawson Hall girls' dorm. Carl and Adrian House were staying in the Olsens' house (previously known as the caretaker's house). There were boys outside our dorm waiting for all the counselors to go to sleep. So I slipped down to the house where my husband and Adrian were to tell them we had fellows outside our dorm. They said they would take care of it.

The Olsens had a parakeet in their house, and they were taking care of it. To make sure they surprised the boys, Carl and Adrian didn't turn on the light before they left the house. Adrian tripped over the cage and the parakeet got out. They were trying to catch it in the dark! They finally did.

Then they came and sat on a log outside Rawson Hall for several hours. The fellows fled to their dorm, so there was no more problem. The next morning, some of the girls asked Pastor Goltz and Adrian, "Why were you sitting outside our dorm?"

I worked under Rocky Schultz and Frank Van Campen when they were youth camp directors. I was dean of women and had the counselors under me. We always went to Winter Retreat, which started the day after Christmas. God blessed in a marvelous way the ministry and all the fun times.

In the 1960s, we Berean pastors' wives had a retreat in the spring (Monday-Wednesday). We did the speaking, chose a theme and divided up the workshops. We had good turnouts and good fellowship.

– Doris Goltz,
North Platte

Pastor Carl and Doris Goltz

Even When Electricity Failed, Camp Was Illuminating

My first experience as a camper at Maranatha Camp was in 1949. I was a very scared youngster, but very much wanted to attend as my older sister had attended even before the camp was at its present location.

The boys slept in a long "bunk house" with a water pitcher pump outside that was fastened to a pipe in the ground, as the water table near the river was close to the surface. The Old Tabernacle was our meeting place, the present "Sweet Shop" was the dining hall. The old "Sweet Shop" was near the tabernacle and sold candy bars and glass bottles of pop for five cents each.

Camp started Monday afternoon in those days and ran through the following Monday morning. The cost was $5.00!

During the week, many of the campers had stomach problems and it was thought that the old tin cup and plates were causing the problems. Creamed peas and soda water for lunch was the solution. I don't know if it was the answer, but we all got better so we didn't have to repeat the menu!

An old gravel pit was the "swimming hole" which was very muddy, but we all enjoyed it. It also served as the baptistery for special services.

As I continued to attend during my teen years, I remember special speakers as "Paul and Bob," Oswald J. Smith who challenged us with "faith promise" giving, and L.E. Maxwell from Prairie Bible Institute. He was preaching with power one evening when the lights all went out due to a thunderstorm. He shouted, "Let there be light!" and suddenly the power came on again!

One Saturday morning Rev. Olsen preached on giving our lives to the Lord for dedication to His will. I was one of those that went forward and we knelt behind the Tabernacle asking God to use us as He chose. That left a profound influence on my life. I later attended New Tribes Bible Institute and Rockmont College and served among the Navaho Indians in New Mexico with Berean Mission.

Between my Junior and Senior year at Rockmont College, I served as a counselor for the children and young people. One of my charges wet the bed every night. While the campers were in services each morning, I secretly washed the bedding and remade the bed. Today he is a grandfather who had raised his family for the Lord. He still calls me as he travels across the country trucking.

I also ran the bookstore for several weeks that summer.

I'm now semi-retired after teaching school for 40 years, I also served for five years as speaker at "Summer Park Ranch" Indian Bible Camp, now "Broken Arrow Bible Camp" near Gallup, New Mexico. My wife and I also served for 20 years at Bonita Park Nazarene Camp near Ruidoso, New Mexico, as nurse and teacher.

I get to visit Maranatha on occasion and rejoice to see how God is still working to reach people for Christ.

– Gary Hasenauer,
Belen, New Mexico

Holy Spirit Eclipses Even Hot Cars, Hum-a-Zoos

Shortly after Scottsbluff Berean Church began, the Wednesday evening Bible study and prayer meetings were held in Ralph and Shirley Scott's home. Pastor Goltz announced the Maranatha Camp schedule. It sounded like fun, but I doubted that I would be permitted to go. To my surprise, my mother gave me the registration fee after the service. Over the next months, I mowed Earl and Effie Walker's lawn with a reel-type push mower (no motor), and did other odd jobs to earn Camp money and 50 cents spending money. My mother went as a counselor too. I think she was as thrilled to attend as I was. My brother, who was too young to be a camper, also came along.

As soon as we completed the registration process, my friends and I toured the bookstore, where we each purchased a hum-a-zoo. Years later, as a counselor and pastor, I was amused by the impatience of adults who were irritated by the incessant hum-a-zoos, as I relived those first joys of Camp.

Camp was all about fun. I don't remember the preaching or classes for the first two years, though I'm certain it all had its impact on my thinking. But the rousing singing in the tabernacle, Cliff Gustafson's energetic song leading, Ruth Gustafson's inimitable piano accompaniment, Gerry Sprunger and Glenn Adams' rendition of "Casey at the Bat," swimming, lizards, and the leaky roof over my bunk are all precious memories that link directly to the Maranatha Camp Song, other Camp choruses and eventually the conviction that God's hand was upon my life.

My first response to an altar call was at Maranatha in my third year as a camper. As an 11-year-old, I made my way to the front of the Tabernacle along with many other junior age kids. I met a missionary, whose name I've often wished to recall. It's strange that I can't remember who the speaker was and I can't describe the missionary or his field, though I think he served in Africa. But, the Holy Spirit has never let me forget the scripture showed me. He sat with me in the old Dining Hall on a long white bench, asked me a few questions, ascertained that I had trusted Christ, and then opened his Bible to Isaiah 43:7. I often wondered why he used such a difficult verse. I really didn't understand it, but I couldn't forget that he applied it to me, telling me I was created for God's glory. From that day I've never doubted that the Lord wanted my full-time service.

Trips to Camp from Scottsbluff and Mitchell are memorable. Once, we made the trip in the tarped grain box of Harold Heinrich's farm truck ... not exactly riding in style. Carlo Pietropaulo devoured salami and cracked jokes as he drove a busload. Adrian House and I made the trip listening to Cassius Clay win a title fight on the radio. My first trip to Camp in my own '55 Chevy was punctuated with spasms until I finally realized it needed a new fuel pump, which I purchased in Sutherland. But, when I arrived, my two-door sedan couldn't compare to Jerry Regier's white and red '57 two-door hardtop with the chromed 327 mill, which he drove from Colby, Kansas. How could we know that Jerry would eventually found the Family Research Council and the Christian Embassy in Washington, D.C., or that he and Sharon would hold Bible studies weekly with David and Julie Nixon Eisenhower? I attended Junior, Junior High and Senior High camps and Winter Retreats. Little by little, leaders like Carlo Pietropaulo, Rocky Schultz, Sid Hendry, and Abe Penner became my role models. After high school, I became involved as a counselor, then as an assistant pastor bringing kids to Camp from Adrian House's church in Cheyenne. Finally, through the influence of my pastors, Carl Goltz, Curt Lehman, Adrian House, Larry Carrier and Darrell Scott, among a host of other preachers, evangelists and missionaries, my wife and I responded to an opportunity to become the founding pastor of Auburn Berean Church. While there, we started the Humboldt Berean Church and learned many lessons of faith, completed training at Grace Bible Institute and gleaned from other missionaries and pastors connected with Maranatha such as Marlin Olsen, Lex de Wit, Sjef Widdershoven, Ed Watke and Sam Dalton.

My first trip to Camp as a pastor, I brought only one camper. He was the meanest little kid in Auburn and the first recruit for our fledgling Sunday school. At Camp, he was assigned to another counselor, then transferred to another. The third day, the Camp dean said to me, "You brought him; you keep him in your cabin." As we drove through Lincoln, he asked lots of questions about the penitentiary. Later, I learned that his mother was serving time.

Adrian House became president of Western Bible College and invited us to join his staff. As a student recruiter, I enjoyed the privilege of preaching in many camp pulpits, including seven successive years at Maranatha. Dr. Ivan Olsen took a personal interest in our work and invited us to conduct evangelistic meetings at North Platte several times. This vote of confidence opened many other doors, eventually making it possible for me to preach in 39 states, including Alaska. Our family has traveled in evangelistic work for 12 years. We have pastored three churches for 18 years, and conducted a Bible institute inside a Tennessee prison for five years. Today, I am a missionary involved in church planting.

In recent years, I have been invited to preach faith promise missions conferences in several churches. My introduction to faith promise was during my first week at Maranatha. Dr. Olsen, as always, challenged everyone to make a faith promise to Camp. The funds raised would build a swimming pool, he explained. I still remember the excitement that swept the crowd at that announcement. Sure enough, when we arrived on the campground the next summer, our first item of business was a visit to see the pool. I learned to swim in that pool! More importantly, I learned the power of faith promise giving through that pool project.

The fourth grader who lay in the upper bunk of the old barracks dormitory at Maranatha could not have imagined how crucial it was that God brought him from a western Nebraska home without a foundation or modern plumbing to spend a week at Camp. Indeed, my whole family was transformed through the ministry of Maranatha and the Berean churches. I will eternally praise God for the faith of Ivan Olsen and Carl Goltz, whose vision reached to an Irish shanty located south of the tracks, south of the river, south of Mitchell, Nebraska.

– C.T. "Lloyd" Spear,
Jacksonville, Florida

Top row: Ivan Olsen helps check in campers on registration day.
Second row, from left: Teen campers hurry to be on time for a chapel service; The Maranatha Book Room was located in the back of the Old Tabernacle.
Third row, from left: This baptismal service was held in the sandpit swimming hole, approximately 1950; The old Sweet Shop was a hot spot on a hot day, 1950s.

Top row, from left: One of the Gospel Teams that promoted Maranatha by visiting various churches during the summer included this trio: Ruby Jansen, LaVerna Krause and Marian Gustafson; Pastor Ivan Olsen dives into the old sandpit swimming hole, late 1940s or early 1950s.

Second row, from left: A moment of fellowship outside a slab cabin (1950s); A quartet practices in the empty Old Tab, date unknown.

Third row, from left: These unidentified boys played ping pong behind the dining hall. In the background is the Olsens' house (later known as "Bethel House") 1950s; This sign marked the entrance to Maranatha on the east property line until I-80 was built. It was almost due north from today's Clark Hall.

Top row, from left: Shuffleboard was a popular recreation option in 1955; Paul Levine (left) and Bob Findlay played mandolin and guitar and sang at Maranatha during the 1950s. Findlay, who was blind, memorized hundreds of songs. Levine was a former professional baseball player who became an evangelist (1950s).

Second row, from left: This group of church women enjoys a good visit while peeling vegetables outside the Dining Hall; A moment from the summer of 1959. From left: Marcella Seymour, Karen Thune, unidentified.

Third row, from left: The unloading point for campers in the 1950s was in front of the dining hall; Campers spend time in prayer between the dining hall and the caretaker's house.

73

Navigator Training Program

One of the unique chapters of Maranatha Bible Camp has to be a program that God raised up to train hundreds of young people to be His disciples during the summers of 1958–1971.

For the first 20 years, every significant event or program at Maranatha had been "homegrown." Although the programming was decentralized — volunteers from various parts of the country had worked together with Rev. Ivan Olsen and his expanding network of people to plan and administer the various camps — it had always been done under the banner of Maranatha Bible Camp. In 1958, the Camp began to act in partnership with a well-known national organization to create something that profoundly affected a generation of young men and women for the rest of their lives.

The Navigators, headquartered in Colorado Springs, Colorado, was an excellent fit with Maranatha. Both were conservative, evangelical organizations that sought to produce life change in young people through systematic teaching and application of the Bible.

The Navigator Training Program not only affected the individuals involved, it left a huge footprint on Maranatha as an organization. It was a model for what later became Maranatha's own Summer Missions program. For decades, people who had gone through the Nav Program wrote the Camp, or returned to visit, relating details to Olsen and his new right-hand man, George W. Cheek, of how they had been established as committed, mature Christians and challenged to serve God fulltime.

"A measure of the success of this program is the number of people I have met at the most unexpected times who tell me with passion what their five-week session meant to them," wrote Cheek, who first arrived at Maranatha about 16 months after the last Navigator session ended. "Again I identify with the gospel writer Luke who felt compelled to write a record, having known personally many eyewitnesses."

The first mention in the Camp board minutes was September 1957, when board president Theodore Epp asked for time in the meeting to explain a burden he had for a program to train young people. He proposed that the event should be several weeks in length, similar to the program he had seen while speaking at Sandy Cove, a Christian conference center in Maryland.

Epp envisioned that the young people would receive "specialized training in Christian life, thus preparing them to meet the issues of life so much better. These same young people will be earning their way through these weeks of camp by doing all kinds of work. They will have special classes in the morning and evening, together with the regular camp. This I believe to be a great forward step."

The Camp board approved Epp's concept as a good idea. Often in ministry board meetings, many good ideas are discussed and approved but are later dropped when the initial enthusiasm fades. Epp and Olsen did not let this concept die on the vine. They agreed to consult Lorne Sanny, president of the Navigators, for help in developing the program. Sanny sent Leroy Eims, a Nav representative, to work out the details with Maranatha.

The original plan was for 10 weeks of training for each student, but it raised so much interest that Olsen proposed dividing the program into two sessions, each five weeks long. The trainees' expenses would be covered, and they each would receive a $3-a-week allowance. "Only those eager to become better acquainted with their Bibles and who want to be more useful in their home churches need apply."

The program started on June 16, 1958. The daily schedule featured Reveille at 6:00 a.m., although by 1966, it was as early as 5:30. The groggy trainees were expected to be up and ready for calisthenics in five minutes. After a 10-minute workout, they showered, had a group prayer time, an individual quiet time and then reported for breakfast.

After breakfast came the morning work shift. Each day included four hours of work for the dual purpose of Camp maintenance and practical training. The trainees were divided into crews. There was the carpentry crew, paint crew, technical crew, electrical crew, mechanical crew, mobile crew, dining hall crew, laundry crew and even the "panic crew," which handled emergency situations. Generally, each person stayed on the same work detail for all five weeks, although when the Berean Fundamental Church in Haxtun, Colorado, donated 351 live hens to Maranatha in 1958, Olsen quickly created a poultry crew, where every trainee got a crash course in killing, scalding, plucking and gutting a chicken.

At midmorning, the students went directly from work to Pastor's Hour, a 60-minute Bible teaching time led by Olsen. ("I don't care what your churches told you," Olsen would tell the trainees. "Can you find it in your Bible? Don't even believe Dr. Olsen. He's only a man. Look in your Bible.") At the conclusion of Pastor's Hour, they had half an hour of personal study time focused on four chapters of assigned Bible reading, followed by 60 minutes of small-group Bible study, and then, lunch.

The afternoon started with another 30-minute personal study session, followed by two hours, 30 minutes of work. During the afternoon work session, Olsen typically would walk or drive around the Camp, stopping to talk with the trainees and answer their questions about his teaching that morning. After the day's work was done, the trainees received 1 hour, 45 minutes of free time, ending with the evening meal. Then came an hour-long "Man to Man" session, which focused on how to share one's testimony and other aspects of personal witnessing. Another personal study time (this time, 60 minutes), which often included a quiz over the day's assigned scripture reading, led into the evening meeting in the Tabernacle, which lasted about 90 minutes. The trainees were required to be back in their quarters with lights out by 9:30.

Each session's trainees also did off-Camp ministry in North Platte, which consisted of evangelism from house to house and in public places such as Cody Park and the bus depot. They shared their testimonies in churches around the region and helped with song leading, teaching and speaking from the pulpit.

It was strenuous. It was designed to systematically teach the basics of Bible study, scripture memory, prayer, personal devotions, obedience and witnessing. Students were trained in time management, organization and motivation. They learned that the Christian life is a disciplined life. The participants called it a "Christian boot camp," but they began to see the value in what they were going through, and the popularity of the program grew.

The program originally was designed for 25 men and 25 women, but soon it grew beyond those bounds. (Olsen was well-known for adding young people to the program at the last minute.) In 1963, 78 attended the first session and 81 the second. In 1966, there were 99 in the first session and 59 in the second.

As the program evolved, Sanny wrote to Theodore Epp on January 22, 1960: "As to our working relationships, I suggest the following:
- "That the training program be called the "Maranatha Training Program," not the "Navigator Training Program." In this way, Maranatha will take the responsibility for who is accepted for training and on what basis. The general purpose of the program as I understand it is to take young people of high school age and training them to be more effective workers to go back into their church.
- "That Maranatha take the total responsibility for financing this program and making suitable arrangements for the finances of the staff, and further that these finances be handled by Maranatha and not The Navigators."

Epp publicized the Navigator Training Program on his Back to the Bible Broadcast and through the Broadcast's magazine, the Good News Broadcaster. Other than that, it was a word-of-mouth promotional campaign.

"We have been asked on some occasions to write up a story of the Teen-Age Training Program, and, admittedly, we are frightened to do it," wrote Olsen in his 1963 report to the Camp board. "This program is outgrowing our facilities already, and if we would dare to publicize it on a national basis, we would be simply deluged."

The Navigators quickly recognized that the system in place at Maranatha was working, and the organization began to send its young members from college campuses all over the nation. "All of the young people that were brought here were those that had just been converted on the university campus," said Olsen. "They had only been converted as recently as two weeks or a month before they came here. They were all babes in Christ."

The growing program soon required new facilities. A large donation by Bert & Ann Needham started a fund drive to build the new Needham Hall Training Center, which was dedicated in 1966. Starting that year, because there were six bunks in each room, the trainees were divided into six-man teams for most of their activities throughout the day.

At the end of each session, the leadership representing the Nav staff wrote extensive evaluations analyzing the strengths and weaknesses of the program. Olsen also kept notes from year to year on what worked best and what didn't. Olsen and the Nav leadership made small adjustments, and the schedule was altered at times depending on the number of campers on the grounds during any particular week, but Maranatha kept the same basic program intact for 14 years.

The program had continuity, mainly because of the Olsens and the Nav leadership who served for several summers. One of the Nav leaders, Russ Johnston, became increasingly prominent. In an evaluation after the 1960 season, Olsen commented, "We are probably most indebted to Russ Johnston who did so much in lining up the leadership. (He) spent much time at Maranatha this year executing these plans and counseling with his leadership as well as with ourselves."

By 1962, the Navigator Training Program was well entrenched in Maranatha's culture. "Year after year, we have a growing conviction that probably one of the greatest things that the Maranatha Bible Camp has ever done has been to have the Teen-Age Training Program," wrote Olsen. "I cannot remember, as Pastor, when my own young people who were in the Training Program have been more zealous for God, and have been more out and out for the things of the Lord, than they are right now. They have their regular witnessing time. They meet regularly in their Bible study times, and have been continuing on in such a way as I have never had the opportunity of observing before, as Pastor, as well as Camp Director. I thank God for the Teen-Age Training Program, and if the Lord tarries, may it continue!"

Alice Olsen also had a well-respected ministry with those who came during the Nav training years. Many former trainees mentioned her willingness to take time with them, showing personal interest. "I really appreciated Mrs. Olsen taking time to pray with me," was a common theme. She also spoke to each session of trainees as a group. One of the students remembered her remarks as "short," but "there is a lot said. The stories of answered prayer prove again to me that God is real."

There is little doubt from reading Olsen's accounts that the Pastor's Hour was the highlight of his 51 years as general director. Navigator trainees wrote that this time of teaching was very special and helpful to them as young college students. "The greatest contact with the Spirit of God of my entire ministry was the Pastor's Hour at Maranatha Camp," said Olsen. "You know, it isn't an easy thing to think of preaching to college-age young people … most of them educated above my own education, but you know, every night the Spirit of God would awaken me and I had to get the message of God for that day, for that group of people, and it was absolutely amazing how God would give me the one-hour message."

One of the most memorable Pastor's Hour messages was in 1969 on the dedication of one's life to God's service. Carter Volle, an architecture student from the University of Kansas who had received his Master's degree, heard the message and his life was changed. The next day, he approached the Camp director.

"Pastor, I've just got to talk with you," he said. "I never made a more sincere decision in my life than I made yesterday. If God tells me, I will go anyplace on earth that He tells me to go. But ever since yesterday, I've been trying to reason out that since I was 12 years old, I've wanted to be an engineer, and all of my high school education, all my college — and now I'm about to get the highest degree in this course — would God have led me this far, could I have been mistaken all these years, and now I'm to go out as a missionary to preach?"

Olsen looked at Volle and remembered the time he had dedicated his own life to God's service more than 30 years ago.

"I was led to say that when I gave my life to Christ, there was only the choice of being a preacher, a missionary or an evangelist, that they were very, very narrow," the pastor said, "but now we're in an hour of specialization, that anyone that wants to bring what is in their hand to God, God will use it like He used Moses' rod, and He'll use their life. If you take your engineering and give it to God, God will use it."

Volle went on to serve Christian ministries in more than half the states in the Union and at least nine foreign countries with his architectural services through Missionary Tech, based in Longview, Texas, and during the subsequent decades, "What's In Your Hand?" became one of the best-known themes ever taught at Maranatha.

Rod Sargent, who served in the Navs' upper-level management, wrote the Maranatha board of directors in the fall of 1967, "The Maranatha Summer Training Program has demonstrated the fact that it is one of the most effective means of training college-age young people we have ever been associated with."

"My wife and I recall the day that summer when we both committed our lives to full-time Christian service," wrote Hyatt Baker in 1970. "We both saw how God used last summer's Navigator Training Program in our lives and in the lives of the other trainees. It was a life-changing experience." Later that year, Jerri Martin wrote, "Thank you for your and Mrs. Olsen's prayers for the trainees." Trainee Bob Freeborn called his experience, "the greatest summer of my life."

Although Sanny urged in 1960 that Maranatha take ownership of the program, especially the financial arrangements, the Navigators soon were eager to claim some ownership themselves. The October 1968 *Navigators Log* reflects that the program indeed had evolved from being a Maranatha-sponsored program for high school youth into a Navigator program for college students. "… The camp has for the last 11 years observed the Navigator-conducted training programs being held there." It was a well-balanced partnership. The Camp leadership acknowledged that without the strong commitment of the Nav staff who came five weeks at a time, plus their nationwide university recruitment contacts, the program would not have grown to the extent it did.

The program flourished throughout the 1960s, but in 1970, with the rise of new Navigator leadership, and the distractions that Olsen faced with his pastorate at North Platte Berean (which was fast approaching a church split), the partnership started to become strained. On a number of occasions people have asked why the Training Program at Maranatha came to an end. Probably the simplest explanation is that God led the Navs to move on to other methods and locations. There is ample correspondence to give insight on the details.

On October 9, 1970, a different Navigator staff member entered the picture. Chuck Strittmatter, an on-site Training Program leader from the mid-1960s who moved up to middle management, wrote, "There are three items I feel we need to discuss regarding next year: 1. the financial arrangement, 2. size of the program, and 3. the control and operation of the program. Because of LeRoy Eims's relationship with you and the program over the years, I've asked LeRoy if he could join us in discussing these matters …"

On November 16, 1970, Lorne Sanny wrote, "We do deeply appreciate the co-laborship with you through the years and look forward to many more …"

On December 9, 1970, Strittmatter wrote another lengthy letter proposing a new financial arrangement, requesting all applications for trainees to go through the Nav offices. He also proposed the discontinuing of Maranatha faith promise offerings with the possibility those offerings could be channeled to the financial support of the Navs' campus staff.

The subsequent correspondence shows that further meetings for realignment took place, confirming that the Maranatha Camp board worked out the first two requests with the regional Nav staff. However, differences in operational preferences between Maranatha and the Navigators' middle management continued to surface. Last-minute acceptances of trainees in the spring of 1971 by an enthusiastic Ivan Olsen, even though Navigator staff already had closed the enrollment, hastened the end of the partnership.

On September 7, 1971, Jack Mayhall, a Nav Divisional Director, wrote Olsen. "We have just finished a Regional Directors planning session where we gave very careful consider-ation to the Lord's leading in regard to training program," Mayhall wrote. "We have concluded that we will not have a training program at Maranatha next summer."

Thus ended a chapter loaded with many fond memories shared by hundreds of young people and those who trained them.

In October 1971, the camp board approved Olsen's plan of returning to a high school training program, but in a June 1972 letter to Carl Yeutter, a retired banker and close friend, he referred to hiring 40 young people at $25 per week to replace the work done in previous summers by the Navigator Trainees. The October 1972 minutes reflect that God had "definitely closed the door" on the high school training program that had been authorized for the 1972 season and that the hiring of young people for work staff had begun. In time, the summer work staff evolved into the Summer Missions program that Maranatha refined and uses into the 21st century.

VOICES OF MARANATHA

He Forgives

I am writing to you by God's grace. As a trainee at Maranatha in summer 1970, I pledged $5.00 per month to the Camp, then lapsed in my pledge. Because He forgives those who confess their sins, I am forgiven for my sinful negligence and I can make restitution with a willing heart. Not being sure of the exact amount I still have not paid, enclosed is $50.00 to cover the remaining amount and a $5.00 check to begin my new pledge.

I am thankful to God for Maranatha. The person I pointed to Christ last year attended second session this summer, and God used the time to revamp his personal habits. It is a joy to see the order of his personal life. More signifi-cant, though, has been Luke 16:12 in his life. God spoke to him through that verse while at Maranatha, and he is to me as Jonathan's armour bearer was to him. Thus far in our dorm ministry at Colorado State University, he has been with me 100% and what a blessing it's been. So I am praising God for His tool, Maranatha, that first helped me and God has used it in the next generation beyond me. Keep preaching the Word.

– Charlie Carson,
Ft. Collins, Colorado
(written in 1971)

Gal to Gal Sessions

In the past year God has changed my heart about the training program until I was honestly at the point where I desired to come. Before I thought I had many reasons (I thought) for not coming. God worked out the specific things: the finances, Scott's job, and a baby-sitter. I know we are in His will by being here.

The highlight of my stay here has been the gal to gal sessions. Just getting to know the girls on my team, hav-ing them share their needs, and then praying together for specific things and watching God give direct answers. How it has strengthened my trust in God. Prayer really works.

– Alma Morton,
Ames, Iowa
(written during the 1960s)

Miracles: 12-ounce Steaks

This account, and the one on the following page, was transcribed from the audio recording of Rev. Olsen's messages, likely given during the 1970s.

I think probably why these Navigator years were so rich to my heart is one verse of Scripture that permeated all 13 years. Every one of the Navigators on the entire campgrounds knew this verse: "Give us this day our daily bread." There were very, very few days that verse wasn't brought out. It was the substance of all our prayers. Everybody knew that whatever they had to eat was what God gave for that day.

"Give us this day our daily bread." Back in those years, we used to get some commodities from the government. Now someone says, "That is how you were able to feed them." Well, the most we ever got was a thousand dollars one year. But we never got anything like meat.

One evening, the leader of the Navigator group, with all of his sweetness — no criticism — came and said, "Pastor, so many have mentioned to us that they are really hungry for a good meal of meat." I wasn't surprised, because we would take two or three pounds of hamburger and 30 or 40 pounds of spaghetti and we had "meat food." We would take a couple of cans of tuna and make a casserole dish to feed 200. We had "meat food," yes, but they were hungry for some straight meat. The Nav leader and I prayed that evening.

It was a sleepless night for me, and by Pastor's Hour at 9 the next morning, my faith had grown.

That morning, I went to 200 college and university students — I tremble as I look back on it — and they came out of backgrounds of doubt. They came out of the university environment. They had been brought here that their faith might be strengthened.

I have heard missionaries tell that they believe God has been pleased to perform miracles on pioneer fields to establish the work the same as He did in the book of Acts. This is what I had the chance to see God do for these 200 students. I went before the young people and said, "Why don't we ask God for a good meal of meat?"

They began to clap their hands and whistle just like university students would do. They made the roof raise when I just mentioned it. We all bowed our heads together and I told them this, "You know, it's not going to be any harder for God to give us a 12-ounce steak for each of us as it is for Him to give us a meatball or a piece of meatloaf. So if we are going to ask Him for anything, let's ask Him for a 12-ounce steak." As pastor, I led those young people to believe that God would provide them with a 12-ounce steak if we asked Him for it.

God bears me witness that when I stepped out of the Tabernacle at 10 o'clock that morning, after we had asked God to provide in that service, Frank and Jessie Shimmin were sitting in their car. They had arrived during the service. I led Frank and Jessie Shimmin to Christ (they were brother and sister). They were ranchers north of Tryon, about 60 miles north of North Platte. I walked directly to their car and Frank handed me a check through the window. He said, "Pastor, Jessie and I have been burdened that we should give you this check so you could use it just for meat."

I was overwhelmed, as you would expect. I went straight to the telephone and called Johnny Thompson, who runs a slaughterhouse in North Platte. I told him of the miracle God had done in answering prayer and providing the money. I said, "Could you just drop everything and cut about 240 steaks of 12 ounces each so we can include the other workers around the campground?"

Well, Johnny is a Christian and a member of our church. He said, "Pastor for a thing like this, I will." He dropped everything and prepared 240 12-ounce steaks. We improvised everything we could and brought them out alongside Lake Maranatha. That evening as the sun was setting, each young person was taking care of his own 12-ounce steak and cooking it just the way he wanted on that outdoor broiler. We enjoyed them with hash browns and onions.

I'm wondering if these young people will ever forget that there is a God in heaven. One of the aspects of the miracle was that even before these young people prayed at 9 o'clock, Frank and Jessie had to leave home about 7 o'clock to get to Maranatha by the time they did. Before we cried or called, He answered. He knew what the need was and He provided.

– Ivan E. Olsen

Miracles: The Electrical Transformer

Let me tell you of the summer when the Navigators had among their faculty or staff a man who was one of the most accomplished electricians I have ever had the opportunity of knowing. He had completed all his university college work and a lot of practical work. When this fellow was among the staff, we realized he would be able to help us here at Maranatha.

Our camp had grown up like "topsy" because we had never planned the camp to have 200 college and university students here. We just adjusted what we had to accommodate them. You should have seen the kitchen over in the old dining hall — a kitchen we had built to take care of a few kids and then suddenly the Lord says, "I want to bring these college and university students." We didn't have it electrically set up, we couldn't plug in and use even the equipment we had — the grinders, the electric toasters and things like that to take care of 200. This fellow proceeded to put in a big enough installation electrically to meet this need.

I'm so stupid as far as electrical and mechanical and construction things go — I don't know a thing about them. We just told the fellow to go ahead and get this thing fixed up. He brought into being the most beautiful things. He had wall plugs all around that kitchen. He had his great big installation there for bringing in the power, and he said, "We'll we're ready to have the transformer brought." Of course, he had to tell me what a transformer was.

I called the Dawson Public Power in Lexington and told them that we had everything ready up here. "When you come, we would like to have you install the transformer for us," I told them. So they came up and investigated to see what kind of transformer we needed. After they had looked at it, they came to me and said, "Why pastor, do you realize what you are asking from us? We only have two transformers that are as big as what you need here. We don't have a transformer available that will do that. If we were to order one now, it would take two years to come."

I stood the next day before these young people and said, "It sounds stupid, I know. The electrician never thought. I just told him to go ahead and make the installation. I didn't know a transformer went with it. Now let's pray and ask God."

We had gone through several days — a week or two — of inconvenience while this fellow was working with the electricity on and off and everything else. We had privations. We had to eat outdoors. We had to have makeshift meals and everything else.

I got a telephone call that afternoon from Dawson Public Power and they said, "Reverend, you're sure in luck." And I thought, "Well, that's the way the world says it." Then he said, "Do you know that after we saw what you needed, we got our records out. We have just gotten a notice that one has arrived in North Platte and it's on the flatcar. Two years ago, we had an order for two transformers and we had even forgotten that at that time, we thought, 'Maybe by the time these get here we might need a third.' And we have a third transformer and it's sitting on the flatcar in North Platte. If it's all right with you, we will be up in the morning and load it up and come right out and get it installed."

You'd say that is enough of a miracle. Beyond that, I had nothing to do with it. Here were 200 college and university students — new converts. We had honestly told them the whole story — the impossibility of getting a transformer. Between 9 o'clock and 10 o'clock when my class was being conducted in the Tabernacle, these students were sitting there and right in the midst of my teaching that morning, there comes a truck with a great big trailer in back of it and the biggest light pole I had ever seen. Here they come bringing it up because installation is right in front of the old dining hall. We call it the Sweet Shop now. It first of all went very slowly by the window. Right in back of it was another great big truck with a great big transformer. And in back of it was another truck with all of the necessary equipment.

As they went by the side of that Tabernacle, there was a holy hush that came over those young people as they realized that what was absolutely impossible was being delivered that morning. I wonder what went through the hearts and minds of these young people as they sat there realizing that God was still alive? He is still in business! That God was ruling in the affairs of men.

— *Ivan E. Olsen*

Miracles: The Mulberry Trees

This account was taken from the transcript of Russ Johnston's 1989 interview with Rev. Olsen and a videotape of the Camp's golden anniversary celebration in 1988.

During the time of the Navigator Training Program, we weren't paying anything for the help, but we had a cook from my church who was a rather nominal Christian, but was able to free herself for the summer. She would use this government-given flour and we had all the butter we could use, so she did nothing all day long but bake bread. She would start early in the morning and make 50 loaves at a time, and these young people would eat all the bread she could bake in one day, so that every day it was fresh and hot.

One morning when breakfast was over, she came over to my home and said, "I get so thrilled watching these young people eat this fresh-baked bread. I don't know, Pastor, why I'm asking this unless it's because I've got a 'mother-heart,' but when I see those young people — I've actually seen a young man eat a whole loaf of hot bread with butter on it — I just feel that it would be so good if we could just have some jelly or some jam or honey or whatever it might be, something that they could put on their bread."

I was led to say to her there in my kitchen, "You know, if God is going to provide it, He'll have to do it, because we give them what we have, and we don't have the money to go and buy jam or jelly, but let's pray and ask God what He would do." And we bowed our heads in that place, about 10:00 or 10:30 in the morning, and asked God that if He wanted to provide some jelly or jam, that He would have to provide this for us.

Now my custom was that after the noonday lunch, I spent my afternoons moving out among these Navigators. They were out working on either the lawn or in the shop on cars or on the trees or wherever they were, and I would move from one group to the other, and they would ask questions about the message I gave in the morning. And we carried on all afternoon. This particular afternoon, I went out into the area where we have the big cross — the 32-foot-high lighted cross — alongside of Interstate 80, and while I was walking there, I saw a big tree of blackberries. I never knew blackberries grew on a tree, and I reached up and tasted them — they were so sweet — they whet my own appetite so that before I realized it, my face was literally black from the juice of those blackberries.

There was a Navigator that was near and I called for him and I said, "Come and see this tree of blackberries," and when he got there, he said, "Pastor, don't you know this is a mulberry tree? These aren't blackberries, these are mulberries." And they were as big as the big blackberries, and juicy and sweet, and when I looked further, there were a total of five mulberry trees in that little group, and all of them laden in the same way. He said, "Pastor, what they do is they lay sheets on the ground and they shake the mulberry trees, and the berries fall on the sheet and they gather them up."

We immediately proceeded to do that. I sent a S.O.S. call to my church in North Platte, and the carloads of ladies arrived around seven the next morning … to make what? To make jam, and to make jelly! It proved that they made pancake syrup, mulberry syrup, and do you know, by the way, they all brought their sugar along with them — that was their donation, besides doing all the work.

One of them said, "Do you know, if this hadn't happened so quickly, it's always best to use rhubarb or apple or something along with mulberries, but we'll just go ahead and make it …" but just about that time, Louis Westcoat and his wife showed up in their little antiquated pickup, and he came to me and said, "You know, Reverend, last night my wife said to me, 'Isn't it a shame that our backyard is full of rhubarb plants, so full, just going to waste? If Reverend Olsen had that rhubarb at Maranatha, every stick of it would be used for pie or whatever they would use it for.'" And they decided that because they had to go to town the next day, they'd rise real, real early so they could cut it, and they cut every stick of rhubarb. It filled the back of their pickup, and they arrived very nearly the same time the ladies arrived. Talk about the timing of God! I can't remember how many gallons of jam, I can't tell you how many gallons of jelly and how many gallons of syrup for pancakes that was made out of that.

Now the punch line is this — we came to Maranatha campgrounds in 1943 (actually 1944), this had to be in the 60s, the incident that I'm telling you about. Don't let anybody ever tell me that five mulberry trees were there all these years, and not a single person on the grounds knew it! I believe God made those trees, just as he made that wine in the second chapter of John, "and it was fully of age." God put those trees laden with mulberries right in those places. You don't have to believe that, but I do. God was able to make those trees fully fruit-laden as He put them in the ground. Our God prepared those, and that was a miracle made in answer to prayer of meeting a provision.

– Ivan E. Olsen

Reveille Over the PA, Flying Feathers, Quiet Time

What Maranatha has meant to me! I have many fond memories of Maranatha that go back 50 some years. When I first knew Maranatha almost all the cabins were one room and built of split cedar logs. I was pleased last year to find one still standing!

I remember swimming in the sand pit lake. I almost drowned there, but fortunately was swimming with Louise McDermott (Crooks), who realized I had slipped out of the inner tube and was in trouble. She pulled me out! I also fondly remember many, many years in the old swimming pool. It seemed so wonderful and big and clean when it was built. Every Friday or Saturday afternoon-late someone had to dive to the bottom and pull the plug so the pool could drain, be cleaned, and be refilled with fresh water.

I remember many services in the Old Tabernacle. I remember *"Onward Christian Soldiers"* being played over the loud speaker for Reveille each morning. I remember when the "modern" Needham Hall was being built!

The most profound effect on my life from days spent at Maranatha, though, was the summer I spent as part of the first Navigator program. I was in high school at the time. I learned about having a quiet time and made a promise then to always having one throughout my life. I have kept that promise, and it has had a deep, abiding influence on my life. It is the most important time of my day! To live without daily contact with the eternal, almighty God, through Jesus, and in the power of the Holy Spirit, I cannot imagine. How empty and futile life would be without it! I remember the teaching of Dr. Epp. That was the first time I had ever heard that God sees us (me) through Jesus' perfection and not through my sinfulness. What an impact that truth has had! How freeing to know that God accepts me because of what Jesus has done for me, and not because of any good I could possibly do!

I remember spending HOURS that summer peeling potatoes behind the old dining room. I have never forgotten the songs we sang together as we peeled with paring knives, mind you!! Then there was the week a farmer donated chickens to Maranatha. I think it was a couple of hundred live chickens! The boys were the beheaders, defeatherers, and gutter-outers! The girls got to finish taking out the hearts, livers and kidneys. Then we split them into their various pieces. I couldn't face chicken for several years after that! But I can still carve a raw, whole chicken in record time!!

These are just some of the memories of Maranatha. I am thankful for them and, even for some of the hard times. As I work now as Director of Children's Ministries in a little inner-city church here in Wichita, I often recall some principle or some event at Maranatha that helps me be more effective in my work. Hopefully, my daily life following Jesus shows the effects of those lessons learned while I was young.

I am so grateful for all the people who took an interest in me and helped me to grow. Thank you, dear Jesus, for allowing a place like Maranatha, to help people draw apart and to get to know you better!

– Joy Parcel Domen,
Wichita, Kansas

She Fed a Lot of Navigator Trainees

Pastor Olsen came to my mom, Betty Smolik, in the spring of 1970 and asked her if she would be interested in being the head cook for Maranatha. She accepted his offer. Pastor Olsen had an account set up just for mom to get gas, as she didn't have the money to put gas in the car.

She had the Navigator girls under her, and she taught them everything about cooking, including how to cut up chickens. She even opened up our home to them so they could go to North Platte and relax and go shopping. All the girls would call Mom before they left at the end of their summer.

Pastor Olsen talked Mom into having fried rabbit and split pea soup; they were two of his favorite meals. He had a nickname for Mom; he called her "girly." Mom knew that she was serving the Lord by feeding the Maranatha crew.

Mom loved Maranatha and before she had her stroke and heart attack, she asked me to see if I could put a donation in to Maranatha in her name, and that is what we did when she died.

– Jackie Smolik Broeder,
Grant, Nebraska

Chicken Killing Was a Character Builder

What wonderful memories I have. I don't know if any one else will mention that one night that summer we had the closest thing to a "revival" I have ever been a part of. Dr. Olsen had spoken to us, I believe, and then a staff woman spoke to us about moral purity and commitment, and I don't remember what else. But there were serious prayer groups all over the room, and serious talks in the staff members' rooms - I remember the prayer the best. It was an amazing experience.

Then there was the infamous chicken killing - I think it was also the summer of 1958. Someone had donated **live** chickens to the camp. One of our training program themes was character development, and I guess someone thought giving each of us a live chicken to kill and clean would build character. I carried mine around by the neck until I could talk some boys into developing more character than I needed that day!

There are also several pictures of the equally infamous "bedbug" incident. Somehow bedbugs invaded the training program girls' dorm. We all had to "take up our beds and walk." The only problem was that they moved out the mattresses as well as the girls before they sprayed. So when we moved back in, so did the bedbugs. Later, they moved us out again and left the mattresses to be fumigated, too. That seemed to take care of the problem. Some unorchestrated character development!

I remember Ruth Gustafson's wonderful piano playing— a trio of girls who I think were pastor's daughters—the Hofrichter family, all those girls with their pony tails tied in knots—no mixed "bathing" (as in swimming)—tug of war across the lake inlet—trying to learn to play tennis with Barbara Bruce from Haxtun—Dwight Olsen playing the piano. I still have several copies of "Maranatha Melodies."

I attended summer camp and retreats for several of my growing up years, and I was in the first two Nav Training Programs—summers of 1958 and 1959. Maranatha was a place of significant spiritual growth for me. I made many serious decisions that impacted my future, and yes, developed character. The things I was learning at home and in my home church (Morrill Berean Fundamental) were reinforced—a love for God's Word, belief that it was the ultimate authority in my life, scripture memory and the desire to make my life "count" for eternity. In 1965 my husband and I joined the staff of Campus Crusade for Christ and worked with that organization for five years. And, after getting my PHT degree at Dallas Theological Seminary (Putting Hubby Through—not particularly politically correct today, I guess) I have been a pastor's wife for 28 years. I am grateful for the part Maranatha had in making me ready to be an effective member of a ministry team, leading Bible studies, teaching leadership and discipleship and speaking to our women.

On my trips back to Maranatha in the 70s (to visit my parents when they lived there—Earnest and Betty Skoog; Mom was the unofficial Camp groundskeeper and beautification committee) and most recently five years ago (to see the waterfront built in Daddy's honor) it has been good to see the progress. But it is sad that the Old Tabernacle is gone and the rickety Sweet Shop gone also.

Another memory, our church youth group came to Camp for a winter retreat (probably winter of 1959-60), and on the way home on Sunday night we all became deathly ill. We barely made it back to Morrill as we had to stop frequently! We found out later that everyone had gotten food poisoning because we ate leftovers that had been stored in the refrigerator in the aluminum cooking pans.

One more: I remember that I was sitting in the old dining room at lunch time when they made an announcement that Russia had successfully launched the first Sputnik!

— Linda Skoog Ewing,
Bixby, Oklahoma

The Navigator trainees got massive dose of chicken killing and cleaning.

Bed bugs infested the Navigator women's dorm in the late 1950s.

A Penetrating Prayer Life

In 1964, Mrs. Olsen spent time praying with the staff girls in the Navigator Training Program–together and individually. Once she said to me, "Shirley, I have a verse for you. Romans 8:1 'Therefore, there is now no condemnation for those who are in Christ...Christ...set me free...'" She didn't know me well, but God spoke to me through her sensitive heart. It was just what I needed.

I noticed that whenever she talked with me, or anyone, her eyes were so intense and penetrating. One day I mentioned that to her and asked, "Is that because you are praying for each person as you talk with her?" She said that it was. No wonder this quiet woman influenced so many. She used few words aloud, but directed her thoughts where it counted most–to the Lord Himself!

– *Shirley Atwood Osborne,*
Newton, Iowa

How God Brought Me Here

Last year Alma and I felt coming here would be an excellent aid in our walk with Christ but God shut the door. I'm certain that He wants me to obey my folks and they were set against it. This year no training of any kind seemed to be opening up. Finally we thought of Maranatha. But there were my folks, my job in Pierre, and a baby-sitter for Beth. Circumstances pointed against it. But both Alma and I got more excited about it.

About the middle of May we were accepted for the second session. Also I found out I was going to be able to quit my job at Pierre. We went to my folks' in the early part of June and amazingly left for Pierre without their saying one word about Maranatha. My mother even suggested I go to a school where I can get credits for religion! And we came to North Platte on July 19 with no idea where we would park Beth, my daughter. After we'd been here four days Carol Booze offered to keep Beth. We were thrilled. But after two weeks Mrs. Booze became ill and we had to bring Beth back. There we were in the same boat again. So we prayed and two days later Precious Olsen told Alma she wanted to keep Beth. Everything worked out.

Alma and I are both closer to the Lord and each other since coming here. We count this training as invaluable. We still plan on "being available" 10 or 20 years from now. I'm not sure we would be if we hadn't come here.

– *Scott Morton,*
Ames, Iowa
(written during the 1960s)

Virginia Epp's Quiet Time

I've heard of Maranatha all my life. Having spent many weeks at the Camp and seeing the trainees running around I figured that I would come out sometime and be a trainee. The problem was when. I have to earn money for college, but my father said I should come and what I lost would be taken care of. It wasn't until I got here that I really got excited about the whole deal, though. I had questions on what I was getting myself into. But now I'm so glad I came—it's really been great!

During the last four weeks I've really learned the HOW of a good quiet time. I had one fairly regular but it didn't do that much for me. Since being here I've had wonderful times with the Lord and really been blessed.

– *Virginia Epp,*
Lincoln, Nebraska
(written in the 1960s)

Using Architecture for the Lord

Letter to George Cheek, March 21, 1989

Dear George:
Greetings in the precious Name of our Lord and Saviour Jesus Christ.

I am thrilled to add my testimony concerning the valuable role that Maranatha Bible Camp has played in my life, with those of many others who are now serving our Lord around the world.

As a shy, lonely architectural student at the University of Kansas in the spring of 1969, I was searching for the reality that would bring meaning and direction to my life. Two fellows from the Navigators ministry befriended me and explained God's plan of salvation. Through my new found friends, I was convicted of my sinful condition before God and prayed to receive Christ as Lord and Saviour.

As I studied and understood God's Word, it became clear that God had a unique and exciting purpose for my life. During that summer I was asked to attend a Navigator Training Program at Maranatha Bible Camp. During those weeks we spent time in concentrated Bible study and in work projects for the camp. One of the definite highlights of that summer was the daily chapel time with Dr. Ivan Olsen. It was during this time that God was planting the seed and cultivating my desire to serve the Lord in missions. Through the wise counsel of Dr. Olsen, I returned to my architectural studies and sought the Lord about how I might serve Him in the future. In the next several years, the Lord gave me a vision for using my architectural educational skills for the furtherance of His kingdom.

Upon graduation in 1972, the Lord brought me in contact with Missionary TECH Team whose purpose is to provide technical services to missionaries and Christian organizations worldwide. God clearly directed in my life to join TECH Team and in the summer of 1975 my wife, LeAnne, and I moved to Longview, Texas to assume our ministry with Missionary TECH Team. Since then I have served in our Facilities Planning Division, providing assistance in various disciplines including long-range master planning, site selection, relocation studies, feasibility studies and architectural design. In the early 80s I was asked to assume the responsibility of Manager of our Facilities Planning Division. This involves coordination and organization of activities and scheduling for the division.

Throughout the 14 years of service with Missionary TECH Team, I have worked on projects which are located in some 26 of our United States, including Alaska, and have traveled and worked in five countries including Mexico, Canada, Guatemala, Ecuador and India. In 1989, I helped produce the master site plan at Maranatha.

I'll be forever grateful to God for Maranatha Bible Camp and for the impact that they have had worldwide for the cause of Christ.

– Sincerely in Christ,
Carter L. Volle,
Longview, Texas

Who Could Forget Ringing the Bell at 2 A.M.?

During my years 1958-1964 as pastor of the McCook, Nebraska, Berean Fundamental Church, I was involved as a counselor in the camps for juniors and youth. Every year we would recruit campers from our community, pile them into my Studebaker, and bring them to Camp. They loved it, and many of them came to receive the Lord Jesus during those years. I specially remember the skit times during the morning sessions, and the camper-counselor sessions out under the juniper trees. Crafts were a big feature, and kids would also flock around the snacks shack.

Dr. Olsen would preach, and many would respond to the invitation. Dinner time was a challenge because of the excited talk, and the softball games were always times of earnest competition. Getting the boys to go to sleep at night was another challenge in my experience. I remember one night these guys rigged up a string through the trees to the Camp bell, and about two a.m. the bell started ringing. Everybody got up and I found the string that led to our bunkhouse. Pushups were then assigned to the alleged perpetrators. They finally all got to sleep in time for the wake up bell!

Every year we looked forward to going to Camp, and when I visit the Camp today, the cedar tree fragrance still brings back fond memories of those happy days of evangelism and discipleship.

– Gerry Sprunger,
Weed, California

The Garbage Crew and the 'Elephant Grave'

I have many great memories of time at Maranatha, the summer of 1964. I was on the garbage pickup crew and we had a saying, "$2 per week and all you can eat." (The Camp paid each trainee back then, $2 per week.) I remember the great singing of some of the great hymns of the church, the "Pastor's Hour" every morning when Pastor Olsen spoke to us. Up at 5:30 every morning, as I remember, for calisthenics. I was also on the surveying crew that surveyed the boundaries of the lake. I remember also having to clean out the old dump site of years of garbage, tin cans, etc. because it would eventually be covered by the lake and they didn't want that pollution in the lake.

I came for the first session and felt God wanted me to stay for the second so I wrote my employer in Minneapolis of my intentions and they told me that they could not guarantee me that I would have a job when I returned. I trusted the Lord by staying and when I did return from Maranatha to my job, it was still there.

The underground cellar, Russ Johnston referred to as the "elephant grave" (he was the Navigator in charge of training). I remember going into North Platte for evangelism in the parks and going from farm to farm doing the same. We were somewhat isolated from the news outside the Camp, but I remember hearing of the three, I think, Civil Rights workers who were killed in Mississippi as well as the Gulf of Tonkin incident, that led to America's greater involvement in Viet Nam.

– Chuck Choate,
Fargo, North Dakota

Calisthenics before 6 a.m. were a daily feature of the Navigator Training Program.

Navigator Program Built Solid Foundations

After receiving Christ in college, I met some of the girls who were with LeRoy and Virginia Eims in the Navigator ministry. They persuaded me to be a trainee at Maranatha in 1959 and I am so grateful they did. It was an important time in establishing me in "basics" of the Christian life and how to seek the will of God. In addition to these, the teachings on the Holy Spirit by Berean pastor, Ernie Skoog, gave me my first real understanding of the third person of the Trinity.

In 1964, I served on the staff of the Navigator Training Program. That year Rev. Olsen asked us to pray as he went to Lincoln to request the highway department to dig on Maranatha property for the sand needed in the creation of Interstate 80. When he returned with the answer "yes" there was much praise to the Lord! Now, whenever we travel I-80 in Western Nebraska, I watch for the big cross and am grateful we had a part through prayer.

Again in 1968 I served on the staff. That year we saw the fruition of those prayers as I-80 was being constructed and we found many dusty detours whenever we ventured from the campground—only a little inconvenience in exchange for a wonderful lake. That year Rev. Olsen delivered his message "The Battle for the Minds of Men." He was among the first Bible teachers to recognize this battle taking root in our country and the world. It was startling but true. Only in eternity will we know how many college students were steered away from entrapments that became more prevalent in the years following.

– Shirley Atwood Osborne,
Newton, Iowa

Living an 'Old Tab' Memory Once Again

My first memories of Maranatha Bible Camp are in the late 1950s and early 60s, prior to the Interstate coming through. We were members of the North Platte Berean Fundamental Church, and Rev. Olsen gave us a challenge: memorize Bible verses, and earn a free week of Bible camp. I still remember reciting Psalm 1, Psalm 23, John 14: 1-6, and other Bible verses (King James Version only back then) to Harold Chapman, our faithful fifth grade Sunday School teacher, with the goal of going to Maranatha.

Back then, the Camp was quite different than today. The lake was a small pond; the Spartan rooms were either in Olsen Hall or the rustic log cabins. Each day began with campers standing in formation around the flagpole next to the dining hall, the smell of pancakes in the air, pledging allegiance to the American flag and the Christian flag, "one nation under God." We ate our meals at the long tables in the dining hall, keeping our napkins on our laps, our elbows off the table and saying "please" and "thank you," as we competed to be picked as the best-mannered table at the end of the meal. The mornings were usually filled with preaching and teaching in the Tabernacle, while the afternoons were full of sports and other fun activities: playing ping pong under the cedar trees, swimming with other boys in the pool's ice cold water, working on leather crafts while listening to music from the camp loudspeakers, buying a pop for a dime at the Sweet Shop.

There were a lot of rules imposed during these camps, and one of the constant dilemmas for spirited young boys was whether to follow or challenge the rules. Most of the time I think we did a pretty good job of being good campers, although I do remember several roommates and I doing pushups in front of the entire camp one day when we "forgot" to make our beds and clean our room in Olsen Hall.

The Navigators were an important part of the Camp during the 60s and after I graduated from North Platte High School in 1969, I spent the second half of my summer in the Navigator program. This was the famous summer of Woodstock, but I have to admit that I had no idea that it was going on, spending my summer memorizing Bible verses at Maranatha (the Navigators were famous for their business-card size Bible verses packets that they carried everywhere). The Navigator program at Maranatha was known back then as the "Christian boot camp," as rise and shine was at 5:30 a.m., and the entire day filled with Bible study, PT, and work programs. Our team was responsible for cutting trees and cleaning brush on the land between the lake and the Platte River.

I have many indelible memories of Maranatha, but if I could close my eyes and for five minutes relive one Maranatha memory, I would be back in the Tabernacle, sitting at the piano, with Louise playing the organ on the other side. It is mid-morning in August, and Rev. Olsen has just finished his morning Bible study. The Tabernacle is filled to capacity with college student Navigators, every one with a Bible in one hand and a notepad and pen in the other. A slight breeze with the smell of cedar cools us through the screened windows of the Tabernacle. Sunlight weaves through the beautiful trees surrounding the Tabernacle.

Rev. Olsen asks the Navigators to stand and turn in their hymnals to *Like a River Glorious.* Louise and I smile, and begin the introduction. Two strong F-chords, then two C-chords, announce the triumphal theme. We pause, and then the voices explode over us like a waterfall. "Like a river glorious..." hits the rafters so hard the roof of the Tabernacle is loosened. We are surrounded by the sound, sung with such vibrancy and gusto that I am transported: the chords give way to arpeggios up and down the keyboard, and my hands and fingers keep playing while I float above the piano. This is pure music, this is pure spirit, this is pure worship: My piano accompaniment fades away; there is only the praise of those powerful voices, singing as one these wonderful words:

Like a river glorious, is God's perfect peace,
Over all victorious, in its bright increase;
Perfect, yet it floweth, fuller ev'ry day,
Perfect, yet it groweth, deeper all the way.
Stayed upon Jehovah, hearts are fully blest,
Finding, as He promised, perfect peace and rest.

It was, I tell you, like a taste of heaven itself.

— *Dennis Fogland,*
Omaha, Nebraska

My Witnessing Career Started at Maranatha

My first experience at Maranatha was at a five-week Navigator Training Session in the summer of 1963. It was between my junior and senior year of high school. I went not knowing what to expect. The spiritual atmosphere was super. The singing was great as all who were there were there to be trained and the spiritual atmosphere was high. We memorized verses and had to keep a strict schedule.

In North Platte, for the first time in my life, I went out witnessing. That was a key thing for me because I never thought of myself as being able to witness since I was timid. But I found out that I could do it. That was life-changing.

At the end of the session there was a call for those who wanted to go forward. I went forward and made a decision to be a missionary. That was a turning point in my life. I had not even thought of what I wanted to be up until then. So I went home so fired up that I went witnessing by myself and sometimes with another guy from my youth group. When I graduated from high school I went to a Bible institute and it has been one big adventure since then. Thanks, Maranatha, for being a turning point in my pilgrimage to serving the Lord.

Our years in Spain have included church planting, camp directing and evangelism and witnessing. Here's one little story. Once I was praying for the salvation of the father of a couple of youth from our church plant in Spain. He was dying of cancer and was in the hospital. I asked them to take me to visit him, but they were afraid to because the woman he had been living with was always with him in the hospital and had said, "If Dan comes to see him, I will throw him out."

I kept praying for him, but nobody would take me to see him. I said to myself, "How am I going to comfort these young people when their father dies?" So when they asked for prayer for him, I felt compassion for him but could do nothing. So one day I kneeled down and prayed, "Lord, may it be when I go to the hospital today, I will meet him in another part of the hospital where this woman is not around. May he be visiting this other patient I am going to see." I went to visit this other relative of his in another wing of the hospital. He was not there, so I was disappointed. I started to go when a nephew of his said "Let's go visit my uncle." So I thought, "Here we go."

We went down a passage way of the basement to the other wing. When we arrived, this man was waiting in the hallway waiting room. His "woman" who had threatened to throw me out was not around. So I talked to him a little and began to explain the gospel. When I got to the decision place, the tears were coming down his face. He said he wanted to receive Christ and then he prayed. I gave him a few verses of assurance and then a whole bunch of people came to see him. So God opened up the way in that space of time where I met him and gave him the life saving Gospel. Then I could go to his son and daughter and say "your father got saved." I did meet them in the passage way of the hospital. They could hardly believe it. They said "How did you do it?" God opened the door. A few months later he died. I rejoiced.

Well, my witnessing career started at Maranatha Bible Camp. I have served as a missionary in Spain and Russia, and as a pastor in Cozad, Nebraska. I have led people to Christ from a number of different countries. It has been thrilling. Keep up the good work at MBC.

– Dan Ashcraft,
Sevilla, Spain

Lessons From Poison Ivy and Mosquitoes

It was unbearably hot. I was full of poison oak and mosquito bites and one totally exhausted 19-year-old "Navigator."

I had thought it would be a great time with other college students at this "Maranatha Camp" somewhere in the middle of Nebraska. But now, my limited vision only saw me crawling across the I-80 exit just before I died!

God hadn't asked me to approve His blueprint for me. I hadn't approved of this place, this oasis, He was preparing for thousands of people to find the peace, joy, rest and hope that comes from being with Him. He knew my small sacrifice was really nothing compared to the results His plan for Maranatha Bible Camp would bring.

Now, 34 years later, I see that I was blessed to be used in His plan, and I pray that He will bless all of you who work so hard. I pray that He will give you great vision, because with our great God, there is always a great plan!

– Karen Overturf Graham,
Talent, Oregon

From Europe to Maranatha and Back

My name is Hans Schneider. I was born in a German colony in Romania. At the age of 3, we went to Germany and lived there because World War II had started. Later on, my parents had to move from Germany to Austria because the bombs had been destroying our house.

In Austria, I went to a Lutheran church for nine years. Every Sunday and every Wednesday we had Lutheran religion class, but during all those years I never heard the gospel. It was an American missionary who came and shared the gospel in a schoolyard. During that time, I first heard that I could have forgiveness and have eternal life and have my past totally erased–all the bad things I had done would never be held against me! And it was wonderful to pray without having to memorize a prayer, praying by my bed that night, asking Jesus to come into my heart. The next day everything was beautiful, much brighter and much better than before because now I could look at people and not wonder if they could tell how bad I was; I had been forgiven and I knew that I was going to heaven.

Shortly after this conversion in my life, my family moved to Kearney, Nebraska. I have two brothers, two sisters, and Mom and Dad–we all came here as immigrants, from Austria in Europe.

A year later, we went to Ohio and that is where I first heard of the Navigators through a Back to the Bible Broadcast. Then a little book that was given to me about how to live for others, the title was *Born to Reproduce*. During the time that followed, I learned how to do Bible study and share the Gospel and give my testimony to others on how I became a Christian.

I came to Maranatha in 1959 and stayed for both of the programs, the first and the second one, and met LeRoy Eims and Rev. Olsen. I was all excited about reaching the world for Jesus Christ in 15 years by sharing the Gospel with one person, and with the two of us, two more, and four with four more, and so on.

I came home from Nebraska to Ohio and my brother said, "Where have you been all this time?" and I shared some things with him and he received Christ. Then the following year I went back again to Maranatha and my brother came with me. It was during that time I heard a message and wanted to give my life to the Lord for full-time Christian service. Maranatha has had a big part in my life, just knowing I could go there and receive training and help in training others myself in Bible study groups and discussion groups, and leading some campers (as a counselor).

Twice I had a group of campers that I taught. We stayed in these little log cabins or old shacks that probably are gone now with the knotholes and the mosquitoes buzzing through 'em. I also came back the second year to be a lifeguard at the swimming pool–I was a lifeguard two summers in a row, and twice a boy almost drowned. I was able to save him and play with him and get him so that he was not scared of the water.

Anyway, Maranatha has been a big help. I remember one time we butchered 300 chickens. Some of these Navigator kids had never even seen a live chicken, let alone butcher one. There were feathers flying all over the woods! We skinned them by pulling the skin off with pliers because the hens were such old hens that we had to make stew out of them and dumplings and stuff.

The Lord used the time at Maranatha to get my heart to *purpose* to serve Him. One of the verses He used was Mark 5:19 where Jesus said, "Go back to your own people and tell them what God has done for you and how kind He's been to you." And I thought, if I obeyed that verse, it would mean going back to my own people, to German-speaking people.

A few years later, I met Helen, now my wife, and she and I volunteered to go and work in Germany with students in Dortmont. Our son was born there, and our daughter was born later during our second assignment in Europe.

Now we're working in Vienna, Austria, in a traveling ministry to Russia. I worked for two years in East Germany, in Dresden and Leitzig, and Poland. And now mainly in the Baltics, in Latvia.

– *Hans Schneider,*
Vienna, Austria

Left: Mr. and Mrs. Bert Needham Sr. sold some farmland and made a substantial donation to Camp. The result was the Navigator Training Program building, dedicated July 17, 1966. It was later named, "Needham Hall."
Right: Navigator laundry and dish washing crews met behind the Dining Hall in the course of their duties.

The Big Chart on the Book of Ephesians

The memory that has blessed me most from my time at Maranatha in 1963 was the Pastor's Hour, when Rev. Olsen taught the book of Ephesians with the chart that he created. I would like to see that chart again.

Thanks for your labors of love for Maranatha.

– Dean Senning,
Reseda, California

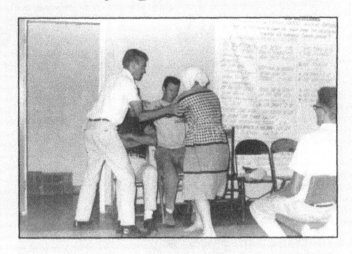

Several trainees take part in a skit in Yeutter Hall near a large chart used by Rev. Olsen to teach the book of Ephesians.

Laundry Crew Veteran Grateful for Camp

Maranatha Bible Camp held a place in my earliest memories. My father was there at the Camp's inception. I attended there as a camper many summers as a child and teenager. Our mother and ladies of the church helped clean the buildings each spring to ready the Camp for summer and we girls helped. I had to memorize verses to earn all or parts of my week at Camp. The folks couldn't have afforded it otherwise.

We were exposed to wonderful godly men and women from around the world.

We loved having "spending money" to use at the Sweet Shop or the Bookstore.

I attended the Navigator Training Program in 1963. To this day I'm an expert at doing laundry (because I was on the laundry crew)!

My fiancee and I were counselors for a few weeks in the late 60s.

– Priscilla Hendricks Millsap,
Kearney, Nebraska

The plan of salvation—a central theme at Maranatha over the decades—is illustrated in classic Navigator style.

Rev. Ivan Olsen and LeRoy Eims at the dedication of the Needham Hall Training Center in July 1966.

Top row, from left: In 1966, a new dormitory was built to accommodate the Navigator trainees. It later became known as Needham Hall; Glen Troyer interrupts a 1961 Navigator Training Session graduation photo for Joy Olsen and Connie Springer.

Second row: Two views of the Navigator laundry crew, mid-1960s.

Third row, from left: Rev. Olsen used the "Pastor's Hour" to teach the Bible to recently converted Navigator trainees. The location is the Winter Tabernacle, later converted into the Camp office; The men's dorm during the 1963 Navigator Training Program.

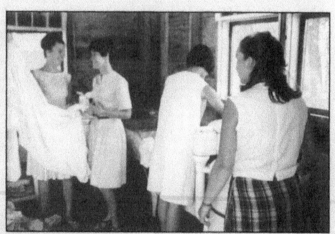

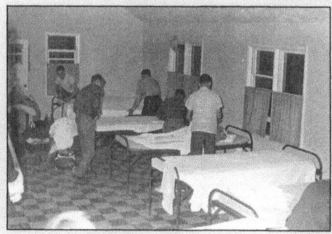

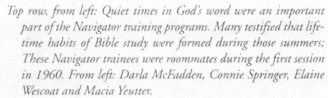

Top row, from left: Quiet times in God's word were an important part of the Navigator training programs. Many testified that lifetime habits of Bible study were formed during those summers; These Navigator trainees were roommates during the first session in 1960. From left: Darla McFadden, Connie Springer, Elaine Wescoat and Macia Yeutter.

Second row: Cleanuup time in the Nav men's dorm, 1961; The hearty Navigator Dining Hall crew is ready to serve another meal.

Third row, from left: Early-morning calisthenics were part of a Navigator trainee's daily regimen; Needham Hall was taking shape in the fall of 1965. Dick Matzke and Ken Blood are behind the table saw.

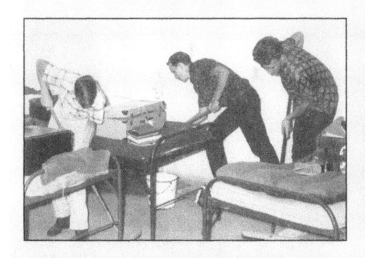

Top row: Staff for the second Navigator session in 1958 included, back row, from left: Hans Schneider, Larry Burke, Ivan Olsen, Jerry DeYoung, Russ Johnston and Dwight Olsen. Front row, from left: unidentified, Patti Brown, Doris Dittum, Doralee Yeutter, unidentified.

Second row: The first Navigator Training Program class to graduate was session one in 1958.

Third row, from left: 1958; First Session, Staff 1958; Second session, 1958.

Fourth row, from left: Second session, 1959; Maranatha Teenage Training Program, First Session, 1960; Maranatha Teenager Training Program, second session, 1960.

Fifth row, from left: 1960; 1961; 1961.

Sixth row, from left: Views from the front (left photo) and back (center photo) of the Tabernacle. Doors could be opened for cross ventilation, and hatches in the roof were opened and closed as needed; Graduation was always a highlight at the end of each session.

Top row: 1962.

Second row: Session one, 1963.

Third row, from left: Session one, 1964; First session 1965; 1966.

Fourth row, from left: 1966; Maranatha Navigator Training Program, first session, 1967; Maranatha Navigator Training Program, second session, 1967.

Fifth row, from left: First session, 1968; 1968 Faculty, first session; Maranatha Navigator Training Program 1970.

Sixth row, from left: Navigator trainees hold their written testimonies. These sheets are part of the Camp archives; Devotional time; Russ Johnston leads a Bible study during the first Navigator Training Program, mid-July 1958.

93

The 1960s

> *"We did everything but go to the governor in person to get him to intervene on our behalf to keep them from putting the Interstate through here."*
>
> – Ivan E. Olsen

For the average American, the phrase "summer camp" brings memories and visual images to mind, and many of those images involve a lake.

Maranatha Bible Camp, located on the Plains of Nebraska, was never a typical summer camp, and it did not have a lake. After the Camp moved to its permanent site in 1944, workers dug a crude sandpit for swimming, but canoeing or fishing took a back seat to more serious concerns about personal salvation and missions work around the world.

But in 1953, while the cement swimming pool was being built, the question arose about what to do with the old sandpit swimming hole. Ivan Olsen decided to carve out a long, shallow pond "two blocks long" that would include the murky old swimming hole, which was located just south and west of the new swimming pool. In 1955, the Camp board voted to make improvements along what secretary Kenneth Blood referred to as the "lake area." The pond, only six feet deep at its deepest point, was stocked with fish, and it became the site of a contest that soon became a Camp tradition — a "tug-o' war" with each team pulling on opposing sides of the pond and the rope extending over the water. The loser was the first team to fall into the shallow water.

"Probably we have needed a lake at our Bible Camp since its beginning, and we are grateful now for this provision," wrote Olsen.

Far away from such carefree pastimes, the nation was consumed by a bewildering array of new issues, from the elimination of teacher-led prayer from public schools to the expanding war in Vietnam, the growth of hippie and feminist culture, no-fault divorce laws and the assassinations of John and Robert Kennedy and Martin Luther King Jr. In Europe, Soviet-controlled East Germany was further isolated by the construction of a cement wall that divided the city of Berlin into eastern and western sectors and kept people from leaving the country.

Bureaucrats in Washington D.C. were deciding on the route that brand-new Interstate 80 would take through Nebraska. Early in the 1960s, the federal government announced its plans. There were two proposed sites under consideration as the construction project slowly moved west toward Lincoln County — a meandering route following the hills at the edge of the Platte valley, or a straighter route along the Platte itself. Though the locals were overwhelmingly in favor of the first option, the government decided to build it through the heart of the valley, roughly paralleling U.S. Highway 30 and the Union Pacific Railroad. This decision raised the anger of local farmers whose land holdings would be bisected by the superhighway, which could be crossed only at viaducts built miles apart from each other. The government would be paying millions of dollars in damages to landowners along the route who were faced with the prospect of having to drive half an hour just to get to the other side of the section of land their family had owned for decades.

In that setting, Maranatha celebrated its 25th anniversary on the weekend of August 17-19, 1962, at the end of Family Week. Theodore Epp was the featured speaker. Beset by the uncertainty of the great highway project, Olsen was glad to see his closest and most trusted friend again. "It was good to have the Epps back on the grounds, and was a great encouragement," he wrote.

As the builders slowly churned their way west through Nebraska past Kearney, Lexington and Gothenburg, they needed dirt — tons and tons of it — to raise the highway above the level of the 100-year flood plain throughout the Platte valley. They condemned land at various sites along the roadbed to dig out sand, gravel and dirt. These newly-formed sandpits filled naturally into small lakes, because the underground water level is so high in the valley.

A crisis mentality was rising at Maranatha Bible Camp and the surrounding neighborhood. The government announced plans to condemn a neighbor's land to use it for a dig site.

"It would have destroyed his whole farm for them to have taken the dirt they needed," said Olsen more than 25 years later. "So this farmer was so angry that he actually said that he would shoot any state man that would come to try to take his farm in that way."

An equally dismayed but more circumspect Rev. Olsen knew that the blueprints for I-80 showed it carving right through the northern portion of Maranatha Bible Camp. It was his nature to immediately take action, but what could he do?

For nearly a quarter century, Maranatha campers had enjoyed the Camp's quiet, peaceful setting, originally on the Talbot farm, then in the Bockus grove and finally at the present site. All three had truly been wilderness environments. Now the Camp's leaders were faced with a scenario of continuous noise from Interstate traffic. What would that noise do to hinder the ministry environment of Maranatha? When Olsen, Clark, Kittle and Carper knelt in the spring of 1944 to thank God for giving them the land, they hadn't envisioned a superhighway running through it.

The Camp board decided to try to get the Interstate rerouted. Board members contacted officials at the local, state and federal level. In 1961, the board authorized Olsen to work with the Nebraska Department of Roads and North Platte Area Chamber of Commerce try to do what they could to get the route changed, but it soon became apparent to the Camp director that the effort would be fruitless.

Something would have to be done to make the best of the situation. In 1962, as Maranatha published the brochure for its 25th Annual Session, the Camp's executive committee started negotiating with the State of Nebraska to demand "just and fair" damages for cutting through the Camp property. The slow-paced negotiations continued into 1965, when the matter went to court. (The issue finally was settled in 1967, when Maranatha received its damage payment from the state.) The highway construction project approached Maranatha and its highstrung neighbor, who had not yet brandished his rifle at any state workmen. Push was gradually coming to shove, and Olsen had an idea. As God took something from Maranatha Bible Camp, was He trying to give it something much better in exchange?

Olsen decided he would ask the Department of Roads to abandon its plan of condemning his belligerent neighbor's farm in favor of using Maranatha's land instead. It was obvious that a sizeable lake could be created if the government could be persuaded to remove enough dirt, sand and gravel.

"When they came and looked at our 70 acres," recalled Olsen, "they said, 'Reverend, you wouldn't have any Camp left after we took the amount of dirt we need. If you can get more land, then we would be very glad to take the dirt.'"

It was time for the Camp to expand, but how could the right piece of land be obtained at almost a moment's notice?

Lester Kittle, a grocer from Maxwell who served on the Camp board, had an idea. He took Olsen to visit an elderly couple, Vearnie & Lily May Anderson, whose property bordered Maranatha's on the east. Anderson's land had been bisected by the Interstate. He was willing — even eager — to sell, and made the deal with Maranatha during the summer of 1964. It was to be one of his final earthly acts; Vearnie Anderson died shortly after the transaction, which cost the Camp less than $4,000, was completed on August 21, 1964.

There were still legalities to wade through. On June 23, Olsen had written the Camp board about his efforts to secure an agreement with the State of Nebraska to use Maranatha's newly-purchased land for a sandpit.

"The story is too long and involved for me to share with you in this letter, but you can be praying that we may, under God, be able to get a required pit here at the Camp," wrote Olsen. "This means that the contractor who makes the bid for the building of the road in this particular area must take his dirt from our pit, thus assuring us of a lake. It all seems to depend upon the one word, 'required.'

"Usually these contractors, when they make a bid, just go up and down the river, and whatever sand bar is the easiest to get dirt from, they can even get it condemned, make it for one or two hundred dollars an acre, and get their dirt so very, very easily. Admittedly, the getting of our dirt would be just a little harder than that; but we have been working from the top down, and from the bottom up. Doing everything we can to show the merits of a lake on Maranatha Bible Camp grounds."

Finally, the state selected Maranatha as an official dig site. At the end of summer, the crew moved in to clear the land of trees and debris, then started digging 20-foot-deep Lake Maranatha, sloping the sides gently to create a beach area. The heavy equipment moved slowly through the water that began to bubble up when the big blades on the earth movers hit water level. The crew established three "haul roads" to haul out the dirt and sand with huge trucks. Olsen, who three years earlier had balked at the thought of earth movers invading Maranatha's property, now watched the progress with tears of joy in his eyes; he would eventually list the creation of the new lake as one of the six prominent miracles that God had performed at Maranatha Bible Camp.

In October 1964, the Camp board commended Olsen for his "hard work and decisive action" in securing the property and his role in the building of the lake.

The Camp's recreation program took a giant leap forward. Campers and staff enjoyed increased fishing, canoeing and the advent of motorboating because of the existence of 43-acre Lake Maranatha. Then, almost immediately, everything was threatened when, for the first time, floodwaters approached Maranatha in 1965.

In mid-June, panic seized the Denver region when a gigantic thunderstorm unleashed 14 inches of torrential rain near Larkspur, Colorado. It caused widespread flooding which devastated homes, factories, roads and bridges in the Denver area, then swept down the South Platte valley into Nebraska. The river, which normally meandered at about 300 cubic feet per second through Denver, swelled to an amazing 150,000 cubic feet per second on June 16 — 500 times the normal flow.

More than 200 miles downstream, the North Platte area had a small window of warning. At Maranatha, a rental group was using the Camp, so Olsen sent the campers home and cancelled the following week's camp (Junior Camp). The Navigator Training Program work crews scrambled to put up a sandbag wall to protect the Camp on the west end, but there was not enough time or manpower to finish the job before the flood was scheduled to hit.

The Navigator trainees and Camp staff prayed for protection from the flood, and God brought heavy equipment in answer to their prayers. State employees who were still at work on the I-80 project a short distance to the west had heard that the Camp was in trouble, and volunteered their time to put up an earth dike west of Lake Maranatha. Shortly thereafter, the county sheriff ordered the Camp evacuated just before the flood crested.

The next morning, when the staff members returned, they saw that the new dike had done its job, protecting the main area of the Camp. They found only one breakthrough — on the south side of the property, where muddy water had swept around and punched its way into the lake. The floodwaters had broken through the nearly one-year-old dike established when the lake construction was finished in 1964. The Navigator trainees fixed the earth dike, and the rest of the Camp schedule went on without incident.

It was a typically busy summer at Maranatha: seven Maranatha-sponsored camps, two Navigator Training sessions and three rental groups used the grounds. Curt Lehman was Junior Camp program director in 1964 and 1965. He was succeeded by Frank Kroeze, who started a nine-year term as Junior Camp director in 1966 and continued through 1974.

Lehman became Maranatha's overall program director (he coordinated the efforts of the various volunteer program directors). His wife, Claudine Lehman, started her 40-plus-year association with Camp during the 1960s.

In 1964, Adrian House took over for Carl Goltz as program director of Young People's Camp. In 1968, that position went to Rocky Schultz.

Campers arrived at Camp in different ways. In the early days, some came by train and got off at the Maxwell station, where someone from Camp gave them a ride the final few miles. That ended with the decline of passenger rail service in Nebraska in the late 1960s. Some campers came by bus. A few came in a private plane from Minnesota with Ernie Skoog. Many came in their family's automobile, but a large number still came via "rural carpool" — they carried their luggage into the back of a common farm stock truck, sat down on hay bales or wooden planks with a dozen or two of their friends and rode to Camp under a tarp, (or occasionally, under the open sky).

In 1967, when the lawsuit involving landowner damages caused by Interstate 80 was finally settled, Maranatha used its portion of the settlement to grow once again, buying more land from its neighbors to the west, Henry & Pauline George.

As the 1960s drew to a close, the world seemed to be changing radically. British groups like the Beatles and the Rolling Stones had firmly established the popularity of rock 'n roll in the United States. In January 1967, the National Football League tried a novel new concept, agreeing to have its champion meet the champion of the upstart American Football League in what would become known as the "Super Bowl." Boys were wearing their hair longer, girls were wearing their skirts shorter and men had walked on the moon. U.S. society was becoming more diverse, and Maranatha Bible Camp would need to respond to meet its needs.

VOICES OF MARANATHA

Camp Kid Graduates to Camper, Staff, Matrimony

Maranatha has been a fixture in my life dating back to my earliest childhood memories. From my Grandpa Krause's cabin, to learning and playing as a camper, to serving on work staff, to meeting my first girlfriend (who is now my wife), God has used Maranatha to bless four generations of my family.

– Jim Childerston,
Hagerstown, Maryland

Children of speakers and workers were part of Maranatha. In this picture are Danny Gustafson, baby Pietropaulo, Tim and Jim Childerston.

The People of Maranatha: Carl Goltz

A tall, steady, man with a voice that sounded a little like John Wayne's soft drawl, Carl Goltz epitomized the conservative, evangelistic values of Maranatha Bible Camp.

He grew up on a farm near the Missouri River in southeast Nebraska. His mother died when he was 4 years old, so Carl went to live with his older brother's family for much of his youth. Like Ivan Olsen, Carl Goltz received Christ as his savior during his teen years.

After graduating from high school, he moved to California, where he was a route manager at a dairy and then worked at a lumber company. He entered the U.S. Army/Air Corps during World War II, where his head was nearly crushed in an accident in Europe. Severely injured, he battled back. After he was discharged from the military, he attended Moody Bible Institute, where he became president of his class before graduating. He planted Berean churches in Torrington, Wyoming, and Scottsbluff, Nebraska, before finishing his pastoral career at North Platte.

Goltz arrived at Maranatha Bible Camp for Christian Workers' Week in the early 1950s. Soon he was helping recruit speakers for that conference. Very quickly, Ivan Olsen and the Maranatha Bible Camp board grew to appreciate the ministry of Carl Goltz. On one occasion, the scheduled speaker, M.R. DeHahn, was unable to attend. At the last minute, Olsen asked Goltz to be the main speaker. "He protested, but Olsen said he prayed about it and the Lord told him Pastor Goltz should take (DeHahn's) place," recalled his wife, Doris. "God blessed the ministry, even though he wasn't Dr. DeHahn."

A man of intellect and wisdom, Goltz brought a great amount of stability to Maranatha. In 1956, he began directing the Young People's Camps. In September 1957, he became a member of the Camp board. He spoke at family camps and singles' retreats. He went on to serve as president of the board for 32 years (1962-94), more than twice as long as anyone else. He also served 28 years as president of the Berean Fundamental Church Council, which Olsen had founded.

Goltz followed in Olsen's footsteps in more ways than one. After Olsen's retirement, Goltz provided so much stability as president that the rest of the board voted not to accept his resignation for four more years.

"I so much appreciated Pastor Goltz's advice on numerous occasions during the years of transition from Dr. Olsen's leadership," said George Cheek.

Although he had a quiet, reserved demeanor, Goltz was a hearty competitor in volleyball, basketball, table tennis or anything else related to sports. He laughingly recalled a footrace he had with other youth camp leaders at Maranatha in the 1950s. "I can't remember who won," he said, "but Pastor Olsen lunged at the finish line and ended up flat on his face, covered with dirt."

Goltz reviewed Maranatha's programs and procedures and suggested improvements in a systematic, thoughtful way. A purposeful administrator, he had an unwavering presence. "When he walked up beside you and put his hand on your shoulder, you knew he had an assignment for you," said Richard Crocker, who worked for many years with Goltz on the Camp board and as a Berean pastor.

In 1988, Goltz wrote Olsen, saying, "We thank the Lord for ever causing our paths to cross." When Olsen died in 1993, Goltz said, "He was instrumental in encouraging me to greater things in my life and ministry, for which I am grateful. We look forward to that day of reunion."

Their reunion came almost 10 years later when Goltz passed away in August 2003 at 79 years of age.

– Tad Stryker

VOICES OF MARANATHA

Married at Maranatha

My wife and I were married at Maranatha July 4, 1952. In 1960 we moved to Maranatha for one week. My wife worked in the kitchen and I did electrical work and telephone repair. We slept in a log cabin north of the old tabernacle. I installed a microphone in or near every building for paging the whole Camp and repaired a switchboard defect.

– Larry Henry,
North Platte

The Maranatha Cross Stands Out

Since 1968, the "Lighthouse on the Plains" has been clearly marked. There's no mistaking that Maranatha Bible Camp is a Christian camp — not with a 32-foot lighted cross standing on the property.

The Maranatha cross, which stands about 75 feet from Interstate 80, is the most recognized feature on the campgrounds. Thousands of cross-country travelers drive by it every day. Like Jesus Christ Himself, the cross is hard to ignore, and it often draws a reaction, whether positive or negative.

As I-80 was built through the Maranatha grounds, many people, including Rev. Ivan Olsen, began to think of ways the Camp could capitalize on its location. The idea foremost in Olsen's mind was to build a large sign in the shape of a cross, and he carried out that plan.

After its construction was completed on June 1, 1968, the cross was lit for the first time. That first night, vandals shot out every light in the sign. "They don't kill me that way!" Olsen responded, and the Camp had the sign repaired. On other occasions, the sign has required repair after windstorms damaged it.

When the cross was first built, the North Platte Telegraph questioned whether the sign was legal (some had asked why the Maranatha cross could be closer to the Interstate than standard billboards, which are kept at least 660 feet from the federal right-of-way line.) The newspaper editorialized about drivers who were "startled" at the sign's size, brightness and proximity to the highway. When its investigation was done, the Telegraph reported that the sign was exempt from the 660-foot requirement because it was built in a "free area" — a place where a highway intersects or runs parallel to a county road, which is the case at Maranatha. The sign was "constructed in accordance with all federal, state and local regulations," the Telegraph concluded. However, others questioned the findings, and Olsen asked for help from Nebraska Gov. Robert Crosby, who defended Maranatha on more than one occasion. Crosby once remarked that Olsen "did more for Nebraska" than anyone he knew, and the governor donated money toward the project.

Some have called Maranatha "God's lighthouse on the plains" because of the way the cross stands out. It is visible at least two miles away to eastbound drivers on a clear night, and some say they have seen it while flying at night between Omaha and Denver.

It's a simple thing to tell people where Maranatha is located by asking them, "Have you seen that big white cross by Interstate 80 that's lit up at night?" It is common to hear truckers honk their horns as they drive by, regardless of the season. In the summer, drivers wave at children walking to and from the Dining Hall.

Occasionally, people stop at the Camp to see what it's all about. A despondent trucker from Denver who was near the point of suicide once stopped at Maranatha, and Rev. Olsen talked to him about Jesus. The trucker accepted Christ and went on his way as a born-again believer.

In the summer of 2000, four young women took a camping trip in Colorado. Three who were already Christians spoke freely of the things of God while in the mountains, praying for God's protection every morning and offering prayers of thanksgiving each night. As they drove home on a warm evening, they talked about how God had been working in their lives. One of them, Monae Quincy of Lincoln, Nebraska, asked the fourth woman if she had ever accepted Christ as her savior. The woman, named Jill, answered, "No." When Monae asked Jill if she'd like to do it, she agreed. Eastbound on I-80, the women saw the Maranatha cross looming in the distance at that moment. The women pulled up, climbed the Interstate fence and knelt at the foot of the cross, where Jill accepted the gift of salvation through Jesus Christ.

– Tad Stryker

The first night the Maranatha cross was lit in 1968, vandals shot out the lights. It has been repaired several times since then, helping identify God's "Lighthouse on the Plains."

Tommy Jackson Killed by Drunk Driver

Tommy Jackson, well-respected at North Platte High School for his character and leadership in the classroom and athletics, was a Maranatha Camper and attended the Navigator Training Program. This is taken from Rev. Olsen's church newsletter.

Seventeen-year-old Tommy Jackson, son of Mr. and Mrs. Arvid Jackson, suddenly passed into the presence of the Lord late Saturday night, or early Sunday morning, April 16 or 17, 1966, as the result of a near head-on automobile accident on the west side of the viaduct near Maxwell, Nebraska.

Returning from a Youth for Christ meeting, Tommy was ran into by a man who has since been arrested, and is being held in jail on charges of homicide. Confused, the man readily told the acting physician that he had been drinking vodka; so confused was he that he was quite sure he was going west, though he was actually traveling east, reportedly with no lights on. Thus, another highway victim, leaving broken hearts and bereaved, who miss their son and brother so deeply.

Victory services were held Tuesday afternoon, April 19, at the Berean Fundamental Church, with the Pastor officiating. The effect of Tommy's testimony among his high school classmates was in evidence at the service Tuesday, when the auditorium, the Annex, the Primary, Junior, Junior High, Cradle Roll and Nursery Departments were all filled to capacity by those who gathered to pay their respects to this young man. Though he lived so short a life, he lived so much of it for Christ.

His last day on earth found him spending the afternoon working at the Maranatha Bible Camp, which he loved very dearly. His loved ones particularly took note that he started the day, as he always did, meditating in the Word of God. His Bible chart revealed that he had completed the reading of the entire Bible, and that the chart was filled; notes which he had taken in the pastor's Home Bible Class on Tuesday night still were in his personal Bible. Not only was his last day on earth filled with activities for the Lord, and about the Lord, but his last week was singularly characterized by the same.

Now we can understand Tommy's entire last winter, when he was so suddenly set aside with a leg injury from football; but which gave him a lot of time to be alone with his Lord. God moved in mysterious ways, His wonders to perform. Greatly to be praised is our God.

Upward of one hundred young people arose to their feet in response to the gospel invitation, following the funeral message brought by the pastor. Only eternity will disclose the possible far-reaching effect of Tommy's death.

– Ivan E. Olsen

Tommy Jackson

That 'Destiny Moment' of Introduction

Dr. Olsen introduced Tom Collins to Arlene Bakewell about 1965 saying, "you need to know one another since you are both attending Kearney State College." We have always included that "destiny moment" in our story of love and marriage. Arlene made critical decisions at Jr. Camp under instruction of Cliff and Ruth Gustafson, Pastor Kroeze and others. Tom and Arlene both profited from the Navigator Summer Training Programs in the 60s.

God has been gracious to give them four children (a son and son-in-law are currently Youth Pastors in KC area) and they are blessed to enjoy six grandchildren who visit regularly.

Tom is chairman of elders of their Bible Church, Arlene is musician and drama coach there.

– Tom Collins,
Shawnee, Kansas

History of the Summerville House

We became acquainted with the Camp in 1958-59 when we became involved with the Berean Fellowship. That year, our oldest daughter, Carol, attended the first Navigator Training Session, which had a real impact in her spiritual walk with the Lord. She is now in Shanghai, China, ministering to women. Our daughter, Jane, attended Camp a couple years, then served as counselor for a few years. Our two boys also attended Maranatha Bible Camp.

In the 1960s, the Berean Church had decided to buy a house in North Platte and move it to the Camp to house campers. Carl and I prayed asking God what part we could have in this venture. I was led by the Lord to purchase the home as a memorial to Carl's parents, Roger and Betty Summerville. Thus it became the "Summerville Home" at Maranatha Bible Camp. They added a second story with a stairway outside the building. During camp time it was lined wall to wall with cots and bunk beds.

In the process of remodeling the home, they found newspapers evidently used as insulation. Among this was the North Platte newspaper which printed the dedication of Maranatha Bible Camp.

Later, George and Jan Cheek came to serve at the Camp and moved into the "Summerville Home." One year all the grandchildren of Roger and Betty put in a fireplace.

The crowning day was when Roger and Betty Summerville's children and grandchildren met at Maranatha for a family reunion. The Maranatha board members made the decision to dedicate the house to the Lord's work. What a wonderful weekend. They also had an open house with refreshments.

Carl and I were (and I still) blessed by the eternal outreach of Maranatha Bible Camp as hundreds of youth have passed through the doors of the Camp to go forth in full-time ministry for the Lord. We have enjoyed having a small part of this wonderful camp ministry.

I stand in awe of an awesome God who planted into the mind of a young, energetic and determined man to obey his heavenly Father to plant a church in North Platte, Nebraska, then to set in progress a Bible Camp to train young people in God's vineyard. Dr. and Mrs. Ivan Olsen are highly revered in their faithful ministry. They had a passion for young people and children. Many of those who labored so faithfully are now in the presence of the Almighty God.

Result: Hundreds and perhaps thousands of young people have gone on to serve the Lord in full-time ministries. God blessed our founders, and continues as George Cheek and his team continue the mighty work for God at Maranatha Bible Camp.

– Mrs. Carl (Dorothy) Summerville,
November 12, 2003

George Cheek in his home for 20 years, the Summerville House.

Mark Skoog, 1969.

June Monk and Sharon Frushour pose near the Old Tabernacle in 1969.

Scott Fasse relaxes near the Dining Hall in 1969.

Five Generations of Summervilles, Eutslers Enjoy MBC

Maranatha Camp has 60 years impact on the Summerville Eutsler family. Roger and Bettie Summerville from Miller, Nebraska spent a week at Maranatha's family camp during the 1940s, the start of a continuing relationship between family and Maranatha. Roger talked about staying in the first cabins they had.

Their daughter, Esther Eutsler, started involvement in '58 when she brought her daughter, Janet, to Junior High Camp. Their son, Dan, spent summers there and accepted Christ at Camp.

Carl and Dorothy Summerville moved a house to Maranatha when the Interstate went through. The Summerville children had a reunion there. They were present when the house was dedicated by Dr. Ivan Olsen. They helped Carl and Dorothy finance improvements on the house. During the 1960s, the Eloe cabin was built and dedicated in memory of Fred Eloe. Fred was a brother of Bettie Summerville. His wife, Sarah Eloe, spent many summers staying in the cabin with her friend, Zenola Burman.

Esther Eutsler attended Senior Adults' and Ladies' Retreats; she also brought grandchildren for Family Week. Especially Chellie and Maurice Wantieg and both accepted Christ there at Camp. All five Eutsler grandchildren spent time at Maranatha Bible Camp.

The last two years, Mrs. Chellie (Wantieg) Gresham from Peoria, Illinois, brought her daughters, Lyn Rae and Tailor to Camp.

This makes five generations of Summerville Eutslers attending.

The Summerville family donated a house, which was moved to Maranatha in the late 1960s.

A Parcel Full of Camp Memories

Leonard and I were classmates of Dr. Ivan Olsen at Denver Bible Institute so we knew about Maranatha Bible Camp from the very beginning. I think Leonard attended one of the first sessions when it was only a few tents in a meadow by the river. We have certainly rejoiced to see God's blessing on Maranatha through the many years since. We rejoice in the enlargement and improvement of the facilities, the variety of programs now being offered, and especially the promotion of God's Word and challenges to spiritual growth that are the highlight of the Camp - in fact its very purpose.

As we were spending time in Congo, Africa, we could not follow all the stages of growth, but we remained close to Ivan Olsen and the Berean Fundamental Church in North Platte; we kept pretty close track and always spent part of our furloughs in the area, if not actually at Camp.

Maranatha became a vital influence to our family. We remember our early visits, sleeping in a tiny "slab" cabin, with plentiful cracks between boards in walls and floor - but it was fun to be in Camp. About that time, I think, I was camp nurse for a session.

I remember helping, one spring, getting Camp ready to open, cleaning the kitchen with ladies from BFC. Then there were meals in the old dining hall, and every group had to take turns with the cleanup - but it was fun. I remember washing family clothes in the laundry, enjoying crafts with Elfrieda Olander in charge, especially enjoying the swimming pool! That first summer with the Navigators we were able to leave our teenagers, Joy and Len (Happy) at camp for the whole summer while we traveled on deputation work. They gained a lot Biblically and spiritually and were relieved that they did not have to do all that traveling. And we were confident that they would be well cared for.

We remember the upgrade to dormitory type halls - they were more comfortable and convenient - and now the almost luxurious motel-type rooms are all the comforts of home, in an environment of fellowship with old and new like-minded friends, wholesome recreation, and Christian doctrine and fellowship. God bless Maranatha!

– Leonard and Hazel Parcel,
Wichita, Kansas

The 'Near Miss' Flood of '65

In the summer of 1965 I was 19 years old and I attended a Navigator Training Session at Maranatha Bible Camp. The Rev. Ivan Olsen was the program director. I was invited to spend the summer there by my friend in Seattle (where I lived), Theodore "Ted" Olsen, who was Rev. Olsen's nephew.

In July 1965, there were great rains on the eastern slope of the Rocky Mountains in Colorado. The South Platte River in Colorado flooded and the floods were moving down the river course toward Nebraska. Nebraska residents had warning of the oncoming floods and preparations were being made. Maranatha Camp was, of course, within the flood plain of the Platte River. Maranatha began preparations by canceling the week's camp and sending the younger campers home. The youth training camp group stayed and began trying to fortify the Camp against the oncoming flood. We had sandbag parties and worked feverishly to construct a wall of sandbags along the western edge of the campgrounds. However, it was a huge task and it seemed hopeless. We didn't have enough people or enough sandbags to build such a long wall. We asked God in prayer to spare the campgrounds from the waters.

The earnest prayers were answered! In the summer of 1965, Interstate 80 next to Maranatha was under construction, but was not yet open to traffic. The workers on the construction of the highway came to the Camp and volunteered to use their heavy equipment to build a dike along the western border to hold back the floods. They did build the dike and the campgrounds were spared. The highway itself, being somewhat raised above ground level, formed a dike along the northern border of the Camp between the Camp and the river and so held back the waters on that side.

The youth training group was initially determined to have faith in God's protection and sit out the flood. However, that evening as the waters were beginning to rise around the Camp, the county sheriff came and ordered us to evacuate. We all grabbed a few belongings, jumped in whatever cars were available, and evacuated the Camp. We drove to North Platte on old US-30 and spent the night in sleeping bags in the basement of a church.

The next morning the flood had passed and we returned to the Camp grounds. We saw many flooded fields near the Camp, but the Camp was spared. The only damage came where there was a small break in the dike and the lake had filled with muddy water. We thanked God for sparing the Camp.

God answers prayer, perhaps not with a bolt from the blue, but by moving men to take action when it is needed.

– Dan Short

This 1965 aerial view shows the still unfinished Interstate 80 and the break in the dike of Lake Maranatha (lower right) due to flooding that year.

Left: This 1955 photo shows that the west end of Lake Maranatha already had been dug out. Beyond it, the old sandpit swimming hole sits unused (the cement swimming pool had been built in 1954). Right: The lake extended only as far east as the swimming pool hill in 1963.

Maranatha an Influence Throughout Life

As I reflect upon Maranatha Bible Camp from the 1960s until today, I must smile. I went to Camp as a child, and I remember the early morning "Reveille" to wake us up and the "Taps" at night to put us to sleep. (I don't think either one worked for its designed purpose.) We always had to have several visits from our dorm counselor to encourage us to go to sleep in preparation for our "busy day" tomorrow. Of course, as the week went on, we didn't need quite as much encouragement to "beat the taps" to bed. We had to walk outside to another building, the bath house, to use the bathroom, showers, and brush our teeth. Who needs convenience when you can be camping? Now that same dorm has become Clark Hall.

We stood in long lines at mealtime to get into the Dining Hall (which is now the Sweet Shop). Swimming and the Sweet Shop were and still are highlights at camp. God's "still small voice" is finally heard, when the stomach is full and the body is tired enough to slow down and listen. I loved the great music and speakers in the "Tabernacle." Since there was no air conditioning, our bodies were wet and our blouses had to be peeled off of the back of the chairs when the meetings were finally over. But, who cared? We all looked and felt the same, and we would soon be on our way to the swimming pool anyway. Many life-changing decisions were made at Camp. I vowed to God that even though I knew I would stumble in my life, my ultimate goal was to follow Him.

A few years later found me at Maranatha again as a Navigator trainee. Rev. Ivan Olsen believed that you must catch people for spiritual training before they get so busy with life. For that reason I was an upcoming freshman in high school at "Nav Training" with college students. I will never forget those endless hours of dish washing for the campers and the even longer hours in the laundry room. We had Quiet Time, Pastor's Hour, Personal Study, Scripture Memorization, and Evening Meetings everyday, while maintaining the Camp and being of service to the campers. After that, I always looked at the assistants at Camp with *much more* respect than ever before. It was great training, and yes, Rev. Olsen was correct about catching a young person before they get too busy with life's activities.

In recent years, Maranatha has also played a large part in my life. My daughters have been going to Camp since their ages allowed them to go. They always fit into their summer schedule a week at Camp, before the summer schedule fills up. My oldest daughter now sets aside one week each summer to counsel, since she is too old to be a camper. Jim and I go to the couples' retreat every year, and I am committed to Ladies' Retreat each year. Maranatha continues to be a place where life-changing decisions are made in my family.

Maranatha Bible Camp has definitely made an impact on my life over the years. I am thankful that there has been a quiet place like this to come away from the fast pace of the world. It is necessary to reflect upon God, to re-examine, and to make adjustments for the future, so that our lives can be more effective for Christ.

– Marlene (Johnson) Davidson,
Lincoln, Nebraska

Driving to Camp on a Summer Evening

The camp has always been a special place because of our kids going there and also because Don and Marguerite Hunt who were our overseers in the faith, had such a vested interest in it. I remember going a lot in the summer evenings. The speakers were from all over, and we got so much spiritual teaching in our early Christian training.

– Lois Buttermore,
North Platte

Early Winter Retreat Memories

In the early 1960s Ruth and I took a load of young people from the Berean Church in Sterling, Colorado, to Camp for Winter Retreat. Our song leader in our church, 40 years later, was one of those campers. While the youth were in classes, I was over at Needham Hall helping insulate the walls. We slept on the cement floor at Needham while we were there (six inches of snow outside).

The spiritual impact Maranatha Camp has had on our youth and my own family is immeasurable.

– Chuck and Ruth Lynch,
Sterling, Colorado

Just Let Us Out at The Cross!

Maranatha Bible Camp is a special place to me. It is what I refer to as my "home away from home." I never missed an opportunity to go to Camp from the first age I could until I was out of high school.

The memories are so many. The earliest would, of course, be Junior Camp. The ride from Scottsbluff seemed to take an eternity. Then Interstate 80 came through and the torture of passing Camp to continue east to the Maxwell exit was what seemed merciless! We pleaded with our drivers just let us out at the cross; they could bring the luggage later!

One of the warm fuzzies that camp offered was the music played over the loudspeaker in the afternoons. I remember feeling as if it were a taste of what heaven will be like. The smell of the cedar trees made Maranatha have that everlasting effect. Every time I smell that type of tree it brings back pleasant memories.

I'm not sure but I think that whoever decided to tear down the "Old Tab" will have to stand before God and account for the move! Just kidding, but it also has special memories. It was great even when it rained and the roof leaked! I miss it to this day when I go to Camp.

Junior High and High School camps were the best. The speakers were always so good. The activities were always so much fun, such as, hiking to Sioux Lookout and polar bear swimming, my personal favorites. Winter retreats were also great but it seemed we just got started and had to leave.

Best of all were the relationships made. My first real "boyfriend" was at Camp. I think my parents felt it was a safe relationship since by this time we had moved to Iowa and he was not anywhere close to there! It was really unusual many years later when my mother finally met him as her physician!

The ultimate happening was the summer of 1972. My personal favorite speaker, Adrian House, was the guest speaker that year. It was in the Thursday night service that I submitted my life to full-time Christian service. I vowed to attend at least one year at a Christian college. The fall of 1973 I began school at Grace Bible Institute, rooming with a close friend I had met at Camp.

God's sovereign control is amazing as I look back and see His hand at work. As a result of my friend, and roommate, Becky Jantz, I ended up moving to Lexington, Nebraska where I met the man who would be the love of my life and my soul mate.

Time took its turn and I strayed a bit in my Christian walk, but when God calls, he also draws you into His will for your life. I never forgot my surrender to full-time Christian service. After 14 years of marriage, my husband answered God's call on his life. We took our first ministry opportunity, wouldn't you know it, a camp position in eastern Ohio! God continued working and eventually convinced my husband that 40 years old was not too old to go back to college. He graduated in 1998 from Calvary Bible College. While I was on staff there, I had the privilege of meeting Torrey House, the son of Adrian House. I was so excited to be able to share with him how much his father meant to me and how God used him to move me to where I am now.

My husband and I were appointed as missionaries to Ecuador, but the Lord had other things in mind as He moved us back to Nebraska to pastor a small church in Newcastle.

I have never regretted the things I learned and did at Maranatha Bible Camp and I thank God for how He used those many summers and memories to shape my life. I also thank God for men like Dr. Olsen and Pastor and Mrs. Carl Goltz, my pastor and second set of parents when I was growing up. God will reward them greatly in heaven.

— June (Monk) White,
Newcastle, Nebraska

Left and center: A hike to Sioux Lookout was a Junior Camp tradition. Right: On Sioux Lookout, Pastor Cliff Gustafson and his son, Danny, gave a memorable rendition of Abraham's preparation to offer his son, Isaac.

The Olanders Became 'Part of Camp Family'

My years with Maranatha started in 1959 when Ivan Olsen invited my brother, Tim, and I to be a part of the Navigator Training Program at the Camp. I had attended church all of my life, but had never made a personal commitment to the Lord. After hearing Ivan Olsen speak at one of the Camp meetings, I realized that I needed a personal relationship with the Lord. The next morning at devotional time I asked the Lord to be my Saviour.

After that I began to notice great changes in my life, to experience hunger for the Word, and I was very anxious to return the next summer.

During the next several summers, Tim and I and our younger brother, Mark, and also our mother, Elfrieda, returned to be a part of the Camp family. Mom ran the Craft Shop, which she dearly loved, and I ran the Sweet Shop. It was an awesome time for us as a family because we spent the summer together as a family, we did jobs around the Camp that we all really enjoyed, and we all grew spiritually by attending most of the meetings. During that time we stayed in the Olander Cabin, which was a memorial to my father, who was a pastor in Iowa.

Several fond memories are Ivan Olsen teaching intensely during the Pastor's Hour, Pastor Olsen sitting on the bench in front of his house with his Lefax planner open looking for people to fill some of the many jobs that needed to be done, floating down the North Platte in inner tubes and going up to Sioux Lookout.

Since that time, I went to Whitworth College in Spokane, Washington where I met my wife, Sandy. We lived for many years in Spokane and moved later to the Seattle area. Sandy and I have both taught elementary school. I recently retired after 34 years of teaching. We have always been active in our church. We were youth pastors for many years, and have been on several leadership teams in the church. One of the favorite things that I do is mentor students at a nearby college who have the call of God on their life to be in full-time ministry.

I will always have a love in my heart for Maranatha because it was where I met the Lord, and where God began to build a foundation in my life in His Word.

– Richard Olander,
Seattle, Washington

Tim, Mark and Rich Olander stand beside the cabin their family helped build.

Campers enjoyed boating on the newly-created Lake Maranatha.

Boating trips on Lake Maranatha were launched from this floating dock.

Maranatha installed trampolines in the early 1960s. They were very popular, but insurance costs forced the Camp to remove them early in the 1980s.

You could find a good ballgame almost daily at Maranatha from the beginning through the 1960s.

River floats down the shallow Platte River have been a popular recreation option for many years.

Finish Strong!

"Adrian, where is Maranatha Camp?"

"It's near North Platte."

"Is it hot there?"

"Yes, sweetie."

"Is it muggy there, Adrian?"

"Yes!"

"Do they have air conditioning?"

"No, we'll take a fan."

"Guess I'll stay home with Mark."

"Nope, it's family camp and we all are going."

"Can I wear shorts?"

"NO!"

"I'll just wear slacks honey."

"No can do, You have to wear dresses, Juanita."

"You gotta be kidding!!!"

"I kid you not!!"

"Whoop-te-doo!!!"

That was our introduction to Maranatha Camp in the summer of 1963. And the beginning of a wonderful ministry. We had the joy of making friendships with some of the "greats" of the Berean Fellowship. Their godly influence has enriched our lives beyond all expectations.

That also was the beginning of the House-Goltz speaking team for youth camp over a period of years.

One of Adrian's greatest joys in the ministry was seeing young people come to know Christ, grow in their walk with Him, and dedicate their lives for His service. George Cheek was one of those young men. I remember being in Adrian's office at Western Bible College. Adrian and George were discussing the possibility of ministry for George at Maranatha Camp. Adrian strongly encouraged him to go!

I continue to hear of Adrian's ministry relating to Maranatha Camp. Hebrews 11:4 says, "...though he is dead, he still speaks."

Juanita House

His challenge to people would be "It's important how you start your Christian walk but it is far more important how you end your walk on earth. FINISH STRONG!!!" Hebrews 3:14 He did!!!

– Juanita House, Denver

God Used Camp to Rescue a 'Burned-Out Soul'

My first real encounter with Maranatha Camp came on May 3, 1989. I was a hard-charging 39-year-old father of three girls, and husband to a Maranatha person whose mother had been involved with the camp since 1941 and still is today. My wife, Marlene, first went to Maranatha around 1959.

I had suffered a "mild" heart attack and was told to break away and get some down time to rest and reflect. Marlene had been at Ladies' Retreat, and my mother-in-law, Eleanor (Bratten) Johnson and her husband, Willard, came 187 miles to Lincoln to watch their three little granddaughters while Marlene was at Ladies' Retreat.

I decided to pick up Marlene. When George Cheek greeted me at Camp, he immediately knew something was wrong with me. I informed him of my health problem, and he gave me a key to the Clark trailer and said for me and Marlene to hang out for as long as was necessary.

We stayed four or five days and God began to blow life into a burned-out soul. I was flat physically tired. We read scriptures, prayed, walked around the lake and began to dream again about God's plan for our lives.

I truly believe to this day had the Camp not been there for us when we needed it, to "get away, be quiet, and listen to the still sweet voice of God...and make decisions," I may have died and left a young wife and three babies.

Since that time I have been called to serve on the Board of Directors for Maranatha Camp and Foundation, and now serve as a co-director of Couples' Conference.

Is Maranatha a place where lives are touched for eternity? Absolutely! What a blessing for 60-plus years. I cannot wait to see how God is going to use it the next 60.

– James O. Davidson, Lincoln, Nebraska

We've Been Drawn Closer to God

Our first contact with Maranatha was in the summer of 1945, when we had been married only a few months. Clarence's aunts, Pauline Yeutter and Rica Timm, had attended meetings at Maranatha and were excitedly telling everyone to be sure and go and get in on the special meetings.

So we went to Maranatha on a Sunday afternoon. The meeting was held in a large tent which was filled to capacity and people standing outside the tent. I think it was Rev. Theodore Epp who was bringing the message. The Back to the Bible quartet sang special numbers. One song that impressed me was "Where is that Stone that Rolled" — and they walked down the aisles while singing. Suddenly one of them "found" the Bible they were looking for. Singing as they returned to the front — "Here is the Stone that Rolled..." It was very impressive to me, such beautiful harmony in their singing. We were blessed by our first service under the tent.

Maranatha continued for some years to have Sunday afternoon services. They were always special to me. We were privileged to hear speakers Oswald J. Smith, from Toronto; Dr. R.R. Brown from Omaha; the early leaders of the New Tribes Mission; Rev. Reuben Lindquist from Berean Mission in St. Louis; Harry Ironside; missionary Marlin Olsen from Africa; and many other missionaries and preachers whose names I can't recall. Dr. Ivan E. Olsen was always there, and usually was in charge of the service.

The inspirational teachings and messages of these dedicated men strengthened my faith. I wasn't getting any other ministry that drew me so close to God at that time.

In the summer of 1947 Clarence and I stayed at Maranatha several days. We stayed in one of the little old log cabins, named "Ruth." We slept fine there. In the morning we had to make a trip to the kitchen to get some hot water for washing and shaving. One morning, there was a little green lizard running around in the wash basin; that explained the scratchy noise I had heard in the night.

The Yeutter Hall was built as a memorial to Clarence's parents, Charles and Emma Yeutter. Clarence's siblings helped on the cost. We have helped with the expenses of repair and improvements to this building as much as we could.

Dr. Ivan and Mrs. Olsen always made us feel welcome with their thoughtful and kind hospitality.

I think Maranatha was always blessed with good musicians. I remember one Sunday afternoon, I was staying in the back of the tabernacle during the service to keep one of my little girls from disturbing others. I watched Eugene Clark practicing for the next song, on the organ in the back of the tabernacle. He was quite young, but was very accomplished in music. As he watched the hymnal, he practiced playing, with his hands over the keys and his feet flying over the foot pedals—but they never made a sound. I enjoyed watching him and admired him.

It was a privilege for us to send our four daughters to Camp at Maranatha. Most of our grandchildren attended later.

Clarence was on the Maranatha Board from 1985-1995. It meant a lot to him to work and plan with these godly and professional men. He realized how much sacrificial time in thought, prayer, and work by these leaders had always gone into what had been accomplished through the years at Maranatha.

When I think of Maranatha, it is like a lighthouse, sending out the beams of past memories, inviting me to return to this peaceful, friendly place and find godly people concerned about our welfare, music that draws us closer to God, delicious meals in a tasteful atmosphere, uplifting messages by Spirit-filled leaders and a chance to visit with these leaders.

We always leave with the feeling that we've been drawn closer to God while at Maranatha and determined to stay that close every day, hoping to return soon.

– Clarence and Dorthea Yeutter,
Lexington, Nebraska

Inspired By a Missionary Challenge

We lived there in North Platte in the 1960s and spent a lot of time at Maranatha Camp having a great time of fellowship. We had opportunity to help and heard some great messages. Our daughter, Deborah Capps, was challenged by the many missionary messages. The greatest challenge was when Marlin Olsen spent some time in our home. Deborah then gave her life to be a missionary. She and her husband have spent about 25 years in the Sierra Madre Mountains of Mexico working with the Mexicans in the town of Guachochi located at 8,000 feet elevation at the edge of the Copper Canyon. They also work with the Tohumarhoe Indians who live on the sides of the Canyon.

– Mel James,
Chaparral, New Mexico

Memories of Maranatha Bible Camp

From the ages of 9-21, Maranatha Bible Camp played a major role in who I am today. Through experiences I had there and the people I met and knew at Camp, I am following Christ now.

First, as a child in the 1950s, the highlight of every summer was Camp. I developed a great friendship with Diana Heinrich (Shaddick) in fourth grade at Camp and we are still the best of friends. Every year I would go forward to the invitation to receive salvation—just to make sure I was going to heaven.

In junior high and high school, my father traveled a lot, so for several summers, my mom and siblings spent it at Camp. Mom helped Mrs. Olander in the Craft Shop and I was a "Camp brat." When it was a Camp week of the age I was, Mom would put me in that program. However, I had a hard time following the rules since I was used to doing what I wanted. One time, during a tabernacle service, I took my friends out on the lake. Two pastors came out in a boat and let us know we were in the wrong place. Highlights of those years were: crush on the lifeguard (Tim Olander), two summers of involvement in Navigator Training Programs, and learning to have a devotional time that lasted more than five minutes.

After high school, the next four summers I worked on Camp staff. I lifeguarded, made the town run, worked in the Sweet Shop, and the book store. My favorite memories were on Saturday afternoons, when the campers left. Camp staff, which included the Olanders, the Olsen kids, Louise Merriman (Crooks) and her children, and myself would raft down the Platte River or go horseback riding.

But what Camp means mostly to me is the people I grew to love who have influenced my decisions and life today. The first person who affected my life was Tom Jackson. He was my "Camp" boyfriend. Tom was killed in a car accident in my senior year of high school. At that time of my life, I was not living for God. At his memorial service, I rededicated my life to the Lord. Tom was the first godly young man I knew. To this day, I am still good friends with his wonderful parents. Whenever I share my testimony, Tom is a part of it.

Second, my best friend during those years was Louise Merriman (Crooks). She was fun, worked hard, and is truly a godly woman. I really admired her and am still in touch with her 35 years later.

Third person I admired and influenced me was my friendship/romance with Mark Olander (Tim's brother). We lifeguarded together for two to three years. He modeled for me what a Christian man should be. He is now serving the Lord with his family as missionaries in Africa.

I saved the best for last. Words can not ever express the love and admiration I have for Dr. and Mrs. Ivan Olsen, founder and director of the Camp. Dr. Olsen believed in me and made me feel special and loved. He defended me when I broke a major rule at a Navigator training program when I was in high school. The head Navigators wanted to send me home and Dr. Olsen came along beside me and fought for me. If I would have had to go home, I do not think I would have ever gone to Camp again. Dr. Olsen gave me lots of responsibilities that others would not have given me. He is the closest person to what I imagine my Heavenly Father to be like. That couple walked the godly life. I count it a privilege and a great honor to have known them and I know they loved me.

God used Maranatha Bible Camp to shape me, give me self esteem and a true love for God. I am married to a wonderful godly man of almost 33 years and have two beautiful married daughters who are serving God. I am the girls' counselor at a Christian high school in California. When I see girls come in my office who are rebellious, I reflect to what I was like and remember the Olsens and their belief in me. It helps me to do the same for these girls.

– June Scott Dobbs,
Fullerton, California

Maranatha Has a Warm Spot in My Heart

I hardly know where to start. For 14 years I took a volleyball team to Maranatha and made many lasting memories.

I started going to Camp in 1958. Each of the following are an important part of my life—Curt Lehman, Carl Goltz, Kenneth Blood, Earnest Skoog, Glenn Adams, Jerry Brandt, Phillip Ewert, Roscoe Schultz, Arthur Van Campen, Ivan Olsen, Adrian House, Cliff Gustafson and many more.

We enjoyed the Christian fellowship. The Lord has been very gracious to me over the years. Maranatha has a very warm spot in my heart.

– Willie Englehardt,
Colby, Kansas

A Day at Junior Camp

7:00	Rise and Shine
7:30	Counselor and Camper Prayer Time
8:00	Breakfast
8:30	Brush teeth and clean up room
8:45	Flag Salutes
9:00	Classes—Doctrine
9:40	Recess
9:50	Classes—Social Problems
10:30	Recess
10:45	Expression Time (Special Music, Choruses, etc.)
11:15	Classes—Missions
12:00	Clean up for Lunch
12:15	Lunch Time
12:45	Resting Time (Reading, Bible Memory, etc.)
1:45	Organized recreation—Clyde White
3:15	Girls Swim—Boys Handicraft
4:15	Boys Swim—Girls Handicraft
5:15	Clean up for Supper
5:30	Supper Time
6:15	Stunt Time
7:00	Evening Evangelistic Service—Curt Lehman
8:30	Surprise Hour
9:30	Devotions and lights out

CLASS TEACHERS:
C. Lehman, C. White, F. Kroeze, J. Sprunger.

RATES:
JUNIOR AND JUNIOR HIGH WEEKS
$8.50 plus $1.00 registration.

YOUNG PEOPLE'S WEEK
$10.00 plus $1.00 registration.

ADULTS WEEK
$2.25 per day plus $1.00 registration.

One-third off for Pastors families, missionaries, and full-time Christian workers. Children under 5 free except for $1.00 registration. 5-14 pay $1.75 per day and registration.

$1.00 per day extra for Prophet's Chamber, or private facilities.

– From the Berean Digest
June 1963

Top row, from left: Junior High Camp, 1966. The camp grew in numbers after being created in the late 1950s; Curt Lehman. Bottom row, from left: Curt Lehman (standing at right) served as program director of Junior Camp during the 1960s; Ministers, their wives, missionaries, children's workers, and all those in full-time Christian work were invited as guests during Christian Workers' Week, July 1963.

Top row: These women, shown at Missions Week in 1963, served in various mission fields around the world. The woman at left is unidentified. The others, left to right: Ruth Peterson Hasenauer (Navajo/New Mexico), Maxine Gordon (Congo), Luella Foster (Navajo/New Mexico and Venezuela), Margaret Buehler (Navajo/New Mexico) and Joyce Owens (Congo).

Second row, from left: Bible teaching time near the swimming pool; Taking time to be quiet and hear God's word has always been an emphasis at Camp; To save on transportation costs, families often sent their children to Camp with dozens of their friends in the back of a large farm truck (1966 photo).

Third row, from left: Dr. Olsen prays with Leonard and Hazel Parcel in the old dining hall on their 25th wedding anniversary. Hazel is wearing her original wedding dress; Cliff Gustafson enthralled Junior campers with his dramatic campfire services; Clothing began to look more casual at Camp during the 1960s.

Fourth row, from left: Two views of how the Camp landscape changed dramatically by the late 1960s after Interstate 80 was completed; Ernie Skoog (left), Doris Goltz and Jerry Swesey handle registrations on the opening day of a Camp week.

Top row: Jerry Yeutter, the Camp recreation director, spent Father's Day 1960 with his parents, Carl and Doralee Yeutter.

Second row, from left: The original Sweet Shop was between the Dining Hall and Tabernacle. Dorothy Dickinson is working behind the counter; Posing in front of Branting Cabin, from left: Cora Swanson, Sarah Eloe, Esther Eutsler, Erma Lee and Zenola Burman; This group won the Senior High Week team competition, which included sports, Bible memorization and cabin inspections.

Third row, from left: As the speaker gave an invitation with the ladies' quartet singing in the background, could it be that the girl near the podium has just made a decision for Christ?; The old "Switchboard" was Maranatha's early telephone system and message center; Free time at the Sweet Shop in 1963.

Fourth row, from left: A microphone hangs ready to use in the old Dining Hall in this 1961 photo; Children gathered each morning between the Tabernacle and the caretaker's home (at left) for the flag ceremony; Elfrieda Olander (left) ran the Craft Shop for many years.

The 1970s

The campers just kept coming in the door.

The dining hall hostess looked at their faces. The children were so excited, chattering to each other as they began their day with breakfast. They gathered around the long wooden tables with linoleum on top. They scraped the wooden benches across the tile floor as they scrambled to sit down.

The crowding wasn't as bad this week, with 11- and 12-year-olds at Camp. It would be worse later on during the teen camps, when there would be more than 400 on the grounds, everyone was larger and the young people would be sitting almost back-to-back.

Breakfast actually didn't seem as crowded as supper would this evening. She knew it would be quite hot and humid inside the dining hall, and her blouse would be sticking to her back, even with the windows open and electric fans running. The roof seemed even lower than usual in the heat of the day. Were the summers getting hotter in the late 1960s than they had ever been, or was she just getting more susceptible to the heat? It was hard to tell.

They were eating in four shifts — first the Navigator trainees, then two shifts of children with their counselors. (Judging by how crowded it was, maybe the Camp leadership should have divided them into three sections, as they sometimes did. But, she remembered, that would give the workers even less time to prepare the next meal.) Finally, the Camp's support staff took their turn. Every shift was allotted about half an hour, so it took a little over two hours just to move people in and out of the dining hall at every meal.

The hostess tried to remember to stop and count her blessings, although sometimes that was hard to do when it was so hot in the building. She had heard about the first year of Camp, when everyone ate outdoors or under a funeral tent when it rained, and about the cardboard kitchen that kept the dirt from blowing into the food as it cooked over the gas range, and she vaguely remembered working in the old slab dining hall in the mid-1940s. This one was much better.

Lela Clark had overseen the dining area in the early years at the Talbot place and the Bockus grove. Then Matilda Krause took over the supervision and handled it for many years. Myrtle Grandy also had helped supervise the food service and dining areas. Regardless of who was in charge, there was plenty of work to do, and women from area churches would come and volunteer a week at a time to make sure that the campers were well fed. Yes, this crowding was a problem that they had all hoped for. They had prayed for good attendance, and God had provided an abundance of campers. But it would be nice to be able to eat in a place that wasn't so hot and crowded.

Everyone had finally come inside and found his seat, and the noise slowly subsided as the children waited for the leader to say grace. It was the third day of the Camp week, so it didn't take quite as long to quiet the campers as it had the first meal or two, when the excitement and anticipation seemed to give them more energy than usual. Everyone waited while the dining hall staff and counselors worked together to serve the meal family-style. As the children finished eating, they took their plates to the dish-cleaning area, where several women helped scrape the plates and passed them along to the Navigator trainee dishwashing crew. The smell of Clorox water permeated the building (it was the least expensive way to conform to state regulations mandating the sterilization of plates and silverware, and the workers used it to wash dishes and wipe tables).

"It was pretty busy days," recalled Alice Olsen, who brought her family for countless meals in the old dining hall located in the middle of the original 80 acres at

Maranatha. "There was never a dull moment. They all kept wiping tables, setting tables. There was activity most every minute."

But try as they might, all the volunteers couldn't keep pace with the changing state laws, which declared the old kitchen as outdated. By 1970, Ivan Olsen was convinced that Maranatha Camp needed a new dining hall. He set about drawing up plans of a larger facility with an expanded, modern commercial kitchen.

And it would have air conditioning. Maranatha had never before seen such luxury.

The plans were approved in October by the Camp board, and Olsen sent out a fundraising letter explaining the need for the improved facilities.

A few days later, Ed Fasse and Carl Yeutter received the letter. The were two supporters of Camp who lived in Dawson County, about 40 miles east of Maranatha. Both had sent their children to Maranatha and donated money regularly, and they were excited about the project. They conferred with each other, and called Olsen, asking for an appointment with him the next day.

Both men agreed with the project in principle, but Yeutter, a banker, questioned Olsen's timing. "Pastor," he said, "we're in a time of inflation. Materials are higher now than they'll ever be. They can't continue this high; they've got to go back down or it'll destroy our nation. If you'll just wait a year or two, you can build this dining room and kitchen for just a portion of what you'd have to spend now." Fasse, who owned a metal building dealership, agreed with Yeutter.

Olsen was not one to wait unless he had to. He explained the crowded conditions of the current dining hall to the men, the "impossibility" of continuing unless the Camp had a big enough place where the children could eat in one shift rather than three.

Yeutter seemed uneasy, and excused himself. He returned home, and so did Fasse. Olsen was dismayed. "I thought, oh, my goodness, I've certainly lost them," he said. About an hour later, he called Yeutter and set up another appointment to meet him for lunch in Cozad the next day.

Olsen prayed for wisdom. How should he handle this situation? He believed God wanted him to move ahead. Was this a sign that he should wait instead? He had no peace about waiting.

The next day, Olsen drove to Cozad. "When I got to the restaurant, God had laid it upon my heart and I said, 'Carl, why don't you provide this dining hall and kitchen?' And he said to me, 'How much do you think it's going to cost?' To show how poor I am at estimates, I said, 'I think I can build it for $30,000.' (It proved that when we finished, it was $120,000.) But he said to me then, 'You know, I have Maranatha Camp in my will for $25,000, but you know there'd be a lot of wisdom to giving that money while I'm alive and then I can see just how it is used, and I can be blessed by that.'"

Olsen then drove to Ed Fasse's place. A trusted friend, Ed and his wife, Eleanor, had donated an airplane for Olsen to use to visit churches and promote Maranatha around the re-

gion. "You know, my wife and I want to give another $10,000 toward this building," he told Olsen. Later, Fasse told Olsen how his family had supported his decision to donate the money toward the dining hall, and that God had restored the $10,000 to him through a surprising turn of events when he sold his corn crop for the year and he received an astoundingly high price per bushel. With tears in his eyes, Fasse said, "You know, God has shown me that I can't even give Him anything. I gave Him $10,000 that I didn't have and God gave it right back to me."

Fasse wasn't finished yet. He looked at the Old Tabernacle and when he heard it had been built out of cinder blocks in the 1940s, he knew its days were numbered. Fasse and Yeutter approached Rev. Olsen again.

"They told me, 'At best, only a few more years will that building be safe to have our meetings in,'" related Olsen. "'Why don't we build a third section? Let's have a kitchen, a dining hall and a sanctuary right in the same building.' And they were the ones who made the decision to build the sanctuary. I convinced them we needed a dining hall, and they convinced me that we needed a chapel."

The dining hall project had just been expanded. The price tag became steeper. The plans were made; the new building would be built on the tract the Camp had bought from Vernie Anderson in 1964. For expediency's sake, it was built on the hard-packed haul road that huge trucks had used to carry dirt from the lakebed.

The finished product was a low-profile, 226-by-60-foot metal building, light blue in color, with a curved roof. It was professionally built for the cost of materials. Rex Shaver, who came with his wife Patsy to Maranatha in the early 1970s to work as caretakers, did much of the labor on the building. It was rather nondescript in appearance, but everyone who had endured the cramped, hot conditions in the old dining hall didn't seem to notice. They were thankful for the big new building, but the project still had a long way to go.

Fasse asked, "What are you going to use to seat the people?"

Olsen: "We'll use the old benches, and old folding chairs from throughout the Old Tabernacle."

Fasse: Oh, no! A brand new building like this?"

Fasse ordered church pews and had them installed. After they arrived, he had another inspiration.

Fasse: "I want to put cushions on those pews."

Olsen: "Ed, I don't even have cushions on the pews in our church in North Platte!"

Fasse: "Well, you don't have to make the Camp what your church is."

Fasse also bought round tables and chairs for the dining room. Dick Christensen bought an organ for the chapel as a memorial to his parents, Mr. & Mrs. Frank Christensen.

Willard Carpenter, a farmer who lived about 200 miles west of Maranatha, near Mitchell, Nebraska, who lived frugally and had no carpeting in his own home, dropped in to see Olsen with yet another idea.

Carpenter: "What are you going to put on the floor of the sanctuary?"

Olsen: "The floor? We've got a cement floor."

Carpenter: "Well, with pews and with a lovely organ, we can't have just a raw unfinished floor. I think you ought to put in carpet."

Olsen: "Man, sakes alive! Where would you get — what would be the cost of the platform and the sanctuary with carpet?"

Carpenter just happened to have carpet samples and cost quotes with him. Olsen brought in a few people who helped him choose colors. Then Carpenter paid for all the carpeting for the dining hall and chapel and hauled it directly from the mill in Georgia. A carpetlayer from the North Platte Berean Church volunteered his labor to install the carpet.

They prepared to dedicate the structure as the Yeutter Memorial Building, in appreciation for the large gift given by the Yeutters, who also had donated a lakeside cabin and by now, had moved to British Columbia. As Ivan & Alice Olsen sat at their kitchen table drinking a cup of coffee, they marveled at the way God was providing for the new dining hall/chapel. Ivan turned to Alice and asked, "Honey, do you think our constituents would feel that we are being extravagant and luxurious if we would put a refrigerated drinking fountain in that dining hall?" All that existed at the time was an outdoor water pipe with a spigot that unleashed a stream of water 10 feet into the air, which then could be turned down to a manageable drinking level.

While they were talking, their telephone rang. It was Willard Carpenter again.

"Pastor," he began, "have you ever considered putting a refrigerated drinking fountain in that dining hall?"

Olsen: "Brother, my wife and I are sitting at the coffee table right now, and I just got through asking her if our constituency would feel that we are being wasteful with their money if we did that."

Carpenter: "My wife and I are ahead of you. We want you to put six of them in that whole building, and send the bill to us."

The Olsens were overcome by the generosity of those who helped furnish and outfit the new dining hall, and they marveled as the interior work progressed. God was providing for the huge undertaking, which looked like it would be finished with no debt. The spirit of excitement prevailed during the summer of 1971.

It was in that atmosphere that tragedy struck Maranatha Bible Camp as unexpectedly as a lightning bolt on a sunny day. Near the end of the 1971 Junior Camp week, two campers were drowned at the climax of the traditional tug-of-war that was contested over the shallow west end of Lake Maranatha. One team had decided ahead of time that everyone would jump into the lake together if it lost, and a boy and a girl were trampled in the resulting confusion. The entire staff was stunned. A grief-stricken Ivan Olsen, who was away from Camp at the time of the tragedy, officiated at one of the funerals. At the time of this printing, they remain the only campers to die at Maranatha Bible Camp.

Progress continued on the new dining hall/chapel, and in July 1972, the Yeutter Memorial Building was dedicated. Five years later, with the blessing of the Yeutter family, it was rededicated as Olsen Memorial Building at the time of the celebration of the Camp's 40th anniversary.

The construction of the new dining hall/chapel building crystallized Maranatha's position as an all-season conference center as well as a summer camp for children and youth. More staff would be necessary to keep the year-round operation going, and they started to arrive in the 1970s.

George Cheek was a fulltime staff member, as were the Shavers. The Camp hired several office workers who stayed a short time and moved on before northeast Nebraska native Ruth Ann Rodgers became a fulltime staff member in 1977. Ruth Ann became the Camp bookkeeper and an administrative assistant to Cheek. Several of the staff learned to use the new Citizens' Band radios that Maranatha purchased for communication as the CB radio craze swept the nation. The fulltime staff members also began to raise missionary support (Personal Support Income) in 1978. This enabled Maranatha to keep salaries low enough to be able to hire more fulltime staff in the future.

Reuben Hasenauer moved to Maranatha in the mid-1970s as a retired volunteer. He would serve for more than 20 years, mowing lawns, stoking wood stoves, cleaning buildings, catching mice and trimming cedar trees. That type of work was rewarded when Maranatha Bible Camp received second place among 603 entries in a nationwide contest designed to encourage beautification along the Interstate highway system throughout the United States.

Nellie Lantz, the widow who allowed the newly-married Ivan & Alice Olsen to live rent-free in her house from 1937-46, died on Thanksgiving Day 1977.

Cheek began forming new outdoor-oriented camping programs such as the Indian Village, and in 1975, he made sure that Maranatha joined Christian Camping International, a professional organization for Christian camps and conference centers. Gil Larsen started in 1975 as Junior Camp director and served 17 years, through 1991. Tom Hunter and Dennis Gingrich were program directors of the new Awana Camps. Frank Van Campen started directing the Youth Weeks.

Training for Christian leaders had been a part of the Maranatha since the early days, and another phase of that outreach became more prominent as pastors' retreats began to gain popularity in the 1970s. While several denominations and church groups have used the Camp's facilities for pastors' retreats, the Berean Church Fellowship has been at Maranatha the most consecutive years.

Ivan Olsen directed most of the early pastors' retreats, assisted by Carl Goltz. In the early 70s, Art Van Campen took over as Berean pastors' retreat director for several years. He was followed by Steve Watson, then Tom Walker. The attendance varied from 50 to 100, which always includes visiting pastors invited from independent churches.

"Having the pastors on the grounds and available for the camp staff to visit with gave some real opportunities for personal growth," said George Cheek. "The good singing, healthy camaraderie and practical teaching has been an encouragement to be around."

Ernie Skoog, who lived at Camp while serving with the Berean Fellowship in the mid- to late 1970s, converted the "winter chapel" (also known as the Mars Chapel) into Maranatha's main office building by the end of the decade. Dick & Marilyn Wiesner of Lexington, who owned several businesses, were among the leading suppliers of lumber and metal building products for Camp during this time.

On January 22, 1973, the U.S. Supreme Court announced that it had discovered a new "right to privacy" in the Constitution that legalized abortion on demand throughout the nation. The decision, Roe v. Wade, would lead to the deaths of more than 40 million preborn Americans during the next three decades.

There was a surge of patriotism in the 1970s as the United States prepared to celebrate its 200th anniversary in 1976. CBS-TV aired nightly "Bicentennial Minutes" in the months preceding the holiday. Maranatha hosted the general public for an Independence Day program on Sunday, July 4, 1976.

In horse racing, there were an amazing three Triple Crown winners during the decade. In August 1977, 42-year-old Elvis Presley died at his home in Memphis of drug- and alcohol-related complications.

Ivan Olsen, having reached age 65 in May 1979, could tell that God had brought along a man qualified to replace him as general director of Maranatha Bible Camp, and started to think about how to prepare for the transition in leadership, while George Cheek, seeing that life and ministry were becoming more complex, suspected that many of the methods that had worked well for Olsen would have to be re-evaluated before the end of the 20th century.

Voices of Maranatha

Life at Camp was Peachy for Skoogs

We started going to Camp in the summer of 1955. Our youngest child was in diapers.

One year we used the Heinriches' farm truck to take our church kids to Camp. We filled the back with church pews and drove down old Highway 30, picking up kids from the churches along the way. It is a wonder we weren't all killed. The kids were told to bring a sack lunch, and we always stopped in Ogallala's city park to eat and rest.

A couple of times, Curt Lehman sent a truck to Colorado to pick up "peach culls"—the truck came back through Nebraska, dumping the peaches off in our front yard and at other Berean churches along the way, for the women to can for Camp. One morning Ernie got up and said, "Look what happened, someone shook my peach tree!" Some of those peaches were pretty squashed, but they were great to eat at Camp! We had peaches three times a day.

At Camp, we all were divided up into teams. Maranatha emphasized Bible memory, and we got points for memorizing verses.

We used to gather by the old Sweet Shop before we went into the dining hall for meals. We all stood there and sang, "Come and Dine."

Afternoons were fun times and free time. We were supposed to also go to our rooms and memorize our Scripture. We used to meet in the Old Tabernacle in the evenings (it broke our hearts when they tore that building down); we would have skits in the evening. Everybody on our teams was supposed to perform or do something to compete to win the Camp trophy. One year, Mark, our son, did a skit.

He laid on the ground yelling, "It's all around me, it's all around me!" He was talking about his belt!

Ernie and I moved to Camp in 1976. Ernie was the secretary/treasurer for the Berean Fellowship. He also took care of the insurance for the fellowship and filled Berean pulpits when churches nearby were without pastors. At Camp we renovated the old Olsen house and remodeled the building where the Camp offices are located. Every week in the summer, I used to mow the whole center of camp - around the house and offices. I enjoyed it! I loved living there when camps were in session but when everyone would leave, it was such a letdown. We lived at the Camp for five years.

My granddaughter, Amber, came to Camp when she was 4 years old. Debbie Wetzig was the leader, and they only let Amber be a camper because we lived there. Amber will never forget that experience. It was one of the experiences that gave her a real love for the Lord.

When the Nav Training Program campers would go home after the summer, they would hate to leave Camp.

When we would go up the valley to minister at Ogallala or North Platte, and we would come back late, late at night we would be so tired. But when we would see the Maranatha cross, we would say, "We're almost home!" How fitting that Camp has marked our lives - our children and our grandchildren - to live for eternity. It makes me think of that song, "Almost home, a night or two at sea...." We'll all be home together for eternity.

— Betty Skoog,
Basalt, Colorado

Maranatha Programs Over the Years

"Programming at MBC was so simple from its beginning, just what a pastor who had never gone to Bible camp would do," wrote Ivan E. Olsen as he reminisced before the Camp's 40th anniversary.

From day one, he set a precedent of distributing the responsibility for programming to volunteers. There was no fulltime staff to plan a week of Camp. Olsen selected people from around the region whom he knew and trusted and asked them to take ownership in Maranatha's programming, which originally was targeted to youth, but quickly expanded to children and eventually, to adults, families and various specialty groups.

The philosophy of daily scheduling at Maranatha's core group of programs has changed very little since the Camp's inception. Bible teaching and a missions challenge in the morning, recreation in the afternoon and chapel sessions in the evening have been the general pattern all along, remaining virtually unchanged into the 21st century.

Maranatha Bible Camp was originally designed for all young people. Young teens came to the Talbot place in 1938, as did people in their 20s. Olsen called it simply "the First Annual Encampment." The philosophy continued unchanged for the next two years, but in 1941, Maranatha continued its Young People's Camp and started a separate Boys' and Girls' Camp, which later would be called Junior Camp.

In 1945, Maranatha expanded its programming to adults when it launched its first-ever Family Camp, although it was not held every year for some time.

The Camp board analyzed the daily programming schedule during its January 1, 1947, meeting in Grand Island. "It was decided that the present plan was good as could be — Bible all morning, recreation in afternoon, revival in evening," Hugh Clark wrote in the minutes.

In the postwar years, those three staples were Maranatha Bible Camp's main summer diet. Attendance at those core programs rose steadily, from a total of 453 in 1945 to 2,310 in 1956. As attendance grew, more weeks of camp were added. In 1956, there were three weeks of Junior Camp and three weeks of Young People's Camp. In 1959, Cliff Gustafson successfully lobbied for a separate Jr. High Camp to be spun off from the Junior Camp.

From 1938 to well into the 1960s, the campers woke up to "Reveille" in the morning and heard "Taps" at night, played by a musical instrument (usually a bugle, but sometimes a trombone). Chalk drawings, flannelgraphs, object lessons, special music, messages and financial appeals were part of campers' daily experience.

Maranatha added variety with other specialized camping programs as demand grew and speakers were available. In the 1940s and 50s, these programs included Ministers' Week, Christian Workers' Camp, Youth for Christ Week (high school/college age), Missionary Week, Music Week, Back to the Bible Camp, Back to the Bible Missionary Camp and Child Evangelism Week. Some programs were dropped as interest waned, and new programs were added.

In the late 1950s, the Winter Retreat ("snow camp") was born. It was held during schools' Christmas vacation for more than 30 years.

The 1960s brought upheaval in the form of sweeping social changes to the United States. At Maranatha, much of the decade was consumed by the big makeover of the campgrounds when the federal government chose to run Interstate 80 directly through Maranatha's property; there was little noticeable change in Maranatha's programming. In 1976, however, the landscape was altered dramatically as George Cheek, who grew up camping and backpacking in the Rockies, started to put his fingerprints on Maranatha.

The Indian Village was the big new attraction in the nation's Bicentennial year. For junior high boys and girls, the Indian Village was promoted as an "adventure-packed campout in the backwoods of Maranatha's grounds." Campers lived in tipis and learned outdoor skills such as building a campfire, knot tying and hunter safety.

The Camp started marketing to the Awana Club organizations at churches throughout the Midwest, and Awana Camp was born in 1976. Its name was later changed to

Present at the Camp board meeting in 1977 were, back row, from left: Hugh Clark, Carl Goltz, Adrian House, Ken Blood, George Cheek. Front row, from left: Ernest Lott, Ivan Olsen, Ed Fasse, Bob Benson, Curt Lehman.

Club Week, and it remained until the early 1990s. Maranatha leaders, ever conscious that the Camp lacked a beautiful mountain setting, added wilderness adventure trips to the Rocky Mountains (similar to the 1941 experiment) to the schedule.

In 1980, Cheek reported to the Camp board that of the 31 camps in Nebraska at that time, Maranatha was the only one to offer at least 15 different programs.

As the Camp grew, its programming became even less centralized. The board appointed a director for each specific program. The program director was responsible for lining up his speakers, musicians and schedule. Many of Maranatha's speakers were well-known in evangelical Christian circles. H.A. Ironside, former president of Moody Bible Institute, taught at Maranatha in 1950, during the final year of his life. Wendell Loveless, a hymn writer who served at Moody, also spoke at Maranatha. Others included Dr. Oswald J. Smith of Toronto, L.E. Maxwell of Prairie Bible Institute in Alberta, Walter L. Wilson of Calvary Bible College in Kansas City, J.C. Brumfield of Denver Bible Institute, Howard Hendricks of Dallas Theological Seminary, Dr. M.R. DeHahn of Radio Bible Class in Grand Rapids, Michigan, and Dr. Clayton "Clate" Risley (well-known in the 1950s-70s as "Mr. Sunday School"). Back to the Bible sent many speakers, including Theodore Epp, J.C. Brumfield, Darrel Handel, G. Christian Weiss, Ord Morrow, Melvin Jones, Warren Wiersbe and Woodrow Kroll. Epp, general director at Back to the Bible Broadcast and a longtime Maranatha board member, used his nationwide radio contacts to help recruit some of the biggest names.

"My husband's desire was to bring in respected speakers to challenge people to consider what God wanted in their lives," said Alice Olsen. "In large tents and later in the Old Tabernacle building, surrounded by those fragrant cedar trees, folks with hungry hearts would come and respond to the offer of the free gift of salvation, and were stirred to give their hearts fully to God's service."

The schedule continued to change at Maranatha. In the late 1970s came other additions to the Camp schedule including Ladies' Retreat, Bike Hike, a Ski Trip for high schoolers and a Choir Clinic. In the 1980s came a Father/Son Camp, a Singles' Conference (sometimes called a retreat, other times an "advance"). The 1990s saw the advent of a new core program — Primary Camp, a one- or two-night camp for children entering Kindergarten through third grade. Specialty camps that appeared during the '90s were Music & Worship Retreat, Single Parents' Retreat, Bowhunters' Archery Camp, Fishing Camp, Ringneck Roundup, Roller Hockey Camp, Basketball Camp, Volleyball Camp, Breakaway River Run, Breakaway Bike Trip and Fasting & Prayer Retreat.

In the 1990s, nationally-known Christian musicians Danny Byram and Steve & Annie Chapman appeared at Maranatha. Byram, an accomplished pianist, guitarist and vocalist, led praise and worship at Youth Week for five consecutive years before going on to coordinate the programming at Promise Keepers men's events nationwide. The Chapmans appeared at Couples' Conferences on two different occasions. Steve also spoke at Archery Camp and Annie at Ladies' Retreat.

In the 1990s, campers were coming to Maranatha from more than 30 states each year, including family reunions.

In the 2000s, Maranatha added high-energy programs like Crossfire Paintball Camp and Wakeboard Camp.

There is written record of Independence Day celebrations being held at Maranatha as early as 1952. The family-oriented celebration has grown to include an open time of boating and recreation at the Waterfront, an Adventure Triathlon, a chuck wagon cookout, hay wagon rides around the grounds and an evening musical program at the amphitheatre, followed by fireworks over Lake Maranatha. It has been a means to introduce newcomers to Maranatha, as have Maranatha's Community Waterfront Days on afternoons during the summer, or Community Gym Events monthly through the winter months. Both are open to the public.

— Tad Stryker

Campers enjoyed the "Indian Village" in the late 1970s.

Repairing Lake Maranatha After the Flood of 1973

This account was transcribed from a message given to Maranatha summer staff.

We had a flood at Maranatha one year. Oh, how devastating it was. I don't think my heart has ever been so crushed or broken. The river broke through the west end of our beautiful Lake Maranatha. It only took minutes to raise the water up so high that the only thing left was for the whole east end to wash out, and that's just what happened. All we had was a river instead of our lake. There was a big hole in the west end and in the east end of our lake. Where could I get dirt that I could use to fill them up? I didn't know. How on earth could we ever replace our lake?

The Navigator students came and I stood before them. *(Although the Navigator Training Program was no longer held at Maranatha, a group of Navigators from Purdue University was on site from May 6-16, 1973, during a period of heavy, prolonged rain and flooding on the South Platte River in Colorado and Nebraska.)* On the first day of the Camp, I told them that I hadn't the least idea of what to do. I know God gave us this lake; the flood destroyed it. Let's pray that God will give us some dirt. We stood in the Tabernacle and we prayed and asked God to give us some dirt. God will bear me witness.

Later that morning when I made my usual trip to town (as I pastored the church as well), I got out and saw the biggest mess you ever saw. There was all the earth-moving equipment you could imagine. The flood had been there and the state had come in with their great big diggers to dig a ditch alongside the road. The flood had almost covered the road and they realized they needed a ditch. They were digging this rich black dirt and throwing it up on the road.

I no more than saw it and realized that this was the answer to our prayer. I called the county commissioner and asked if we could have some of the dirt. He said, "Reverend, it doesn't belong to me. I'm sure you can't have it. We've already tried to get it and they turned us down."

I asked him who owned it and he said, "The state owns it." I asked him who was in charge and he said Harold Easom in North Platte was. *(Easom was the district engineer for the state highway department.)* I went to the telephone and called Harold Easom and told him the predicament that we were in, and that we hadn't been government-financed at all, but were trying to make a go of our camp project and that we had a devastating flood.

He said, "Reverend, I haven't given the dirt to anyone. How much do you need?" How do you answer a fellow when you have a situation like this? So I said, "I think I need all you have." He said, "Reverend, I'm going to give it to you. I won't let anyone take one load of dirt until you have all you need."

God provided for us in the midst of an almost impossible situation — the flood had been so devastating through here that every dump truck and everything else was in use. But God provided. Yet that day, we had our dump trucks there and they were loading the dump trucks as they were throwing the dirt out. We had our scoop there so that after the state finished working, we could continue to work right around the clock. We had to first of all dump the dirt in the west end and make it wide enough so that we could go across it (in a truck). We hauled that rich, easy-to-pack dirt and filled all of that, and filled all of (the east end), and there was still a little left.

Some of our roads were very low, so we went through the campgrounds and built all of our roads up. You know that by the time we hauled the last truckload, we had used up all they had. It was just enough.

Do you think things like that just happen? There is a God who knew just how many yards of fill dirt we needed there. Miracles at Maranatha! Maranatha has been a miracle work of God since its beginning.

– Ivan E. Olsen

The flood of May 1973 took considerable time and effort to clean up. Workers built a large dike at the east end of Lake Maranatha, which was severely damaged. Right: This crew helped protect the new Dining Hall/Chapel building when flood waters threatened.

This Happened to Mary at Camp

I first experienced Maranatha Bible Camp when I attended in 1965. I had just completed the eighth grade at Adams Junior High in North Platte, Nebraska. My Great Aunt Jessie Shimmin volunteered to pay for my cousin's (Connie Shimmin) and my way to Camp. My Aunt Jean Shimmin drove us to Camp. I remember how hot it was through the week. I didn't see much of Connie that week because she was "boy crazy" and she was always talking to boys. While I was attending Camp, I do not recall hearing about how Jesus could save me from my sins. I guess I just wasn't ready to understand the plan of salvation.

My family had moved next door to Clyde and Erna Northey. Mrs. Northey was helpful to monitor all three of us after school. My mom would get off from work at about 4:00 PM so there was 30 minutes in which to listen to Mrs. Northey. One day she asked my sister, Joanne, and me if we would like to go to Sunday school and church with them.

I knew if I attended church with Mr. and Mrs. Northey, I would have a ride home. I began attending the Berean Church and was taken to the Junior High classroom. When I walked in I saw some of the girls that I knew from school, Linda Cook, Susan Renfroe, Faith Olsen, and Nancy Johnston. I was so happy to find my friends attending this church.

The summer before my sophomore year I again attended Maranatha Bible Camp. We were meeting in the "Old Tabernacle," sitting on old wooden pews and when we walked across the floor it creaked. Pas-

God worked in the hearts of Jessie and Frank Shimmin, a sister and brother who ranched in the Sandhills, to answer the prayers of 200 hungry Navigator trainees.

tor Curt Lehman was speaking in an evening service I attended with my friend, Linda. He explained about hell and how I was going there unless I accepted Christ as my Savior. I went forward, along with several others, to accept Christ and we were all sent to a side door to go outside.

As we walked out the door there were college students lined up and as we walked by, hands would reach out and take a child. Joy Olsen Lucht took my hand and we went to the dining hall, now the Sweet Shop, and sat in a booth where she explained to me how to become a Christian. I can still show you which booth and the exact spot I became a Christian.

I began my sophomore year at North Platte High as a new Christian. I was fearful of the student that had ruined my freshman year, but the Lord took care of it because I hardly ever saw him and he was not in any of my classes.

I wanted others in my school to know I was living a life serving the Lord, so I carried my black leather Bible to every class each day. Two young men seated behind me in English class were the only ones that ever teased me about my Bible. It happened only once and I just ignored them. Years later one of them was married, and I later heard they had lost a new born baby. I wondered then if he thought the Bible was so funny. The other died at the age of 50 with a liver disease. I wondered if he had time to think about what the Bible is all about, but I never knew if he had made a decision for Jesus. I met his Aunt and she wondered if he had put his trust in Christ.

When I arrived home from Camp, I immediately tried to learn the Bible verses explaining the plan of salvation that led me to accept Christ as my Savior. I read the booklet over and over but never felt confident to share it. One day I took our dog, Mitizi (rat terrier), down to the bedroom in the basement and together we sat on the bed while I practiced the verses once again. I decided to pretend that Mitizi was someone that I wanted to share Christ with, so I placed her across from me and I practiced telling her about Jesus. She was so attentive to what I was saying, I thought if only the person I was going to witness to would be this interested then I could easily share Christ's message!! I laughed after our session because Mitizi had a look on her face that could only mean "what happened to Mary?" Indeed!! Do you know what happened to Mary? New life in Christ!!

– Mary Shimmin,
North Platte

Maranatha Led to Marriage, Then Thailand

Maranatha Bible Camp means a lot to me. It was there that I found the Lord. It was there that I met the lovely girl who would become my wife. It was there that I first began to learn the joy of serving Jesus.

Without that foundation, it is unlikely I'd be serving as a missionary in Thailand today.

– Charlie Shimmin,
Thailand

Tragedy Strikes at Maranatha Bible Camp

This account is taken from Rev. Olsen's church newsletter in July 1971.

After 33 successful summers with no fatalities, in our 34th summer season we sustained two drownings, a 10-year-old boy, Joseph Kohl, son of Mr. and Mrs. Gale Kohl and an 11-year-old girl, Kathy Rhoden, daughter of Mrs. Joy Rhoden, all of North Platte. The accident occurred Friday, July 9, 1971.

On July 12, Pastor Olsen conducted the funeral for the boy. It was very significant that, under the preaching of Rev. Curt Lehman, who is uniquely gifted to preach to junior children and who had been having a remarkable revival with the children this year, on Wednesday evening Joseph came forward making a decision to accept Jesus Christ as his personal Saviour. The fact that of his own initiative, without being prompted, this boy declared less than two days before he went to be with the Lord that it was his desire as best he understood to become a Christian. He wanted to follow the Lord Jesus. This fact was a great comfort to the parents.

The little girl was in the DVBS of our church and also during Camp came forward and made a decision for Christ. Her counselors felt that it was a decision for reassurance. It was their feeling that Kathy had made a decision for Christ.

Naturally everyone has asked how it happened. Let me briefly explain. Though I was not actually present, talking to most of the adults that were witnesses of the occasion, we have gleaned these basic facts. First of all, there were approximately 45 adults. This includes counselors, both men and women, and many of the parents. This was a Camp-sponsored game in which everyone was present. The children that were not participating were watching. The game was called rope pull. It was not intended as a water game. The rope was stretched across the narrowest place of the lake. Two equal sides - one on each bank. If we use the term "tug-of-war," most would understand what was meant. The rules of the game were very carefully laid out to all, and they all understood. No one was to get into the water. The winning side was the side that pulled the other to the water edge. The moment the losing side touched the water they lost. Nine pulls determined the winner. Eight pulls had been completed.

Excitement was running high. The adults were just as excited, if not more, than all of the children. The ninth pull determined the winner. In the excitement of having won, the winning side gave a hard jerk merely to show they were the winners. This was all it took to plunge 12 or 15 children into the water. This along with the fact that some of the children who were able to swim wanted to swim anyway, many of the losers just jumped into the water to swim. The first moments of the hilarity didn't even frighten the adults. Among the adults who were observing the game, there were none who even had apprehension or question or fears. It was something that had been done many times over many years. In fact, it was one of those games that continued from year to year where everyone was present. The swimming period from 2:00 to 3:00 was forfeited for the sake of everyone seeing this game. The water between the two pulling sides was part of the psychological excitement with the rules having been made definitely clear; no one was to get into the water. The touch of the water declared the loser. There was only a couple feet of water near the shore.

In just moments, the adults all realized the danger and those able jumped into the water and threw the children on the shore. The two that were lost must have been toward the front, and with the crowded condition were pushed out to the deeper water. College Navigator trainees were near at hand and immediately were in the water. The lifeguards were present to do what they could. The fire truck with the resuscitator, similar to the one used by the North Platte rescue unit, was there. The nurse was there. Artificial respiration was given for 30-40 minutes after the sheriff pronounced the little ones dead. Cardiac massage, mouth-to-mouth resuscitation, plus the clearing of breathing passages and nose and throat of mucous were all done.

It must be kept clearly in mind that the tragedy was not a lack of safety, but of over excitement with the game on the part of the children which caused them to forget the rules. Heroism on the part of counselors was manifested in the control of the approximately 300 children who were watching. All of them were kept from going into the water in their attempt to "rescue." The counselors immediately got all of the children assembled in their units so they could get an absolute report of the number missing. It took four minutes to discover that the one boy and one girl who had already been brought in from the water and were being worked on were the only two missing. It was amazing the quick thinking on the part of counselors and leadership.

It is so easy to "look back;" "If we had done this or that." An automobile tragedy on the Interstate could do the same. A playground at a public school could do the same. If this had been a tragedy involving children who were not observed or adequately cared for, it would have been a different thing. We always attempt to have one adult to eight children. Few camps anywhere in the United States can boast of the high counselor-camper ratio and as dedicated, consecrated. Most of them are ministers and their wives, full-time Christian workers, missionaries, etc. Rev. Frank Kroeze is the director of the Junior Camp, having directed it so successfully for so many years. Rev. Franklin Curtis was his assistant. Rev. Curt Lehman, the evangelist and Rev. Sam Lehman, the director of recreation. Probably in all, more than a dozen pastors and their wives and a couple dozen adults, and these the choicest of all of our churches. To question the game at all would be to question the discernment of all these counselors and adults standing on the shore excitingly following the game.

Literally hundreds of prayers were going up daily, most of which were praying for God's protection. Parents who had children here, pastors, Sunday school teachers, the staff at Maranatha constantly pray to this. In the light of this we can only leave this entire matter with God. He knows best. Our deepest appreciation to the pastors from all over this area who have called and expressed their heartfelt sympathy and their prayer support for Pastor and his wife, the Camp staff and our church, also parents and friends who called. These supporting phone calls have held us up during this very trying time.

Maranatha leadership commits itself to a greater attempt than ever before to continue to do everything in our power to continue to command the confidence of all of the parents who entrust their children to us. It should be said that boats were in the water at the scene of the tragedy. Never have we permitted any camper to go in any boat at any time without a life jacket on. We have scores of them on hand. Pray with us that we may find God's purpose in having permitted this tragedy.

– *Ivan E. Olsen*

As these 1960 photos illustrate, the tug 'o' war across the lake was a Camp tradition until a tragic accident resulted in the drownings of two campers in 1971.

The Light of the Cross

We were driving on a cold winter night.
My husband and I just had such a fight.
My eye was swollen and I had a black and blue chin.
I always kept my prayers deep within.
Oh Lord, I need a sign that your love's still mine.
The hurt and shame I felt it came from within.
Not from you.
The night so black
The stars so few.
Oh Please dear Lord
It is I, Where are you?
Confused and alone here with this man.
Help me Lord if you can.

When off in the distance on the side of the road
Is that a Cross I see showing just for me?
I've been on this road hundreds of times
Never seeing it, was it always there?
Truly Lord your spirit is near.
I thanked the Lord for the cross that night
For it showed he cared even when I lost sight.
Out of the depths of confusion and sin
The cross gave me hope and faith anew.
Look up and see the cross shines bright for you and me.
Now come to the cross. Find your Savior and friend.
He will show you the path.
So no matter what happens you'll have peace within.

– *Dianna G. Hawkins,*
Fremont, Nebraska

God Uses Camp to Transform Both the Prankster and the Meek

I was so excited when I got the summer of 2003 *Newsline*, the newsletter of Maranatha Ministries. Like so many others, I have a history at your Camp, one that I would love to share.

I began attending the Berean Fundamental Church in Cheyenne, Wyoming as a senior in high school in 1973 and also as a new Christian. Immediately I got involved with the youth group. Bible Camp was a hot topic for the other students, so I decided I would love to participate with my newfound friends in Christ. About a dozen of us boarded vans and drove to Nebraska. I was amazed at the friendship and fellowship that abounded at Camp. I don't recall the speaker that year, or much of anything else, except for the hard oatmeal, the wonderful ice cube machine that helped cool us down, and the heat. The last day of camp was riotous. It seemed that the Lincoln, Nebraska, group and our group had an ongoing battle for supremacy. I was very shy and completely taken off guard when my Cheyenne friends unleashed their cans of shaving cream and slyly filled water balloons. Soon, the white lather was everywhere. It was in hair, on clothes, down backs, in sleeping bags, pillowcases and suitcases and even in the now empty dorm drawers. We were quickly shoved into the vans for the return trip. "We got away with it!" my fellow passengers snickered all the way home.

Of course, we returned for the high school winter retreat and again I was amazed with the warmth of friendships formed. I am sure that there were a few shenanigans, but I was still shy and as a new Christian I tried to keep a low profile.

As a newly graduated high school student, I decided I needed to go to Senior High Camp, just one more time. Our first evening at orientation, the emcee asked that the Cheyenne kids please wave. As we did so, he then asked us to keep our shaving cream where it belonged and as my buddies chuckled, I felt like slipping under my chair.

I recall this camping experience very vividly. First off, our main speaker in 1974 was Lloyd Spear. As he spoke, I soon lost my heart to the passion he had for the Lord. Not only did he challenge me spiritually in a way that I had never experienced before, yet he had such practical advice for teenagers. During one of his messages, we had a terrific hailstorm come through. The noise was so loud from the stones hitting the corrugated metal roof that we had to wait for half an hour for him to continue. When he was able to go on, he spoke of the secular song, Anticipation. (Anticipation, is making me wait.) He talked about the free love that our society deemed acceptable. He talked face to face to us about retaining our virtue, what was appropriate in the clothing we wore, in our speech and in our lifestyles. He touched a place in my heart that had never been touched before. I rededicated my life to the Lord that week, as did many others. I honestly know that God used that man in so many special ways. I watched my friends closely over the next month. They were so on fire for the Lord. When some of them began to slip back into their old ways, it broke my heart and I remember pleading to God that that would never happen to me.

I need to back up, just for a moment now. There was a young man, Bryan Kirk, who was also attending Camp with me. He was from the same youth group that I attended. He had always treated me rather badly at school, because he was a "jock," and still holds many of the high school records, while I was the shy geek. One day at Camp, I was walking out of Needham Hall when he called me from his dorm room window. My friends went on without me as I stepped back to where he was. He stuttered around a little, than he blurted out, "Will you go with me to the banquet on Friday night?" Feeling rather weak in the knees, I nodded yes. He leaned out of the window and gave me a light kiss on the cheek. And as they say, the rest is history. Bryan and I married several years later and have been married for 27 years this coming September. We were both pure on our wedding day and I know that Pastor Spear's devotion and dedication to the Lord helped make that possible. I still claim that I got my first kiss at Camp!

I have family that lives in Kansas, so each year as we make our trek to see them, we pass Maranatha Bible Camp with a beep and a wave and a tenderness of heart.

Many of Bryan's family as well as my own have attended various events sponsored by Camp Maranatha. My husband came back as a counselor several years after we were married and he recalled to me the other day the response that he got from some of the permanent staff members. They remembered him well as a student and they were rather disturbed with the fact that this young man who was always on K.P. for his pranks actually had the audacity to come back as a counselor. They were teasing him of course and he proved to be a worthy addition to the Camp because as he told his youngsters, "I've been here, I've done it, so don't even try it." My niece worked for the Camp last summer and as I write this, I think of the young man from my youth group who is currently on staff. Also, my daughter returned home just last week with her tales of Maranatha as a counselor. As we visited, I discovered that many changes have taken place and she has convinced me that next summer as we drive by, instead we should stop by to see the wonderful blessings God has provided at Camp. Oh yes, my daughter was able to lead one of her students to the Lord during her week as counselor! Praise God!

Thank you so much for being a wonderful part of my early development as a Christian. I walk very closely with my Lord and He has led me through some amazing and awesome adventures. 1) I lost my sister in a domestic violence attack in 1986 and since then have been working closely with her murderer, my brother-in-law to stop such attacks, as well as promoting abstinence from drug and alcohol abuse. 2) Bryan and I worked for a combined 28 years in three different AWANA groups. Most of that time was spent as director and commander. 3) I was able to work for several years in Teen Challenge Christian Academy where girls were sent as an alternative to jail. 4) I worked for many years in a nursing home as the Christian advocate in the social service and activity department. I was encouraged to share my faith with those dear old folks and even got to help in the full immersion baptism of two of them. 5) I now work at one of our local high schools with students that are considered to be "at risk" as well as those that are handicapped. And, because of my close involvement with the youth ministry at my church, conversations about my faith in Christ happen frequently in a public school! 6) I was blessed with leading both of my children to the Lord at young ages, their daddy was blessed with baptizing them. Our son and daughter are faithfully serving God in our community.

I believe that God answered the prayer that I prayed so many years ago that I remain faithful to Him. I believe that because of the strong foundations given to me through my church and the work of your faithful servants at Maranatha Bible Camp, I can testify of His faithfulness to me, to my husband, my children and all that we stand for. Thank you seems rather pale in comparison to how I truly feel. Be blessed as you have blessed.

– Susan (Wilson) Kirk,
Cheyenne, Wyoming

Friends at Senior High Camp 1974. From left: Rhonda Lerninger, Kathy Remser, Carol Bates, Larry Lerninger and Darlene Hueftle.

Left: Susan Wilson, 1974. Right: Lloyd Spear, 1974 Senior High Camp speaker.

Shavers Kept Maranatha Maintained and Fed

My Daddy and Mom (Rex and Patsy Shaver) felt the will to serve the Lord at Maranatha when Rev. Olsen expressed the need for a man who could work as a leader in the completion of the new kitchen/dining hall and chapel - now known as Olsen Memorial. He also put in the fireplaces still in use.

He laughs when he said he was a "jack-of-all trades and master of none" as he tried to keep up with repairs of all types and "making do" with the resources available. Memorable moment - Flood of '73 as he had to organize the volunteers and navigators present to sand-bag and do whatever necessary to protect the Camp.

Mom served as a cook, baker, canner and hostess to many campers and Christian workers who needed food and rest.

They were there from 1970-1977. Mom went to be with the Lord in 2000. She took her gift of sharing her faith seriously wherever she was.

They both enjoyed their time at Camp and have a full appreciation of the hard work of all of those who now are in service at Maranatha.

– Mary Matzke,
Ellis, Kansas

Left: Patsy Shaver kept Maranatha's campers and workers fed throughout the 1970s. She is shown here with Bill Rogers. Right: Rex Shaver installed the septic system for the new dining hall/chapel building in 1971.

Struggling Up Sioux Lookout Changed Her Life

I found it a slightly dangerous thing to begin reliving my many memories of Maranatha. I was amazed at how many emotions came back with them. Youth is such an intense time of grappling with relationships, values, and how you view yourself, God, your world and your future. I found my memories of those times to be centered mostly around the people I met at Camp. While the grounds themselves were conducive to fun - and great times of devotion in the morning! - it is the people who had the deepest impact on me. And surprisingly, it is not so much the good teaching I remember, but the spontaneous moments of encouragement, confirmation, and challenge.

I met one of the dearest friends of my life at Camp, Sue (Slagle) Reisman. Her acceptance and affection is something I still treasure. I was amazed to find I could still remember the words to one of the songs we learned from Joe Costantino as we sat singing along with his guitar on a picnic bench during High School Week. The song went, "I wanna be a more righteous man, I wanna be a godly man, Teach me to do what I can to follow closer to you." As I remembered Joe singing that song I realized what drew me to friends like that. They shared the same longing to know God and to be what He wanted us to be. We had our struggles with our sinful natures like everyone else, but God had given us the desire to be different from the rest of the world by living godly lives and doing great things for Him, and it was sweet to express that desire with our friends.

One of my other strong memories is of climbing up Sioux Lookout. It's not much of a mountain, really, but I had a hard time anyway, and it got harder every year. The doctors would not diagnose my SMA until later in college, so I had to struggle with physical challenges like climbing without knowing why. But every time I struggled up that hill, there was always someone who hung back with me and kept telling me I could make it. Sometimes it was someone I didn't even know, God bless them. With the progression of the disorder, climbing is out of the question now, but I have memories of getting to the top and feeling the sense of having persevered. It didn't matter that I wasn't one of the first to the top. I believe that struggle was just another little piece of what God used to make me the person that I am.

Since my days as a camper and counselor at Maranatha I earned my BA in education and spent three years teaching in a mission/international school in Dakar, Senegal, West Africa. When I returned I became involved in the youth ministry at my home church in Sterling, and I enjoy helping these teens grow through those teen years that helped shape me.

I am grateful for the part Maranatha Bible Camp played in my life.

– Donna Lynch,
Sterling, Colorado

Sue Slagle (left) and Donna Lynch at Winter Retreat 1978.

Family at Maranatha is a Happy Memory

I worked in the kitchen in the late 1960s or early 1970s. I came out right after school closed and left for home before school started in the fall.

My daughter, Othelia, worked with crafts and my son, Tim, worked with boats. My daughter, Arleta, baby-sat.

Those are such happy memories for me! I thank God for my memories.

– Hulda Goossen,
Colby, Kansas

Winning the 'Battle for the Mind'

While I was in junior and senior high, much of my time was spent at Maranatha. My father was involved in many building projects at Camp and the whole family helped whenever possible. We attended chapel services each morning and stayed on in the evening whenever there was a special speaker. The teaching I received there helped form a foundation for my life. Truths learned from Dr. Olsen's sermon "The Battle for the Minds of Men" have been a particular help to me.

At Camp I met the young man who later became my husband. Our family has served in Thailand as missionaries with New Tribes Mission since 1981.

– Debbie (Wagner) Shimmin,
Thailand

The Story Behind the Playground

I don't know if you ever look around the Camp and wonder how or why something is there. I do because I know the rest of the story behind the playground pieces that are scattered around.

As a young girl, I was determined to rebel against my Dad. Most of the time I managed to barely stay out of trouble, but rebellion was a weed that had taken over the garden of my heart. When we moved to a new community and Dad forbade me to go to a particular church, I went as soon as a friend invited me.

Stubborn, rebellious, angry, wild were all words that Dad used to describe me. When my church friends invited me to go with them to Camp, I fussed, whined, begged and pleaded for a year for my parents to let me go. Probably just to shut me up, they acquiesced.

I couldn't tell you what the speaker said that week, but I knew without a doubt after the first night that if I died right then I would be going to hell. Every night we sang a song that seemed to pierce me to the core, but the weed of rebellion gripped my heart so that I thought that somehow I could fool God and be okay. Finally on the fourth night I walked to the front of the chapel to meet with a counselor who walked me through scripture and prayed with me as I asked Christ to take care of my sins. I had no idea how that would change my life! The counselor who talked with me said that I was now a new creation in Christ. I couldn't really see any difference, but Mom and Dad did when I arrived home. Rebellion was slowly being replaced by respect. Involvement in the church replaced the rebellious activities.

Dad had never been one to like "religious" people or places, but he said many times that whatever changed me at Camp was a very good thing. As I got older, the pastor of our church and his family became good friends. We talked a lot and he began to feel a real burden for my Dad, so he devised a scheme. Since he knew that Dad would never come to church, and a relationship between the two of them wouldn't just happen, he would get Dad to help him with a project. The project needed to be big enough to give them plenty of time together. Dad had made swing sets, teeter-totters, and monkey bars before, so how about if he could get him to do that for the Camp? Pastor came up with some new, creative ideas as well. This would give them time together to build a relationship. Through this Dad grew to respect and admire Pastor. Along the way Pastor would talk with Dad about Christ. Dad would always get angry and rude with Pastor when he talked about Christ, but Dad would say that Pastor was a respectable man.

The playground equipment is a reminder to me not only of a Savior who changed my life, but of a Pastor who cared, and a Dad who still needs a Savior. There are many kids who come to camp with friends and meet a Savior who changes their life, but when they go home they go back to homes that may be antagonistic to Christ. As you see the playground equipment remember them and pray for them. Pray that they will continue to grow in Christ. Pray that they will have a loving pastor who will be burdened for their families. Pray. Pray for the counselors who will be working with the kids. Pray for the kids who will be bringing friends. Pray for the friends who will come. Pray for the work to continue.

– Ruth Krehbiel,
Sterling, Colorado

Camp 'Cop' and Nurse Remember Involvement

Our Camp memories go back to the 1960s and early 70s. I know Arthur spent many hours fixing and helping build housing or making major repairs. He also helped at the Junior and Senior High youth camps for several years (Camp Policeman!).

I was Camp nurse in a tiny old building near the swimming pool for two or three summers (no major injuries). It was a nice change for me to go to Camp. At that time, we had five children who enjoyed their freedom and the activities (a relief from Mom's child care at home). We had no air conditioning—accommodations were rather primitive compared to now, but the Lord did great works there and blessings made it all worthwhile.

Our four older children all spent several weeks there, either at Camp proper or with their Dad.

I am thrilled about all of the progress in buildings, rec facilities and growth in numbers of camps and numbers of people. A lot of this is due to George Cheek's faithful work over the years. The speakers, of course, have been really top-notch. So I give praise to God and thanks to Dr. Ivan Olsen for his foresight in beginning a great work. May it continue until He comes.

– Mary Van Campen,
Dallas, Texas

Art and Mary Van Campen

Top row, from left: Indian Village operated for several summers on the south side of the lake with directors Warren Cheek, Larry Harper and Tom Collins; The confidence course was built in the 1970s by Lincoln Berean Youth under the direction of John and Debbie Wetzig.

Second row, from left: Hikes to the top of Sioux Lookout were a regular feature into the 1970s; One of the old "slab cabins" was converted into a boating equipment storage building; Wanda Anderson (left) and Grace Lehman have a minor disagreement during Winter Retreat 1976.

Third row, from left: Tom Walker (left) and an unidentified young man try to stay warm during Winter Retreat 1976; Camp board member Duane Norman and his son, Jonathan, at Camp during the 1970s; Tom and Janet Walker led a Maranatha sponsored missions trip to Canada.

Fourth row, from left: Three couples whom God used to help build a new Dining Hall in the early 1970s. From left, Ivan and Alice Olsen, Carl and Dora Yeutter, Ed and Eleanor Fasse; Two views of the new Dining Hall/Kitchen/Chapel building was authorized in 1970 and completed and dedicated in 1972, originally named the Yeutter Memorial Building, it was renamed the Olsen Memorial Building in 1977.

Top row, from left: Junior campers hike up the eroded hillside leading to Sioux Lookout; Curt Lehman listens during a meeting in 1979.

Second row, from left: Two views of recreation time at Junior Camp 1975 included a bucket and brigade-style relay and a frog-jumping contest; Prepared to depart from Colby, Kansas, for Junior Camp in 1976 are children, from left: Bonnie Barrett, Audrey Weed, Beth Siebert, DeAnna Dean, Keith Horney and Jeff Faber. Adults, from left: Becky Engelhardt, Keith Jones and Pastor Fran Harwerth.

Third row, from left: Glenn Ashcraft cast a menacing shadow during Winter Retreat 1976; Campers listen closely during an orientation session at the 1973 Junior Camp; Progress is evident on the new Dining Hall building in 1971.

Fourth row, from left: In the 1970s Gil Larsen took over as program director of the Junior Camp; Junior campers watch a skit in 1978; Claudine Lehman surveys the Platte River Valley as she climbs Sioux Lookout.

127

The Cheeks

In 1965, a 12-year-old boy from the mountains of Colorado heard a distinct call from God, and he determined in his heart that he would follow it for the rest of his life. George Walter Cheek had grown up enjoying the outdoor life with his father, Merle, and his younger brother, Warren. Hiking, backpacking, camping, hunting, fishing — they loved it all. Especially memorable was the 10-day, 100-mile hiking and camping trip over the Continental Divide and back that George took with Warren, starting and ending the trek in their back yard, using no vehicles. They packed and prepared their own food along the way.

"He was probably 16 that summer," said George's mother, Stella. They loved camping and fishing. Merle took them fishing from the time they were little guys."

Nearly a decade before that trip, George had sunk his roots deeply into Christian camping. From his elementary school days, George attended summer camps at Mt. Elim Bible Camp, a rustic, 60-bed camp located in the Yampa River valley near his family's home in Steamboat Springs, Colorado. "I clearly remember names, faces and lessons of speakers and missionaries who had a part in these weeks," George recalled. "They were certainly very developmental in my decision-making process."

So were his parents, who were strong supporters of Christian camping. Merle, a board member at Mt. Elim Camp, had moved with his family from Illinois to Routt County, Colorado, at age 7 and eventually attended high school in Steamboat Springs. Merle, who grew up in an unchurched home, accepted Christ as his Savior at age 17 through the intervention of a Sunday school teacher. After high school, Merle spent four years in the Army Air Corps. Stella, a native of Kansas, also moved with her family quite early in life to the High Plains of northeastern Colorado. She accepted Christ at age 14. Stella met Merle at Rockmont College (formerly Denver Bible Institute), and they married before their senior year in college. After their graduation, they moved to Steamboat Springs and raised their family there.

Merle & Stella raised their children in an evangelical household. George accepted Christ as savior at home when he was very young, and made a recommitment at Euzoa Bible Church after watching a gospel film.

Merle & Stella attended Euzoa Bible Church in Steamboat Springs, and soon George was involved in the music ministry there, joining the choir as an eighth-grader. "For awhile, he was the only man in the choir," his mother recalled. "In 10th grade, he and some of his friends organized a gospel singing group, and they went around to different places and sang."

George started singing for funerals when he was 16 years old and has sung at well over 100 since then.

George, as well as Warren and their sisters, Lavon and Donna, spent a lot of time at camp. "After they got out of second grade, they could go," said Stella. "I think they might have missed one year in all that interval in going to Mt. Elim Bible Camp." It was at Mt. Elim that George felt the call from God. He committed his life to serving God through Christian camping, envisioning that his life's work would be somewhere in the Rockies.

As a high school student, George spent weeks at a time volunteering at Mt. Elim and other Christian ministries. After graduating from Steamboat Springs High School in 1971, George left home, moved to Mt. Elim and commuted 30 miles one way to work in a coal mine. When he got off work at 4 p.m., he returned to do volunteer work at the camp until dark.

George entered Western Bible Institute in the Denver metro area and joined a men's quartet, where he sang bass. In 1972, at a retreat at Horn Creek Ranch in

Colorado, George talked with Russ Johnston, who had led Navigator Training Program sessions at Maranatha for years. "You ought to spend a summer at Maranatha," said Russ. "You could learn a lot from Ivan Olsen. And they just built a brand-new dining hall by the lake!" George, imagining a rustic log-framed lodge with vaulted ceilings, agreed that it was worth a try. He would get valuable experience at Maranatha before he moved on to the place that God would show him. That winter, he traveled to work at Maranatha's Winter Retreat.

George Cheek first arrived at Maranatha in December 1972. On his first tour of the grounds with Rev. Olsen, he saw a long, low-profile metal building with a rounded roof. "I was surprised that they had a paved parking lot by the maintenance shop," he said. "Then, we went inside and I was surprised that the hallway was carpeted."

To his surprise, it turned out to be the dining hall/chapel building, and Cheek knew he wasn't in the Rockies any more. Over the years, he would become more accustomed to the frugal western Nebraska mindset.

Adrian House was president of Western Bible Institute when George began attending there. He also was on the Maranatha Camp board at the time. When George made an appointment to ask advice about coming to Maranatha for the summer of 1973, Adrian told him it would be a good thing for the summer, but not to expect the job to last much longer than that because it was his observation that "no one stayed there" very long. Over the ensuing years, they reminisced about that conversation several times. More than 30 years later, in a conversation with Adrian's wife, Juanita, George agreed that where God leads, He enables.

George needed wisdom to adapt to his new surroundings. "When he came here to Maranatha, he said, 'That's not running a camp; that's running a motel.' His idea of camping was camping outdoors," said Stella Cheek. Nebraska summers were hotter and more humid than George had known in Colorado, but he adapted to both the new environment and a different style of camping.

There were more surprises ahead. When Cheek started working at Maranatha in 1973, Olsen didn't break him in gradually. Cheek immediately shouldered "more responsibility than I ever thought I'd have so soon." Most of the daily supervision of the summer workers fell to the 20-year-old Coloradoan, who assumed the title of staff coordinator. The much-heralded Navigator Training Program had ended in 1971.

Cheek had plenty to do besides organizing the summer staff. Olsen assigned him responsibility for the day-to-day administrative operations of the Camp as well, and he responded with vigor. He set standards of cleanliness in dormitories, restrooms and the dining hall, complete with detailed checklists. He planned recreation schedules for various Camp programs, and evaluated the programs themselves. He had ideas for skits and group singing at camper mealtimes. Cheek suggested that "outstanding camper" awards be given, based on points to be allocated for performance in Camp games, cleanliness and Bible memory work.

Cheek made checklists for yearly Camp promotion and cataloged prospective camper-sending churches within a 100-mile radius of Maranatha. He made checklists for opening Camp buildings in the spring and closing them in the fall. He created daily summer checklists for himself that included everything from observing staff work crews to food preparation to collecting money from pop machines and the Sweet Shop. He was in charge of recruiting and hosting rental groups. He assumed responsibility for preparing the Camp brochure in 1974, after only a year on the staff. Cheek even familiarized himself with fundraising, which had been Olsen's turf.

"George Cheek was sent of God to us, to train for camping," wrote Olsen in his 1973 report to the Camp board. "He felt led of God to stay over a full year after the summer was over. George is a born leader, with real capability. He is easily followed, and deeply spiritual. The summer staff … was one of the brightest spots in the entire year. George Cheek immediately led them. We did not have five minutes of problem all summer, and their work was done unbelievably well."

By the end of the summer, Olsen invited Cheek to stay on "at least through next summer." He continued to work at Camp that winter and commuted to Mid-Plains Community College in North Platte, where he continued some of his studies. He could see much more that needed to be done at Maranatha, but Olsen also asked for his help at the Berean Church in North Platte, where Cheek began serving part-time as youth pastor in the fall of 1973. He also took a leadership role in the church's ministry to children, serving as commander of the AWANA program, a post he would hold for 15 years. Colorado seemed a distant memory.

Cheek's multiple ministries continued throughout the winter, but he refocused on Maranatha as summer approached. Olsen and Cheek recruited a capable 1974 summer staff, which included future pastors Dan Lehman, Doug Shada, Tom Walker and Bryan Clark. That staff tested the serious young staff coordinator with several pranks. One night, several of the young men picked up Cheek's tiny green two-door Honda automobile and, using bridge planks at strategic points, maneuvered it into the shallow west end of Lake Maranatha to spend the night on a small sandbar.

"He gave us no pleasure at all the next morning," said Walker. "He just showed up at breakfast and announced that he needed his car to go to town that morning. He never even cracked a smile."

"The funniest part of that whole deal was that it didn't faze him," remembered Clark. "We didn't even get a rise out of him. We were kind of wanting him to holler or scream or something."

People were watching as George Cheek dealt with boisterous summer staff, guest group recruitment, maintenance issues and his responsibilities at the Berean Church. Ed & Alice Felgate lived at Maranatha and did much volunteer work throughout most of the 1970s. They had been observing the young man with the wire-rimmed glasses, light blond hair and sideburns.

"A handsome young man lived next door to us, and what a pleasure it was," recalled Alice. "He dropped by at mealtime, and we were so happy to have him sit and eat with us. My, he ate anything — no fuss. He became general director of the Camp. We knew he was a dedicated young man and willing to do all things, and very capable, too."

Cheek eventually did every type of job on the Camp, then started supervising them all. He began to diversify Maranatha, making it more outdoor-oriented. He was on a fast track toward high-level leadership.

By the fall of 1974, George had been given the title of Camp manager. He was spending less time with the Felgates because he needed to prepare for his wedding. Three years earlier, he had met a young woman from Redlands, California, named Jan Rush, at Western Bible Institute. George & Jan were married in September and moved into Summerville House, a two-story structure that had been moved from North Platte. The Cheeks would live in that house for more than 20 years.

Jan immediately got involved in Camp life, doing painting and housekeeping and serving in the kitchen, Craft Shop and the Switchboard (later referred to as the Information Center).

George continued his schooling, eventually getting an associate's degree from Mid-Plains in 1976. Earlier that year, Jan gave birth to their son, Kris. In the fall of 1977, their daughter, Tara, was born.

At the time of Tara's birth, the Cheek family was commuting from Maranatha to Denver, where George was taking classes at Western Bible Institute and Rockmont College. A friend let them use a house in Denver from Monday through Friday, and they drove back to Camp on weekends until the school year ended the next spring. George finished his schooling by correspondence and received degrees from both W.B.I. and Rockmont.

"Some time after that, the process of Dr. Olsen asking us to stay on for 'one more summer' came to an end, and we agreed to give plenty of notice should we decide the Lord was calling us to a different ministry," said Cheek.

Even before his children were born, Cheek seemed to have put down roots in Nebraska, but to most close observers, all doubt was removed after the Camp Board meeting of October 1976. Cheek gave reports on income projections and future site development. Along with program director Curt Lehman, he recommended that a new rate structure be put in place. Later at that same meeting, Cheek was voted a full member of the Camp board at 23 years of age, joining president Carl Goltz and board members Ivan Olsen, Curt Lehman, Ed Fasse, Ernest Lott, Hugh Clark, Adrian House, Don Hunt, Max Fogland, Kenneth Blood and Ralph Scott. By then, Cheek had worked for two years with Theodore Epp, who retired from the board in 1975.

"To a close observer, the stamp of George in Maranatha Bible Camp is by increased camping outreach," wrote Olsen, who marveled at the way Cheek was using canoeing, backpacking and Indian Village programming to reach young people.

In just a few years, Cheek had earned Olsen's trust. It was only a matter of time, he knew, before Cheek would be ready to take over the entire operation. In fact, Olsen, having worked closely with the young leader, was getting ready to retire many years before the Camp board was ready to let him go. The board had difficulty imagining the existence of Maranatha Bible Camp without Ivan Olsen and his fundraising ability.

"The public needs to gain a respect and confidence, which only time and acquaintance can bring about," Olsen told Cheek. Relations with the Camp board were every bit as vital: "I cautioned a few years ago, having watched me take liberties as I did, you would have to be very careful you did not try to be me," said Olsen, "because you must earn their confidence before they will let you go ahead."

Cheek, with his new title of executive director, essentially ran Maranatha Bible Camp beginning in 1977, with Olsen doing most of the fundraising.

That fall, with Cheek having served at Maranatha less than five years, Olsen spoke openly about his desire that George Cheek be his successor "when he would retire or at such a time as he might be unable to continue his ministry in this capacity." The board voted that fall that Cheek should be made interim director if a health issue arose which would keep Ivan Olsen from continuing in his role.

Cheek waited patiently for the Camp board to decide his future with the Camp. Olsen had planned to retire as early as 1986, but the board voted to retain him through the Camp's golden anniversary celebration in 1988, and after that, asked him to stay on through March 1989, when it finally accepted his resignation as general director. The board named Cheek as interim general director, then seven months later, approved him as general director.

Once fully in charge, Cheek continued to be a hands-on, detail-oriented leader who was committed to cooperating fully with the Camp board and the board of management.

Cheek, knowing that God had led him away from the Rocky Mountains to Nebraska, kept track of what he referred to as "God sightings," situations where God had intervened and answered prayers or provided people to do His work. When Cheek was introduced at a Maranatha event, he often commented, "I came for a summer, and I'm still here." That was at least partly because he loved life at "Midwest campground." He has always enjoyed stopping to appreciate his surroundings, as was evident in the July 1989 receipt letter that he wrote from Summerville House:

"A new day is unfolding here at Maranatha. It's 6:30 a.m., and I'm watching the robins bouncing across the lawn looking for breakfast. A young rabbit just hopped through the lawn and not one bird flew up in alarm. The recent abundance of rains has turned the Camp as green as if it were late May. A few minutes ago, many of the summer staff walked down the sidewalk on their way to attend the daily 6:30 a.m. staff meeting. At 7 o'clock, I'll be taking the family campers that are interested on a 'boundary walk,' an optional activity before breakfast. Soon, the whole Camp will be alive with campers and the sound of laughter will be coming from the Dining Hall. This morning is donut morning, so the smell of donuts will greet them as they approach the Dining Hall."

His enjoyment of Camp life has been immense. Whenever a summer camp was in session throughout the 1990s, he would turn up unexpectedly in his golf cart, often with a potential donor sitting beside him. George relishes befriending people and giving them a firsthand look at what God is doing at Maranatha. He and Jan host visitors on an increasing basis as he delegates more authority to departmental directors and transitions to a less "hands-on" role as chief executive officer.

His family grew up at Maranatha, living on site the entire time with the exception of the Denver commute of 1977-78, whereas the Olsen family had spent much of every year living at the Berean parsonage in North Platte. Kris and Tara attended school at Maxwell, where they were involved in sports and many other school activities. George & Jan saw their children go to Christian colleges and return to live in Nebraska. Kris founded a sports evangelism outreach called SportReach, which became affiliated with Maranatha in 2001, and Tara does volunteer work with SportReach.

After the children moved out of their home, George & Jan agreed to give up Summerville House to be used by a large family that was about to join the staff. In 1997, at the urging of the Camp board, they began to raise money for a large cabin on the south shore of Lake Maranatha that would be owned by the Camp and serve as the director's home. They moved into the finished house in November 2002 and dedicated it debt-free, completely paid for by designated gifts.

Just as Olsen had at least two or three ministries going on at any particular time, so does Cheek. Besides his involvement at North Platte Berean (where he is an elder, a choir member, sings in a men's quartet and is a member of the Christian education committee), he is a board member of Christian radio station KJLT in North Platte.

In the 1990s, another passion began to energize George Cheek. Having been involved firsthand in ministry to various ethnic groups at Camp, he explored opportunities for evangelizing foreign countries. India has been his main interest. He chairs the Berean Fundamental Church Council's foreign church planting committee, which established a partnership with Campus Crusade for Christ for the purpose of starting 300 churches by the year 2006. He helped organize the structure of the church planting effort, making six trips to India by January 2004, meeting with Campus Crusade staff and interviewing prospective pastors.

Cheek and his old friend Russ Johnston developed a common interest in helping start a Christian camp in Russia; they traveled there in May 2003.

In the fall of 2003, Maranatha Bible Camp, the Maranatha Camp Foundation and SportReach were reorganized into a larger entity, Maranatha Ministries, and George was named CEO. Having established a strong leadership team to run the day-by-day needs of the organizations, he has begun a more active role in fundraising with the goal of eliminating the ministry's debt and updating the Long Range Plan.

VOICES OF MARANATHA

Creating an Oasis in a Secular, Material World

I think one of the most obvious indications of God's love for and blessing upon Maranatha Bible Camp had to be His bringing the Cheek family to this area. (You are *all* so special!)

How exciting to watch your vision for a missionary outreach become a reality—indeed, to prove how God is able to do the "exceedingly above" all that we ask or think!

In the early 1970s Max and I purchased the mobile home and installed it there at Camp. Not too long afterwards, Maranatha took it over and it has been Ruth Ann Rodgers' home since. There is such a heavenly, peaceful atmosphere out there, it certainly is an oasis in a world saturated with the material and secular.

I remember helping in the kitchen in the 1950s and occasionally with some cleaning after that. Max did donate many hours helping with the construction of the main dining hall and chapel; I know he was happy to do it.

Dennis, Dan and Steve all attended Camp there and recall both humorous and serious times. I don't believe anyone could come away untouched spiritually. I personally heard many unforgettable messages that challenged me to live for that which has eternal value.

God bless you. With leadership like yours, I'm sure the Lord will continue to smile on Maranatha.

– Fern Fogland,
North Platte

Maranatha, a 'Great Way to Invest Our Lives'

Jan Cheek, who has worked with her husband since 1974 to expand the ministry of Maranatha Bible Camp, wrote this in 2004.

I came to Maranatha as a new bride in the fall of 1974. George had been working here for two summers already. Maranatha has been a place that has inspired me to grow in my walk with the Lord.

We've raised our two children here and they in turn have made life-changing decisions and commitments because of the many people who have come across their paths (i.e. speakers, leaders, cabin leaders and peers, as well as those who have labored alongside us over the years in this thing called ministry).

We came for a summer, and now, 30 years later, we're still finding it satisfying to challenge those who come for a weekend, a week, for the whole summer or just once for a short time, to make Jesus the Lord of all in their lives.

Living and serving at Maranatha has been a great way to invest our lives.

– Jan Cheek

Maranatha's Influence Around the World

In the fall of 1983, I was glad to be through the summer of flooding from the North Platte River. This had been a controlled flood released from Lake McConaughy, which lasted six weeks. There was also a good response financially from Maranatha's friends to help with the financial loss of camp cancellations and flood-related expenses.

Jan and I had been prayerfully considering if we should stay at Maranatha longer or move on to other Bible Camp ministries who where calling, writing or sending leaders to stop by and "visit." I also wondered about exploring the possibility of moving to another country to be involved in a similar work.

The summer ended with a new group of campers from the Christian & Missionary Alliance's Hmong district, and they were excited about returning in the year ahead. They brought the prospect of a new missions dimension to our ministry.

During that year, a vision came into focus for me. I realized we could document that our efforts here were actually touching the world. It was that concept that God used to help Jan and me decide to set the anchor and stay right at Maranatha for the foreseeable future rather than accept other invitations.

At that time we identified 220 countries from the resource book *Operation World*. The year 2000 was intriguing to many. We announced that we would like to document by letters of testimony how many of the countries of the world would have been served by a camper who either accepted Christ or made a commitment for missionary service while at Maranatha.

George W. Cheek arrived at Maranatha in 1973 with the intention of staying for the summer. Within five years, he was responsible for the Camp's daily operation. This photo with his wife, Jan and children, Kris and Tara, was taken in 1980.

Thus the 220 by 2000 Project was born.

By the time we reached the end of 2000, our letter file showed 55 countries were touched under the above criteria. There were a number of others who checked in who had been at Maranatha Camp and went on to serve outside the country, but had come to that decision independent of their Maranatha experience. Only heaven will tell the complete story!

– George Cheek

Left: George Cheek often found himself "multitasking." Here he instructs Camp staff how to line up the Maranatha's entry in the 1980 Nebraska-land Days parade before he appeared in the parade with an Awana entry (Cheek was Awana commander at North Platte Berean Church for many years). Right: A crossroads in the history of Maranatha: Pastor Ivan Olsen (front row, right side) lines up for one of his final group photos in the still-unfinished gymnasium, a building he raised much money for. George Cheek (far left) finished the gym and took the Camp into the 21st century.

The Director's House Project

Part of Maranatha Bible Camp's Long Range Plan includes a set of cabins on the south shore of Lake Maranatha. The cabins are to be built and donated by friends of Camp who will have first priority to schedule vacation times and weekends in the cabin their family built. Otherwise, the cabins will be available for scheduling by the Camp office for individuals who want to spend time at Maranatha.

Jan and I asked the board for permission to raise designated funds for a house that we would live in as long as we are a part of Maranatha Ministries. Permission was granted and we started some fund raising quietly among a small group of friends and family, rather than using a broad appeal. The first gift was from Scott & Kim Fasse, a second-generation Camp family encouraging a second-generation Camp leader. The Fasses' gift helped get the infrastructure in place for the new housing area.

Other primary contributors included Russ Johnston (who first told the Cheeks about Maranatha more than 25 years earlier), the Max and Harriet Hasenauer Foundation (former college friends of George's parents), and longtime friends at AK Acres Farms near Imperial. In all, about 50 households contributed to enable the project to be dedicated debt-free in November 2002.

One of the major "God sightings" came in December 1999. The project was drawn up, the funds were half in, but no building start was scheduled. Chuck Lawson, a friend from college days and a Maranatha alumnus, called me from Chicago. He related that Aurora Christian School annually does a missions project during Easter vacation with contractors and students totaling about 100 people. Their upcoming project had just cancelled and was the house project at Maranatha ready to start? That was just the push we needed to get going. Their group did a "barn raising," and when they left, the plywood was on the roof.

The house has two unusual features. First it is built on a bridge made of 48 wooden utility poles and rail bridge timbers. This solves the problem of being in a flood plain with sandy ground. Such construction is common in coastal states, but may be the first such house in Nebraska.

The second unique feature is that the ceiling and window trim of the main room are made of native Maranatha cedar. A tornado passed through the Camp in 1998, and about 150 trees were lost. We saved most of the logs and allowed them to dry in the pile for two years. Then we brought in a portable sawmill and cut them into rough lumber and properly stacked them under the house to be dried

for another year. Jan and I, along with other volunteers, planed, edged, sanded and sealed the boards with urethane before nailing them into place.

In addition to the Aurora, Illinois, group, about 90 volunteer households helped with the work of building the house over a three-year period. Bruce Stucky acted as the general contractor, assisted by Mark Swesey and David Jones.

We moved into the house in November 2002. The home is a busy place of ministry, including my office and two guest rooms. Already by the end of June 2004, more than 1,000 people had signed the guest register.

– George W. Cheek

George and Jan Cheek used this machine to plane the cedar boards for their vaulted ceiling.

The director's house on the south shore of Lake Maranatha was built on poles.

Gift Shop, Maintenance are Enjoyable Retiree Responsibilities

We first heard about Maranatha Bible Camp when George came to Winter Retreat in 1972 with a Western Bible College quartet.

Our first trip to the Camp was with our family in 1973 when we were invited to visit George after he came on staff. We spent a few days at the Olsen home here on the grounds.

George and Jan were married in 1974. From that time until 1987, we visited Camp at regular intervals. Donna, Warren and Lavon all came and worked at Camp as summer staff at different times.

The summer of 1987, Dr. Olsen and George invited us to come to Camp as volunteer retirees. After prayerful consideration, we agreed to come. The following week, the Sanders donated a mobile home to Maranatha and moved it to Camp that fall. This has been our home at Camp.

We felt we needed to accomplish three things before we moved. We saw Lavon settled in new living quarters; final arrangements were completed for a KWBI repeater in Steamboat Springs; and our home sold to the first young couple who looked at it. We were free to move to Camp early in October 1987.

My responsibility (Stella's) from then until March of 2002, has been managing the Gift Shop. At that time I retired from being manager, but have continued to be a helper. Merle has worked at grounds maintenance, painting, and other odd jobs.

Our years as Camp volunteers have been rewarding and fulfilling. We will continue as the Lord gives us health and the ability to serve Him here.

– *Merle and Stella Cheek,*
Maranatha Bible Camp

Retired volunteers, Merle and Stella Cheek, are surrounded by their family on their 50th wedding anniversary. Back row, from left: Jeff Kautz, George Cheek, Kris Cheek, Elaine Cheek, Warren Cheek, Gary Mahnken. Second row, from left: Tara Kautz, Jan Cheek, Natalie Cheek, Lavon Cheek, Carol Cheek, Donna Mahnken. Front row, from left: Michael Mahnken, Charissa Cheek, Katie Mahnken, Silas Cheek.

Jan Cheek was a familiar face in the Switchboard (later renamed the Information Center). Mary Osler is at left.

George's sister, Donna Cheek Mahnken.

During the 1990s, George Cheek was commonly seen in his golf cart. Here he enjoys a conversation with Bob and Mary Harmon and Fred Gaymon.

George and Jan Cheek with Kris and Tara, 1983.

Doug and Farrol Shada and George and Jan Cheek enjoyed the 1984 Couples' Conference.

4-year-old Kris Cheek shows that he's at home in the wild West.

The 1980s

The first day of summer staff training is always hectic. There are dozens of new staff members who need to be welcomed and have many questions answered before they begin their summer of ministry, but George Cheek had been through 10 staff training weeks already, and as he prepared to start his 11th, his mind was on the task at hand. Every year, he had refined his training schedule to make it more efficient and to address problems that came up year after year. This year's would be the best so far, he hoped.

He had worked on the training schedule with John Meschke, the staff coordinator for the summer of 1983. John would be working directly with the summer staff as George had done his first few years at Camp. With George in charge of day-to-day operations of the entire ministry, he was glad to delegate this summer responsibility to John. He knew the pressures that the young man would face, and was ready to listen to him at a moment's notice.

So early on that morning of Monday, June 6, Meschke had Cheek's full attention when he returned from his run around Lake Maranatha and delivered an unexpected report: a stream of water was running into the lake on the west end. Other staff members quickly confirmed that Meschke's report was true. Exactly 45 years after Ivan Olsen and his supporters launched Maranatha's First Annual Encampment on the Ralph Talbot place, the flood of '83 had begun.

That stream of water changed the complexion of the entire summer at Maranatha Bible Camp. Much of the staff training schedule was out the window. The focus shifted from campers to sandbags, from discipleship to damage control.

It was not a big surprise. Out in Wyoming, trouble had been brewing. The previous few years had been wetter than normal, and the water levels were high at the various reservoirs all along the North Platte River. In addition, there had been huge amounts of snow that winter in the Wyoming Rockies.

"The various irrigation and government agencies were not working in sync," said Cheek. "All the dams were full, and they had to start releasing water."

All the water eventually flowed into the west end of Lake McConaughy, located on the North Platte River near Ogallala, Nebraska. The level of the lake raised to dangerous levels, and Kingsley Dam, on the east end of the lake, was threatened. A dam break would be catastrophic to the residents of the Platte Valley, so the stewards of the giant lake had to relieve the pressure on it by doing what their counterparts upstream had done: systematically release the water downstream for someone else to worry about.

The result was a controlled flood that lasted for six weeks.

After more than 25 years of no flooding problems, this was the third legitimate high-water alert that threatened Maranatha in less than 20 years. The near-miss flood of 1965 was the Camp's introduction to the drawbacks of owning property in a flood plain, but there had been only minor damage to the lake that year. In 1973, the lake had suffered major damage at both ends, but a miraculous gift of huge quantities of dirt from the State of Nebraska had helped solve that problem. Neither of the first two floods impacted the main part of the Camp grounds. This one did, in a major way.

Floodwater covered many roads around Camp in 1983, turning them into canals. Staff members could (and often did) travel more than a quarter-mile by boat from Needham Hall to the Olsen Memorial Dining Hall, but the water never quite rose high enough to damage any buildings. The Camp road was washed out and was impassable by car for more than a mile east of the grounds. Staff members parked their cars along the road at the last dry place and rode back and forth from the Camp to their cars via a four-wheel drive vehicle loaned by Berg Motors of North Platte and manned a retired volunteer named Loyal Willard. There was a 10 p.m. staff curfew so Loyal could go home and sleep.

Campers came to Maranatha for the first two weeks of the summer schedule, but the water kept slowly rising and the battle to save the property eventually became too consuming. It devastated the schedule. Five Camp weeks, including Awana Camp and two major guest groups, had to be canceled. Sandbagging became the main pastime for the summer staff of 1983.

It was not a dramatic flood, with bridges being smashed to rubble and cars being swept away by raging waters. There were areas in the region where water rushed powerfully across roads, but mostly, it was a seeping, slow-moving, low-key flood that kept coming at you, wearing you down with its sheer persistence.

"It was just unbelievable," said Cheek. "It was very controlled. Once it got up as far the sidewalk by the dining hall, it varied only one or two inches. You could see it rising and falling on the side of the sidewalk."

Throughout the United States, the 1980s had begun on a large wave of patriotism when the U.S. men's ice hockey team upset the powerful team from the Soviet Union on George Washington's birthday and went on to win the gold medal at the Winter Olympics in Lake Placid, New York. Later that year, Ronald Reagan was elected president and ushered in an era of optimism in America, overhauling many of the liberal social and economic policies of the previous two decades. In 1987, he challenged Soviet leader Mikhail Gorbachev to tear down the quarter-century-old Berlin wall, and amazingly, by the end of the decade, it had fallen.

The "we-can-do-it" attitude also prevailed at Maranatha, where the staff rolled up its sleeves and began to make some long-overdue updates to the Camp property and facilities. "We tackled a lot of renovation projects with aging buildings that needed to be remodeled and bathrooms that needed to be added," said Cheek, who hired three fulltime staff members to work in properties. In 1982, Bruce Stucky, a summer staffer from Kansas, stayed on year-round to supervise the day-to-day management of Maranatha's properties. By mid-decade, the Camp added Nebraska natives Mark Swesey and David Jones, who also had served on the summer staff. The three men, with the help of many volunteers, remodeled and insulated buildings, replaced septic systems, buried new electrical and phone lines, re-shingled dozens of roofs and built two new buildings – a bathhouse and a large workshop/storage facility.

In 1984, Ed Fasse's wife, Eleanor, spearheaded a drive to landscape the area around the Olsen Memorial Building. It improved the stark cement-and-metal look of the exterior immensely.

Cheek and his staff started to think long-term about site development. The Camp board authorized Cheek to begin working with former Navigator trainee Carter Volle and the Missionary Tech organization to develop a long-range site plan for Maranatha.

Some of the "can-do" spirit was fueled by God's provision of income through a new guest group. The Hmong tribe had begun using Maranatha for large rallies nearly every year starting in 1983. Crowds of 1,000 and more were common during Hmong weeks, and they helped the Camp's cash flow.

Cheek continued to build the fulltime staff. In 1982, he had hired Meschke, who did promotional work in addition to serving as staff coordinator. Meschke left by mid-decade, but in 1986, Jo Ann Beetem, a summer staffer from southeast Nebraska, came on as secretary and registrar. Wyoming native Joe Dapra was food service director for much of the 1980s. In 1989, Tad Stryker, who grew up about 50 miles from the Camp, joined the staff to oversee the housekeeping department, but soon took over many of the promotional responsibilities that Meschke had handled.

Ivan & Alice Olsen began to spend their winters in Florida, and Cheek, with the assistance of a newly-created Board of Management, ran the Camp, although Olsen continued to do the bulk of the fundraising. At the 1983 board meeting, Olsen announced his intention to retire in 1986. The board took no action at that time, but two years later, voted to retain Olsen as general director until Maranatha's 50th anniversary celebration was completed in 1988. It seemed to be a natural move, and Olsen accepted.

In 1984, the Camp board began to discuss the upcoming 50th anniversary of Maranatha and how to commemorate it. Olsen had celebrated the 40th anniversary a year early (in 1977, after just 39 years of operation), but decided to celebrate the golden anniversary in over the Independence Day weekend in 1988, after a full 50 years had elapsed.

As thoughts began to turn toward the upcoming celebration, God laid out another opportunity for the Camp. At about 6:30 a.m. during a busy Hmong youth week in August 1986, real estate agent Robert Martin of North Platte called Cheek with exciting news. The land adjoining Maranatha Bible Camp's eastern property line was coming up for sale.

Cheek, who had been praying the "prayer of Jabez" from 1 Chronicles 4 (almost two decades before the book came out), perceived that God was giving Maranatha another opportunity to expand its borders.

Cheek told Olsen about the phone call, and Olsen immediately called the landowner, Cal Miller, who lived in Canada. The two came to a tentative agreement during that phone call, and soon, a committee designated by the Camp board approved the purchase of the 167-acre tract of farmland and river bottomland. The Camp launched a fund drive to bring in the money to pay for the land, which has been used for outpost camping, a sporting clays course and a paintball course. It also produces crops of alfalfa in the 40-acre field that has not yet been developed.

The 50th anniversary occupied Olsen's thinking for months. He wrote a letter to Cheek making it clear that he would take personal responsibility for planning the major details of the weekend. Olsen wanted it to be a time of thanking God for His faithfulness, and he wanted it to be a Bible conference. He wanted Back to the Bible to be involved, as it had been when Theodore Epp was the main speaker at the silver anniversary celebration in 1963. Epp having died in 1985, Olsen invited his successor, Warren Wiersbe, to be the main speaker and asked Ward Childerston to return from Maryland to lead music. Olsen chose Louise (Merriman) Crooks, who had been active at Maranatha for many years, to be the main accompanist for the weekend.

A good writer, Olsen began to be more prolific as the golden anniversary year began, recording his remembrances of major events of the past, especially the miraculous intervention of God throughout the Camp's history. He had gotten rid of his typewriter and didn't own a computer, so he filled many pages with his own handwriting.

Maranatha celebrated its 50th anniversary during the hot, humid weekend of July 1-3, 1988. Olsen and Cheek worked together to script the entire program, which was built around six lengthy chapel sessions. They included Sam & Ella Becker and their daughter, Darlene, who sang throughout the weekend, as did Alice Olsen and Inez Maline. George Cheek sang two of his trademark songs, "The Lighthouse," and "People Need the Lord." Ward Childerston, and Louise Crooks (piano) worked together to lead congregational singing. Dwight Olsen gave up a European trip to play the organ at Camp.

Former state Sen. Maurice Kremer of Aurora, Nebraska, and a longtime friend of Maranatha Camp, spoke on patriotism. Wiersbe spoke five times throughout the weekend. Board president Carl Goltz spoke on the changing of the guard to a new generation of leaders that would step forward and lead the ministry into the future.

Olsen raised money throughout the weekend, taking several offerings ("Could I ask you to give the largest amount that you find it possible to be able to give?"). He also spoke about the "Miracles of Maranatha." The final gathering was a musical service and was themed around Maranatha's goals of salvation, discipleship, Christian service and patriotism.

Participants were thankful for the air conditioning on a steaming hot Sunday evening. The program led off with the Eugene Clark chorus, "Nothing Is Impossible." It included several songs by Dwight Olsen, who accompanied himself on the organ

George Cheek, whose bass voice by then was well-known throughout the region, sang "Water From the Rock" and his trademark solo, "People Need the Lord." Tad Stryker, who was less than a year from joining the fulltime staff, sang with his wife, Jean, in a Berean Church vocal group called the "Melody Messengers," led by Louise Crooks.

As the last service came to a close, Ivan & Alice Olsen stood together at the pulpit. The memories of half a century of hopes, dreams, work, prayers, victories, disappointments, changed lives and Christian fellowship welled up inside them.

"We have not done anything more than anyone could have done, had he stayed long enough," said Ivan. "The source of our strength has been the deep, deep prayer ministry of our companions, that I have been so grateful for. I want to thank all of you who have been so kindly disposed throughout the years. Each of you has made a contribution.

"We have new friends and we have old friends. The new are like silver, and the old are like pure gold. I thank God for those of you who have had so many, many years of investment in our life."

Alice Olsen also expressed her appreciation.

"I want to thank every single one of you who has made a sacrifice to be here. We thank you for making this 50th anniversary celebration a highlight in our lives," said Alice. " 'Maranatha,' in 1 Corinthians 16:22, means, 'Jesus is coming soon.' Let's get out there and reach the world for Christ."

The past had been celebrated. The future lay ahead. George Cheek had essentially run Maranatha Bible Camp during the decade of the 1980s. He had taken care of countless behind-the-scenes details before and during the golden anniversary weekend. Then he waited another 20 months to take over as general director while the Camp board slowly transitioned Olsen out of leadership. By the end of the decade, Cheek had become quite familiar with Olsen's methods of operation. He also knew that with society changing at a rapid rate and families facing new pressures, ministry was becoming more complex.

Throughout 1989, Cheek frequently referred to "this year of transition." That would become the theme for the entire next decade.

VOICES OF MARANATHA

Blessed by Maranatha

We have been blessed by Maranatha Bible Camp since 1962. Rev. Olsen would come to Lexington Berean Church. George and his brother would sing. They would share about Maranatha. Our prayers for support to Maranatha have been a blessing.

We have attended the July 4th picnic.

Our daughter, Barbara, has gone to Ladies' Retreat, enjoying the "Gift Shop," worship service, good food and fellowship. The joy of having a small part in helping Maranatha Ministry has been gratifying.

— Harold and Irdell Chase,
Lexington, Nebraska

Family Reunions at Maranatha

When space permits in the schedule, Maranatha Bible Camp hosts family reunions. Most families request a summer weekend, which can fill up rather quickly (non-summer weekends work well and are easier to schedule).

One of our requirements, because of our tax exemption for religious purposes, is there needs to be a Bible devotional for each overnight stay by a guest group such as a family reunion. Sometimes, the families plan their own structured worship services. If the family desires, a member of our staff speaks at the occasion, which sometimes takes place at the close of breakfast while the family sits together around the tables. These are often special times.

Some reunions are very small and casual, while others are fairly large and structured right down to different-colored T-shirts for descendants of various siblings.

An unforgettable event happened during the Mann Family Reunion one fine Saturday evening in July 1996. The family was enjoying a cookout at the basketball court near the horseshoe pits. A few children were playing on the giant swing set nearby as most of the family went through the food line at the chuck wagon. As it traditionally does, our staff was waiting for the guests to go through the line first.

One of the guests was a woman named Nancy, a relative of the Mann family, who had married an aspiring young coach. Her husband, who had become prominent in the world of college football over the next three decades, had arrived earlier that day, causing a fair stir of excitement among any of the staff who had interest in football. In fact, we instructed our people to not ask for autographs until the last day.

One of our retired volunteers, Reuben Hasenauer (who didn't concern himself with sports) came for supper and joined in line. The reunion included people from several states, so Reuben, who was legendary among our staff for his comically unsophisticated outlook on life, of course was getting acquainted. After several moments of discussion with the man next to him in line, Reuben was heard inquiring if it was the camper's first time to be in Nebraska. As staff and family members tried to hide their laughter, Tom Osborne, who had just won two consecutive national football titles as head coach at the University of Nebraska, politely replied that it was not.

– *George Cheek*

Maranatha has hosted family reunions—both large and small—for many years.

Fifty Years of Miracles

Rev. Olsen wrote this as he prepared for the 50th Anniversary Celebration at Maranatha in July 1988.

The lifetime story of Maranatha Bible Camp can best be told by the miracles that have occurred:

Miracle No. I: That God chose a man in his twenties, in his first pastorate of less than fifty members, and one who had never attended one day of any Bible Camp, to be the Founder and Director for fifty years of Maranatha.

Miracle No. II: God surrounded this young, impoverished, nondescript person with giants like Theodore Epp and the Back to the Bible Broadcast, the Navigators and the Berean Church Fellowship of pastors, such associations.

Miracle No. III: God miraculously provided, through faith and prayers, money to build, and food to eat "In the Wilderness." More than half of all the labor during these fifty years has been volunteered without remuneration.

Miracle No. IV: Forty-three-acre lake, twenty feet deep, filled with fish.

Miracle No. V: God sent conference speakers to Maranatha, such as Dr. H.A. Ironside of Chicago, Dr. Oswald J. Smith of Toronto, Wendell Loveless, Dr. M.R. DeHahn, Dr. Howard Hendricks, to name but a few.

Miracle No. VI: Thousands saved, and hundreds in full-time Christian service. Fifty years conducting a revival campaign at each Maranatha Conference, and a commitment of lives. Maranatha stuck to God's purpose for which He raised it up. Possibly the greatest miracles during these fifty years have been the spiritual responses in individual lives.

God took Moses to the top of the Mount, to review his forty years. On July 1 through 4th, at our "Mountain Top Experience" here at Maranatha, we shall look back at fifty years of miracles, and praise, worship and adore the God Who did it all.

– Ivan E. Olsen

Left: Terry Jensen prepares to get a pie in the face during Father-Son Retreat, 1989. Center: These Junior High Camp staff members are caught preparing for some water balloon mayhem in 1988. Right: A large delegation from the Dunkard Brethren Church met every four years at Maranatha throughout the late 20th century. This photo was taken in 1989.

Left: Occasionally, Lake Maranatha freezes solidly enough for ice skating, as it did for Winter Retreat 1981. Center: Senior High Camp friends at Needham Hall in 1982. From left: Rhonda Dolan, unidentified, Peggy Welsh, Brenda Lines. Right: Bryan and Patti Clark play a mild-mannered married couple during a skit at Couples' Conference 1987.

The Hitchhiker Showed Up, the Zip Line Went Up

As a child in the early 1960s, I couldn't wait for Junior Camp at Maranatha. I looked forward to everything: skits by Pastor Frank Kroeze, browsing in the bookstore at the back of the Old Tabernacle, the awards we would earn for scripture memory, cabin clean-up and what God would do in my life through the messages. My father, Gerry Sprunger, was a Berean pastor in McCook, Nebraska, at that time and he would be there too.

In 1964, our family moved to Omaha, Nebraska. I was in the sixth grade. One of the top priorities in my life was figuring out how to get to Camp. God was so faithful to give me my heart's desire. Somehow, I made it to Maranatha every year except one until I graduated from high school. I even rode the Greyhound bus by myself one year.

In 1969, between my junior and senior year in high school, I had a boyfriend who came to Omaha from Indiana. He was a cousin of a friend and was hitchhiking to California. I really wanted him to go to Senior High Camp that year so I told him that if he really cared for me, he would hitchhike back and meet me in the front of the Old Tabernacle at 4:00 p.m. on the first day of camp. Nervously, I went into the Tabernacle at the appointed time. There he was! Of course, we wanted to spend a lot of time together and of course, Pastor Art Van Campen was on our case not to have any display of affection. Mrs.

Goltz also kept us in check. Later in my life, I was so thankful for the godly people who influenced me in life.

In 1974, I married John Wetzig who was from Iowa and attended many weeks of Bible Camp growing up. By the fall of 1976, we were on staff at Lincoln Berean and of course got very involved in Maranatha. We began by taking our youth to Winter Retreat that year. In the summer of 1977, we both were counselors at four weeks of camp. That was a stretch for a newly-married couple! During the next four years, we were heavily involved in the planning of the youth camps and I was working closely with Claudine Lehman on Ladies' Retreats.

Highlights from those years include a huge hailstorm at youth camp during a banquet in Olsen Memorial, taking our youth on a missions trip to build the zip line in 1980, a trip to Indiana to attend the camping convention with George and Jan Cheek, and seeing many children and youth come to the Lord and follow Him through the programs at Maranatha.

Maranatha will always be special in my heart for it is the place where God met me many times to encourage me to follow Him.

– Debbie Wetzig,
Grenada, California

The zip line was a popular recreation option in the 1980s.

A Camp For All Stages of Life

My memories from Maranatha Bible Camp will be forever etched in my heart. My first memory of Maranatha is when I was just a toddler. As a family, we looked forward to getting away each summer and spending our vacation at Maranatha attending Family Camp. As a toddler I spent my early days at camp playing at the "kiddie campus." As I grew, our family continued to attend Family Camp each summer. My sister, Linda, and I made lots of lasting friendships, played fun pranks on George and Mac Welsh and daughters, Peggy and Patti, and just enjoyed the water activities, jumping on the trampolines, mini golf and most of all the Sweet Shop.

I attended Junior Camp when I was 8 years old. My mom, Bethene Lines, was my cabin leader for the week. I attended Junior Camp for a couple more years and then I was old enough to go to Junior High Camp. It was at this camp that I rededicated my life to Christ and prayed that

Tim and Brenda Malmkar and sons (from left) Tanner, Michael and Ethan.

He would use my life for His glory. I really enjoyed attending Senior High Camp and stayed in the same room with several girls that I had developed friendships with since we were 8-year-olds at Junior Camp.

During that time I also was a cabin leader for several of the Junior Camps. My sister, Linda, and I also worked on the Camp staff for several summers. While attending college, several friends and I went to Maranatha to a weekend singles' getaway. It was at this camp in 1986 that I met the man that I would someday marry.

Tim Malmkar and I were married on August 20, 1988. Tim and I have continued to attend various camps at Maranatha. We had the opportunity to organize and help plan the first fall couples' retreat. We enjoy the men's, ladies' and couples' retreats. I enjoy the scrapbooking retreats, this is a relaxing weekend to create lasting memories for my family.

Now that Tim and I have three sons, we are continuing the Maranatha tradition. Michael, Ethan and Tanner have all attended Primary Camps with dad as their cabin leader. I had the opportunity this summer to attend Junior Challenge Camp along with two of my boys. I was the cabin leader for two of the girls who I had led to the Lord and built a relationship with through Awana at church. As I look toward the future, I'm excited that my three boys will be able to reap the wonderful benefits that I did as a child, teenager and adult as I attended Maranatha. Because of Maranatha I was able to continue to grow in the Lord. Thanks for the memories!

– Brenda Malmkar,
North Platte

Family Lines Up in Favor of Camp

Because of Maranatha Bible Camp, Bethene and Leo Lines accepted Christ, as did their three children: Jerry Lines, Linda Lines Shoemaker and Brenda Lines Malmkar. When our children were very young up until they were in high school, we scheduled our summer vacation most years at Maranatha Bible Camp.

We have all created special and lasting memories from our days at Maranatha. The friendships that have developed from the different camps are priceless. Bethene was a counselor at Junior Camp for 20 years. Our son, Jerry, met his future wife, Harla, at Junior Camp when they were both counselors. Linda and Brenda attended all the camps they

possibly could growing up, starting as infants at Family Camp, then Junior Camp, Junior High Camp and finally Senior High Camp. They also spent many years as cabin leaders during their junior high and high school years. Linda and Brenda worked on the Maranatha staff for several summers. Brenda met her husband, Tim Malmkar, at the Singles' Conference at Maranatha. Our seven grandchildren have attended various camps at Maranatha and have made important decisions and all have received Christ because of Maranatha.

– Leo and Bethene Lines,
Imperial, Nebraska

Maranatha Influenced Bill Rice Ranch

This is an excerpt from a 1982 letter to Rev. Ivan Olsen, written by Cathy Rice, wife of the founder of the Bill Rice Ranch in Tennessee.

I can almost tell you the first time Bill was with you. I guess all we women remember events by the birth of our babies. And Bill was with you there in North Platte, Nebraska the first time when Bill III was born. That was 1942. So, that would have been in the very early part of your ministry there in Berean Church. I remember you made a real impact on Bill and was an influence on him throughout his life. He always remembered eating breakfast at your home and seeing the sign on the wall that said, "If we do not have time to read the Bible and pray, we do not have time to eat." And he always told in his message on the home of being in your home for breakfast and reading the Bible and praying before you ate.

I was with Bill when we went to visit you and to pick your brain on having a camp ground. I was with you and Bill as you traveled over the grounds together. I remember, also, your telling him of Paul Levin and Bob Findley. That very next summer, we had Paul Levin and Bob. From that time on, Dr. Paul Levin has been with us for our youth weeks. Only eternity will reveal the young people that have been saved and the lives that have been changed from the influence and the preaching of Paul Levin. The first year he was with us was 1956. And he has been with us every year since that time!

We are opened all year long now. Besides our summer camp season which last thirteen weeks, we have retreats all through the fall, winter and spring months. This year, in spite of many people being out of work, was our largest summer in the history of the Bill Rice Ranch. We had 10,087 in attendance this summertime. We averaged 1,012 in each of our youth weeks. We have five weeks for young people. We have two weeks for the deaf and two weeks for junior-age boys and girls, besides our family weeks. We had far more than our capacity, so we were packed and jammed to the gills. And, as always, we are needing to build.

– Cathy Rice,
Murfreesboro, Tennessee

Memories of Maranatha

When I think of Maranatha Camp, my mind is filled with memories. My first memory is of living in a little cabin before I was old enough to be a camper. My grandmother, Nina Havens, worked as a cook or kitchen helper several summers and I had to stay with her. Once I remember having other kids in our cabin, so I think she may have counseled some also. I then became a camper and it was the highlight of my summer. I have MANY fond memories of my years as a camper. My first year of "solo" camping, my grandparents came out to see me and asked if I was homesick and I replied, "No way, but I did want to see you."

The Hofrichter family and Carlo Pietropaulo were at the top of my list of things I enjoyed. I always hoped I would be able to like the Hofrichter girls. Several life-changing decisions were made in the Old Tabernacle and dining hall.

As I became a teenager, Pastor Goltz was an important figure at Camp. I always figured he had a personal visit with God each night to find out what we teenagers were doing or thinking so he could speak on that topic the next day.

I also enjoyed Camp as a counselor for Primary and Junior Camp. What a blessing to be able to be a part of the spiritual growth of young children. I appreciated the impact Maranatha Camp had on my daughters as well. Charity began going to camp as a 2nd grader and loved it.

We spent three summers on staff. It was the best experience of our lives. Charity was part of the Sweet Shop staff and learned what it meant to have a job. Amy was always a "go-for" girl and had many different experiences. It was a real growing spiritual experience for my daughters and myself to be a part of Prime Time and work daily in a Christ-centered atmosphere. I have only had the privilege of attending Ladies' Retreat one time, but I still remember the praise and worship time with Claudine Lehman as a most memorable experience.

I am so thankful for the privilege of being a part of Maranatha through the years.

– Sheila Slack,
North Platte

It Was Like a Small Piece of Heaven

Maranatha was a very special part of my life growing up. I began attending camps as soon as I was old enough for Junior Camp (continuing on through Senior High Camp).

I have so many memories and met so many great Christian friends. High school camps and Winter Retreats were some of my favorites, getting to see the friends I had met from other towns. Camp was like my second home; I used to ask my parents if we could move to Camp!

After high school, I worked as counselor to all camps and worked two years on summer staff. Those were awesome learning experiences and I had the time of my life - it was almost like I'd moved to Camp! So many memories, friendships and lessons I took from Camp! Being at Maranatha was like a small piece of Heaven to me. You were surrounded by a Christian example everywhere—Christian friends and staff, Bible lessons and worship daily, chapel—it was always very hard to leave. I felt a little empty when returning home. But, I think that's what makes it so special to go back ... a little more of Heaven each time!

I have since enjoyed going to Ladies' Retreats and the Fourth of July celebrations, which I've been able to share with my family.

Thanks for all the wonderful years of great Christian service and commitment. Maranatha made a huge difference in my life! God bless you and many more years of heavenly service!

– Linda Lines Shoemaker,
Oakley, Kansas

A Part of Life

I can't remember a day when Maranatha wasn't a part of my life. From my earliest memory I have the most amazing recollections of summers spent at Maranatha. Camp was just as important to my Dad (Curt Lehman) as his local church ministries were to him and he allowed us to see that commitment to Christian camping lived out in many ways.

I looked forward to spending all my summers at Camp when I got old enough to join the staff as a worker. I can't believe what Dr. Olsen entrusted to a bunch of "young adults/ teenagers," but his faith in us built a lasting confidence in me that has carried me through many trials as an adult.

My faith in God at Maranatha was built, molded, refined and challenged during my formative years. How I thank God for the many people on those Camp grounds who showed me what it was to live daily for Christ.

– Cindy MacGray,
Steamboat Springs, Colorado

Above: Senior High Camp, 1988. Right top: Cliff and Ruth Gustafson (front row, at left) directed the Senior Adults' Retreat (this one was in 1987). Right bottom: The Maranatha Camp board members in 1988 were, back row, from left: Richard Crocker, El Streyle, Carl Goltz, Hugh Clark, George Cheek, Duane Norman. Front row, from left: Curt Lehman, Ernest Lott, Clarence Yeutter, Ivan Olsen, Cliff Gustafson, Don Hunt.

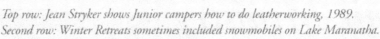

Top row: *Jean Stryker shows Junior campers how to do leatherworking, 1989.*

Second row: *Winter Retreats sometimes included snowmobiles on Lake Maranatha.*

Third row, from left: *Clark Hall eventually was used for adult housing; Nothing could be better than pizza during Winter Retreat 1988. Kris Cheek is seated at right (dark T-shirt and glasses); Junior High campers in 1989 enjoyed a beach ball game.*

Fourth row, from left: *Senior High Week campers at Needham Hall in 1984 included, back row, from left: Lee Anne Nation, Stacy Schwamb, Kim Yeutter, Jennifer Dods. Front row, from left: Angie Clark, cabin leader Connie Yeutter, Theresa Schafer; Church buses, fishing poles and anticipation of a fun week of Camp make for good memories; An early morning aerial view of Camp, summer 1988.*

Fifth row, from left: *Maranatha utilized the Valley View Ranch, owned by Les and Shirley Ross, for many years. This is a 1987 photo; Dave Wyrtzen (left) joins the soccer game at Senior High Camp 1984; If you heard piano music at Maranatha during the 1960s or later, there was a good chance that Louise was at the keyboard. Louise McDermott Crooks served the Camp as lifeguard and bookkeeper, but is best known for her musical accompaniment.*

Sixth row, from left: *Don Hillis was a Family Camp speaker in the 1980s; Glenn Adams, here with his wife, Norma, was a program director and speaker at a variety of camps, including Junior High Camp and Singles' Conferences; Ernest Lott (shown here with his wife, Annie) served more than 40 years on the Maranatha Camp board; Bethene Lines and her daughters, Linda Shoemaker (left) and Brenda Malmkar, pause during a Ladies' Retreat; Earnest Skoog was a pastor who taught many years at Camp, then moved to Camp to help remodel the current office building. The Waterfront was named in his honor.*

145

Ethnic Ministry

It had been a long, and sometimes discouraging, fight. The staff of Maranatha Bible Camp had fought a tiring battle against the floodwaters that covered much of the grounds for six weeks during the summer of 1983.

The staff had resigned itself to the loss of many goals that had been set for attendance and salvation decisions. With half the summer schedule having been cancelled by the flood, it seemed that the year would be forever defined by that event.

Then, early in July, a few of the staff who were filling sandbags outside the dining hall saw an unusual sight. A vehicle pulled into the Camp, and two Oriental men climbed out and splashed through the standing water to the dining hall. They said they were from a tribe of people known as the Hmong, and he was looking for a place to hold a large camp meeting later that summer.

"Because of their difficulty in speaking English, it took some effort to come to a complete understanding of the arrangements," said George Cheek, who welcomed the two men. "Providentially, the group wanted to come during a week that another organization had abandoned because of a misconception of what the high water might have done to the Camp." (Actually, no damage was done to any of the buildings.)

Jerry Soung was a youth leader in the Hmong District of the Christian & Missionary Alliance Church. Disregarding the standing water on the grounds, Soung reached a verbal agreement with Cheek to hold a youth camp at Maranatha that August.

On July 22, Soung wrote a letter to Maranatha. "How about the flooding?" he asked. "I passed there about a week ago. I saw water covered all camp ground. I wonder if water will dry by the 14th of August. If not, could we buy boats and use for transportation back and forth from the chapel to the cabin! Or can we swim back and forth? Hopefully, by then I won't have to swim because I do not know how."

Soung's joking comments belied the fighting spirit his people have. The Hmong were natives of the hill country in northern Laos. Some also lived in Thailand and China. Many of them had swum for their lives across the Mekong River escaping persecution in Laos, because the Hmong had fought against the Communists during the Vietnam War, so they were targeted for destruction after the United States pulled out of Southeast Asia in 1974. Those who could do so, escaped to the United States, where more than 40,000 had taken residence by the mid-1980s.

The first Hmong youth camp was held August 14-20, 1983. There was much anticipation about how many people would show up. Cheek and the Hmong youth leaders had prayed that 200 would arrive, but by the time everyone had been accounted for, there were 323.

The first meal on Sunday evening revealed a problem, however. Nearly one-third of the people did not eat their barbecued beef sandwiches, baked beans, fresh vegetables and jello salad.

"Later that evening in a brief meeting with the leaders, we discovered that many of the Hmongs were still eating rice three times a day. They would become ill if they strayed too far from their eating habits," Cheek said. "Consequently, we sent a car to North Platte and bought all the rice we could find. The group ate it for breakfast the next morning.

"In the meantime, one of our board members arranged to bring several 100-pound bags of rice to Camp from the Thai Market in Denver."

The Camp kitchen staff had to improvise on the fly. With the help of several Hmong women, food service director Joe Dapra and his staff learned to prepare stir-fry dishes served with a side dish of meat that appealed to the Hmong.

By the end of the week, the two cultures were beginning to mesh. More importantly, God had been at work. About 50 Hmong young people received Jesus Christ as savior that week. When added to the 50 people who had been saved at Maranatha during the flood-shortened schedule earlier that summer, the staff saw God answer its prayer of more than two months ago — that 100 people would accept Christ at Maranatha that summer.

The Hmong week was a godsend in other ways. In June 1983, Maranatha recorded just 784 camper-days. In July, the number increased to 1,486, but it jumped to 4,006 in August. Of that total, 2,289 camper-days (36 percent of the summer's total) were from the Hmong camp. It saved the summer financially, and launched one of the most amazing chapters of Maranatha's history.

With Soung as the chief spokesman, the Hmong youth camp became well established at Maranatha. It returned with more than twice the turnout in 1984, and kept coming every year for more than a decade. Crowds of more than 1,000 became common. Their adult sponsors enjoyed themselves so much that they organized a Hmong adult camp for many years as well.

In 1984, the Hmong youth overflowed the dining hall at mealtime and had to sit outside at tables that Camp staff set up on the paved parking lot. Soon, with the help of Nebraska Third District Congresswoman Virginia Smith, Maranatha located tents and cots to borrow from the U.S. Military. The Camp also rented a large circus tent to enable 1,000 Hmong to eat meals under cover in the parking lot.

The Hmong camp attracted people from all over the United States. On several occasions, close relatives who were separated by Communist persecution a decade earlier had a happy reunion at Maranatha.

While the Hmong camp was going strong, two friends of Maranatha challenged Cheek to consider doing a ministry to the Spanish-speaking community of the Midwest.

Bob Kracht and Aaron Jewett, both on staff of Rio Grande Bible Institute in Edinburg, Texas, pledged their help, and Maranatha moved to expand its outreach. "The Hmong is something that the Lord just brought into our laps," said Cheek. "The Hispanic was something we intentionally went out and recruited for."

God opened a relationship with Pastor Eliseo Hernandez, his family and church in the Denver Metro area. Pastor Hernandez and George Cheek traveled to RGBI for a planning session in 1987, and that summer, Maranatha held its first Hispanic camp. RGBI sent students and staff, including a singing group, to help with programming. Jewett, who in his teenage years had received Jesus Christ as his savior while at Maranatha Camp, acted as a go-between for Maranatha and Pastor Hernandez.

It took the form of a family camp. Because the Hernandez family was from El Salvador, most of the attendees were also from that country. It did not grow as the Hmong camp had.

After several years, the Hispanic camp moved on to use a Bible camp in Colorado.

"There were three years of Hispanic ministry, then Maranatha turned it over to lay leadership and it faded out," said Cheek. "They didn't hold in like the Hmongs."

The Hmongs indeed were a strong presence at Maranatha. During the years when they brought two camps (generally, a youth camp in early August and an adult camp two weeks later), the Hmong accounted for about one-third of Maranatha's gross income. They are the largest-attended Camps in Maranatha history (the Camp had to bring in extra tents and portable toilets to accommodate the large crowds). Maranatha annually recruited extra volunteers to cook, wash dishes and make cold beverages to serve the huge numbers of people. Eventually, the Camp staff had its routine down pat, and it was common for more than 1,000 campers to leave the chapel, fill their plates at six buffet lines in the dining hall, walk to the parking lot, take a beverage and enter the circus tent to eat, all within 30 minutes.

The momentum began to fade in the early 1990s, when the adult conference left Maranatha for another conference center. Maranatha hosted its final Hmong youth camp in 1996. As the Hmong people became more Americanized, they wanted more spacious accommodations than Maranatha was able to provide. Although many Hmong youth felt sad at leaving their "home" camp, they moved on to larger conference centers during the succeeding years.

In 2002, another ethnic ministry found its way to Maranatha Bible Camp through a strategic partnership with a nationally-known ministry.

The story began when George Cheek attended a symposium on the plight of the American Indian, held in Lincoln, Nebraska, on a wintry night in 2000. It was led by Ron Hutchcraft, the nationally-known youth ministry leader, and Ron Brown, the receivers coach for the University of Nebraska football team and founder of Mission Nebraska. This led to another meeting with the Hutchcraft ministry team in 2001, which led to Maranatha's invitation to bring an outreach camp for Native Americans to Maranatha.

In July 2002, 107 youth and Christian sponsors came from 20 tribes to Maranatha's first Warrior Leadership Summit. "This was so encouraging to everyone!" said Cheek. Ron Brown, a household name across Nebraska, came to help, adding to the excitement of the event.

Months later, the WLS staff put together a promotional video to get the word out about the next summer's event. It promised that if Native American youth could get to Maranatha, their time at Camp would be paid for by the friends of Hutchcraft Ministries. The prayer was for God to bless by doubling the attendance.

In July 2003, God showed how He was answering those prayers. When everyone was counted, there were 240 Native young people representing 45 tribes. "One of the highlights for me was to visit with a missionary family and some of the 25 Eskimo youth who had traveled all the way from the Bering

Sea coast in Alaska," said Cheek. "Their village is 400 miles from Russia and 500 miles from the nearest road!"

Before the week was over, 50 of the young people, representing 32 different tribes, were invited to go on a one-month outreach tour to seven reservations. Hutchcraft sent eight e-mail reports to supporters of his ministry. Then e-mail #9 arrived in hundreds of computers around the nation:

"... based on the records we have kept throughout this month, it appears that something unprecedented — almost unbelievable — has happened," it read. "In the Summer of Hope 2003, these young warriors have helped 841 NATIVE AMERICAN YOUNG PEOPLE BEGIN A PERSONAL RELATIONSHIP WITH JESUS CHRIST! " (Caps are Hutchcraft's.)

Dr. Pat Blewett of Grace University, Omaha, Nebraska, an eyewitness to these events, marveled at what God was doing.

"Having grown up on a reservation, I was dumbfounded at the Warrior Leadership Summit ... by sheer numbers, this summit was miraculous. ... I had the opportunity to see a spiritual harvest on a reservation that perhaps has not taken place in 500 years! It was miraculous!"

That word has echoed at Maranatha for more than 60 years. No one knows how God will choose to work through this latest ethnic outreach, but it is evidence that He continues to use Maranatha in unlikely ways to change the hearts and lives of countless people.

VOICES OF MARANATHA

Glad to Help Teach Choruses to Hmong

Our association with the Camp spans more than 40 years. Gil brought his own Hammond organ to Maranatha Camp and played for the "Big" Sunday School Conventions beginning in 1957. These meetings were held in the Old Tabernacle building. In those days, Howard Hendricks and Clayt Risley were on hand for teaching, preaching, etc.

Dr. Howard Hendricks is now a well-known Christian author and speaker. Clayt Risley was once known as "Mr. Sunday School" and traveled all around the country in behalf of better Sunday Schools. He is now at home with the Lord.

After these meetings were no longer held, Dr. Ivan Olsen invited Gil to come to Maranatha and play for Family Camp in August of 1960. We were expecting our first child at the same time as the Camp was scheduled, making it necessary for him to decline the invitation.

Later, when the Nebraska Gideon Retreats were held over Labor Day at the Camp, our family (by then we had three young sons) came for the weekend and Gil played the Camp's organ for these meetings. Dorothy played the piano for a few years, as well. They continued coming to these retreats for several years.

When the Hmong conferences and camps were held at Maranatha, we helped with the music as George Cheek taught the Hmong folks to sing hymns and choruses in English. After two or three years, they began taking care of their own music and brought their own accompaniment so we were no longer needed in this area. However, there was a lot of work needing to be done with approximately 1,000 campers and staff on the grounds.

Gil began to help in the Gift Shop and Dorothy worked at the Switchboard (now called the "Information Center"). We both enjoyed volunteering in these areas. In fact, we continued spending a good part of our summers serving in these areas until the year 2000.

We have fond memories of Maranatha and have enjoyed lasting friendships directly related to the Camp and staff. Over the years we have seen the Lord accomplish His purposes in many different ways through the ministry of Maranatha.

— Gil and Dorothy Glad,
Central City, Nebraska

He Met Wife During Hmong Camp

I thank God for Maranatha Camp. I attended the HLUB summer conferences in 1993, 1994, and 1996 held by the Christian Missionary Alliance Hmong District. Each year strengthened my walk with Christ. I still have vivid memories sleeping in Needham Hall, nearly drowning in the lake, and (eight years ago) meeting Linda for the first time in the Sweet Shop. She is now my wife. She was from

South Carolina and I was from Michigan! Who would have known that God would use a camp in Nebraska to unite us?

Thanks God and thanks Maranatha Camp for the great, and sometimes scary, memories!

— Daniel Yang,
Ann Arbor, Michigan

Proclamation

WHEREAS,	Nebraska needs leadership to promote AOD prevention and to role model healthy lifestyles and
WHEREAS,	Nebraska Ethnics Together Working on Reaching Kids and Cultures of Color Youth Leaders are developing that leadership August 19-23, 1992 by sponsoring "Our Leadership Makes the Difference: Multi-Cultural Youth Leadership Retreat" at Maranatha Bible Camp, Maxwell, NE and
WHEREAS,	Multi-Cultural Prevention Strategies will be developed at the retreat to minimize the risk of Nebraska Youth becoming involved in AOD issues and behaviors.
NOW, THEREFORE,	I, E. Benjamin Nelson, Governor of the State of Nebraska, DO HEREBY PROCLAIM August 19-23, 1992 as

AOD PREVENTION LEADERSHIP DEVELOPMENT WEEK
FOR YOUTH OF COLOR AND MULTI-CULTURAL YOUTH

IN WITNESS WHEREOF, I have hereunto set my hand, and cause the Great Seal of the State of Nebraska to be affixed this Third day of August, in the year of our Lord on thousand nine hundred and ninety-two.

Attest:

_____
Secretary of State

_____
Governor

Letter From the Congress of the United States

VIRGINIA SMITH
3d DISTRICT, NEBRASKA

2202 RAYBURN BUILDING
(202) 225-6435

APPROPRIATIONS

SUBCOMMITTEES:
AGRICULTURE
ENERGY AND
WATER DEVELOPMENT

Congress of the United States
House of Representatives
Washington, DC 20515

July 20, 1987

Mr. Glen Rodman
Headquarters 89th Army Reserve
3130 George Washington Blvd.   Attn: AFKB-AC-CL-LG
Wichita, Kansas 67210-1598   Mr. Rodman or Mr. Burnett

Dear Mr. Rodman:

This is to inform you that I have been advised that the
Maranatha Bible Camp, east of North Platte, Nebraska, will be
the site of a Youth Conference for the refugees of the Hmong
Tribe of Laos who have been granted sanctuary in the United
States. The conference dates are August 9 through August 15.

As you may know, the Maranatha Bible Camp is a non-denominational camp available to all church groups. Mr. George Cheek
is its Executive Director. The camp has been in existence for
many years, and I am well acquainted with its fine facilities
and its excellent reputation.

It is my understanding that the camp facilities will have
to be supplemented with extra tents and cots for at least
200 of the 1,200 people expected for this conference. I also
understand that a request has been made to you for this extra
equipment to take care of the overflow crowd. It is my sincere
hope that you will be able to comply with this request, and to
provide the equipment several days prior to the opening date
of the conference. It appears to be a cause worthy of our help.

With best wishes,

Sincerely,

VIRGINIA SMITH
Member of Congress

VS/cc

150

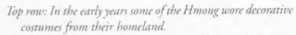

Top row: In the early years some of the Hmong wore decorative costumes from their homeland.

Second row: Too many Hmongs to fit in one photo! A three-photo composite from one of the many Hmong Youth camps.

Third row, from left: Maranatha hosted Hispanic camps in 1989; and in 1992; Big crowds took on a new meaning in the 1980s and 90s when the Hmong camps were held. Groups of 1,000 were common year after year.

Fourth row, from left: The flood waters having receded, the first-ever Hmong group at Maranatha prepares for its banquet in August 1983; Aaron Jewett (left) helped organize Hispanic camps at Maranatha; Inside the big dining tent in the parking lot, Hmong Camp 1986.

The 1990s and Beyond

Ernest Lott started leading music at the Bockus grove, during Maranatha Bible Camp's Sixth Annual Session in 1943. He joined the Camp board on January 1, 1945, less than a year after Maranatha moved to its permanent site. He saw the construction of the first dormitories, the Tabernacle and the original Dining Hall. He produced Camp brochures and was in charge of promotion during the 1950s. He prayed and pondered with the rest of the board when Interstate 80 was built through the Camp, when the new Dining Hall and Chapel were constructed and rejoiced to see Maranatha evolve from a one-week-a-year operation into a year-round ministry. Lott was an inquisitive man who did his best to keep up with ongoing changes in technology and society. During much of the 1990s, as the ministry went through one transition after another, he regularly phoned George Cheek and often showered him with questions and encouragement. He continued to not only serve as an active board member, but also as a member of the board of management, well into his 90th year. After Lott closed his final board meeting with prayer in October 1997, he lived to see the 21st century before he died in Lincoln on May 28, 2001.

The decision to go year-round, a move which had been long anticipated by Ivan Olsen and which had come to fruition largely through the impetus of George Cheek, presented an important philosophical question. Was Maranatha still a camp for children and youth, or was it now an adult conference center? The question was important as Cheek continued to develop the Long-Range Plan. What kinds of buildings were needed? Should they be built for young people, or to accommodate adult retreats?

Early in the 1990s, with Olsen and Hugh Clark having recently retired, the median age of the board that was making these philosophical decisions had become much younger. At that point, nearly half of its members had served fewer than 10 years.

This new Camp board decided that Maranatha was still primarily a camp for children and youth, and secondarily a conference center. Then it set about applying its philosophy to upcoming decisions about bricks, mortar and lumber. One visible result was the development of simple fourplex cabins, located near the existing bathhouse. They were built with baseboard heat and ceiling fans, and the cement floors were left unfinished. By the end of the decade, four new cabins had been built; they were named after Curt Lehman, Carl Goltz, Don Hunt and Adrian House.

The cabins stand in the center of the Camp grounds, near the place where Olsen, Clark, Carper and Kittle knelt and prayed in 1944, but 50 years after that impromptu prayer meeting, a much-beloved structure long associated with that section of Camp stood no more. The Old Tabernacle was torn down.

The old cinder block building had become unsafe. Ed Fasse had warned Olsen that it would eventually happen, and 20 years later, a structural engineer confirmed it. In 1989, the board (fully cognizant of the Camp's increasing indebtedness) decided that "no more major funds should be spent on it ... realizing structurally, its days are numbered." The Old Tab was demolished in the spring of 1994.

As the old went down, the new continued to go up. In March 1991, the board held a five-hour brainstorming session, which identified a need for Camp to improve its indoor recreation facilities. The board decided to build a large multipurpose building that would include a high school-size gymnasium, locker rooms, meeting rooms and a spa. Even though the Camp already was facing a significant debt, the board members believed the need was vital enough to press forward with a half-million-dollar building project. The metal building was to be attached to the Olsen Memorial Building with an enclosed hallway.

George Cheek, Ivan Olsen and the Camp board took several shined-up shovels and broke ground for the new multipurpose building on a chilly October evening during the 1991 board meeting. Fundraising began in earnest with both Cheek and Olsen concentrating their efforts on the new project.

After nearly a year of fundraising, the Camp started construction of the new building in late August 1992. As his health deteriorated, Olsen looked on with approval as the shell of the building started to take shape. When he and Alice returned from Florida in the spring of 1993, the building already had been used for basketball and volleyball at several retreats, although the finish work would not be complete until the next year. Olsen continued to raise money for the project until a sunny September morning when, with the ash trees along the Camp road sporting their full autumn color, he passed away at age 79 due to complications from his heart condition and kidney dialysis.

Alice Olsen began living at the homes of her daughters, Joy, Faith and Precious, during the non-summer months. After recovering from a bout with severe arthritis, Alice started volunteering at a city mission in the Kansas City area, spreading the gospel message to single mothers in the region. She continues to spend part of each summer at her home on the shore of Lake Maranatha.

Cheek, having been officially confirmed as general director by the Camp board on March 15, 1990, had been overseeing the entire operation for years. He led Maranatha into an era of change. Technological advances changed the way the office functioned. Computers and the Internet replaced typewriters and reduced the number of letters being mailed out. A large designated gift enabled the Camp to replace its antique 1940s-style switchboard (which had plug-in extensions) with a new telephone system. Tad Stryker developed a Maranatha Web site (*www.maranathacamp.org*) and began to use it as a marketing tool. Cheek, known to his staff as a gadget enthusiast, stopped dictating letters with his handheld tape recorder and began sending e-mail. He fully endorsed all the new technology, and efficiency and productivity increased.

There were many other improvements around the Camp, including the installation of a new peaked roof on Needham Hall and comprehensive remodeling of Clark, Becker and Lott halls to make them more adult-friendly. The most noticeable improvements to most campers were the 30-foot climbing wall, which was built onto the gym's east wall in 1998, and the development of the Skoog Memorial Waterfront from 1999-2004. The Camp turned what once was a cedar-choked shoreline into a sandy beachfront area with a 100-foot waterslide, 25-foot water trampoline, power boating, canoeing, kayaking, paddle boating and swimming in a roped-off area along the beach. Swimming in the lake without a life jacket had not been allowed since the two campers drowned during Junior Camp in 1971.

The Camp developed a nature trail in the early 1990s; it runs south and southwest of Lake Maranatha, following the path of the south channel of the Platte River, which crosses the Camp's property. Part of the trail is on land belonging to longtime Camp neighbors Ralph & Doris Craig.

Maranatha's other neighboring landowners are Aaron & Janice Schad (who own various motels and have donated enough furniture to Camp that most of our guest rooms contain something they used to own), Lonnie & Londa Gosnell (who share the longest private fence line with Maranatha … second only to the Interstate 80 fence) and Mark & Shawn Loostrum (who own land on both sides of Maranatha Road, and can see all the cars and buses as they rattle along the gravel road that leads into the Camp grounds). During the 1990s, the Camp staff began a December tradition of going Christmas caroling at the homes of neighbors in Maxwell and the surrounding rural area, and has enjoyed a good relationship with them for decades.

Much less noticeable to the neighbors was another change in the ownership of the Camp's land. In 1994, after four years of legal preliminaries, the board voted to incorporate the Camp independently from the Berean Fundamental Church Council, just as it had been before 1949, and all the property was transferred to Maranatha Bible Camp, Inc. For liability reasons, the BFCC had become increasingly concerned about the risk of owning a camping ministry.

There was no denying that the face of Christian camping was changing. Cheek began to give increased emphasis to outreach to unchurched people. In order to reach out to those who shy away from church, Maranatha developed targeted retreats for adults, including Fishing Camp, Archery Camp, Ringneck Roundup (pheasant hunting and sporting clays), Single Parents' Retreat and Making Memories Scrapbooking Retreat. For youth, the Camp held basketball and volleyball camps (Scott Wilson has directed these camps for 15 years).

Attendance rose at Maranatha and operational income continued to climb, but so did operational expenses. Then, in 1997, the Hmong leadership decided to take its annual summer rally to a larger conference center. This decision cut off about one-third of Maranatha's gross income, ushering in years of financial pressure and tight spending. Board president El Streyle met regularly with the departmental directors, both to encourage their spiritual growth and to brainstorm about improving the recruitment of campers and the Camp's bottom line. The debt, which had been accumulating for more than 15 years, had grown to half a million dollars; Cheek and the board were concerned and began to discuss strategies to reduce it.

The fund drive for the gymnasium/multipurpose building ended in the late 1990s with the building totally paid for. A significant portion came through a large donation from the estate of Hugh Clark, who died in 1998.

The Camp board decided that it would be in Maranatha's best interest to designate someone to work on fundraising fulltime. In 1996, Maranatha hired Mark Geist as executive director of the newly-formed Maranatha Camp Foundation. Geist resigned from his family business to lead the Foundation, working with people to set up long-term estate planning strategies that would benefit both their family and Christian ministries. He also raised donations for the camper scholarship fund through golf events. He also arranged for the construction of houses with volunteer labor, with the profits going to the scholarship fund when the houses were sold.

The face of Maranatha was changing rapidly. During the March 1991 brainstorming session, the board had decided to hire a fulltime staff member to coordinate all Maranatha-sponsored camping programs. That position was filled first by Harald Bjerga, then by Joel Ondrejack and at present, Rodney Thiessen. Bjerga, Ondrejack and Thiessen took the existing summer staff program and built it into a 12-week missions program, working to increase the average age of the staff and raising expectations for all participants. Several different colleges were well represented over the 1990s, including Grace University in Omaha, Moody Bible Institute in Chicago, Calvary Bible College in Kansas City, Frontier School of the Bible in Lagrange, Wyoming, and Prairie Bible Institute in Alberta, but no school sent more students to Maranatha's Summer Missions program than Briercrest Bible College in tiny Caronport, Saskatchewan.

Thiessen and another new staff member, Adam Stuart-Walker, developed a two-week discipleship program called "Teens in Training" for young people ages 14-17. Maranatha held six sessions of TNT during the summers of 2002-04, and planned to develop an intermediate level to take TNT graduates and incorporate them into the Summer Missions program.

More longtime Maranatha leaders were leaving the picture. Curt Lehman, the former program director and board member, and Carl Goltz, the longtime Camp board president, died in 2003. So did Faye Ward, who had served for more than 50 years as Ivan Olsen's personal secretary. A generation was passing away.

Possibly nothing symbolized the changes of the 1990s more than the rise of the computer age. The greater availability of information made the world seem like a much smaller place.

As the long-anticipated year 2000 drew closer, Maranatha staff faced a concern that had spread throughout much of the world. By that time, nearly all economic and utilities infrastructure was computer-based, and it was feared that a flaw in the programming of Microsoft Windows-based computer software could result in widespread power failures that would disrupt utilities and shut down banks and grocery stores. The Camp directors developed a plan for preparation and response to possible "Y2K" incidents, put it into place and waited to see what would happen.

On the unseasonably mild evening of December 31, 1999, Maranatha hosted a large youth rally that was organized by many area churches. More than 300 teens and youth leaders showed up to hear the Christian ska band "Buck" and celebrate the end of the millennium. At midnight, the electrical power continued on without interruption at Camp, as it did almost everywhere else around the world, and the youth celebrated the start of the year 2000 with a fireworks show over Lake Maranatha.

One year later, December 31, 2000, marked the end of Maranatha's "220 by 2000" project. At that time, the Camp documented that Maranatha "graduates" had reached at least 53 nations. At the same time, there was a noticeable increase in missions enthusiasm among campers at Junior Camp, Jr. High and Sr. High Camp.

In the spring of 2001, 25-year-old Kris Cheek, son of George & Jan Cheek, teamed with his friend Matt Janssen to start SportReach, a sports/adventure outreach and later that year, Maranatha Camp added it as a branch of its overall ministry. During the next three years, SportReach began to target its programs to the unsaved, and emphasized world missions. Working with Pastor Juan Barrientos, who was a featured missionary at Junior Camp in the late 1990s, SR had sponsored three missions trips to Lima, Peru, by March 2004. About 40 people raised their own financial support to make the trips. SportReach plans to increase its involvement in Peru and around the world.

As Maranatha Bible Camp finishes its seventh decade of ministry, it is in a stronger position than ever to evangelize the world and encourage young people to become full-time missionaries, two goals that Ivan Olsen, Hugh Clark and thousands of people who have worked, prayed and donated to Maranatha would wholeheartedly endorse.

VOICES OF MARANATHA

Scholarships Are Appreciated

My fondest memories have always been of attending Maranatha Bible Camp since I was 11 years old. Now I have to thank you especially this year for allowing my three children: Travis Bates, Amanda Bates, and Aleah Bates, to attend camp on a scholarship. I know that they had a great time there because I always did. Thank you very much! I appreciate the caring giving spirit at this time in my life.

– Lori Bates,
Beatrice, Nebraska

The People of Maranatha: El Streyle

In 1986, Elton Streyle of Scottsbluff joined the official board of Maranatha Bible Camp. He became the fourth president of the board in 1994. Of the first three presidents, two were pastors and the third was a radio Bible teacher. Streyle was an insurance agent, and the Camp benefited from his practical outlook.

As a businessman, one of his key contributions was to get Maranatha into the habit of using a systematic budget-based list of projects to be accomplished in the coming fiscal year. Early in the spring, each department head calculates those costs. Then we add the projected fixed overhead, which results in our anticipated need for the coming year. The next objective is to set goals for income from registrations, other group fees and donations. Once those decisions

El and Joyce Streyle

are made by the department heads, bookkeeper Ruth Ann Rodgers (along with others who help with data entry) produces the first draft of the budget. Then the department heads and board treasurer Terry Jensen, vice president Royce Norman and other interested board members gather for a meeting to evaluate the first draft and recommend changes – usually budget cuts. This helps provide a reality check. The changes from that meeting are made in the budget, which then is presented to the full board at the April meeting.

Besides his comprehensive recommendations on our budget, El was also faithful as president to arrange strategy meetings for setting intermediate goals and accountability in light of the annual objectives. These principles are still in use by the management team.

In 2001, Streyle resigned as president of the board and later retired from his insurance job. He continues to serve as a Camp board member and provides the staff with his valuable insight.

One of the most noticeable hallmarks of El's tenure as president was his concern about the spiritual health of Maranatha's fulltime staff, and his willingness to invest time and energy to communicate with the staff face-to-face.

– George Cheek

Former Maranatha Camper Killed as Missionary

As a camper at Maranatha in the 1960s, Stephen Welsh once listened to missionary speakers in the Old Tabernacle. He took their message to heart.

In the 1986 Stephen began serving as a missionary in Colombia with New Tribes Mission. By the early 1990s, he was in charge of construction at a missionary school about 55 miles from Bogotá. He lived at the school with his wife, Sandy, and children Shannon, Shad and Scott.

Because of the unstable political climate in Colombia, the Welshes knew they were serving in harm's way. But no one was prepared for what happened in January 1994, when Stephen and his co-worker, Tim Van Dyke, were kidnapped at gunpoint by the leftist rebel group Revolutionary Armed Forces of Colombia.

Negotiations between New Tribes and the guerrillas took place for the next 15 months, but just when it seemed that the hostages would be released, Stephen and Tim were

found shot to death on June 19, 1995, in what was believed to be a clash between guerrillas and the Colombian military.

His parents, George & Mildred Welsh of North Platte, had been involved with Maranatha for many years. At the time of Stephen's death, they were serving as volunteers for Maranatha, delivering supplies on "town run" three times a week.

"We know he was trying to serve the Lord in a place that the Lord wanted him to be," said George Welsh.

Sandy Welsh, who was evacuated from Colombia after her husband's kidnapping, said she loves the people of Colombia and she never questioned the commitment she and her husband had to the work there.

"His whole heart was down there in that work," said Sandy. "He wanted to be there; he wouldn't have wanted to be anywhere else."

– Tad Stryker

The People of Maranatha: Dave Wyrtzen

"I had come to Nebraska to celebrate Christmas with my in-laws, the Van Campens, in Broken Bow, but my brother-in-law asked, "Dave, will you be our speaker for snow camp at Maranatha?!" That was more than 30 years ago. Then, when Frank Van Campen became the director for the Senior High summer camp (1978), he asked me to come along as Bible teacher. "

So began the long association of Dave Wyrtzen, the son of Jack Wyrtzen, founder of the Word of Life Camps in New York. Wyrtzen is one of the most prolific speakers in the history of Maranatha.

"Young people, listen to me," he cried out — and they did. His shoot-from-the-hip, gut-level style of teaching appealed to all kinds of youth for more than a quarter century, although his non-traditional musical style and his lack of emphasis on how campers dressed tended to make Ivan Olsen and some of the "old guard" a bit uneasy.

"With Mrs. Olsen sitting in the back of the auditorium, we started strumming our guitars and trying to communicate with young people in a language that they would respond to, but firmly based upon intimacy with Jesus Christ as revealed in the Scriptures," said Wyrtzen. "Mrs. Olsen persuaded her precious husband that we were not heretics, and this opened the door for years of ministry with Maranatha."

Wyrtzen's ministry at Maranatha expanded from youth camps to couples' retreats and then to pastors' retreats. His ability to use Greek or Hebrew and common American street language in the same sentence captivated listeners of all ages.

Wyrtzen occasionally made trips overseas to teach the Bible to pastors and Christian workers around the world. He settled in the Dallas suburb of Midlothian, Texas, becoming the senior pastor of a large Bible church. Soon he was sending dozens of the youth from his church to Maranatha, even when he was not the featured speaker.

"One of the precious gifts of grace for this New York-New Jersey kid is that the Holy Spirit used the teaching of His Word and a team of incredibly gifted men and women to impact so many lives, including the lives of my own four children, underneath the cross alongside Interstate 80, deep in the heart of Nebraska," said Wyrtzen. "Thanks for the years of opportunity at Maranatha."

– Tad Stryker

VOICES OF MARANATHA

Notes for Missionaries

In July, 1995, we came as Camp missionaries to Maranatha, working with the Juniors and Primaries. I featured Juan Barrientos, a missionary in Peru, and had them praying and giving for him to get a car. I also had them write some little notes, and here are three samples (spelling not changed):

"Dear Missionary,
I like the way you explain things so that kids can understand. You are a great speaker and I am sure you will make a good pastor some day."

"Dear Missionary,
You make it so interesting Usually I get bored. Hearing you speak is one of my most favorite things to do at Maranatha Camp. I really look up to you for going to different places and sharing the gospel. I hope I can do that sometime. P.S. I will be praying for Wanchi (Juan)."

"Dear Mr. Broan,
...I would like to do what you do but I don't really know if I'm good at it. But I hope that I can do somthing that involves christchan. P.S. This dollar is for Juan's car."
– Richard "Brom" Cowser, Bessemer, Alabama

Richard "Brom" and Betty Cowser, longtime missionaries to Curacao. Brom was a regular speaker at Junior Camp.

The People of Maranatha: Bryan Clark

First a builder, then a musician, and finally, a pastor-teacher. Bryan Clark, the son of Eugene & Ferne Clark and the grandson of Hugh & Lela Clark, is continuing in the tradition of Clarks who served prominently at Maranatha Bible Camp. He has been a Camp speaker, program director and volunteer for much of his life.

Bryan and his brother, Bruce, grew up coming to Camp. Bryan began a friendship with Patti Pierson in the mid-1970s while serving on the Maranatha summer staff. Their parents were both in ministry and were glad to have their children serving the Lord in what was for both, their first job away from home. Eventually, they were married and had three daughters, Ashley, Bobbi and Jayme.

After graduation from Moody Bible Institute and Talbot Seminary, Bryan and Patti returned to Nebraska to pastor the Broken Bow Berean Church. In 1990, Bryan launched the Fishing Camp at Maranatha and served as its program director for several years.

In 1991, Bryan was invited to join the Maranatha board. Later, the Lincoln Berean Church asked Bryan to come back home to join the staff there. In 1995, he succeeded Curt Lehman as senior pastor.

The church had already become the largest single source of campers to Maranatha-sponsored programs and continues that tradition today under the team that Bryan leads.

Bryan & Patti have been a part of the program for many years in the youth camps, where he served as speaker in main sessions and seminars as well as being part of the leadership team, contributing to the growth of these weeks throughout the 1990s.

— George Cheek

Spontaneous camper-led prayer meetings around the flagpole were an encouraging sight during Junior High Camp 1998.

VOICES OF MARANATHA
Meeting His Mate at Maranatha

During the summer of 1995 I met a beautiful, young, red-haired woman who was working at Maranatha. Her name was Jodie Shada, and little did I know that her energetic personality and love for the Lord would become such an integral part of my life. Jodie and I started dating the following winter, and in May of 1998 we were married.

We've spent many weeks at Maranatha and done everything from take photographs to paint buildings. I grew up enjoying birthday parties and fishing trips with Kris Cheek; Jodie grew up attending every camp Maranatha had to offer. We enjoyed some tremendous times of prayer and renewal while serving as counselors for senior high week. But we will always treasure that wonderful summer of 1995 when we first met and the Lord began a friendship that will last a lifetime.

— Gregg Madsen,
Auburn, Nebraska

God Spared the Camp During Tornado of '98

Portions of this eyewitness account were published in the Fall 1998 issue of Newsline, the camp newsletter.

If you've never thought about God's hand guiding a tornado, consider the events of Saturday evening, June 13, 1998, at Maranatha Camp.

A tornado swept through at 5:50 pm., uprooting or damaging 150 trees, but causing almost no damage to buildings. Most importantly, no one was injured. No one could have hand-picked a path for the tornado to cross the main Campgrounds and cause less damage.

"This was the closest we've had a tornado strike in the 25 years I've been here," said George Cheek. "Even the adjustor who came to look at the buildings was totally amazed that with all the trees that fell down and around the buildings, there was hardly a scratch."

Girls' Volleyball Camp was in session the day the tornado struck. There were fewer than 50 campers and program staff, and they all were in the Dining Hall for the evening meal at the time of the tornado.

There was little time to prepare beyond making a quick sweep of the grounds to alert staff members to the tornado warning. Once they arrived at the Dining Hall (the Camp's top-priority storm shelter), many of them took a few steps out the main door and watched the angry-looking skies over Interstate 80, north of the Dining Hall, when suddenly the tornado came swooping down upon Lake Maranatha behind them, from the south. It passed between the Olsen home and the Fasse cabin, then evaded the Crooks mobile home, ripping up cedar trees along the way. It entered the parking lot at a point less than 100 feet from the Dining Hall, picked up the Camp's small bus and carried it about 200 feet to the northwest, slamming it into a row of parked cars owned by Maranatha Summer Missionaries.

The tornado — a relatively small one — crossed I-80 and went another half mile north, where it knocked a house off its foundation before dissipating.

"A small tornado is kind of like minor surgery," said Tad Stryker, who saw the storm coming over the lake. "It's not small or minor if it happens to you. I've lived all my life in this area, and I'd never seen a tornado on the ground before. I hope I never see another one."

The staff surveyed the damage in the growing darkness, and thanked God for His protection of the Camp. There was virtually no structural damage to any buildings; only a screen door and some shutters were ruined, and some trees had gently leaned up against the Olsen house, causing minor indentations in the shingles.

That evening, the call went out for volunteers to help clean up the twisted trees. About 150 workers showed up on Sunday afternoon to saw branches and drag them into piles while Camp staff shredded them to make cedar mulch that would cover paths around the Camp. Some of the volunteers came from as far as 60 miles away.

"Some of them, I didn't even know," said Cheek. "It was very gratifying to see so many people show up."

Besides an increased feeling of goodwill between Maranatha and the community, the storm provided another benefit. A few years later, Cheek sawed some of the larger trees into cedar paneling to make the vaulted ceiling for the director's house, which was finished in 2002.

For the staff, it was an opportunity to see God at work, whether guiding a tornado away from buildings or motivating volunteers to spend a day cleaning up cedar branches.

I believe one of the lessons we need to learn is that this is God's camp," said staff member Cal Carter. "He has His hand of protection on it. He's going to do with it what He pleases."

— Tad Stryker

The tornado that struck Maranatha Bible Camp on June 13, 1998, moved the Camp bus about 200 feet and tossed it into a row of parked cars. The bus remained useable for years afterward.

As nearly as Camp staff can estimate, these trees (just south of the main parking lot) were directly in the path of the tornado.

The Resurgence of Youth Camps

A dramatic rise in attendance in youth camps occurred at Maranatha starting in the mid-1980s. Several key people should be mentioned during this time period. Frank Van Campen directed Sr. High Camp for several years and Russ Matzke directed Jr. High Camp. Beginning in 1990, Doug Shada became the program director. For several years under his team's leadership, the Jr. High and Sr. High camps were merged. Eventually, attendance outgrew the housing and chapel. Again the age groups were divided and the momentum carried through until 20-man Army tents were needed to handle the overflow housing for campers.

Predating this time period was Dave Wyrtzen, who in 1977 began as featured speaker and continued for more than 20 years, becoming the longest-running consecutive youth camp speaker Maranatha has seen to date. Bryan Clark also joined this program team, both directing and speaking.

Many others should be mentioned, but three longtime associates, all of Lincoln Berean Church, have been important in recruiting cabin leaders and providing their talents.

Dan Lehman has influenced hundreds of collegians to give one or two weeks in cabin leading and then provided training. Paul Lucks, through his team in junior high ministry, has recruited hundreds of young people to Maranatha, as has John Matzke and his team in senior high ministry.

Dave and Mary Wyrtzen were a familiar sight at Couples' Conference. Dave also spoke at youth weeks for many years.

You can't mention youth camps without talking about "Mr. Wizard." Pete & Cindy Vasek of Laramie, Wyoming, have had the longest running specialty involvement in chapel services of anyone in recent years. Pete was a lifelong science teacher. He brought demonstrations with an application to the Jr. High and Sr. High camps from the early 1980s to the present. The Vaseks also brought their water ski boat and taught the sport to campers for a number of years.

Duane and Carol Porter of Laramie first started bringing their children in the 1970s. They enjoyed coming with their camper and ski boat to help with the youth weeks. Their interest in Maranatha, the staff and the Camp scholarship fund for youth has continued to this day.

Dave Wyrtzen's church, Midlothian Bible Church, began sending its youth on the long trip to Maranatha from near Dallas, Texas. Sometime late in the 1970s, a carload or two filled with youth and sponsors from Midlothian drove to Maranatha with Dave for a Senior High Camp. In subsequent years, Youth Pastor Wes Ooms organized larger groups. The annual migration to Nebraska grew under the leadership of Pastor Tim Wallace, who took over for Ooms in the mid-1980s. Tim and his wife, Becky, have achieved the task of raising funds to bring busloads of youth year after year. The trip includes an overnight stay both ways at Sterling College in Kansas. Volunteers have traveled up for work projects. The church's annual fundraiser, among other projects, has been very successful.

The Texas accents are a source of good-natured teasing from the predominantly Midwestern campers (and the Texans usually give it back as quickly as they receive it). Many lifelong friendships, including a few weddings, have resulted.

This longtime relationship with the good people of another "MBC" is certainly one of the "God sightings" we've seen along the way!

– George Cheek

VOICES OF MARANATHA

Foundations

Our three children: Tyler (19), Xavier (17) and Tiana (15) attended your camps while we belonged to Lincoln Berean Church. The Marines needed us in North Carolina for the past few years and recently I was deployed to Kuwait/Iraq. Because of that experience, God is seen in our lives more and more each day. Thank you for the foundations you built for us and our children.

– Kerry Quinn

Director, Speaker, Playground Maker

My (Barb) first time on the campground was in the summer of 1966 or 1967, when my brother and his wife were preparing to go to the mission field. Little did I know at that time that our lives would be involved with MBC.

We were in two Berean pastorates for more than 20 years. During those years we would send our Junior/Senior high youth to the Camp, and would send along some counselors also. We would always have ladies go to the retreats. While pastoring in Haxtun, Colorado, John was the Awana Camp director for several years. The latest involvement with the Camp is the family camp—Biblical Concepts Family Conference. John has been the director of that week as well as the speaker.

John also was the one who designed, and with the help of some other men, made the playground equipment. A group of men from the Haxtun church helped to cement it into the ground.

Our children remember the time well when they had gone with John a day early to get ready for Awana Camp, and got there only to find out it was flooded.

John Regier, director of Biblical Concepts in Counseling, spoke at family camps and volunteered many hours painting children's playground equipment at Camp.

We have had the privilege for two summers now, to bring our family to the Camp and have our own reunion. Our children would walk the grounds sharing memories with each other. It was special for them to share with their own children about things that they remembered of the Camp.

God has done many special things in the lives of the people who have attended Maranatha. We are privileged to have been a part of what He has done. We know that what has been accomplished through the ministry of MBC will last for eternity.

– John and Barb Regier,
Colorado Springs, Colorado

The Regier family enjoys a reunion at Maranatha.

We Watched Many Little Lives Be Influenced

I will never forget the first year of involvement at MBC after I came on staff at Lincoln Berean. The first year I was a cabin leader at Junior Camp. The next 10 years, I came back as the director of Junior Camp. Go figure.

My wife, Mary, and I watched many, many little lives be influenced over those 10 years. We saw many committed adults serve their hearts out, and while so doing their lives were etched with God's influence as well.

The ripple affect was that our kids were affected as well. We brought them to Camp every year, and they grew to love the environment. The result has been that their lives have been influenced in later years as they attend youth camp. They would not miss it, and now serve back as cabin leaders and worship team members for Junior Camp.

God, in His grace, continues to bless many families through the ministry of MBC. As a family, we count it a great blessing to have been a part of ministry that continues to affect lives for eternity.

– Donn Stoner,
Lincoln, Nebraska

Christian Music, Missions Interests Born at MBC

I spent the whole summer of 1990 at Maranatha doing various things around Camp. I had just finished my class work at Kearney State College and was waiting to do my internship the next fall. I think my brother, Tad Stryker, who had joined the staff at MBC the previous year, suggested that I apply for a Core Counselor position.

I had never attended a Camp at Maranatha before then, but I decided to apply. I was accepted and began the summer with nine others, including John and Beth Matzke from Lincoln Berean, who were leaders of the Core Counselors.

The counselor training was led by Tim Lehman from Kansas. One thing I particularly remember from the training is singing "Awesome God" by Rich Mullins for the first time as Tim led us on his guitar.

For six weeks the 10 of us were the main cabin leaders for the different camps that came to Maranatha, ranging from elementary through high school kids. We also assisted with child care for the family camp.

After the six-week counselor assignment was done, I decided to remain at MBC and work as a lifeguard. I also ended up working in the recreation shop, kitchen, and in housekeeping.

I look back on the summer of 1990 with fond memories. It was very challenging, yet rewarding. I met so many great people and really grew in my walk with God. I was exposed to great Christian music from artists like Michael W. Smith, Steve Camp, Steven Curtis Chapman, and DC Talk.

I will never forget all the Hmongs that came that summer and all the rice we went through! The adults came one week and the youth the next - probably 2000 people between the two weeks. They set up huge tents around camp and piled into them at night. I remember while washing dishes after one of the meals, I sprayed hot water into the container which had held the Hmong hot sauce. The vapor made me cough for several minutes. Needless to say, I never did that again! And I thought Mexican food was hot!

During Youth Week, I particularly enjoyed the teaching of Dave Wyrtzen and Danny Byram leading worship. I have a memory of a re-enactment of Elijah and the prophets of Baal around the campfire by the lake trying to call down fire from heaven. I don't recall that happening but it certainly wasn't because John Matzke, Karl Yeutter, and the rest of the guys didn't try!

I remember being especially challenged by Dan Lehman's mission presentations during Youth Week. I decided I wanted to participate in a missions trip. I found out the Lincoln Berean college group, led by Dan Lehman, was going to inner-city Los Angeles the following summer for six weeks to work with World Impact, so I decided to raise support and go. What a blessing it was to see the money come in from so many people who were also praying for my experience there.

The summer of 1992, after being challenged by Ben Sawatsky, now head of EFC Missions, I went to Romania with a group from my church in Kearney to do street evangelism and show the Jesus film, which Campus Crusade for Christ has shown to millions all over the world. The next year, I went to Kansas City with a youth group from Kearney EFC to do some work projects for Calvary Bible College.

I enjoyed my experiences on all three trips and my world vision was broadened. I strongly believe in the value of short-term missions trips and recommend them to everyone. It is fair to say that I may never have gone on any of the trips if I hadn't been at Maranatha that summer. That is where my interest in missions began.

Since marrying Daren Popple in December of 1994, we have attended Couples' Getaway at MBC almost every year, and always look forward to seeing friends there. I like not having to cook! Through the years, we have enjoyed getting to know the speakers, Richard and Toni Crocker, from Cheyenne. The program staff adds humor, creativity, and special touches which make for an enjoyable weekend.

Daren and I love Maranatha and pray that it will continue to transform lives as it has done for decades.

– Jeana Popple,
Holdrege, Nebraska

Family Fun in the Pool

Our family loves Family Camp at Maranatha, including the grandparents, parents and children.

One of our favorite activities is swimming. We overheard this conversation between our two daughters (ages 3 and 5 at the time):

3-year-old Kori: "Kaylynn, do you have your googles?"
Kaylynn: "No, Kori, not googles—GOGGLES!" Such fun memories for us.

– Kari Schott,
Sterling, Colorado

Maranatha's Eternal Impact on the Knott Family

God has used Maranatha Bible Camp to impact our family for three generations. We first heard about Maranatha through my family's involvement in the Berean Church in Haxtun, Colorado. My father, Albert Knott, who was a music teacher, began serving in 1964 as a counselor and director of music at Junior Camp. As I recall, he continued that ministry every summer until he died from Lou Gehrig's disease in 1972. The Lord used him to impact lives at Camp, but I also know that he grew spiritually through those days of ministry.

I got involved at Maranatha one year before my father did. I first attended Camp in 1963, the summer before I entered third grade and continued to attend for the next eight years. I still remember godly speakers, tiny cabins, the slamming screen doors of the Tabernacle, great singing, and how good a bottle of pop at the Sweet Shop tasted on those hot summer days.

Two words come to mind when I think about Camp: "significant decisions." During my junior high years, I was really struggling with peer pressure and was making a lot of wrong choices. I wanted to be accepted by my friends, but I also knew that the Lord wanted me to walk with Him. It was at Camp that I made significant decisions to serve the Lord with my life. It was at Junior High Camp that I said to the Lord, "Here am I, send me." Every time I am on the Camp grounds, I remember that commitment, and I know

The Paul Knott family in 2001. Counter clockwise, from back left: Tiffanie, Jason, Paul, Brianna, Joshua, Betty, Caleb.

that decision made so many years ago is one reason I am serving as a pastor today. I also know that my younger sisters, Janelle and Ruth, were impacted in similar ways by their involvement at Camp over the years.

In 1995, my wife Betty and I were living with our five children in Newman Grove, Nebraska, where I was pastoring a Bible Church. Our oldest son, Jason, was 16 years old, and was just finishing his sophomore year of high school. He was walking with the Lord, however, he was facing quite a bit of discouragement due to persecution from those who did not share his faith. That summer the Lord opened up the opportunity for him to serve as a lifeguard at Maranatha. It was exactly what Jason needed. He had all kinds of fun, made some wonderful friends, was mentored spiritually by godly college-aged young men, and saw the Lord at work in his life and in the lives of the campers and staff. His life has never been the same.

Every summer since 1995, one of our children has been on summer staff at Maranatha as a lifeguard. Each of them could share similar testimonies to that of Jason. Josh, Caleb, and Tiffanie have all grown through their involvement at Camp. They have returned home at the end of each summer with a deeper understanding of God's Word, a deeper love for their Lord, and a renewed commitment to walk in obedience to Him. As a parent, I can think of no greater blessing.

I thank God for the ministry of Maranatha Bible Camp. It has made an eternal impact on my family for three generations, and for that I will be eternally grateful.

– Paul Knott,
Hastings, Nebraska

The Albert Knott family in 1963. From left: Janelle, Albert, Marian (holding Ruth), Paul.

Bringing Friends to Christ at Camp

I had lots of fun this year (2003) at Camp. I brought my best friends to Christ by bringing them! I decided Maranatha probably needs money more than I do, so I paid $2 extra. (Whoopty do) but I hope it will help a little.

– Tiffany Dahlkoetter

Welshes Have Seen Maranatha From Many Angles

My first acquaintance with Maranatha was the first Camp at Bignell, Nebraska, across the river south of Maranatha.

My sister, Rose (McDermott) Robinson and my brother, Don McDermott, went to one of the first camps.

Later my sister, Esther and I went where Camp is now; they had tents and it rained, but that was fun for us. We were both baptized that year and dedicated our lives to become missionaries. I remember all sitting in a circle on the ground. Rev. Theodore Epp was one of the pastors.

My sister and I didn't become missionaries, but Esther's son was in missions work and our son, Stephen Welsh, was a missionary in Columbia (was martyred in 1995 by the guerrillas).

We sent Stephen's two sons (age 8 and 9), Shad and Scott and our daughter, Betty and Chuck Wretling's son, Stephen (age 9) to Camp. What a great time for them. Shad and Scott now are missionaries with their families in Peru.

Our daughter, Betty, attended the Navigator Program in the 1960s. It was a very spiritual training program with lots of discipline. Our daughter and several others later went to Bible school.

Our son-in-law, Chuck Wretling, went to Navigators at Maranatha. Also went on to Bible school and was a pastor later.

Ladies' Retreat was always so great. We had very good speakers and a lot of spiritual help, fellowship and sharing times. Some times our teenage daughters came. Mrs. Olsen and Inez Maline were so much fun in Needham Hall.

Later on, we started going to Family Camp. Some of our married children and families joined us. It was a refreshing time worshipping together and also the games, swimming and sharing.

Then there was couples' retreat. Steve and Sandy and George Jr. and Sandy, our sons came. It was so great to be all together. There were the fun times and the serious learning times about marriage.

Since the 1990s our son, George Jr. and Sandy and sons, attend Family Camp every year; they take their vacation at Family Camp. George Jr. is the pastor in a Bible Church in Neligh, Nebraska.

We have our family reunions at Maranatha, usually stay two days. It is a very good place for reunions, no cooking, cleaning, all kinds of recreation, climbing wall, basketball, soccer. A time to have just our family share and spend time together.

Maranatha has been a great spiritual blessing to our families having a part in their lives and making decisions to go into Christian work. Plus making strong Christian families. Camp has very good leadership and a caring staff.

We have also done town run, which is getting groceries, parts for cars, swimming pools, laundry supplies or whatever they need. We have done town run three times a week every summer since the 1980s.

Maranatha has made a large imprint in our whole family in different times of our lives.

Praise God for Rev. Ivan Olsen and God leading him to start Maranatha and choosing a faithful leader in George Cheek to continue after his retirement.

— *George and Mildred Welsh,*
North Platte, Nebraska

'Dear God' Letter Made All the Difference

I went to your spring ladies' retreat about encouragement. I had a GREAT time and grew and learned so much. I really enjoyed just "getting away" too! To me it was like going up to the mountain top! At the end of the retreat we wrote "Dear God" letters. It was such an incredible time and I wrote mine on God's faithfulness, His ability to be trusted, and just how great He is! We turned them in and they were to be mailed to us at an unspecified time.

Over the past year and half my "father" came into my life (I am 27 years old now and he never had anything to do with me). He is not a Christian and neither is his new wife.

Things did not work out and he "dumped me" with a letter. My heart was broken again! (It is his pattern to run and abandon.) But I still felt such a sting of rejection. That same day I got his letter I also got my "Dear God" letter! What an awesome moment that was. I just went off by myself and read it and just cried in God's arms! It was definitely from God to get that on the same day!

Thank you for being such an instrument for God's plan and such an encouragement for all people. I will definitely be back next year!

— *Bree Wilson*

'Mr. Wizard' Grateful for Years (and Miles) at Camp

The first time we ever went to Maranatha, we didn't go. Cindy and I were waiting in Laramie with about 30 Awana kids who were packed and ready to go. The Camp was flooded in 1983, and we were waiting for a phone call from Duane Porter who was already at Maranatha. There was no possible way to have Camp due to the high water so we sent all of our campers home without even getting on the road to Maranatha.

Pete "Mr. Wizard" Vasek grabs the attention of youth campers with his entertaining science experiments.

The next year, we finally made it to Maranatha. It would mark the beginning of nearly 20 years of different kinds of camps. Our first one was an Awana Camp which exposed us to extreme heat, night time tornadoes, and Doug Shada. We were hooked after that.

As our children, Bethanne and Nathan, continued to grow, we moved along with them to Junior High and High School camps every summer. We led all sorts of caravans to Camp filled with kids from Laramie. We always found some way to help out. The lake just begged for use, so we bought a boat and started bringing that along for extra recreation. I don't know how many miles that Dean Ostrander, Duane Porter, and I have drug kids around the lake on tubes or water skis. The highlight would be if we could get Dave Wyrtzen around for a barefoot run.

We cannot remember or explain how the ministry of "Mr. Wizard" began for the youth weeks. It has been one of the great adventures for me to share physics demonstrations and a resulting Biblical application.

Probably the greatest memories are the people we have met at Camp. We have developed an incredibly large extended family composed of people from Camp staff, Lincoln, Midlothian, all over Nebraska, Colorado, Wyoming, and other parts of the country. Our son, Nathan, wound up at the University of Nebraska as a result of the relationships at Camp. Now we are bringing our grandchildren for the next level.

Maranatha is not just a Camp for us. It is a focus point for our ministry.

– Pete Vasek,
Laramie, Wyoming

A Cycle of Investing in the Lives of Campers

My earliest memories of Maranatha Bible Camp are from the summer after third grade when I came out for Awana Camp.

I don't remember exactly what all the speakers have said over the years. What I do remember is that there were people at Camp who loved me.

As I grew older, I realized that these people were investing their lives in the campers. This investment cost them something. Some of them took vacation time from work, some of the college students would simply take a week off from working. I didn't understand why until it was my turn.

Now I am grateful that I could serve the Lord in this way and know that He would be faithful to me by providing for my needs. It was important to me to come and be a part of the weeks that gave an opportunity to shape the lives of some young people. So many people had done the same for me.

My family has been integral in my Maranatha experiences. My dad and mom have been bringing kids out to Camp all of the years that I have been coming out. My dad baptized me in Lake Maranatha.

Last summer, I married Paula. She had never been to Maranatha before. We had been married two weeks when we came out to spend two weeks at camp. Paula is a nurse and came out to be a Camp nurse. She loves the kids and had a wonderful time. At the end of the two weeks, we were laughing and saying that we had spent half of our married life at Maranatha. Not many people could say that. We look forward to serving in the future.

I look back and am so thankful for my counselors, the program staff, and the Camp staff for all that they did for me and the other campers over the years. People who have given their lives to serve the Lord. I can honestly say that so many of these people have opened my eyes to the Kingdom of God and what it means to be a Kingdom worker.

– Nate Vasek,
Laramie, Wyoming

Top row, from left: Sports camps caught on in the 1990s, and after the gym was built, they enjoyed better facilities; Cal Carter (center, back row) started Roller Hockey Camp in the 1990s. Cal and his family traveled from Canada to be on the Summer Missions staff several years, then joined the full-time staff in the late 1990s; Primary camps had a Hawaiian theme in 1994.

Second row, from left: A long run of Singles' Conferences come to an end with this group in 1995; Scott Wilson began directing sports camps at Maranatha in 1990. This is the first Volleyball Camp. JoAnn Wilson (back row, sixth from left) also was an instructor and director; The Couples' Getaway was a theme-oriented autumn weekend program, usually with wacky overtones.

Third row, from left: Primary camps added a new dimension to Maranatha's schedule, 1990s; Maranatha held a Single Parents' Retreat throughout much of the 1990s. Steve Demoret (back row, second from right) was program director; The Ringneck Roundup attracted men (and a few women) for a weekend of hunting and sporting days, with the gospel message mixed in.

Fourth row: Praise and worship music, here shown during Senior High Camp 1998, was a big feature of all youth programs at Maranatha during the 1990s and beyond.

Top row, from left: Starting in 1994, many Camp registrations were held in the gym; Nationally-known Christian musicians Steve and Annie Chapman gave two concerts in conjunction with Couples' Conference (this one was in the Camp gym in 2002). Steve also spoke at Archery Camp and Annie at Ladies' Retreat.

Second row, from left: The Camp opens the gym to the public during the fall and winter for roller skating; Two views of the Old Tabernacle, which was used for overflow camper housing in the late 1980s and early 1990s.

Third row, from left: Jorge and Elodia Pacheco (left) and Mark and Jo Schafer enjoy the Couples' Conference banquet in 1999; Paula Dishmán, Jeanette Andrew, Jan Cheek and JoAnn Beetem are ready to serve an English High Tea during Ladies' Retreat 1992; The "One Way" quartet from George, Iowa, was a regular feature at Family Camp.

Fourth row, from left: Water tubing; Sand volleyball; Cabin leader Todd Nighswonger and his campers appear to be re-energized by their lunch.

Top row, from left: This Junior Camp cabin leader is about to take a chilly plunge; Gregg Most is one proud papa after his twin sons, Trapper and Tyler, bagged pheasants at the 1998 Ringneck Roundup.
Second row, from left: The bicycle jump into the lake was a popular spectator sport at Senior High Camp; Cabin leader Jeff Thompson and three campers enjoy a peaceful moment at the Waterfront during Junior High Camp 1999; July 4 at the waterfront.

Third row, from left: Campfire services like this one (Junior High Camp 1998) have been the setting for life-changing decisions throughout the history of Maranatha; Two campers collide during an innertube sumo wrestling match at Junior High Camp 1998; Fred Gayman and his grandson, Jordan Johnson, enjoy fishing on Lake Maranatha in 1997. Within two years, the Camp cleared this area for the sand beach area of its new waterfront.

Fourth row, from left: Lowland flooding in 1995 was a nuisance, but did not damage any buildings or affect the Camp's scheduled events. This is a "ferry boat" just north of Clark Hall; Candy Presley, program director for Primary Camp, and Lance Gerry, Maranatha's food service director, whip up a batch of cotton candy during a carnival in 1996.; Donn Stoner (front row, left end) and Mark Geist (wearing cap next to Donn in the front row) were directors of Archery Camp during the 1990s.

Staff Members

Kenneth Blood was no slacker, but he could tell that he was falling farther behind. In the late spring of 1969, Ken and his wife, Sophie, came to live at Maranatha Bible Camp to help Ivan Olsen by serving as Camp managers. They also worked at the North Platte Berean Church.

Blood was a staunch supporter of Maranatha. For nearly 20 years, he had served on the Camp board, much of that time as secretary. But during his time on site, he got a new appreciation for how much work was required to maintain the Camp facility, let alone spending part of every work week at the church. For 15 months, he had served "with a full measure of time and effort," but by then, he had come to realize that his list of responsibilities was longer than his health could stand. He decided to write a letter of resignation to Olsen.

The main reason he was leaving, he wrote Olsen, was "none other than the matter of never being caught up, so that there is the mental strain of an unfinished task continually." He proposed that either Olsen begin working fulltime for the Camp, or that he hire someone else to do so because the workload had become so great.

Olsen had seen Camp managers come and go for many years, but this time he appeared to take Blood's recommendation to heart. He knew that the ministry had grown dramatically, and he hoped to see its growth continue. Olsen began to look into the possibility of hiring fulltime help at Maranatha.

Within three years, Olsen hired George Cheek. By the end of the 1970s, there were others on staff. By 1999, there were 10 fulltime staff members, each one raising financial support to be at Maranatha. As of this writing, seven fulltime staff members have served 15 years or more.

Here is a capsule of each current fulltime staff member, taken by year they joined the fulltime staff:

Ruth Ann Rodgers (1977) came for the first summer to help as the dorm supervisor and head of housekeeping. Her college training and experience as a bookkeeper for Pepsi in Lincoln made her qualified to accept a position working part time for Maranatha and part time for Ernie Skoog's office under the supervision of the Berean Fundamental Church Council. Later she also worked as administrative assistant under George Cheek. When the Cheeks traveled promoting and recruiting for Camp, she was also the primary child care provider in the evenings and days school was not in session. Ruth Ann saw the office evolve from mimeograph to copy machines, from bound ledger books to computer programs and electronic banking.

Bruce Stucky (1982) first heard of Maranatha at Calvary Bible College when recruiter John Meschke told him of the need for someone to help in property maintenance. Bruce came for the summer and found his ability was needed. Bruce already was engaged to Rachel Fahl, and they decided to begin their life together in ministry. Time flew by, their daughter Esther was born and raised at Camp, graduating from Maxwell Public School in 2004. Bruce's abilities grew with the job including building good relationships with volunteer workers. Except for his first three years, he has been assisted by Mark Swesey and David (Bubba) Jones.

Jo Ann Beetem (1982) had graduated from Nebraska Wesleyan University with a teaching degree and her summers were open. She was on the summer staff several years before joining the staff fulltime. Her job has always involved registrations of campers and data management. Her secretarial responsibilities look quite different now with the advent of e-mail and Internet availability. The late spring and first half of summer are especially full for a camp registrar, and Jo Ann has served faithfully.

Mark Swesey (1985) grew up coming to Maranatha as a camper from Alliance, Nebraska, where his parents were in the pastorate. One winter after the potato harvest ended, Mark came to help get Camp ready for winter retreat. He still remembers the first meal Jan Cheek served the first day on the job as a volunteer. Because help was needed for the projects already underway, Mark stayed on through the summer and then continued on as seasonal help, which developed into fulltime. Some of his responsibilities have included lawns, sprinkler systems, mowers and mechanical.

David Jones (1986) first saw Maranatha as a volunteer with a Broken Bow, NE youth group led by Bryan Clark. He accepted an invitation to return that summer as part of the properties crew. This he did for two summers and then stayed for the winter as a seasonal worker to help with some building projects. Part of his responsibilities became lock smithing, plumbing and CDL bus driver as needed.

Tad Stryker (1989) had a journalism degree from the University of Nebraska-Lincoln and experience in the newspaper business, so he and his wife, Jean, assumed that God would lead in that direction. At the time, Camp needed help in housekeeping for year-round quality and continuity and there was a part-time need for brochure production and marketing. Tad was willing to apply for the job, but George wanted them to wait until their second child was born. Within weeks of that event, Tad had been accepted. George remembers Don Hunt wanted to know why Tad would leave a "good-paying job" to come to Maranatha. Later Don commented several times how God had blessed the Camp and the Strykers as they stepped out in faith.

Tad became director of marketing in 1998. Jean has supervised both the Craft Shop and Sweet Shop at different times, served as interim food service director from 1999-2000 and contributed with creative landscaping and interior decorating ideas over the years. Their children, Jake, Micah and Abigail, have grown up at Camp.

Rodney Thiessen (2000) and his wife, Leila, sold their new home near both sets of their parents in the Frazier Valley of British Columbia and moved with their three children (Braedon, Emily & Christian) to Saskatchewan to attend Briercrest Bible College. In only a few months, they met Maranatha recruiters Carol & Ken Dyck, who told them about a Summer Missions opportunity in the U.S. The Thiessens looked at a map to be sure where Nebraska was, and believed that the Lord led them to apply for an internship position. They subsequently were accepted.

Upon their arrival in May, an unfortunate staff situation made Rodney's "internship" experience much more hands-on than anyone had planned. Leila helped with health care and soon the couple's giftedness had made room for them. By the end of summer they were invited to stay on. The Thiessens have invited a steady stream of friends and family members who come to join in the work force each summer. The Teens in Training program has been enhanced with the help of the Thiessens' friend, Adam Stuart-Walker, who was on the fulltime staff from 2001-03. The Summer Missions program continues to grow in quality. In 2002, Rodney was appointed director of programming.

Ron Prohaska (2001) met his wife, Bonnie, when they were at Maranatha as members of the 1983 summer staff. Bonnie was recruited from Biola University by John Meschke. Ron was attending college in Iowa. That was the summer of the six-week flood, and Ron stayed on a few months to help with restoring Lake Maranatha.

Several years later, after they had managed a camp ministry in Iowa, they returned to North Platte to work for Norman Refrigeration, owned by friends they had met during their first time at Maranatha. During the following years, Bonnie served part-time on Summer Missions staff several times.

Their desire to be in fulltime ministry intensified and they joined the Maranatha staff, where Ron became the director of conference center. This position involves oversight of the facilities including the gym, classrooms, locker rooms, chapel, dining hall, kitchen and dishwashing area. As a department, it has the largest budget and staff. His prior experience was a real asset in preparation for this responsibility.

Scot Cockson (2002) and his wife, Carla, had lived in several major cities as they followed their careers, Carla in marketing and Scot in department store management. They sensed that God might be calling them into some type of ministry before they moved to Minneapolis, where Scot was general manager of Bloomingdale's in the Mall of America. When they heard about the director of operations position being created at Maranatha, their hearts were prepared. After visiting Camp, their interview process was completed when George Cheek and Richard Crocker visited them two days before September 11, 2001. The Cocksons spent the next four months raising support and preparing to make the move to Maranatha with their four sons (Andrew, Paul, David, and Daniel).

The transition went fairly smoothly for Scot, George Cheek and the department heads at Maranatha. In 2003, George became CEO of Maranatha Ministries and Scot was appointed executive director of Maranatha Bible Camp.

Two other vital staff members are serving at Maranatha on an hourly basis. Marlys Gosnell and her husband, Ivan, are ranchers who live only five miles east of Camp. In 1999, Maranatha had advertised the need for bookkeeping help in several area church bulletins. Marlys was commuting to North Platte for the same type of job and immediately applied. The type of work was a great match and she fit in well with the office team and area businesses we have accounts with.

That same year, Kathy Sprague saw another advertisement Maranatha had placed in several area church bulletins for a year-round part-time housekeeping manager. After her interview, she knew this was a job she would like. Kathy is a real people person and in the summer has a number of staff working for her part-time. Her thoroughness and dedication have taken the cleanliness of our housing facilities to a new level and the Camp has received many comments of appreciation. Kathy and her husband, Roger, live in North Platte.

When anyone comes to Camp, two questions are utmost in mind: Where am I going to stay and what time is the next meal? Food service is such an important part of the ministry. The following are people who served more than one summer as head of food service since the early 1970s. Patsy Shaver, Hazel Anderson, Cindy Lehman, Kathy Fellows, Jeanne Foster Huntley, Jean Aerhart, Evan Schrenk, Dennis Jewert, Amanda Berry, Lance Gerry (also worked in technological development and insurance management) and Dorothy Grafton (also served as housekeeping manager and guest group coordinator).

Joe Dapra ran the Maranatha kitchen for several summers during the 1980s; he also took a spiritual leadership role in the summer staff programs during that time. John Meschke was a promotional specialist for Maranatha and was summer staff coordinator in the early 1980s. Warren Cheek (George's brother) served as staff coordinator in the mid-80s, and Bob Bulkley was staff coordinator in the late 80s.

There have been paid staff members working in the properties department since 1947, when Maranatha hired Rev. & Mrs. Joseph Switzer of Maxwell to serve as Camp caretakers. The Switzers served until the mid-1950s, and were succeeded by Mr. & Mrs. Kenneth Martin (approximately 1956-59), Mr. & Mrs. Wendell Williams (1959-early 1960s) and Gordon Thrash (the mid-1960s). Rex Shaver followed Kenneth Blood as caretaker, but Shaver's role was more focused on mainte-

nance and grounds. He helped build the new kitchen/dining hall/chapel. Tim Harder also served on the properties staff for a short time.

In the 1970s, the Berean Fellowship temporarily opened an office at Camp. Ernie Skoog worked out of that office and did some work for Maranatha as well. The Waterfront on Lake Maranatha is named for this longtime friend of Camp. Bob Benson, a reserve running back for the Nebraska Cornhuskers during the 1930s, served the BFCC as Stewardship Director, and during the 1970s and 80s, maintained an office at Maranatha. Several inheritance gifts have come to Maranatha as a result of his work. The flagpole by the conference center was installed with the memorial funds given in his honor after his death in 1991.

Many people have worked fulltime in the Camp office for less than five years, including Connie Lutes, Bernice Smith and Brenda Harder (1970s-80s) and Harald Bjerga, Joel Ondrejack, Cal Carter, Jamie Flinchbaugh, Evie Bagley, Mark & Karle Weiderick, Adam Stuart-Walker and Angela Berry (1990s-2000s).

Laura Kramer and Tobias Davis served as kitchen managers (assistants to the director of conference center) in the early 2000s.

Mark Geist has served as executive director of the Maranatha Camp Foundation since 1996. His office has been in Lincoln, and sometimes out of his home. His wife, Suzanne, and children Alexis, John Mark and Derek, also have been involved in Camp for many years.

Kris Cheek is executive director of SportReach. He and his wife, Natalie, live in Lincoln. They raise all their own support, as do the other members of the SportReach staff — Pete Kirchhoff (and his wife, Donna, and children Joshua, Rachel and Calvin) of Woodland Park, Colorado, Jacqulyn Miller (husband, Shane and daughter, Annalee) of Lincoln and Gayle Gerkensmeyer, also of Lincoln.

We Sure Enjoyed the Maranatha Community

God has given us some very special memories from our time serving at Maranatha Bible Camp. Earl started working at Maranatha seasonally, mostly in the kitchen, from 1984 to 1990. Nita came to Maranatha the summer of 1987 to visit Karen Millheim and work in the kitchen for two and one-half weeks, met Earl and became engaged. June of 1988 we were married in Minnesota. George and Jan and Kelly Willis were there for our big day.

We lived at Maranatha for two years and our first son was born at the North Platte hospital. We sure enjoyed the Maranatha community. Nita taught kindergarten at Platte Valley Christian school but during the summer served in the Sweet Shop, Craft Shop and the switchboard. One of our favorite things to do was to walk around Lake Maranatha.

— Earl and Nita Grover

Strykers Blessed by Step of Faith

In April 1989, I drove the Camp pickup and flatbed trailer packed with my family's belongings from our home in North Platte to Maranatha Bible Camp. I remember thinking, "What in the world am I doing, God?" It turns out that we were taking a step of faith and allowing God to work on us in ways we never dreamed of.

Jean and I had talked and prayed about joining the staff at Maranatha. We believe it was God's will for us to go, and we have never regretted our decision. It has been a growing experience all the way.

Our sons were young (Jake was 2 1/2 years; Micah was 3 months) when we moved to Camp. Abby was born a year and a half later. Our kids have grown up and our marriage has been enriched at Maranatha. The wide variety of godly men and women we see at Camp every year have taught our family that God's church includes all races, backgrounds and personality types.

Jean has shown versatility by managing the Craft Shop, Camp kitchen and Sweet Shop at different times during our years at Maranatha while she kept our family cared for.

I have communicated the story of Maranatha through various media. I was eager to start working on Camp brochures when I arrived, and soon I also was working with video. In 1989, I'd never heard of the Internet, but not many years later, I was in charge of Maranatha's Web site.

I have enjoyed working with other staff members with different abilities and being part of God's work — something that is much bigger than any of us. Just being part of the history and heritage of Maranatha is something I will always treasure.

Living at Camp is a privilege. I walk across the grounds and around the lake whenever I can. I like to look at the place where I used to play football with my boys, or the spot I went camping with them by the south channel of the Platte. I remember taking Jake, at about age 4, out to the big lighted cross by Interstate 80 so he could view it up close on about a dozen different occasions. I remember helping Micah learn a gutsy skateboard maneuver on a plywood ramp at the cement court near Needham Hall. I remember tossing 7-year-old Abby on my shoulders and setting a personal speed record running for the Dining Hall when I saw the tornado of 1998 coming at me from across the lake!

The Camp is usually a lot more peaceful than it was that evening. In fact, people have come here for decades to get away from their routines, hear from God and make life-changing decisions. We have a slightly different perspective; as a staff family, we view Maranatha not a destination, but as our home turf and workplace. Still, for us and for many others, Maranatha is holy ground.

– Tad & Jean Stryker,
Maranatha Bible Camp

The Tad Stryker family in 2000. From left: Jake, Tad, Abby, Jean, Micah.

Hard Kitchen Work Taught Valuable Lessons

It is hard to recount my memories of Maranatha in just a few short paragraphs, I'm afraid. I worked at the Camp for six summers and on lots of week-ends during the winter months for a number of years. My experiences varied from happy, funny times to humbling, learning experiences and challenges.

I met a lot of people at Camp who influenced me in many ways. One example is the number of Bible college students that spent their summers working for God. Because of their influence and example, I decided that Bible college was where I would start my higher education. I also made a lot of friends from my time at Maranatha. Some were friendships that I asked for the summer months and a little more, but they will be renewed in Heaven. Other friendships have survived the challenges of time and distance, lasting until even now. Those friends include Cheri Geise, Donna (Cheek) Mahnken and Nancy (Shull) Rogers.

My time at Maranatha was spent primarily in the kitchen and dining room. I remember fixing pounds of potato salad, heaps of hamburgers, and scores of pancakes. The days were long, often hot and never dull. Most of us in the kitchen were young, often led by a more experienced cook. The cooking skills that I acquired at Maranatha allowed me to "cook my way" through college and I know it was part of God's plan to do this.

In the first few summers that I worked at Camp, Rev. Olsen was actively involved in running day-to-day activities. One time he came back from town with "good" news. A semi had overturned and it was carrying ice cream; we could have as much ice cream as we could gather before it melted. It seemed like we ate ice cream (a real luxury) for weeks, but I don't know if it really lasted all that long.

Working at Maranatha taught me discipline and dedication. We had jobs to do and we needed to do them in a timely manner. That included serving meals on time and doing the best job as we could. It was a challenge to keep a good attitude (which I didn't always do) when the kitchen was hot, we didn't have much time for a break, or we had to clean the kitchen at the end of the day.

In just remembering things that happened, I remember serving picnic suppers out in a field or along the lake, in the evening cleaning the kitchen and listening to the campers sing in the chapel, and being exposed to diverse groups of people.

Of the different groups that would attend Camp, I fondly remember the Dunkards, who came every four years. One summer, when I was working in the kitchen, we had 500 Dunkards. The Dunkards, like most groups, helped clean tables and do dishes after meals, but this group also helped peel potatoes which we needed a lot of during their week. Then, one morning, the dining room began to slowly fill with smoke. At first, we thought the smoke

Joanne Shimmin (right) shares a laugh with Cleo Farmer (left) and an unidentified kitchen worker in 1978.

came from the grills in the kitchen, but soon we realized they weren't the source. People had to evacuate the building; some of the Dunkard men helped our staff search for the cause of the smoke while most of us waited anxiously outside. The problem was discovered (some smoking rags) and we were let back into the building. Needless to say, the dining room smelled of smoke and the tables were grimy. We had to start lunch. Many of the Dunkards formed teams, helping with the cleaning of the tables and meal preparation. It was a time of sharing.

My involvement at Maranatha was not without the support of my parents. When I would get tired and feel worn out from the work, they would encourage me. When I worked in the kitchen on winter week-ends, by myself as cook, my mother would give me menu ideas or help me with recipes. Years later, my father made wooden swings for Camp so people could sit and enjoy watching the lake or other parts of nature.

I remember my last summer at Maranatha (1983). That year I did not work in the kitchen, but had other jobs helping with various projects. It was also the year that Maranatha was flooded. One of my vivid memories of Maranatha is filling sandbags. It seemed that we worked for days filling sandbags in an effort to keep the river and lake from flooding the camp. One day, the water broke through and flooded the chapel in the dining hall. When the water was discovered, George called my parents to ask them to bring out some equipment to vacuum up the water in the chapel and clean the carpet.

Finally, I am glad that I worked at Maranatha. It has a special place in my heart, not only for the time that I worked there, but also for its mission.

— *Joanne Shimmin,*
Lincoln, Nebraska

A Training Stop on the Way to West Africa

It was June 1975. I arrived at Maranatha not knowing where I was nor what I would be doing. I only knew that the Lord had led me there. I had been working on the Union Pacific floor of the old St. Joseph's Hospital in Omaha. A patient by the name of Frank Watkins from North Platte suggested that I spend a summer at Maranatha. He had impressed me by his witnessing to everyone who came into his room and by spending his week-long hospital stay memorizing the book of Ephesians. Amazingly I had a Christian nursing supervisor who helped me to get a leave of absence for the summer.

I arrived at Camp as a fairly new believer, and the summer was one of stretching and growth. There was the daily Pastor's Hour with Dr. Olsen and the opportunity to hear many good speakers. At the end of the summer at a singles' retreat with Pastor Curt Lehman as speaker, I dedicated my life to serve the Lord however and wherever He desired. I was baptized in the lake along with several others. Then the Olsens invited me to move to Maranatha.

I lived at Camp year-round for two years and served on staff for six summers. There were not only opportunities to serve, but also to learn from Dr. and Mrs. Olsen, Ed and Alice Felgate and Rex and Patsy Shaver. It was my time at Maranatha and in the North Platte Berean Church that gave me the foundation of my Christian walk. I met many missionaries, pastors, and godly men and women who influenced my life.

It was only a few months after I had moved to Maranatha that Dr. Olsen said, "Cheri you need to go to Bible school." Being 22 and somewhat independent, I thought, "How dare he tell me what to do!" But I kept my thoughts to myself. He was right, and in less than two years I was in Bible school. After more years of growing, education, and experience, the Lord led me to Cote d'Ivoire as a missionary. I have been with CBInternational since 1986.

The first memories that come to mind from my time at Maranatha are the special times with the Lord and the friends that I made. Here are just a few others:

- Eating in the dining hall. Was that chicken or rabbit?
- Sweeping the parking lot with a push broom in 100-degree heat.
- Husking pick-up loads of corn.
- Doing mountains of dishes.
- Eating potatoes at almost every meal.
- Living with the ants and spiders in the dispensary. (It was good missionary training.)
- Praying for something different for dessert and having an ice cream truck break down on the Interstate next to Camp. Then having all the ice cream we could eat.
- Praying for specific campers and rejoicing in their testimonies at the end of the week.
- Grilled steak suppers for the staff behind the Olsens' house.
- Staff outings to Lake Maloney.
- The little girl who swallowed a staple while picking her teeth in chapel.
- The little boy who swallowed his offering money before the plate arrived.
- How a little TLC and a free pop from the Sweet Shop did wonders for homesickness.
- Walking across Camp with the snow untouched and heavy on the cedar trees.
- A deer by the lake in the morning mist.
- Memorizing over 100 verses during my second summer at Camp.
- Visiting Bert Needham in his little house.
- Reuben Hasenauer faithfully mowing lawns and keeping the wood fires burning.

– Cheri Geise,
Cote d'Ivoire

Discovering That It's All About God, Not Me

When I came to Maranatha (May 18, 2003) I was depressed. On my second day of Camp I had an encounter with God during Prime Time while we were singing "The Heart of Worship." When we sang the verse "Cause it's all about You, it's all about You Jesus" I realized that my pain didn't matter because it's not about me, it's about Jesus. Right then I was healed and years of pain dissipated in my tears.

Since my encounter with God, I've had peace and joy and have learned and grown more than ever before. I now look forward to the future with excitement and anticipation, thanks to the incredible staff here at Maranatha.

– Stephen Harris,
Summer Missionary 2003

I Met My Wife at Maranatha Bible Camp

I served on Summer Missions Staff at Maranatha from 1992 through 1996. God taught me and grew me up in Christ significantly while I worked doing dishes, cleaning toilets and mopping floors. A considerable portion of my spiritual training came from relationships with other summer staff. Some of those relationships persevere even now, which I am glad for.

The financial pressures of college kept me from continuing my summer tenures at Camp. I found "real jobs" while home from the university. However, I still visited Camp—since some of the people I served with during my five years were still working there. I drove out to camp for a wedding on Memorial Day weekend in 1998. I got there Saturday, and while eating with friends in the Dining Hall, noticed a girl I didn't recognize. This is not too unusual. But she was cute—blue eyes and curly blonde hair for starters. I asked the others at the table who she was. Her name was (and happens to still be) Hannah, which I had long ago established as one of my favorite names.

The next morning I worshipped at the Berean Church in North Platte, the congregation I grew up in. Hannah happened to be there as well. After Sunday school, I introduced myself to her and asked if she wanted to sit together for the worship service. She didn't raise any objection.

Now, you have to understand this was the first time *ever* that I approached a woman because I was attracted while thinking, "I wonder if she's dating material." During high school, I experienced no desire to date anyone, and was shy as well. College, though, changed me.

After the service, I asked her to lunch. She accepted this invitation as well. Another friend was along too, but my intentions seemed clear to Hannah after a while! And because I wanted to take her out, my other friend and I missed the wedding I was there for—which was to take place Sunday afternoon. I did help out with decorations for the reception instead.

My summer allowed for one or two more trips to Camp that summer. The only other we remember for sure was at the Fourth of July. We saw each other a while then, but she was headed to New York City for the MacWorld expo. Even with such limited time together, I pursued her. After the summer ended, I acquired her e-mail address and started writing occasionally.

And then I started sending her snail mail.

And then she moved up to Nebraska to be near me.

And then her father asked, "What's he waiting for! Why don't you have a ring yet?"

We were married 28 July 2001, which is my parents' anniversary as well. That wasn't planned.

– Paul Nielsen,
Siloam Springs, Arkansas

'Just Couldn't Stay Away' from Camp

My first trip to Maranatha Bible Camp was in the summer of 1975, when I was asked to come be a counselor for Awana Camp. I was living in Lincoln at the time and attending Lincoln Berean. I returned the following summer as a counselor as well. I had never counseled before and learned a lot those two weeks.

Little did I realize that the Lord would completely change my direction a few years later and plant me here at Maranatha.

I had graduated from Nebraska Wesleyan University in Lincoln in 1973 with a degree in teaching. In 1977, I left Lincoln to pursue further training, this time in Tennessee at Bryan College in Dayton. At the end of that year, I pursued my teaching career, landing a job at Berean Christian School in Olathe, Kansas.

I worked on staff the summers of 1978, 1979 and 1980. Those were very good summers. I did a variety of things, including town run three days a week. I chose to take the summer of 1981 and stay in Olathe thinking I would find odd jobs and be able to get some debts paid off. The Lord had other plans. My father passed away very suddenly at the end of June and I spent the rest of the summer with my mother. I did come to Maranatha toward the end of that summer to help with Family Camp, working in the nursery. Just couldn't stay away completely.

Through various circumstances, I was contacted about the possibility of coming to work full-time. I didn't commit right away, in fact I came "just for the summer" 21 years ago. It's been a long summer. It has been good. The Lord has taught me much and continues to teach me. I have seen many changes in that time. I have handled thousands of registrations, some even being second generation.

May the Lord continue to use Maranatha for His glory till he comes - Maranatha!

– JoAnn Beetem,
Maranatha Bible Camp

Lifelong Friendships Form at Camp

My first summer at Maranatha was orchestrated beautifully by the Lord months before I even knew of Maranatha. I had my heart set on going to Hungary for a year with Campus Crusade for Christ to serve on the campus at Budapest. My training was complete and then inexplicably, I was denied. That is when my mother asked me to check out Maranatha. I did, and that led to several summers working as support staff as well as two years as full-time staff. And oh, what a ride it was!

My first summer, I was the resident assistant for the women. Basically, I was supposed to "keep them in line." I was older than most and feared that my roomie would be young and less than enjoyable. (I did not have a great attitude at first). I was greeted with a wonderful young woman named Trisha Freedman (now Baker) and we hit it off immediately. I went into the "big room" at Mary and Martha and promptly tripped, fell and bounded back up to regain my composure and introduce myself to the Mary and Martha girls. I was greeted with a round of very girly-sounding machine gun fire. It was Beth Roesch (now Christensen) pretending to be I guess a bad imitation of a machine gun. I mention these two names because they are two women who have been my friends for about 10 years.

There are so many stories that could be told that would show how much these two women mean to me. Like when Trish and I were the featured act at the synchronized swimming trials for one of the camps, or when Trish, Beth and I decided that jumping into the pool fully dressed was a great idea, or when Beth and I decided to get some sun, and also use some tan accelerator and ended up looking like a couple of tomatoes. But I think the most beautiful thing about our friendship is what has happened since we all left Maranatha and went our own way.

Trish, Beth and I over the years have been in contact with one another. We have shared sad times and beautiful times, like both of their weddings. These two women have been joyful, silly, encouraging spirits in my life for about 10 years. How could I have even guessed, or dared to ask for two such wonderful friends. God had our friendship in his heart long before we were born, long before we knew about Maranatha, and long before that fateful summer when he brought us together.

I made another profound friendship there, her name was Christy Householter. She shared a cabin with Trisha and I for a summer and I have since lost contact with her. She and Trish were such a joy to be with. I have thought of her over the years and have been remiss about trying to contact her. As I write this letter about Maranatha it reminds me that the excuse of being "too busy" is just that, an excuse. And I am going to look for her to try and restart that friendship again.

Maranatha is truly a place where people can get away from the world and get a fresh look at our God. Our magnificent God who cares about finding lost souls at Maranatha also gives the added gift of building lifelong friendships. What an incredible place is Maranatha; I am truly thankful for being a part of it.

– April Adams,
Norfolk, Nebraska

Beth Roesch, Trish Freedman and April Adams keep the Dining Hall well supervised.

By the Way, This is My House

A fun day—living in the staff girls' dorm (Mary and Martha house), my friend and I enjoyed a day when we decided to rename the dorm. So whenever the phone would ring, we would sweetly answer, "Hello, this is Christine & Kari."

We even put our names on the sign outside the door just to make it officially fun!

– Kari Schott,
Sterling, Colorado

A Chance to Say the Right Thing

I was so blessed, back in the mid-90s, that a lady from my church (Central Christian Church) in Ocala, Florida, was looking for someone to go to MBC with her! It seems that Sally Giles' grandson had experienced Camp at Maranatha and wanted his grandmother to go, too! I never did get to know Sally very well; however, simply by "word of mouth" I got the message - talked with Sally and we decided to go to camp for six weeks - needless to say, by the time six weeks was over, I was *not* ready to leave!

Leota Bailey

I'm pretty sure it was the very next summer that Sally and I drove to Camp again, for a *larger* commitment, this time. We shared housing with Dorothy Grafton and had a summer of Camp that was beautiful in every way, until Sally fell and had to be taken home; I stayed on until my commitment was completed.

When summer rolled around again, MBC just seemed the thing to do! It *calls* me every season! It is such a thrill to see the youth "praise the Lord," and realize the changes that (obviously) take place within them from year to year. One can just "feel" it in some of them. Their smile "glows" from within; not just a "facial" smile.

I returned for the summer and worked in the Gift Shop again, and always feel *needed* and *wanted*!

One incident that thrills me is when I (obviously) said the right thing, at the right time to one young lady and two of the young men. I didn't even know what they were talking about, but they were having a disagreement; I couldn't help but detect *that* part. (I was working in the Dining Hall at the time.) All I said to them was: "Wait a minute! Don't you know things are not *always* the way they look?" There was an instance of silence; all *three* of them looked at me and surprisingly smiled, came and gave me a *big hug* and said "Thank you." I never did know what it was all about, but I sure seemed to have the answer they needed! Praise God! I will never forget that incident. I've always felt if I could say the right thing, at the right time, to just *one* camper during the season, my presence there would be *worth it*!

— Leota "Lee" Bailey,
Ocala, Florida

From Family Camp to Full-Time Missions

My history with Maranatha started in 1993 as a camper at Family Camp. My parents were going through some struggles at the time, so we went on vacation and finished our last week at Maranatha before heading home. There are few things I remember about that time except for the musical ministry of "One Way." I enjoyed their music so much that I decided that I wanted to invest more of my time in music and be able to do just what they did, minister to others through music.

The Camp staff and the people of North Platte reached out to my family so much, that we moved to North Platte the following year and started getting involved in the Camp ministry. We started attending the yearly July 4th celebration and looked forward to the swim and cookout that were involved. My dad was influential in designing the four-plex cabins (Lehman, Goltz, Hunt, Adrian) and helping the Cheeks plan for the director's house across the lake.

As for me, I was a camper for a number of years and then started working at Maranatha. From Junior Camp through a TNT session and on to eventually working as Craft Shop and Gift Shop managers, God had things for me to learn and grow in. It was at Maranatha that I felt God leading me to pursue a life of full-time missions after college. I was also able to learn what it meant to work and function around other Christians my age. This was a major thing in my life, because I was home schooled as a child, and had never been around a lot of people my age.

There have been many hard times and struggles as well throughout the past 10 years, but I've come to believe that the reason was Satan. He has seen and knows the work that God is doing at Camp, and wants to stop it. There have been many times, especially in my summer work, that I've wanted to throw in the towel and just leave. As a matter of fact, I did for two years, but God helped me through it and led me right back to Maranatha.

I thank God for Maranatha and the people that work there. Even through the hard times, they are there to lift you up both in prayer and friendship, and to point you back to God. I know because I've experienced this support both as a staffer and a camper. Praise God for Maranatha.

— Christie Whistler,
Colorado Springs, Colorado

Maranatha Brought Healing into Her Life

Several years ago I was talking with a fellow Christian who said, "Christian camps don't really impact a person's life. While there you spend time in an out of the world environment, hit a mountain top experience, make unreal promises and leave. Within a week you hit a valley and are worse than you were before."

Although I very strongly disagreed, I kept silent and never told him my story. Going to camp was the first step in many that would radically change my life. I was 12 years old when I arrived at Maranatha for the first time. The week before arriving at Camp I had been grounded due to being caught in sexual activity. Although it was embarrassing to be caught, it had very little meaning to me as I had already been sexually molested by four different men in my world. As the week progressed, the reality of my sinfulness hit me. On Thursday night I went forward to ask Christ into my life. I went home changed, a new creation in Christ.

Throughout the next several years, my life appeared fairly normal. I went to church with a friend and her family. I was an average student who struggled with identity issues. I went to Camp for a week every summer. I also tried to find ways to avoid the daily incestuous relationship with my dad.

Silence was my code of conduct. Fear was my lifestyle. One night in total terror, I finally told a friend the horrible secret and she began to pray with me that I could find a safe haven for the summer. God's answer was for me to spend the next three summers working at Camp. One of those summers there was a family that all the summer staff kids adopted as "Mom" and "Dad." They loved and cared for all of us. It was my first experience of a normal parent/child relationship and I was 18 years old! One day I was overexhausted and fell asleep in a pew in the back of the chapel. "Dad" saw me sleeping and later gave me a hug and asked me if I was okay. The memory of that sticks out so in my mind because it was the first good touch that I had experienced from a man that I could remember.

Yes, being at Camp was a mountain top experience for me because it was there that I met the Savior. It was also a mountain top experience for me because at Camp I was safe. It was there that I learned up close about healthy family lives, sexual purity, forgiveness, love, and so many other things that a life crowded with fear couldn't learn otherwise.

Camp was the beginning of the end of the cycle of abuse that had plagued my family for generations. Christ took me out of that cycle. He gave me His perfect love. Later at Maranatha, He brought a young man into my life who would later become my husband. Now our children go to Camp and come home with their lives changed from the lessons that they have learned at Camp. The cycle changed from a cycle of abuse and broken lives, to a cycle of growing in Christ. Psalm 25 always reminds me of this important time in my life.

Thank you, Father for people who would give their time, money and energy to the Camp. Mine is a life that was changed, may other lives be changed, made new, and rescued from the consequences of sin in the world.

— A grateful Maranatha camper and staffer

Keeping Close Tabs on Camp Speaker

Al Rasmusseson was speaking at Maranatha for a few weeks in 1981. The staff didn't always get to go to the chapel services, but we sometimes had our own theological discussions with the speaker after services, especially with Al, since he was always willing to talk with us. After speaking at Maranatha one week, Al went to Midwest Bible Camp in South Dakota where my brother was. I saw him there when I went with my parents to pick up my brother. The next weekend Al was going to Bloomfield, New Mexico, where Peggy and Sue Bachert lived. He asked me if I was going to be there, too and I told him maybe, but if I couldn't make it, I would send someone else from Maranatha to see him. When I got back to Maranatha, Peggy told me she was planning to go home for the weekend and she would stop to see him. The next spring, I saw Al in Bridgeport, Nebraska and told him that it was just a little reminder that, wherever Al Rasmusseson goes, if a Maranatha staff member is not there, there will always be a Maranatha staff member thinking about him and praying for him.

I learned how to play the guitar in high school and I was trying to find someone at Maranatha to play guitar with. I almost gave up but I went to talk to George Cheek first. He said that Duaine Gingrich played the guitar, so I went to see him. We sat out on the grass along a major walkway and played guitars most Friday nights. We played at the Sweet Shop one night and as much as we could for anyone who made a request over the summer. One of our biggest audiences was some of the Dunkard young people.

— Mary Wahl Hillegas,
Miltonvale, Kansas

She Survived Town Run Escapade

I grew up at MBC and have so many memories it is hard to pick the best. Four generations of my family have worked at MBC. My grandfather, Martin McDermott, helped in the beginning years with the very first permanent buildings. My mother, Louise (McDermott) Crooks worked at MBC as the bookkeeper and bookstore manager. This was during my childhood and I spent my summers living at Camp and having a great time. I worked at MBC starting in seventh grade. I worked in the kitchen, housekeeping, craft shop, and managing the bookstore when the dining hall/chapel was first built. My three oldest children: Sarah, Joshua, and Rebekah, have worked at MBC. My husband, Rich, spent one summer working at MBC and proposed to me there.

One of my fondest memories was when the Navigators came every summer and Pastor Olsen led Pastor's Hour every day. The best part of this service was Mrs. Olsen's talk. She usually talked about how God answered prayer for some impossible item at Camp. One of her stories involved my sister, Tami (Littrell) and I. Precious Olsen and I went to N.P. every day for the "Town Run" to get supplies for Camp and the Navigators. One day, my sister came with us. On our way back to camp on I-80, the brakes went out on the car. We could not slow down or stop. The car began to pick up speed. Precious was getting nervous and told us to pray. As we got close to the Maxwell exit with no way to slow down, my sister said, "Why don't you just turn the key off?" Precious did just that, the car rolled to a stop on the exit ramp. Precious asked Tami what made her think to turn the key off and she said, "I prayed and God gave me the idea."

One of my funniest memories happened the first year George Cheek came to Camp to work. He was a college student from Western Bible College at the time. Every day after work, the staff would go to the pool. George came up to see everyone and we decided to throw him into the pool to initiate him to MBC. He claimed that he could not swim. We didn't believe him because everyone said that, so they wouldn't get thrown into the pool. He was carried to the end of the diving board and thrown in, yelling, "I really can't swim." He was telling the truth. His head bobbed up, he sputtered, "I can't swim" and sank. Two of the guys jumped in to save him. Poor George. He did come back to Camp the next year, and stayed.

The best times of my life have been spent at MBC.
— *Cheri Lorenz,*
Littleton, Colorado

Maranatha Kitchen a Place of New Life and Growth

In 1992 I came to Maranatha just for a couple of weeks to get my life together, but stayed for seven and one-half years!! It was a great experience. Maranatha is a great place to grow up in the Lord. It was here that I came to know the Lord in my life and began the journey of understanding what the Lord wants for me, what He expects of me as a believer.

The years I spent working in the kitchen, training the summer kitchen staff, were great years. The opportunity to get to know these young people, to listen to their problems, stories and sometimes to be able to help them in the process of growing through their teen years was a great blessing. In the process I learned much from them, importantly patience and tolerance. There are a few that stand out in my memory, especially, Laura, Lisa, Toby, Jason, Kari and so many others, all good kids and wanting to find their way and grow in their faith. They were in the right place.

At Maranatha I formed some friendships that I know will last a lifetime, each one of them contributing in their own uniqueness to my growth in the Lord. My walk with the Lord is a wonderful journey that I take a day at a time and at the start of this journey my friends at Maranatha supported me and gently showed me the way, especially Mrs. Olsen, Stella and Merle, Hank and Evelyn, Jack and Virginia, Dick and Bonnie, George and Jan and particularly my daughter, Jean and her husband, Tad. Thank you, my friends ... Maranatha will always be a special place for me.

— *Dorothy Grafton,*
Kearney, Nebraska

Long-Distance Romance Started at Camp

During the summers of '94 and '95, Shelley Chaboyer worked at Maranatha Bible Camp on the Summer Missions Team. A native of Canada, she came from her home church in Oak Lake, Manitoba.

During this same time frame, Keith Ruenholl, residing in Hastings, Nebraska, started attending the singles' retreats at MBC. Although we were both at Camp in '94, they did not meet until the summer of '95.

A spark developed and Keith soon returned to Camp and our first date was a trip to the county fair in North Platte. As summer ended so did Shelley's time at Camp. She returned to Canada and a long-distance relationship became longer. Shelley soon returned to the U.S. to attend the fall at McCook Community College for her intermediate EMT course. Dating continued when Keith was home from his days off as an over-the-road truck driver based out of Hastings.

Keith enjoyed a mid-December trip to Shelley's home to meet her parents, braving a snowstorm through the Dakotas along the way. Although there are no language differences, it was interesting to learn some of the cultural differences and hear the accent because of two different countries.

At the '95 singles' New Year's Eve party, Shelley accepted Keith's marriage proposal at midnight while everyone else was busy watching the fireworks going off over the lake. We returned to Camp three and a half months later to be united in marriage on April 14, 1996. Travel was difficult that day (especially between Kearney and Lincoln) due to a snowstorm, so several people were unable to attend.

During the summer of '97, we moved to the Kansas City area. Although we have not been to Camp for a while, we get to see Mrs. Olsen when she visits her daughters in the Kansas City area.

– Keith and Shelley Ruenholl,
Kansas City, Missouri

'God Drew Us Together' at Camp

It was the spring of 1996 and Lincoln Whitehead and I came to serve at Maranatha together. The person who was to become my partner through life greeted us with a smile from behind the Switchboard.

I was able to serve the staff through music and I also had the opportunity when needed to run the sound board. It was during free time and housekeeping duties that Linda (Malm) and I were able to get to know each other.

You see, working at Maranatha you have a choice to either serve God and be blessed or toil under the relentless demands of the summer schedule. It was while serving God, He drew us together and later we purposed to serve each other and Him throughout our lives.

Linda traded her four letter last name for mine (with 11) in May 1998, around the same time of the month we met in 1996. We chose to have our reception in the same building where we first met. It's ironic that God gave us two beginnings in the same place.

Maranatha is a place that harbors special memories and meaning to each of us. We haven't been back for a while but I'm sure we'll have more memories there in the future.

– James and Linda Blaszkowski,
Rapid City, South Dakota

James and Linda Blaszkowski held their wedding reception in the Dining Hall in May 1998, two years after they met on Summer Missions staff.

Just Like Family

In the spring 1976, a friend of mine in Awana at Lincoln Berean (JoAnn Beetem) told me that she thought I would enjoy going to Maranatha Bible Camp and being a cabin leader for a week of Awana Camp. Jack and Virginia Ashcraft and Jim and Charlene Ellis all of Lincoln Berean were the leaders who worked with me that week of Camp. They shared with me that I would be with four Chums (third-through fifth-grade girls) for the week. Well, they ended up short on cabin leaders and I had eight Chums for the week. What an experience!

That week changed my life and I knew that I wanted to come back the next summer and be a part of what was happening at Camp. As the summer turned into fall, and then winter I started thinking about being there for the whole summer. I quit my job of eight years in the spring of 1977 as a bookkeeper at Pepsi, not knowing what the fall would hold for me. I arrived May 23rd, 1977 for a summer. More than 26 years later, it's been a long summer!

The first two and one-half years I did guest groups, housekeeping, gift shop, cooking (winter), Sweet Shop and office work. Mainly, my responsibility since 1980 has been bookkeeping (with a few other hats thrown in here and there). Some of my favorite times, are being in the Snack Bar and being closer to the campers. It's been a very rewarding ministry as I have had the privilege of hearing and reading testimonies of how God has worked in many lives over the years. I get excited over the notes that teenagers send in with their faith promises. It's exciting to hear how God is working in their young lives.

It was a privilege to have had the chance to serve with Dr. Ivan Olsen, Pastor Ernie Skoog, Bob Benson, and Faye Ward in my early years out here. The current Maranatha team is just like family.

– Ruth Ann Rodgers,
Maranatha Bible Camp

'You Truly Worked' in Maranatha's Kitchen

Life at Maranatha for me was a time of real growth. Life at Maranatha was at times, fun, trying, tiring and exciting. If you worked at Maranatha, you truly worked! I remember working long hours in the kitchen and cooking everything from scratch! Maranatha is not an eight-to-five job, it is truly a place of ministry.

I think I worked in every department of Camp at one time or another during my two years there. I was at Camp when the Hmongs came for the first time, now that was an experience I will never forget! Putting up all those huge tents and all the rice! Rice, rice, rice! We cooked rice three times a day for a week. I was also there during the big flood. We spent hours filling sand bags and stacking them along the banks. There were many different emotions during that time - it was fun and scary at the same time.

Many special friendships were formed during my time at Camp that to this day I hold dear.

My experience at Maranatha led me to work at another camp years later in California. It was there that I met my now husband of 14 years.

But the most important thing I remember about Maranatha is my growth as a person. It was at Camp that I realized the importance of the Christian way of life. Thank you George Cheek for your patience!!

– Sandy Amaya Kay,
Frazier Park, California

Sandy Amaya (right) takes a break with her roommate, JoAnn Beetem.

Leadership Position Made It a 'Hard, Great' Summer

Results of experiences are often not immediately recognized. The summer I spent as head of housekeeping for Maranatha Camp was not fun. Overall, I did not enjoy the summer. However, blessings resulting from that season have been revealed to me gradually since.

I met my husband at Camp that summer of 1998. I didn't know he was my mate until three years later when we wed.

I persevered. I didn't like the job, but I did not quit. Pressing on is a God-given ability I learned that summer that I've needed more than once since.

I practiced management skills. I was probably not very good at the beginning of the summer, but by the next time I was in management, I knew what not to do.

I learned grace, too. I wasn't qualified to do the job, and that must have been clear to the Camp leadership. They stuck with me, though, encouraging me to keep on.

I had the chance to listen to God, and He revealed Himself to me. Coming into the summer I'd prayed for passion, for vision. I knew what I was working toward was empty, but I had no clue what to replace it with. God showed me, in part through one summer at Camp, that only He is worth living for and spending myself on. God gave me passion for the nations, for the glory of His name.

I had a great summer. I wonder what He'll show me I learned next.

– Hannah Wahlgren Nielsen,
Siloam Springs, Arkansas

He Started as a Primary Camp Counselor

Maranatha has meant much to me over the years. Not having been a frequent camper, my first real exposure to what Camp was like was through Primary Camp. I came to help out as a counselor at 13 years of age. That really impacted me and I wanted to come back to work on staff. And though I would prove to be somewhat mischievous, I was graciously tolerated and over time became more refined.

Maranatha would come to mean more and more to me. Camp is where I met my wife, a former summer staffer as well, and God revealed to me that ministry is where He wanted me. Though at that time a pastoral ministry wasn't what I had in mind!

Pastor Tom Walker often jokingly teased me about becoming a permanent fixture at Camp as I continued to come back summer after summer. And indeed they even wanted me to come on as part of the team full-time to work in the kitchen as kitchen manager under the direction of Lance Gerry, food service director at the time.

My wife, Sarah (Berger) Busch and I have been obedient to God, as He has led us into pastoral ministry to rural America. I wish I could tell you just how much Maranatha's ministry has impacted and impressed the work of our Lord Jesus Christ into my life. May God continue to bless and use Maranatha Ministries for His glory.

– Charlie and Sarah Busch,
Brewster, Kansas

Left: Cindy Lehman (left) enjoys a laugh with a kitchen staff friend in this 1970s photo. Right: Tim Roesch (left) served many years as a Summer Missionary, as did his brother, Dan, and sister, Beth.

Top row: Serving the meals at Ladies' Retreat 1990 were, from left: Earl Grover, Beth Porter, Rod Kihlthau, David Jones, Dennis Jewert and JoAnn Beetem.

Second row, from left: John Meschke was staff coordinator in the early 1980s. Bonnie Patterson did an internship through the University of Nebraska; Rodney Thiessen led Maranatha's Summer Missions program into the 21st century; Staff pool time, 1974. From left: Bruce Clark, Terry Dougherty, Warren Cheek, Dan Lehman.

Third row, from left: Sheryl Trembly perfected the art of making donuts with this amazing machine; Bruce Clark usually worked outdoors, but was in the kitchen here for some reason; Staff members enjoy a rest during the summer of 1986.

Fourth row, from left: Ken Chezik was a familiar sight at Maranatha during the 1990s. He was a summer missionary who became a full-time staff member; Adding the restrooms to Yeutter Hall in 1983 were, from left: Hank Wambolt, Reuben Hasenauer, Matthew Melchart and Bruce Stucky. Allen Solomon is on the roof; Bruce Stucky is ready to head deeper into the trees in this 1987 photo. Mark Swesey is at left.

Top row: Maranatha residents met weekly for prayer and information. This late 1990s residents' meeting included (clockwise around the table) George Cheek, Kathy Sprague (partially hidden), Rachel Stucky, Tad Stryker, Ruth Ann Rodgers, Fred Gayman, Pauline Tallman, Stella Cheek, Merle Cheek, David Jones, Bruce Stucky, JoAnn Beetem, Ken Chezik and Reuben Hasenauer.

Second row, from left: Mark Ellis bids a fond but sticky farewell to his fellow summer staffers in 1978; Sweet Shop attendants Beth Shada (left) and Rose Spracher, mid-1970s; Brenda Taylor was on the 1981 summer staff.

Third row, from left: Christy Olsen and Karl Yeutter put a bacon face on a pizza in 1985; David "Bubba" Jones (left), Reuben Hasenauer and Mark Swesey rarely gave each other a moment's peace throughout the 1980s and 1990s; Stan and Jan Spiess were "Dad and Mom" to summer staff in the early 1980s.

Fourth row, from left: Summer staff friendship around the campfire in 1987. Clockwise, from left: Deanna Herman, Brad Stover, Karl Yeutter, unidentified, Leonard Purdy and Bob Bulkey (wearing hat). Mark Swesey has his back to camera in right foreground; Paul Kroeze spent several summers doing a variety of jobs, including driving the life boat; David Jones introduces himself during staff training week, 1989. Bertha Pleger also is standing.

Top row: Summer Staff, 1981.

Second row: A Christmas party for staff and volunteers in 1987.

Third row, from left: These 1973 kitchen staff members have the meal ready to go! Foreground, from left: Debbie Clark, Sue Garner, Pam Richmond; Megan Fitzgerald (left) and Anne Masten served on the Summer Missions staff in 2000; Ed Felgate reviews the shopping list with Kathy Fellows.

Fourth row, from left: Diane Clark sweeps up around the dining hall, mid-1970s; David "Bubba" Jones, a full-time staff member since 1986, serves as plumber, locksmith and general maintenance man. He often helps run the Camp's climbing wall; Summer missionary Jonie Gosnell ran the Craft Shop in 1998.

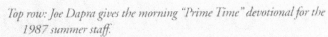

Top row: Joe Dapra gives the morning "Prime Time" devotional for the 1987 summer staff.

Second row: Summer Staff, 1985.

Third row, from left: Emily Niver's form is somewhat suspect as she tries a back dive in 2000; John Meschke and Roberta "Bert" Garrett met on summer staff 1981 and were married in 1982. They were on full-time staff from 1982-84; Three generations served God together at Maranatha in 2000. From left, Shirley Gayman, Rosemary Johnson and Justina Johnson.

Fourth row, from left: Staff coordinator George Cheek awoke one summer morning in 1973 to find his Honda beached on a small island in the west end of Lake Maranatha. Another morning, the Honda mysteriously appeared in the north entrance to Needham Hall. Both times, the car was retrieved by staff members who "wondered how that car got there"; During a break in the Camp kitchen, Becky Weir and Tara Rasmussen hopped into a pair of overalls that belonged to a co-worker. The photo was taken in the late 1970s; Summer Missionary Adam Stuart-Walker (right) worships the Lord during Prime Time in 2000. Adam joined the full-time staff and worked with Rodney Thiessen to organize and lead the Teens in Training program. John Trammell is in the foreground.

The Growth of Maranatha

It was inevitable that what Ivan E. Olsen once described as a "plain, humble, simple Bible camp" would grow, and Maranatha has done so. God has given an increase of at least a hundredfold over what originally took root in the dry Depression years.

Some use facilities to measure growth. Maranatha's buildings and grounds, when compared to many smaller camps in Nebraska, are spacious and offer plentiful conveniences, but they do not begin to compare in size or beauty to many camps and conference grounds around the United States.

Some use statistics to measure growth. The group of campers, donors and prayer supporters who consider themselves "friends of Maranatha" grows each year. It's impossible to determine the number of people who have accepted Christ as their Savior while at Maranatha. Still larger is the number of those who made other types of life-changing decisions while on the campgrounds, including rededications and service to God.

It has proven easier for the Maranatha staff to document the number of nations that have been ministered to by Maranatha "graduates" — that is, the number of former Maranatha staff members, Summer Missionaries or campers who made decisions while at Maranatha to serve God in a foreign nation. At the end of the 20th century, Maranatha had reached more than 50 nations in this manner.

It cannot even be speculated about how many people have been reached for Jesus Christ by those who had their lives changed at Maranatha, but it is certain that God has used Maranatha in a dramatic way for the expansion of His kingdom.

Some use financial figures or attendance to measure growth. Camper attendance, camper registration fees and the annual budget can be analyzed to show where the Camp has been and where it is headed. Maranatha is in the top 25 percent of Christian camps nationwide in attendance.

Maranatha Bible Camp was started during the Great Depression, and from the beginning, the Camp board decided to operate as inexpensively as possible and keep camper registration costs low.

From the very start, Maranatha's operational costs exceeded its operational income. The philosophy was not to charge campers what it actually cost to run the Camp, but to subsidize the camping program with donations from people who believed in the ministry. "No one has ever been turned away due to lack of funds," was the policy that Olsen lived by. He raised money to provide Camp scholarships to those who had financial need. Donations from churches also were solicited, although no church or denomination ever underwrote Maranatha Bible Camp, even during the years when the Berean Fundamental Church Council owned the property.

The Camp could not have paid for labor in the early days. Volunteers built Maranatha and kept it running, and no one could recruit volunteers like Olsen. "I've never seen anyone get so many people to work for free," marveled Theodore Epp.

Campers paid $3.50 apiece to come to the first week of Camp in 1938. The following year, the board authorized a price increase to $4 for registrations by June 1, or $5 for those registering after that date. By 1951, the price was $6 per week.

At the end of the First Annual Encampment in 1938, there was $10 left in the treasury. The Camp leadership decided to spend it on silverware. By the following spring, the Camp also had purchased 125 plates and cups.

Government commodities were a source for staples like flour and butter, but there were many days when Rev. Olsen drove to farms in the area asking for meat and garden produce to serve to campers.

Times were tough financially in the 1930s, but Olsen and the Maranatha board were convinced that God would grow the camping outreach larger as the years went by.

It appears that they never seriously considered scaling back the ministry, although they tried to manage it carefully.

"When deciding whether to launch a venture or not, I never worry about finances," Olsen said. "Once I'm certain the matter is in the Lord's will for me, I plunge ahead, trusting Him to supply the funds. That doesn't mean, of course, that I can handle the Lord's money carelessly. I feel a grave responsibility to watch every phase of our activities even more than a businessman watches the departments of his firm."

When Olsen plunged, the board usually raced along with him, often making adjustments in course as they went down the road. By the late 1940s, they decided to build permanent structures on the Camp property to replace the old dormitories and slab dining hall that had served since the early years.

First to be built were the boys' and girls' dormitories. John Kile, pastor of the newly-founded Ogallala Berean Church, was a block layer and he did much of the work in building the first dormitories and a girls' bathhouse out of cement blocks.

The Tabernacle was a much larger building (50 by 80 feet) and would be costlier than the Camp could afford to build. The solution? Hugh Clark and his other railroader friends loaded piles of burned coal into pickup trucks and hauled them to Camp, where the sooty substance could be mixed with cement. "We broke off those cinder blocks for a penny a block," said Olsen. It cost $3,750 to build the large structure, which had windows and doors on three sides and an open-beam ceiling with trap doors in the roof to help the air circulate.

Despite all the donated labor and his best efforts to find low-cost building materials, Olsen found himself writing a fundraising letter in November 1947 asking for approximately $2,000 to finish paying lumber bills for the buildings, plus $245 for 100 single beds bought at a war surplus outlet.

Construction continued. By 1953, there were eight major buildings on site: the Hasenauer Memorial Tabernacle (later known as the "Old Tabernacle"), the Dining Hall, the boys' dorm (later known by a variety of names, including Olsen Hall, Daniel's Inn and finally, Lott Hall), two girls' dorms (later known as Clark Hall and Wesley Hall, although Wesley was renamed Becker Hall in the 1980s), a bathhouse located between the two girls' dorms, the Prophets' Chamber (later renamed Rawson Hall) and the caretakers' house (later named Bethel House), located next door to the Dining Hall. During various summers, the Olsen family lived in the caretaker's house, but it often was used for other Camp leaders.

There also were a campfire circle, a tennis court, a sandpit swimming pool, a baseball field and areas for shuffleboard and volleyball. There were slab cabins for speakers' and pastors' housing, and a scattering of small cabins that families had built. In 1954, the Camp replaced the sandpit with a cement swimming pool that would be used for more than 50 years. (The pool bathhouse was built in 1962.)

The board continually faced the reality of paying the bills, and looked for ways to raise more income. In the beginning, all "faculty members and workers" were exempt from fees. By 1957, counselors were charged a fee to come to Camp. Amounts were to be left up to program directors. Still, the camp found it necessary to raise rates for campers.

By the 25th summer of camping (1962), the price had risen to $9.50 for Junior (grades 4-6) and Jr. High Weeks, and $10 for Young People's Weeks. In 1977, the cost had tripled, jumping to $27.50 for Junior Camp and $37.50 for Senior High Week. By the 50th summer of camping (1987), the prices had risen to $57.50 for Junior Camp and $75 for Senior High Week, and annual cost increases had become a way of life as the prices of insurance, utilities and food soared. Maranatha's cost increases generally were tied to the nation's rate of inflation.

A philosophical shift on the Camp board occurred during the 1990s. More began to believe that camper fees should pay for all Maranatha's operating costs. In 1999, it cost $169 for Junior Camp and $196 for Senior High Camp. However, the Camp continued to cultivate a scholarship fund to help those who could not afford to pay the entire fee and raised money for it more vigorously than in previous years.

The Maranatha board agreed that controlling operational expenses was paramount. In 1941, the board voted to pay Olsen $10 per month for expenses incurred as general director. Apart from that, for nearly the first 20 years of its existence, Maranatha did not pay salaries or honorariums, or cover expenses for speakers, workers or anyone else associated with Camp. The Camp was built and maintained on volunteer labor, and volunteers worked in the kitchen and other behind-the-scenes jobs.

For many years, Olsen dreamed of the time when the Camp could be maintained year-round for programs in non-summer months. Converting Maranatha to a year-round facility meant that maintaining the operation became a much more absorbing task. In fact, by 1965, running the Camp was becoming so complex that Olsen divided the operation into various departments (financial, personnel, physical, planning, program, promotional and training) and started recruiting volunteers to run each department.

It also meant that money had to be raised to winterize existing facilities and construct new buildings. While the costs of the building themselves came from designated offerings, the costs of maintaining those buildings added to the operational expenses.

"There is not a single church in the world (including the one that I have pastored for 40 years), that has any obligation to support Maranatha Bible Camp," said Ivan Olsen during the 1970s. "Anything they do, they do of their own free will. There is not one man or woman that has an obligation other than the Holy Spirit telling them, 'I want you to send a gift to Maranatha Bible Camp.'"

As expenses mounted, the Camp looked for other sources of income. In the early years, the board expressed a preference that the Camp not rent its facilities to any outside group, but in the 1954, the board changed course and began to allow rentals. By the early 1990s, rental income far surpassed income from Maranatha-sponsored programs.

By the early 1950s, Maranatha had started to borrow money to pay bills that came due during non-summer months. The Camp paid back the loans with summer income.

As camper numbers increased, construction continued at Maranatha, which raised funds and built two new dormitories:

Yeutter Hall in the 1950s and Needham Hall in the 1960s. Needham Hall was built for the Navigator Training Program, but after the Navs left Maranatha in 1971, Needham served as the Camp's largest dormitory. This was fortunate, because more than 7,000 campers attended Maranatha during the 1971-72 camping year.

The new dining hall/kitchen/chapel building was completed in 1972 and dedicated as Olsen Memorial Building in 1977. Ground was broken in 1991 for a gymnasium/multipurpose building just east of the dining hall, and the buildings were linked with a covered walkway upon completion of the project in 1994. Both these projects were paid for with designated donations.

In 1973, George W. Cheek joined the staff and assisted Olsen for the next several years. In 1977, he was appointed executive director while Olsen maintained his title as general director. By that time, Cheek had assumed responsibility for day-to-day operations of the Camp.

The fulltime staff was enlarged in 1977 when the board decided that others could be hired fulltime if they raised part of their own financial support (Personal Support Income). Camp provided housing and utilities (except telephone), health insurance and meals while the dining hall was open for campers. More fulltime staff members were added over the next few years as the Camp built more facilities and started to raise its standards in maintenance, housekeeping and programming.

Over the last quarter of the 20th century, a considerable debt accumulated as year-round operation of the Camp's program and facilities became more costly. Significant expenses from the flood of 1983 also were included in the debt. Cheek and the Camp board began to re-examine Olsen's policy of "plunging ahead" when new facilities were needed.

To expand ministry and increase income, Maranatha hosts groups that fit within its parameters as a non-profit ministry. In addition to hosting outdoor education groups and other non-profits, the Camp works with church groups that can agree with its doctrinal statement, which is similar to that of the National Association of Evangelicals.

Groups that Maranatha currently works with or recently hosted long term include the Nebraska District of the Nazarenes, Nebraska, Kansas & Colorado districts of Wesleyan Churches, Westside Baptist Church of Omaha, the Awana Youth Association, Grace University of Omaha, and once every four years since 1973, the Dunkard Brethren National Convention.

In the 1980s, Maranatha constructed a large bathhouse near the Old Tabernacle, which was being used mainly for storage and overflow camper housing, and was rapidly deteriorating. In 1987, the staff moved a large inventory of maintenance supplies (which had been stored in the Old Tab) to a newly-constructed metal building.

By the mid-1990s, the Camp board had decided to accept Cheek's recommendation that Maranatha expand its facilities only when designated donations were in hand, unless safety or health issues were involved. Using the new policy, the Camp built four large fourplex cabins (Lehman, Goltz, Hunt and Adrian) without adding to the operational debt load.

By the end of the century, Maranatha Bible Camp had become a large non-profit enterprise with a million-dollar budget. The cost of maintaining and insuring more than 50 buildings and paying health insurance premiums for its fulltime staff had become quite high. Increased governmental regulation of the camping industry also raised costs.

Deciding that it needed to provide a stronger base for the financial future of the Camp, the board in 1996 authorized the creation of the Maranatha Camp Foundation and hired Mark Geist as its executive director. The Foundation's purpose was to raise long-term gifts by educating and assisting people in developing long-term estate planning strategies designed to help both their families and Christian ministries. The Foundation also became a strong supporter of Maranatha's camper scholarship fund.

In 2001, the Camp added a sports/adventure ministry called SportReach, which had been founded that year by Kris Cheek and Matt Janssen. Kris, the son of George & Jan Cheek, is the executive director of SportReach, which hosts outdoor adventure programs and provides mobile sports outreaches in partnership with local churches. SportReach also has launched sports-related overseas missions trips whose primary purpose is evangelism. Almost from the beginning, SR staff members have raised all their own financial support.

By the late 1990s, the Camp board, which had generally been a hands-on management board, decided to change its philosophy and instructed the fulltime staff to organize its own management team, consisting of directors of various departments (operations, promotion, properties, conference center, program) at Camp. The departmental directors, along with the board treasurer and three other board members (including the general director) met in monthly finance committee teleconferences to manage large expenditures.

In 2003, George Cheek and the departmental directors developed the concept of Maranatha Ministries, which combines Maranatha Bible Camp, the Maranatha Camp Foundation and SportReach as separate branches of a single entity. George accepted oversight of the entire organization and assumed the title of chief executive officer. Scot Cockson, who joined the Maranatha staff in 2002 as director of operations, was promoted to executive director of Maranatha Bible Camp.

Freed from day-to-day management of the Camp, George grew increasingly determined to attack the long-term debt. He proposed that 50 percent of all undesignated gifts be used to pay down the debt, and that policy was implemented. The directors looked for ways to achieve the much-discussed goal of raising enough operational income to pay all operational expenses for the first time in the history of the Camp.

The directors also realized that controlling costs was only part of the equation in balancing the budget. They continued to recognize the need to increase the number of campers. Part of their goal was to develop new "key alliances" with large churches and other Christian ministries, much as the Camp had done with the Navigators in the late 1950s. Throughout 2004, the Maranatha leadership worked to develop a new vision statement that would take them well into the 21st century.

The People of Maranatha: Richard Crocker

Richard Crocker, who moved from Torrington, Wyoming, to Cheyenne to serve as pastor of the Berean Church there, has served on the Maranatha Camp board since 1986. In 2001, he succeeded El Streyle as president.

The first year in his position, Richard brought the staff together for an evaluation, teambuilding and vision-building retreat in Estes Park, Colorado, at the lodge owned by Camp board member Mark Hewitt. It was a pivotal moment in the ministry's history.

During Dr. Crocker's watch, one of the key components has been the transition to a broader approach to the outreach of the Camp, as reflected in the name change of the overall organization to "Maranatha Ministries."

In the October 2003 board meeting, George Cheek's title became CEO of Maranatha Ministries, recognizing that others now carry the day-to-day operations. Other new titles included Maranatha Bible Camp Executive Director (Scot Cockson), SportReach Executive Director (Kris Cheek) and Maranatha Foundation Executive Director (Mark Geist).

During his time as vice president in the 1990s, Richard and his wife, Toni, also did a very commendable job of helping the board and our fulltime ministry staff walk through some difficult personnel issues.

Richard and Toni Crocker

Many children of Maranatha staff members remember Richard as the man who offered them a dollar if they could remember his middle name. (Sometimes, Richard gave them the dollar regardless of whether they got his name right.)

Additionally the Crockers have been involved as camp speakers and program directors. Most notable has been Toni's long term as director of the Ladies' Retreat. Toni also was on summer staff in the early 1970s.

– George W. Cheek

The People of Maranatha: Doug Shada

Doug & Farrol Shada first came to Maranatha in the summer of 1974 after graduating from college, teaching and coaching in Nebraska. Doug had recently accepted Christ under the ministry of Art & Mary Van Campen who, in turn, recommended them to Ivan Olsen as summer workers. The Shadas often refer to that summer as one of their fond memories.

They moved to Lincoln to attend the Berean Church and be discipled by Curt & Claudine Lehman. Doug worked as a counselor at the Nebraska State Penitentiary. After a few years, the church asked Doug to join the staff fulltime.

In the 1970s, Doug & Farrol began directing the annual Maranatha Couples' Conference. Summers saw him helping as a cabin leader at Junior Camp, but soon, youth camp became his area of interest. His leadership abilities were put to work there, and he became program director of the combined Jr. High and Sr. High weeks in 1990. Known as "The Bear" to thousands of campers over the years, Doug Shada has been able to recruit a working team of youth pastors and sponsors, then keep them coming back and pulling together year after year.

The combined Jr. High and Sr. High weeks soon grew to the point where they had to be held separately. By the summer of 2000, the Sr. High Camp had grown to an all time high of 562 paying campers plus program staff. The same year, Jr. High Camp had 466 paying campers. Both camps have since leveled off to about 400 campers.

In 1991, Doug was invited to join the Camp board and continues to be a source of energy and insight for Maranatha Ministries.

– George W. Cheek

Doug "The Bear" Shada directed Junior High and Senior High camps in the 1990s and beyond.

Businesses and Organizations of Area Assisted Maranatha

Several area businesses have had a long-term relationship with Maranatha Bible Camp. Again, to name a few is to risk omitting others.

The longest continuous dealings have been with four generations of the Keenan family who until the early 2000s owned the Coca-Cola franchise. Right behind them are Pearson Appliance (Pearson and Kittle families), Pearson Propane (Milroy family) and Hipp Wholesale (Hipp family). Others include the Berg family (office supply and auto dealership) and the Chrisp family (Home Telephone Co. of Brady). All of the above have supported the Camp financially out of personal funds, in addition to offering the Camp generous purchase discounts.

Many other area businesses from Ace Hardware to Bill Summers Ford support the Camp scholarship fund annually.

Local branches of national companies such as Wal-Mart and Cabela's help with in-kind gifts and have been a tremendous resource. The regional food bank in Kearney has assisted.

Public services such as the Dawson and Nebraska Public Power Districts have served Maranatha well and keep Camp informed of cost-saving incentives and rebates, which led to the installation of several heat pump systems in 2000 and beyond.

Lincoln County has provided assistance as able, including emergency situations. Maranatha Road is the most traveled gravel road in the county and requires special attention.

As part of the rural Maxwell community, Maranatha has received service beyond the call of duty from the Maxwell Volunteer Fire Department and ambulance crew. Recently some of the Maranatha staff, including Leila Thiessen in 2003, have joined the team.

The Maxwell Public School has been a real encouragement to the Camp families, many of which have sent children to be educated there. Maranatha and the Maxwell school have made several reciprocal arrangements related to gymnasiums and equipment.

The Post Office staffs at Maxwell and North Platte have been helpful over the years. Postal management told Camp staff that the fees Maranatha pays for mailings of brochures and First Class postage have helped keep the Maxwell Post Office open.

The area media outlets have been very generous in using Maranatha's press releases as public service announcements.

KJLT AM-FM, as a Christian broadcasting station, has faithfully been serving North Platte and the surrounding region for almost as long as Maranatha. Without its help, many of Camp's events would go unnoticed. Current staff members are John L. Townsend, Gary Hofer, Roger Olson and Sonja Boyles.

Ivan & Alice Olsen were friends of the late John & Dorothy Townsend, founders of KJLT. Beginning in the 1990s, George Cheek has served on its board as well.

– George W. Cheek

VOICES OF MARANATHA

Kind Words Were Never Forgotten

There were three unusual things which I remember about Maranatha. The first year of Camp, in 1938, when it was held out south of North Platte, we used a cardboard shack for cooking and dish washing. I was helping with the dish washing, and we had to throw our dishwater outdoors. I headed for the door with the pan of water, and just as I got to the door, it slipped out of my hands, and the water landed in the lap of a visitor who was sitting just inside the door. It has been things such as this which have kept me humble.

Years later when we moved to this present location, I had been staying in one of the log cabins. The morning after the Camp season was over, I thought I would try to rest a little bit later. But it was necessary that all the mattresses be picked up and stored in a safe, dry place. So you can guess what happened! That morning early, the truck came to my cabin to pick up my mattress, and I didn't get my rest.

Another time, when we had the bookstore in the Old Tabernacle, I took care of it for a while. One noon I was getting ready to go over to the dining hall for lunch, when Mr. T.J. Bach came by. He was the speaker that week, and he was head of the Scandinavian Alliance Mission, now TEAM Mission. He said, "God bless you, sister." I said "Oh, are you leaving, Rev. Bach?" He replied "No, I just like the way you do your work." This I have never forgotten, as you can well imagine!!

So thankful that in the early days of Maranatha, I had the privilege of helping with the dining room, cooking, book store (everything but counseling). This included taking care of the registrations, both before Camp, and on the opening day. Thankful that God gave the vision of Maranatha Camp to Pastor Olsen.

– Faye Ward,
North Platte

Top row, from left: Maranatha broke ground in 1998 for the Adrian House four-plex cabin. Doing the honors are, from left: Mark Geist, Bruce Stucky, Alice Olsen, Carl Goltz, George Cheek; Local fireman, Bob Turner, helped secure this truck for Maranatha's fire protection.

Second row, from left: Louise Crooks (at left) directed this small orchestra at the Golden Anniversary celebration in 1988; The construction of the gymnasium from 1992-94 was a key step in the growth of non-summer programming at Maranatha; Photo taken early September 1992 from top of Dining Hall. Gym building is east of Dining Hall and is connected to Dining Hall.

Third row, from left: Ward Childerston leads the singing of hymns during the 50th anniversary celebration service, Sunday, July 3, 1988; Pouring the cement floor for Adrian Cabin required much help from several volunteers in the spring of 1998; Maranatha built its first four-plex housing unit (Lehman Cabin) in 1994.

Fourth row, from left: Later renamed Kittle Cabin, this is one of many cabins on the Camp property; Camp residents often are treated to the sight of deer, especially in the quieter non-summer months. This photo was taken near the west end of Maranatha's property; This group of campers used newly-built Adrian Cabin at Junior High Camp in June 1998, just days after a tornado struck the Camp.

Afterword

I t would be difficult, if not impossible, to count the number of souls saved and to quantify the people who have made life-changing spiritual decisions at Maranatha Bible Camp. Ever since that quiet prayer meeting on March 15, 1938, God has used a small, independent Bible camp in a sparsely-populated area of the United States to make a disproportionately large impact on the world.

It surely has not been the work of one man. Ivan E. Olsen attested to that fact late in his life, writing, "The 'tender tree of God's planting in a dry and barren land' was nourished by many similarly led pastors and leaders." Many of those leaders stayed with the task 30 years or more. The list is long. As Paul said in Hebrews 11:32, "... and what shall I more say, for the time would fail me to tell of Gideon, and of Barak, ..."

"God, the Book Keeper, has the 'labors not in vain' done for Him by lay people and missionaries and all," wrote Olsen. "It has been, in every way, a faith work. Only heaven will be able to tell the success story of lives set afire and sent to the four corners of the world.

"We talk about 8, 9, 10 percent and more, interest. In the Bible, we read 40, 60 and 100 fold. Mr. Dick Zoet invested part of his effort, leading me, Ivan Olsen, as a 16-year-old boy, to Christ. As a result, he will have a share in anything that has been accomplished through these years. We wish that we could convince you, who have stood by Maranatha faithfully with your prayers and your financial gifts, and whatever else, that when the rewards are handed out, you will get dividends from your investment."

Another man who made an investment in God's work at Maranatha, Hugh Clark, made near-prophetic comments in his 1938 prelude to the many years of Camp board minutes he took.

"God in His wonderful guidance and blessings has really made the Camp a possibility for man," Clark wrote. "Doors have been opened that we had not realized could be opened. Material needs provided such as we never had expected. We must thank God again for His wonderful protection and care.

"May God use Maranatha Bible Camp to His glory, and continue His guidance and provision for the needs of Camp. May we who have been entrusted to this task be faithful in giving God the glory, in thanksgiving, in prayer and the work of our hands, till Jesus comes or takes us to work elsewhere or to be with our Savior forevermore."

– Tad Stryker

Authors of book were eyewitnesses of much of the history in this book

Hundreds of old photos

Maranatha Bible Camp scrapbook compiled by Tammy Hofman

Transcripts of Olsen "Pastor's Hour" sermons to Navigators

Transcript of Russ Johnston interview with Ivan Olsen in Florida, 1989

Transcript of Pauline Tallman's interview with Alice Olsen, 2004

Videotape of George Cheek's interview with Hugh Clark, May 1995

Scrapbooks of NP Berean bulletins and NP newspaper clippings compiled by Estelle Hocquelle, 1932-1979.

Testimonies sent by friends of Maranatha

Bernard Palmer in February 1950 issue of *Christian Life* magazine

Camp newsletters (*Newsline*)

Original Camp brochures

Original summaries of early Encampments

POWER Team prayer bulletins

Videotape of Olsen funeral

Video testimony from Curt Lehman, Ruth Gustafson Gibson, Alice Olsen

Tad Stryker's interviews with Alice Olsen, 1997, 1998 and 2004

Story by Eric Seacrest in North Platte Telegraph Family Weekend, June 27, 1969

Flood of 1973: North Platte Telegraph, May 10-15, 1973

Ivan Olsen obituary and story in NP Telegraph, Sept. 22, 1993

Story about Stephen Welsh murder in June 22, 1995, NP Telegraph

The Berean Digest, Sept-Oct 1965 edition

Navigators Log, October 1968

Handwritten notes by Ivan Olsen in preparation for the 40th and 50th anniversary celebrations of Maranatha

Real estate records, Office of the Register of Deeds, Lincoln County Courthouse

Letters of Ivan E. Olsen

Letters of Theodore H. Epp

Fundraising letters by Ivan Olsen (Nov. 19, 1949) and other correspondence

Hmong article by George Cheek in September 1987 issue of *Confident Living* magazine.

Web site for City of Littleton, Colo., www.littleton.gov, for information about the flood of 1965

Lincoln Berean Church Web site, www.lincolnberean.org

Maranatha Camp Staff

1976

Allen, Larry
Archer, Lillian
Ashcraft, Glenn
Benson, Amy
Berg, Karan
Campbell, Shelly
Cheek, Donna
Cheek, George
Cheek, Jan
Cheek, Warren
Clark, Bruce
Clark, Bryan
Clark, Diane
Coleman, Teresa
Cook, Amelia
Cook, Joe
Dalrymple, Edith
Dalrymple, John
Ellis, Beth
Felgate, Alice
Felgate, Ed
Garner, Susan
Geise, Cheri
Hanus, Karen
Harper, Larry
Hasenauer, Reuben
Herrick, Cindy
Hokenson, Rhoda
Johns, Martha
Lanka, Julie
Lehman, Doug
Lutes, Connie
Lynch, Robin
Mays, Cathleen
McClintock, Chris
Merriman, Cheri
Miner, Gary
Patterson, Betsy
Potter, Mark
Rhoda, Inez
Rhoda, Irvin
Richmond, Sheri
Schneider, Peggy
Schrenk, Evan
Schrenk, Virginia
Scott, Patty
Seiver, Ann
Shaver, Patsi

Shaver, Rex
Shimmin, Joanne
Simmons, Jon
Simmons, Karen
Simmons, Paul
Williams, Nancy

1977

Ashcraft, Glenn
Becker, Brenda
Benson, Amy
Campbell, Shelly
Cheek, George
Cheek, Jan
Clark, Bruce
Clark, Bryan
Clark, Diane
Coleman, Teresa
Cook Amelia
Cook, Joe
Felgate, Alice
Felgate, Ed
Foster, Jane
Geise, Cheri
Hasenauer, Reuben
Hollenbeck, Barb
Joedeman, Cindy
Johnson, Dave
Johnson, Tammi
Lehm, Jim
Lynch, Robin
McCall, Kathy
McClure, Mary
Merriman, Cheri
Merriman, Louise
Merriman, Tami
Olsen, Alice
Olsen, Ivan
Olson, Sally
Partridge, Laura
Phillips, Rita
Pleger, Marie
Rasmussen, Kari
Rasmussen, Tara
Rhoda, Ervin
Rhoda, Inez
Rodgers, Ruth Ann
Schneider, Peggy
Shimmin, Joanne

Shive, Donna
Shive, Loran
Shull, Nancy
Siebert, Jeannie
Simmons, Jon
Simmons, Sharon
Smith, Jim
Smith, Al
Smith, Margaret
Twiggs, Karen
Williams, Roberta
Zechin, Kevan

1978

Anderson, C.U.
Anderson, Rozan
Atchison, Liam
Atchison, Precious
Baleno, Flo
Beetem, Jo
Bennet, Sanda
Bryant, Pat
Carter, Jeff
Cheek, George
Cheek, Jan
Church, Matt
Clark, Kelly
Cole, Cindy
Coley, Karen
Cook, Joe
Dible, Paul
Dible, Ruth
Dick, Jo
Drake, Dana
Egolf, Dawn
Ellis, Mark
Farmer, Bruce
Farmer, Cleo
Farmer, Paul
Farmer, Wanda
Felgate, Alice
Felgate, Ed
Geise, Cheri
Harder, Brenda
Harder, Tim
Hasenauer, Reuben
January, Randy
Lehman, Doug
Lehman, Steve

Merriman, Tami
Millheim, Karen
Nielssen, Norm
Norris, Tamara
Okken, Al
Olsen, Alice
Olsen, Ivan
Overby, Steve
Overby, Sue
Partridge, Laura
Pestal, Chris
Phillips, Brenda
Phillips, Donald
Rasmussen, Lori
Rasmussen, Tara
Rodgers, Ruth
Saathoff, Nancy
Shimmin, Joanne
Shull, Nancy
Siebert, Jeannie
Slaughter, Donna
Suiter, Michelle
TerBerg III, Garrett
Weir, Becky
Wolff, Bill
Wright, Doug

1980

Anderson, Alice
Arehart, James
Arehart, Jean
Arehart, Lee
Arehart, Lori
Arehart, Mark
Arehart, Teresa
Bachert, Susan L.
Beetem, Jo
Benson, Bob
Breck, Evelyn
Carlson, Gloria
Cheek, George
Cheek, Jan
Cheek, Kris
Cheek, Tara
Coleman, Gordon E.
Coleman, Teresa
Compton, Sara
Crow, Joyce
Davis, Chrystal

Deaver, Paul
Dible, Ruth
German, Laura
Glad, Jim
Grieser, Amy
Groh, Laurie
Hascall, Glenn A.
Hasenauer, Reuben
Herrera, Roseann
Keller, Jennifer
Kihlthau, Rod
King, Shawn
Kyne, Jay
Macken, Steve
Maline, Steve
McCarley, Chris
McClure, Cheryl
Merriman, Tami
Meschke, John
Millheim, Karen
Morehead, Rosemary
Needham, Bert
Norris, Tami
O'Kane, Amy
Persson, Lydia
Rawson, Rich
Regier, Marcella
Rodgers, Ruth Ann
Sandin, Beth
Shimmin, Joanne
Skoog, Betty
Skoog, Ernie
Smith, Bernice
Smith, George
Uber, Ruth
Van Timmeren, Steve
Wachtel, Chris
Walters, Sherry
Wedel, Terry
Whitbeck, Bonnie
Young, Mary

1981

Anderson, Alice
Ashcraft, Jay
Bachert, Peggy
Bachert, Susan
Benson, Bob
Benson, Peggy

Cheek, George
Cheek, Jan
Cheek, Kris
Cheek, Tara
Correll, Dennis
DeBoer, Mindy
Delehoy, David
Durnell, Jill
Foster, Jeanne
Garrett, Bert
Gingrich, Duaine
Goodnough, Dana
Goodnough, Monica
Grover, Gail
Hasenauer, Reuben
Horan, Chris
Hunter, Dilean
Hunter, Dwight
Johnson, Julie
King, Shawn
Kouris, Julie
Lehman, Steve
Lines, Linda
Maline, Lori
Marks, Shirley
McClure, Mary
Merriman, Tami
Meshke, John
Needham, Bert
Olsen, Alice
Olsen, Ivan E.
Pledger, Marie
Regier, Marcella
Rodgers, Ruth Ann
Ruybalid, Rod
Schneider, Joyce
Shimmin, Joanne
Skoog, Betty
Skoog, Ernie
Spiess, Elizabeth
Spiess, Jan
Spiess, Julie
Spiess, Scott
Spiess, Stan
Springer, Brenda
Taylor, Brenda
Tiffany, Marvin
Tonkin, Steve
Uber, Ruth
Wachtel, Chris

Summer Staff, 1973

Summer Staff, 1981

Wahl, Mary
Walters, David
Walters, Sherry
Wambolt, Evelyn
Wambolt, Hank
Wiebe, John

1982

Amaya, Sandy
Ashcraft, Glenn
Ashcraft, Sue
Ashcraft, Jay
Bachert, Peggy
Bauer, Becky
Bauer, Duane
Bauer, Edna
Bauer, Sam
Beetem, JoAnn
Benson, Bob
Benson, Peggy
Buck, Laurie
Campbell, Bonnie
Cappel, Dorothy
Cheek, George
Cheek, Jan
Cheek, Kris
Cheek, Tara
Clevenger, Paula
Coleman, Gordon
Dapra, Joseph P.
DeKing, Jeff
Durnell, Jill
Foster, Jeanne
Hall, John
Hasenauer, Reuben
Hunt, Jayne
Hunt, Rachel
Krehbiel, Michael
Lucht, Jeff
Maline, Lori
Marks, Shirley
Massey, Daniel
McCall, Coni
Meisbauer, Peggy
Merriman, Tami
Meschke, Bert
Meschke, John
Needham, Bert
Olsen, Alice
Olsen, Christy
Olsen, Debbie
Olsen, Ivan E.
Olsen, Rick

Phillips, Brenda
Rodgers, Ruth Ann
Sandeen, Steve
Sandin, Beth
Schmidt, Janice
Stucky, Bruce
Tiffany, Marvin
Wambolt, Evelyn
Wambolt, Hank
Welsh, Patty
Welsh, Peggy

1983

Amaya, Sandy
Bachert, Peggy
Bauer, Becky
Bauer, Duane
Bauer, Edna
Bauer, Sam
Beetem, JoAnn
Benson, Barry
Benson, Bob
Benson, Peggy
Bourgeios, Gayzel
Cheek, George
Cheek, Jan
Cheek, Kris
Cheek, Tara
Clevenger, Paula
Dapra, Joe
Delehoy, Dave
Friesen, Cathi
Geise, Cheri
Hasenauer, Reuben
Holtorf, Tina
Kaufman, Kent
Kroeker, Lynette
Lamb, Bonnie
Lindquist, Glen
Lindquist, Olive
Lines, Brenda
Lines, Linda
Lynch, Dennis
Maline, Kathy
Maline, Lori
Marks, Shirley
Merriman, Tami
Meschke, Bert
Meschke, John
Meschke, Matthew
Millheim, Karen
Ogden, Carla
Olsen, Alice

Olsen, Ivan E.
Prohaska, Ron
Rodgers, Ruth Ann
Shimmin, Joanne
Sloan, Dollie
Sloan, Jerry
Solberg, Kirsten
Solomon, Allen
Stucky, Bruce
Stucky, Rachel
Tracy, Mark
Wagoner, Eric
Wambolt, Evelyn
Wambolt, Hank
Welsh, Patti
Willard, Dorothy
Willard, Loyal
Willson, Paula

1984

Amaya, Sandy
Anderson, Collin
Bachert, Peggy
Beetem, JoAnn
Benson, Bob
Benson, Peggy
Bulkley, Bob
Bulkley, Bob Jr.
Bulkley, Jan
Cheek, George
Cheek, Jan
Cheek, Kris
Cheek, Tara
Collison, Leslie
Dapra, Joe
Garrett, Wayne
Grover, Bob
Hasenauer, Reuben
Lamb, Bonnie
Lindquist, Glen
Lindquist, Olive
Lynch, Dennis
McCall, Dorothy
Melchert, Matthew
Meshcke, Bert
Meshcke, John
Meschke, Matthew
Millheim, Karen
Myers, Bobbi
Myers, Byron
Myers, Linda
Myers, Luke
Myers, Joe

Myers, Josh
Myers, Ted
Naeve, Glynda
Nienkamp, Deb
Olsen, Alice
Olsen, Christy
Olsen, Danny
Olsen, Ivan E.
Olsen, Jamie
Olsen, Judy
Olsen, Ted
Prohaska, Ron
Rodgers, Ruth Ann
Sawyer, Sheryl
Schwindt, Suzy
Solomon, Allen
Spiess, Scott
Springer, Kathleen
Stover, Miriam
Stucky, Bruce
Stucky, Rachel
Tracy, Mark
Vanderwal, Relinda
Voss, Dan
Wambolt, Evelyn
Wambolt, Hank
Welsh, Patti
Willard, Dorothy
Willard, Loyal

1985

Amaya, Sandy
Amen, David
Bachert, Peggy
Beetem, JoAnn
Benson, Bob
Benson, Peggy
Berg, Don
Breiner, Doug
Cheek, Carol
Cheek, Elaine
Cheek, George
Cheek, Jan
Cheek, Kris
Cheek, Tara
Cheek, Warren
Cheek, Silas
Cramer, Cindy
Dapra, Joe
Dible, Jeanette
Dible, Ruth
Diederich, Chad
Duncan, Floyd

Empson, Laura
Finnan, John
Gerry, Lance
Giles, Sally
Gillespey, Mark
Gore, Tracy
Graf, Matt
Grover, Diann
Grover, Earl
Gurney, Tammy
Hall, Rich
Hamilton, Genevieve
Hand, Dan
Hasenauer, Reuben
Herman, Deanna
Jones, David
Kaltenbach, Barb
Kienitz, Cindi
Kienitz, Tim
Koch, Jeff
Littrell, Glenn
Lowrey, Anita
McGill, Angela
McGill, Bonnie
McGill, Nathan
McGill, Tim
Melchert, Matthew
Merrimam, Tami
Millheim, Karen
Moore, Ron
Morris, Delline
Nekuda, Andi
Olivas, George
Olmsted, Stuart
Olsen, Alice
Olsen, Ivan E.
Olsen, Kristy
Pace, Esther
Peterson, Karen
Pietzyk, Laurie
Porter, Brian
Rodgers, Ruth Ann
Siebert, Beth
Solomon, Allen
Spiess, Scott
Stover, Brad
Stover, Miriam
Stucky, Bruce
Stucky, Esther Lorraine
Stucky, Rachel
Tallman, Neil
Tallman, Pauline
Turner, David
Vanderwal, Relinda

Voss, Dan
Wagoner, Lynn
Wahl, Mary
White, LeAnn
Williams, Erin

1986

Andersen, Collin
Babcock, Jason
Bachert, Peggy
Beetem, JoAnn
Benson, Bob
Benson, Peggy
Berg, Don
Borba, Jane
Bottorff, Alexis
Brindle, Bob
Cheek, George
Cheek, Jan
Cheek, Kris
Cheek, Tara
Coady, Nat
Cramer, Cindy
Dapra, Joe
Douglas, Rob
Fabik, Craig
Fabik, Nancy
Garcia, Scott
Geise, Cheri
Gerry, Lance
Giles, Sally
Gillespey, Mark
Grover, Diann
Grover, Earl
Groves, Mary Lynn
Hasenauer, Reuben
Hayden, Chris
Haynes, Karen
Herman, Deanna
Jones, David
Kaltenbach, Barb
Kienitz, Cindi
Kienitz, Grace
Kienitz, Joy
Kienitz, Ruth
Kienitz, Terry
Kienitz, Tim
MacKenzie, Jason
Manuel, Denise
Meaders, April
Meaders, Crystal
Meaders, Irene
Meaders, Johnny Mike

Summer Staff, 1983

Summer Staff, 1984

195

Meaders, Roy
Melchert, Matthew
Millheim, Karen
Millsap, Tyler
Nelson, Mike
Olsen, Alice
Olsen, Ivan E.
Ostrander, Dean
Ostrander, Marilyn
Ottun, April
Ottun, Philip
Pace, Esther
Peterman, Jeffrey
Phillips, Jeff
Porter, Beth
Rodgers, Ruth Ann
Scranton, Bronwyn
Springer, Kathleen
Stover, Bard
Stover, J.J.
Stover, Miriam
Stover, Wendi
Stucky, Bruce
Stucky, Esther
Stucky, Rachel
Swesey, Mark
Tallman, Neil
Tallman, Pauline
Tomihama, Lynette
Vilt, David
Voss, Dan
Wagoner, Lynne
Walker, Dale
Wambolt, Evelyn
Wambolt, Hank
White, LeAnn
Willis, Kelly

1987

Bachert, Peggy
Barnes, Tammy
Beetem, JoAnn
Benson, Bob
Benson, Peggy
Britton, Julie
Bulkley, Bob
Bulkley, Jan
Cheek, George
Cheek, Jan
Cheek, Kris
Cheek, Tara
Coady, Nat
Colison, Leslie

Cramer, Cindy
Dapra, Joe
Douglass, Rod
Empson, Laura
Enns, Daniel
Garcia, Carrie
Garcia, Scott
Geise, Cheri
Gerry, Lance
Grover, Diann
Grover, Earl
Hall, Karen
Hasenauer, Reuben
Hayden, Chris
Herman, Deanna
Jones, David "Bubba"
Koch, Jeff
Kremer, LeeAnn
Larson, Dawn
Macken, Steve
Mackenzie, Jason
Manuel, Denise
Meadors, April
Meadors, Crystal
Meadors, Irene
Meadors, Johnny Mike
Millheim, Karen
Morris, Lester
Nekuda, Andrea
Nelson, Nita
Olsen, Alice
Olsen, Ivan E.
Peck, Shane
Peterman, Jeff
Porter, Beth
Purdy, Leonard
Rodgers, JoAnn
Rodgers, Ruth Ann
Spiess, Julie
Springer, Kathleen
Stover, Brad
Stover, J.J.
Stover, Miriam
Stover, Wendi
Stucky, Bruce
Stucky, Esther
Stucky, Kenneth
Stucky, Rachel
Swesey, Mark
Tallman, Neil
Tallman, Pauline
Tomihama, Lynette
Wagoner, Mike
Walker, Dale

Wambolt, Evelyn
Wambolt, Hank
White, LeAnn
Willis, Kelly
Wilson, Lisa
Yeutter, Karl

1989

Barnes, Tom
Bauer, Becky
Beetem, JoAnn
Benson, Bob
Benson, Peggy
Brush, Barbara
Bulkley, Bob
Bulkley, Jan
Cheek, George
Cheek, Jan
Cheek, Kris
Cheek, Merle
Cheek, Stella
Cheek, Tara
Crider, Pat
Dapra, Heidi
Dapra, Joe
Dapra, Miriam
Dericksen II, Stan
Eliphaz, Abraham
Feay, Bonnie
Feay, Dick
Gontjez, Pauline
Goodrich, Steve
Grover, Earl
Grover, Nita
Gustafson, Ruth
Haase, Betsy
Hasenauer, Reuben
Hunt, Melissa
Jewert, Dennis
Jewert, Jennifer
Jewert, Joshua
Jewert, Randi
Jones, David
Krahn, Bona
Larsen, Colleen
Maline, Nikki
Martin, Kathy
Miller, Mark
Nichols, Timothy
Olsen, Alice
Olsen, Craig
Olsen, Ivan E.
Peck, Shane

Pleger, Bertha
Rodgers, Ruth Ann
Rowe, Kent
Rowe, Michelle
Ruff, Rhonda
Schirmer, Kim
Schnell, Roger
Slack, Amy
Slack, Charity
Slack, Sheila
Stackhouse, Kevin
Stover, Brad
Stover, J.J.
Stover, Wendi
Stryker, Jake
Stryker, Jean
Stryker, Micah
Stryker, Tad
Stucky, Bruce
Stucky, Esther
Stucky, Rachel
Swesey, Mark
Van Mark, Janet
Vandenbos, Jean
Wambolt, Evelyn
Wambolt, Hank
Yates, Mike
Yeutter, Connie
Yeutter, Karl
Yeutter, Kim

1991

Ashcraft, Jack
Ashcraft, Lindy
Ashcraft, Matt
Ashcraft, Virginia
Beetem, JoAnn
Boettcher, Andrea
Boettcher, Deb
Bottorff, Jason
Buckley, Ben
Bulkley, Bob
Bulkley, Jan
Cateine, Christine
Cheek, George
Cheek, Jan
Cheek, Kris
Cheek, Merle
Cheek, Stella
Cheek, Tara
Chezik, Ken
Crooks, Scott
Dapra, Heidi

Dapra, Joe
Dapra, Miriam
Eliphaz, Rev. M.A.
Feay, Bonnie
Feay, Dick
Ganow, Tim
Gerry, Lance
Gerry, Sherry
Griffiths, Robyn
Gustafson, Ruth
Hasenauer, Reuben
Herrick, Vanji
Jensen, Laurie
Jones, David "Bubba"
Kassebaum, Noel
Kimble, Benny
Littlejohn, Ron
Jantz, Hugh
Lucht, Jill
Maline, Nikki
McDaniel, Becky
McGee, John
Meyer, Jenny
Motakatla, Daniel
Munro, Duane
Munro, Janet
Munro, Jesse
Munro, John
Munro, Peter
Norman, Janelle
Norman, Jonathan
Olsen, Alice
Olsen, Christy
Olsen, Craig
Olsen, Ivan E.
Olsen, Misty
Olson, Kael
Olson, Leif
Olson, Roxie
Patterson, Mike
Rodgers, Ruth Ann
Roesch, Dan
Scheidegger, Muriel
Schenk, Sandy
Slack, Amy
Slack, Charity
Slack, Sheila
Smith, Naomi
Soares, Andy
Sommers, Amy
Sommers, Dan
Streeter, Sally
Stryker, Abbie
Stryker, Jean

Stryker, Jacob
Stryker, Micah
Stryker, Tad
Stucky, Bruce
Stucky, Esther
Stucky, Rachel
Swackhamer, Brent
Swesey, Mark
Swoboda, Abram
Tallman, Neil
Tallman, Pauline
Taylor, Karen
Trantham, Donna
Van Mark, Janet
Vance, Debbie
Waldo, Debbie
Waldo, Peter
Wambolt, Evelyn
Wambolt, Hank
Wardyn, Becki Hiser
Yates, Mike
Yeutter, Karl

1992

Aeschliman, Mike
Alexander, Tammi
Ashcraft, Jack
Ashcraft, Virginia
Atkinson, Jane
Baxter, Corene
Beetem, JoAnn
Benson, Peggy
Bottorff, Jason
Buckley, Ben
Cheek, George
Cheek, Jan
Cheek, Kris
Cheek, Merle
Cheek, Stella
Cheek, Tara
Clang, James
Dapra, Heidi
Dapra, Joe
Dapra, Miriam
Feay, Bonnie
Feay, Dick
Fread, Robin
Gerry, Lance
Gerry, Sherry
Grafton, Dorothy
Gustafson, Ruth
Hasenauer, Reuben
Hunt, Don

Summer Staff, 1986

Summer Staff, 1988

Hunt, Marguerite
Jantz, Hugh
Jenner, Stephanie
Jones, David
Lamb, Carole
Littrell, Tami
Malm, Linda
McGee, John
Meadors, April
Moog, Sue
Morey, Renee
Motakatla, Abraham
 Eliphaz
Motakatla, Daniel
 Eliphaz
Nielsen, Paul
Olsen, Alice
Olsen, Ivan E.
Olson, Kael
Olson, Leif
Olson, Roxie
Olson, Shad
Prohaska, Bonnie
Radtke, Nelson
Roberts, Kari
Rodgers, Ruth Ann
Steele, Todd
Stryker, Abigail
Stryker, Jake
Stryker, Jean
Stryker, Micah
Stryker, Tad
Stucky, Bruce
Stucky, Esther
Stucky, Rachel
Swesey, Mark
Tallman, Neil
Tallman, Pauline
Turner, Becky
Van Mark, Janet
Waldo, Peter
Wambolt, Evelyn
Wambolt, Hank
Welsh, George
Welsh, Millie
Yates, Mike

1993

Adams, April
Ashcraft, Jack
Ashcraft, Virginia
Beetem, JoAnn
Bjerga, Harald

Buckley, Ben
Burbach, David
Busch, Charlie
Carrier, Steve
Cheek, George
Cheek, Jan
Cheek, Kris
Cheek, Merle
Cheek, Stella
Cheek, Tara
Chezik, Ken
Cotten, Kathy
Danielson, Brian
Davis, Chester
Davis, Felicia
Dishman, Casey
Donaldson, Joan
Donaldson, Mike
Feay, Bonnie
Feay, Dick
Floe, Geri
Fread, Robin
Freedman, Trisha
Gerry, Lance
Gerry, Sherry
Grafton, Dorothy
Grafton, Scott
Gustafson, Ruth
Hanken, Dina
Hanken, Todd "TJ"
Hasenauer, Reuben
Hofman, Jim
Hofman, Tammy
Hurley, Becky
Johnson, Ben
Johnson, Rosemary
Jones, David
Kelley, Christine
Lamb, Carole
Leach, Sheri
Littrell, Tami
Lucht, Jill
Meadors, April
McKim, Jennifer
Moog, Sue
Morey, Renee
Morphew, Jim
Morris, Kelley
Morrow, Jerrold
Munro, John
Nighswonger, Todd
Olsen, Alice
Olsen, Ivan E.
Patterson, Corey

Patterson, Mike
Pike, Trevor
Prohaska, Bonnie
Reid, Maxine
Roberts, Kari
Roesch, Beth
Rodgers, Ruth Ann
Smith, Naomi
Sommers, Dan
Stover, Brad
Stryker, Abigail
Stryker, Jake
Stryker, Jean
Stryker, Micah
Stryker, Tad
Stucky, Bruce
Stucky, Esther
Stucky, Rachel
Sullivan, Kim
Sullivan, Mike
Swesey, Mark
Tallman, Neil
Tallman, Pauline
Thompson, Sally
Turner, James
Unrau, Becky
Van Mark, Janet
Wambolt, Evelyn
Wambolt, Hank
Yates, Mike

1994

Adams, April
Ashcraft, Jack
Ashcraft, Lindy
Ashcraft, Virginia
Babcock, Colleen
Beetem, JoAnn
Bjerga, Harald
Bjerga, Kim
Bjerga, Sarah
Buckley, Grace
Burbach, David
Busch, Charlie
Carter, Cal
Carter, Kristen
Carter, Kayla
Carter, Reegan
Carter, Heather
Chaboyer, Shelley
Cheek, George
Cheek, Jan
Cheek, Kris

Cheek, Merle
Cheek, Stella
Cheek, Tara
Chezik, Ken
Davis, Chester
Davis, Felicia
Deets, John
Dishman, Deb
Donovan, Clyde
Donovan, Rachel
Every, Deanna
Fasse, Eleanor
Feay, Bonnie
Feay, Dick
Floe, Geri
Floe, William
Floe, Deanna
Fread, Robin
Freedman, Trisha
From, Derek
Gerry, Lance
Gerry, Nathan
Gerry, Sherry
Gikaru, Mike
Glad, Gil
Glad, Dorothy
Gompert, Kate
Gosnell, Tonda
Grafton, Dorothy
Hasenauer, Reuben
Haynes, Donna
Hermsmeyer, Heather
Hermsmeyer, Spring
Hofman, Tammy
Householter, Christy
Hurley, Becky
Jones, David
Johnson, Ben
Johnson, Rosemary
Koole, Melanie
Koole, Melissa
Malm, Linda
Masten, Anne
Masten, Barry
Masten, Brent
Masten, Connie
Masten, Nick
McDermott, Marty
McDermott, Stephen
Meadors, April
Moog, Sue
Morey, Laura
Morey, Lisa
Morey, Renee

Nanninga, Kip
Nelson, Rachel
Nielsen, Paul
Olsen, Alice
Olsen, Shad
Patterson, Corey
Patterson, Michael
Pike, Trevor
Presley, Abby
Presley, Alec
Presley, Candace
Presley, Candy
Presley, Rosie
Presley, Lauren
Presley, Loran
Presley, Meggan
Radtke, Nelson
Rodgers, Ruth Ann
Roesch, Beth
Stryker, Abigail
Stryker, Jake
Stryker, Jean
Stryker, Micah
Stryker, Tad
Stucky, Bruce
Stucky, Esther
Stucky, Rachel
Swesey, Mark
Tallman, Neil
Tallman, Pauline
Thomspon, Sally
Tidquist, Heather
Unrau, Becky
Unrau, Cindy
Wambolt, Evelyn
Wambolt, Hank
Yanitski, Aaron
Yanitski, Amber
Yanitski, Barry
Yanitski, Charlene
Yates, Mike

1996

Adams, April
Adams, Arline
Ashcraft, George
Ashcraft, Virginia
Bank, Jodi
Banks, Deb
Banks, Jacki
Barker, Emily
Beetem, JoAnn
Berger, Sarah

Bjerga, Hagan
Bjerga, Harald
Bjerga, Kim
Bjerga, Sarah
Blaszkowski, James
Bostwick, Jake
Braun, Krista
Brito, Irma
Busch, Charlie
Carlson, Jessica
Carter, Cal
Carter, Heather
Carter, Kayla
Carter, Kristin
Carter, Reegan
Chapman, Summer
Cheek, George
Cheek, Jan
Cheek, Kris
Cheek, Merle
Cheek, Stella
Cheek, Tara
Chezik, Ken
Chotvacs, Amy
Christensen, Beth
Crooks, Michele
Danielson, Brian
Davis, Ethne
Demoret, Jessica
Dishman, Steven
Donovan, Clyde
Donovan, Rachel
Fasse, Eleanor
Feay, Bonnie
Feay, Dick
Fogland, Fern
Foord, Diane
Foord, Roy
Friesen, Lance
Gardner, Jamie
Gerry, Lance
Gerry, Nathan
Gerry, Rebekah
Gerry, Sherry
Gibson, Ruth
Gibson, Walter
Glad, Dorothy
Glad, Gil
Gonell, Marlys
Gonzalez, Pedro
Gosnell, Jonie
Gosnell, Londa
Gosnell, Tonda
Grafton, Dorothy

Summer Staff, 1989

Summer Staff, 1990

Gumb, Megan
Gumsey, Jason
Hardt, Christi
Harlow, Josiah
Harmon, Bob
Harmon, Mary
Hasenauer, Reuben
Henry, Larry
Hofman, Jim
Hofman, Tammy
Hunt, Don
Hunt, Marguerite
Jones, David
Kamau, Mary
Kiger, Laurie
King, Shelli
Knapp, Amy
Knott, Jason
Kramer, Lisa
Lawson, Adam
Lawson, Joshua
Lawson, Rebekah
Leach, Sarah
Leach, Sheri
Lehmkuhl, Daniel
Lehmkuhl, Mark
Lehmkuhl, Rachel
Lehmkuhl, Rebecca
Lehmkuhl, Renee
Lightfoot, Sharon
Lingbloom, Ryan
Lingbloom, Tammy
Lorenz, Sarah
Madsen, Gregg
Malm, Linda
Masten, Anne
Masten, Nick
McDermott, Felicia
McDermott, Steve
Meadors, April
Miller, Beneth
Miller, Pam
Moog, Erika
Moog, Holly
Moog, Sarah
Moog, Sue
Morey, Laura
Morey, Lisa
Ngugi, Veronica
Nielsen, Paul
Niver, Rachel
Norman, Jamie
Norman, Jonathan
Olsen, Alice
Patterson, Corey

Patterson, Mike
Peer, Murray
Peterson, Sarah
Prohaska, Bonnie
Reisner, Jenifer
Rodgers, Ruth Ann
Roth, Ryan
Rouse, Wayne
Salsman, Danny
Sauls, Jennifer
Schiffner, Mark
Schmidt, Reba
Slack, Sheila
Sprunger, Ben
Steele, Todd
Steiner, Jason
Stewert, Sara
Stodden, Andriele
Stryker, Abbie
Stryker, Jacob
Stryker, Jean
Stryker, Micah
Stryker, Tad
Stucky, Bruce
Stucky, Esther
Stucky, Rachel
Swesey, Mark
Tallman, Pauline
Thomas, Andrea
Thompson, Jeffery
Thompson, Sally
Timson, Levi
Townsend, Heather
Townsend, Jennifer
Townsend, Jessica
Townsend, Marcia
Townsend, Staci
Unrau, Becky
Utterback, Melinda
Vandevenne, Jean
Vandevenne, Tom
Wambolt, Evelyn
Wambolt, Hank
Welch, Linda
West, David
White, Joy
Whitehead, Lincoln

1997

Adams, April
Adams, Arline
Ashcraft, George
Ashcraft, Virginia
Babcock, Colleen

Bauley, Justin
Beetem, JoAnn
Bjerga, Ellie
Bjerga, Hagan
Bjerga, Harald
Bjerga, Kim
Bjerga, Sarah
Box, Dan
Brennfoerder, Aaron
Busch, Andrew
Busch, Charlie
Butler, Denise
Butler, Don
Cape, Sharon
Carlson, Jessica
Chapman, Summer
Cheek, George
Cheek, Jan
Cheek, Kris
Cheek, Merle
Cheek, Stella
Cheek, Tara
Chezik, Ken
Christensen, Beth
Cook, Jessica
Crooks, Michele
Danielson, Brian
Danielson, Melissa
Danielson, Sarah
Darr, Cindy
Davis, Ethne
Demoret, Jessica
Detamore, Ken
Donovan, Clyde
Donovan, Rachel
Dorsey, John
Dyck, Carol
Dyck, Ken
Dyck, Kendi
Dyck, Vanessa
Fasse, Eleanor
Feay, Bonnie
Feay, Dick
Floe, Geri
Gallagher, Terry
Gayman, Fred
Gayman, Shirley
Gerry, Lance
Gerry, Nathan
Gerry, Rebekah
Gerry, Sherry
Gibson, Ruth
Gibson, Walter
Glad, Dorothy
Glad, Gil

Glassbrenner, Jeff
Gosnell, Brandon
Gosnell, Jonie
Gosnell, Tonda
Grafton, Dorothy
Harder, Mike
Hardt, Christi
Hasenauer, Reuben
Herr, Julie
Hutton, Mary Jo
Jackson, Amy
Jackson, Brandon
Jackson, Kindan
Jackson, Noah
Jackson, Taylor
Jackson, Tom
Johnson, Rosemary
Jones, David
Kaiser, Bryce
King, Andrea
Knudsen, Don
Kramer, Lisa
Laboso, Mary
Lehmkuhl, Renee
Lingbloom, Tami
Lorenz, Sarah
Lucht, Jill
McClellen, Keri
McDermott, Amy
Miller, Pam
Moog, Holly
Moog, Sarah
Moog, Sue
Nickerson, Kyle
Nielsen, Paul
Niver, Emily
Niver, Rachel
Norman, Janelle
Olfert, Nathan
Olsen, Alice
Olson, Amy
Ottoson, Bryan
Patterson, Corey
Pierce, Nicki
Prohaska, Bonnie
Reisner, Jenifer
Rodgers, Ruth Ann
Roesch, Beth
Roesch, Tim
Rogers, MeShell
Sauls, Jennifer
Schleicher, Tammy
Sheets, Rashae
Slack, Charity
Slack, Sheila

Smith, Jen
Steele, Todd
Stodden, Andriele
Stryker, Abbie
Stryker, Jacob
Stryker, Jean
Stryker, Micah
Stryker, Tad
Stucky, Bruce
Stucky, Christina
Stucky, Esther
Stucky, Rachel
Swedberg, Brock
Swesey, Mark
Tallman, Pauline
Thompson, Jeff
Thompson, Sally
Timson, Levi
Townsend, Heather
Townsend, Jennifer
Townsend, Jessica
Townsend, Marcia
Townsend, Staci
VanLear, Jake
Wambolt, Evelyn
Wambolt, Hank
Welch, Linda
Whistler, Christy
White, Joy
Williams, Heidi
Wiswall, Travis

1998

Albano, Rachel
Ashcraft, Andrew
Ashcraft, George
Ashcraft, Matt
Ashcraft, Virginia
Atchison, Hope
Atchison, Jesse
Bauley, Justin
Baxter, Elizabeth
Beetem, JoAnn
Bennett, Marty
Blackmon, Melissa
Bralick, Andrew
Brodock, Deren
Busch, Charlie
Carlin, Roxanne
Carter, Cal
Carter, Heather
Carter, Kayla
Carter, Kristin
Carter, Reegan

Cheek, George
Cheek, Jan
Cheek, Kris
Cheek, Merle
Cheek, Stella
Cheek, Tara
Christensen, Colleen
Christensen, Patrick
Codgill, Chris
Crocks, Michele
Curtis, Sara
Davis, Ethne
Davis, Gary
Davis, Julia
Davis, Toby
Demoret, Jessica
Detamore, Ken
Donovan, Clyde
Donovan, Rachel
Dowell, Ross
Dyck, Carol
Dyck, Kandi
Dyck, Ken
Dyck, Vanessa
Enyeart, Beckie
Etter, Kristi
Fasse, Eleanor
Feay, Bonnie
Feay, Dick
Freedman, Ben
Freedman, Joshua
Gayman, Fred
Gayman, Shirley
Gerry, Lance
Gerry, Nathan
Gerry, Rebekah
Gerry, Sherry
Gibson, Ruth
Gibson, Walter
Gosnell, Jonie
Gosnell, Marlys
Grafton, Dorothy
Harder, Daniel
Harmon, Mary
Harvey, Jennifer
Hasenauer, Erin
Hasenauer, Reuben
Hutton, Mary Jo
Jensen, Eric
Jensen, Erica
Jensen, Lindie
Jensen, Melanie
Jensen, Spencer
Johnson, Jordon
Johnson, Justina

Summer Staff, 1992

Summer Staff, 1993

Johnson, Rosemary
Jones, David
Kaiser, Bryce
Kihlthau, Benjamin
Kihlthau, Dina
Kihlthau, Rod
Knapp, Amy
Knott, Josh
Kunnemann, Christel
Leach, Sheri
Livingston, Christine
London, Brandon
Lorenz, Joshua
Lorenz, Sarah
Maginn, Leslie
Manley, Charla
Manley, Chelsea
Manley, Greg
Manley, Nathan
Martin, Candace
McClellen, Keri
Miller, Pam
Moog, Bob
Moog, Erika
Moog, Holly
Moog, Nola
Moog, Sarah
Moog, Sue
Morgan, Lisa
Murray, Amber
Neff, Keila
Nekuda, Andrea
Neth, Kevin
Neufeld, Abe
Nickerson, Kyle
Nighswonger, Josh
Niver, Emily
Norman, Jamie
Northup, Merry
Northup, Nadia
Northup, Nathan
Northup, Samuel
Olsen, Alice
Oman, Levi
Oman, Marilyn
Ondrejack, Diane
Ondrejack, Jane
Ondrejack, Joel
Ondrejack, Katie
Ondrejack, Mary
Ondrejack, Philip
Osler, Marilyn
Ottun, Sterling
Pacheco, Jackie
Prohaska, Adam

Prohaska, Amanda
Prohaska, Bonnie
Pyykkonen, Paul
Reinhard, Jeff
Reisner, Jenifer
Rodgers, Ruth Ann
Roesch, Tim
Rogers, Tim
Roth, Tim
Russell, Susan
Seadore, Joy
Shamburg, Erica
Shearer, Rachel
Shook, Tara
Slack, Sheila
Squier, Kenna
Squier, Marcus
Stodden, Andriele
Stodden, Daniela
Stryker, Abbie
Stryker, Jacob
Stryker, Jean
Stryker, Micah
Stryker, Tad
Stucky, Bruce
Stucky, Esther
Stucky, Rachel
Swedberg, Brady
Swedberg, Jeanne
Swesey, Mark
Tallman, Pauline
Townsend, Heather
Townsend, Jennifer
Townsend, Jessica
Townsend, Marcia
Townsend, Staci
Van Mark, Jean
Van Mark, Jim
Wahlgren, Hannah
Wahlgren, Sarah
Wahlman, Scott
Wambolt, Evelyn
Wambolt, Hank
Welch, Linda
Williams, Heidi
Williams, Melody
Wood, Tara

1999

Albano, Rachel
Albano, Ryan
Armbruster, Andy
Ashcraft, Jack
Ashcraft, Virginia

Austin, Bill
Austin, Kristen
Austin, Clarissa
Austin, Katie
Austin, Lydia
Austin, Rachel
Beetem, JoAnn
Butler, Holly
Carlin, Roxanne
Carter, Cal
Carter, Heather
Carter, Kayla
Carter, Kristin
Carter, Reegan
Castor, Faith
Castor, Jake
Chapman, Cassandra
Cheek, George
Cheek, Jan
Cheek, Merle
Cheek, Stella
Chezik, Ken
Chitwood, Sue
Christensen, Colleen
Christensen, Patrick
Crooks, Michele
Davis, Chester
Davis, Ethne
Davis, Toby
DeBuc, Nathalie
Dechtiarenko, Joe
Demoret, Jessica
DesEnlants, Ty
Dickinson, Amber
Dickinson, Pam
Donovan, Clyde
Donovan, Rachel
Dovenbarger, Brad
Dyck, Carol
Dyck, Ken
Dyck, Kendi
Dyck, Vanessa
Enyeart, Beckie
Erickson, Hans
Fasse, Eleanor
Feay, Bonnie
Feay, Dick
Flinchbaugh, Jamie
Franssen, Katie
Freswick, Keith
Gayman, Fred
Gayman, Shirley
Gibson, Ruth
Gibson, Walter
Glad, Dorothy

Glad, Gil
Gosnell, Ivan
Gosnell, Jonie
Gosnell, Levi
Gosnell, Marlys
Gosnell, Shane
Grafton, Dorothy
Green, Matt
Hall, Cindy
Hall, Lucas
Harder, Daniel
Hasenauer, Erin
Hasenauer, Josh
Hepp, Gabriela
Hepp, Lucas
Hofer, Joshua
Hunt, Sally
Janssen, Matt
Johnson, Jason
Johnson, Jordan
Johnson, Justina
Johnson, Rosemary
Jones, David
Kaiser, Bryce
Kibwaa, Sam
Kihlthau, Benjamin
Kihlthau, Dina
Kihlthau, Rod
Knott, Caleb
Knott, Josh
Kort, Heather
Kort, Paula
Korthuis, Suzanne
Kramer, Corey
Kramer, Julie
Kramer, Laura
Kramer, Lisa
Krehbiel, Tad
Leach, Sheri
Loe, Monica
Lorenz, Joshua
Lorenz, Rebekah
Maginn, Leslie
Malsbury, Joe
Martin, Matthew
Masten, Anne
Mayo, Paul
McClellen, Keri
Meschke, Jessica
Miller, Jan
Miller, Jim
Moog, Erika
Moog, Gordon
Moog, Holly
Moog, Sarah

Moog, Sue
Mudde, Robert
Neth, Kevin
Niver, Emily
Olsen, Alice
Ondrejack, Diane
Ondrejack, Jane
Ondrejack, Joel
Ondrejack, Katie
Ondrejack, Mary
Ondrejack, Philip
Osler, Marilyn
Ostrander, Ryan
Otis, Sara
Ottun, Sterling
Pacheco, Jackie
Preston, Amanda
Prohaska, Bonnie
Pyykkonen, Paul
Rodgers, Ruth Ann
Roesch, Tim
Schulte, Sarah
Seadore, Joy
Shamburg, Erica
Shearer, Rachel
Shook, Tara
Smith, Kristin
Sprague, Kathy
Squier, Marcus
Stodden, Andriele
Stryker, Abbie
Stryker, Jacob
Stryker, Jean
Stryker, Micah
Stryker, Tad
Stucky, Bruce
Stucky, Esther
Stucky, Rachel
Sughroue, Katie
Sutton, Katie
Swedberg, Ben
Swedberg, Brady
Swedberg, Brittni
Swedberg, Brock
Swedberg, Jeanne
Swesey, Mark
Tallman, Pauline
Thompson, Jeff
Tickle, Greg
Tickle, Linda
Townsend, Heather
Townsend, Jenny
Townsend, Jessica
Townsend, Marcia
Townsend, Staci

Turner, Angela
Van Mark, Jean
Van Mark, Jim
Wahlman, Scott
Walker, Esther
Walker, Hannah
Wambolt, Evelyn
Wambolt, Hank
Ward, Travis
Weiderick, Karle
Weiderick, Mark
Whistler, Christie
White, Adam
Wilson, Jordan
Wood, Reydan
Workman, Joshua

2000

Ashcraft, George
Ashcraft, Virginia
Bailey, Lee
Bartsch, Erica
Beetem, JoAnn
Berry, Amanda
Boorman, Mike
Brumm, Randy
Cheek, George
Cheek, Jan
Cheek, Merle
Cheek, Stella
Chitwood, Sue
Christensen, Colleen
Christensen, Patrick
Coffey, Jessica
Conour, Jessica
Conour, Laci
Crocker, Rachel
Crooks, Michele
Dean, Brandon
Dechtiarenko, Joe
Delaplane, Katy
Dickinson, Amber
Donovan, Clyde
Donovan, Rachel
Dovenbarger, Alice
Dovenbarger, Brad
Dunbar, Katie
Dyck, Carol
Dyck, Ken
Dyck, Kendi
Dyck, Vanessa
Edwards, Alica
Elias, Kirbylynn
Fasse, Eleanor

Summer Staff, 1994

Summer Staff, 1995

Fear, Pam
Feay, Bonnie
Feay, Dick
Fitzgerald, Ashley
Fitzgerald, Meghan
Flinchbaugh, Jamie
Freeouf, Luke
Gayman, Fred
Gayman, Shirley
Gibson, Ruth
Gill, John
Glad, Dorothy
Glad, Gil
Gosnell, Ivan
Gosnell, Levi
Gosnell, Marlys
Gosnell, Shane
Green, Matt
Habermas, Liz
Halfpenny, Joe
Harder, Daniel
Hasenauer, Erin
Hofer, Joshua
Jensen, Tyce
Jergensen, David
Johnson, Jason
Johnson, Jordan
Johnson, Justina
Johnson, Rosemary
Johnston, Jillian
Johnston, Susan
Jones, David
Kaiser, Bryce
Kaiser, Mitch
Kaiser, Zach
Karr, Rhea
Kautz, Jeff
Kautz, Tara
Kihlthau, Benjamin
Kihlthau, Dina
Kihlthau, Rod
Knott, Caleb
Kramer, Laura
Krehbiel, Tad
Kunnemann, Sam
Lorenz, Joshua
Lorenz, Rebekah
Maginn, Leslie
Malsbury, Joe
Marquardt, Sheila
Martin, Candace
Martin, Matthew
Masten, Anne
McCormick, Jonna

McDade, Jamie
McIntosh, Angela
McKinnon, Joanne
McLean, Jennifer
Merry, Dustin
Miller, Jan
Miller, Jim
Moog, Sue
Nguei, Veronica
Nickerson, Kyle
Niver, Emily
Nordin, Matthew
Olsen, Alice
Ondrejack, Diane
Ondrejack, Jane
Ondrejack, Joel
Ondrejack, Katie
Ondrejack, Mary
Ondrejack, Philip
Osler, Marilyn
Pacheco, Jackie
Paulus, Andy
Petersen, Nathaniel
Prohaska, Bonnie
Ravenscroft, Laura
Rodgers, Ruth Ann
Roesch, Beth
Roesch, Tim
Schlosser, Chandel
Schwindt, Shayla
Shambough, April
Shamburg, Erica
Slack, Sheila
Sprague, Kathy
Stohlman, Aren
Stryker, Abbie
Stryker, Jacob
Stryker, Jean
Stryker, Micah
Stryker, Tad
Stuart-Walker, Adam
Stucky, Bruce
Stucky, Esther
Stucky, Rachel
Sughroue, Katie
Swedberg, Brady
Swedberg, Brittni
Swedberg, Jeanne
Swesey, Mark
Tallman, Pauline
Thiessen, Braedon
Thiessen, Christian
Thiessen, Emily
Thiessen, Lelia

Thiessen, Rod
Tickle, Greg
Tickle, Linda
Townsend, Jessica
Townsend, Staci
Trammell, John
Turner, Angela
Van Mark, Jean
Van Mark, Jim
Vaquero, Jerrilyn
Vaquero, Santiago
Vaquero, Vanessa
Verner, Sharon
Walker, Esther
Walker, Hannah
Wall, Natalie
Wambolt, Evelyn
Wambolt, Hank
Warzeha, Craig
Weiderick, Danna
Weiderick, Karie
Weiderick, Katie
Weiderick, Mark
Wekesser, Bethany
Wekesser, Britney
Welch, Amber
Welch, Linda
Welsh, Kayla
Wheeler, Clint
Whistler, Christie
Whistler, James
Wilson, Jordan
Woodill, Sarah
Workman, Jennifer
Workman, Joshua

2001

Anderson, Jodi
Arnold, Bryce
Arnold, Daniel
Ashcraft, Andrew
Ashcraft, George
Ashcraft, Virginia
Atchison, Jesse
Baab, Emilee
Bagley, Evie
Bailey, Lee
Beetem, JoAnn
Berry, Amanda
Berry, Angela
Bratt, Karron
Brumm, Randy
Cheek, George

Cheek, Jan
Cheek, Kris
Cheek, Natalie
Cheek, Merle
Cheek, Stella
Christensen, Colleen
Christensen, Patrick
Clapper, John
Compo, Paul
Conour, Jessica
Conour, Laci
Crooks, Michele
Daeley, Justin
Davis, Ethne
Davis, Hosanna
Davis, Sophie
Davis, Toby
Dickinson, Amber
Dickinson, Amy
Dowenbarger, Alice
Driscoll, Hannah
Dyck, Carol
Dyck, Ken
Dyck, Kendi
Dyck, Vanessa
Fasse, Adrienne
Fasse, Eleanor
Feay, Bonnie
Feay, Dick
Fitch, Jeremy
Forrester, Renee
Forrester, Rod
Forrester, Rusty
Forrester, Ruth
Gayman, Fred
Gayman, Shirley
Geiger, Cynthia
Gibson, Ruth
Gill, John
Glover, Katie
Gosnell, Ivan
Gosnell, Levi
Gosnell, Marlys
Gosnell, Shane
Graham, Charles
Harkness, Lucretia
Hasenauer, Erin
Holscher, Joshua
Huebner, Becky
Huebner, David
Hunt, Joselyn
Johnson, Darlene
Johnson, Jason
Johnson, Jordan

Johnson, Justina
Jones, David
Kaiser, Bryce
Kaiser, Mitch
Kaiser, Zach
Kihlthau, Ben
Kihlthau, Dina
Kihlthau, Rod
King, Melissa
Klassen, Karl
Knott, Caleb
Knott, Tiffanie
Knox, Chris
Kramer, Laura
Krehbiel, Beth
Krehbiel, Tad
Kroeker, Tyler
Larkin, Melissa
Little, Graham
Lorenz, Joshua
Lorenz, Rebekah
Marshall, Miles
Masten, Anne
McCormick, Jonna
McDade, Jamie
McIntosh, Angela
Moog, Erika
Moog, Sue
Nickerson, Kyle
Niver, Emily
Norman, Janie
Okoye, Brian
Olsen, Alice
Ondrejack, Katie
Ostrander, Chris
Petersen, Nathaniel
Prohaska, Bonnie
Prosser, Wesley
Ravenscroft, Laura
Rivera, Tom
Rodgers, Ruth Ann
Roesch, Tim
Ruppert, Amy
Ruppert, Angel
Ruppert, Dustin
Ruppert, Mathew
Ruppert, Mikael
Schroeder, Kirsten
Schueman, Liz
Scott, Jana
Shamburg, Erica
Shamburg, Richard
Shearon, Lauren
Shouldice, Russ

Smith, Becky
Sprague, Kathy
Spresser, Kelsey
Stryker, Abby
Stryker, Jake
Stryker, Jean
Stryker, Micah
Stryker, Tad
Stuart-Walker, Adam
Stucky, Bruce
Stucky, Esther
Stucky, Rachel
Sughroue, Katie
Swedberg, Brady
Swesey, Mark
Tallman, Pauline
Teske, Forrest
Teske, Ross
Thiessen, Braedon
Thiessen, Christian
Thiessen, Emily
Thiessen, Lelia
Thiessen, Rod
Townsend, Heather
Townsend, Jenny
Townsend, Jessica
Townsend, Staci
Trosell, Rose
Van Mark, Jean
Van Mark, Jim
Vike, Jessie
Visser, Mandy
Walker, Esther
Walker, Hannah
Wall, Natalie
Wambolt, Evelyn
Wambolt, Hank
Ward, Jena
Wentworth, Maira
Willems, Jacob
Winn, Rebekah
Workman, Jennifer
Wyckoff, Cody
Yonnie, Jerilynn
Yonnie, Marie Lynn

2002

Anderson, Jodi
Arnold, Bryce
Asenov, Claire
Asenov, Pavel
Ashcraft, George
Ashcraft, Virginia

Summer Staff, 1998

Summer Staff, 1999

Avis, Natalie
Beard, Joseph
Beetem, JoAnn
Berry, Amanda
Berry, Angela
Bhikoo, Josh
Boorman, Mike
Boyle, Brian
Boyle, Megan
Bratt, Karron
Briscoe, Jessica
Brown, Journey
Butler, Brittany
Canfield, Danae
Castor, Faith
Castor, Jake
Cheek, George
Cheek, Jan
Cheek, Kris
Cheek, Merle
Cheek, Natalie
Cheek, Stella
Childs, LylaJo
Christensen, Colleen
Christensen, Patrick
Cockson, Andrew
Cockson, Carla
Cockson, Daniel
Cockson, David
Cockson, Paul
Cockson, Scot
Conour, Jessica
Conour, Laci
Cook, Tara
Cromer, Brenda
Cromer, Gabriella
Cromer, Madeline
Cromer, Ray
Crooks, Michele
Curtis, Dustin
Davis, Ethne
Davis, Sophie
Davis, Toby
Davis, Zanna
Dechtiarenko, Joe
Dyck, Carol
Dyck, Kendi
Dyck, Vanessa
Fasse, Eleanor
Feay, Bonnie
Feay, Dick
Fitch, Jeremy
Forrester, Rod
Friesen, Brett

Garton, Joe
Gayman, Shirley
Geist, Alexis
Geist, Derek
Geist, John Mark
Geist, Mark
Geist, Suzanne
Gentile, Andrew
Gibson, Ruth
Gosnell, Ivan
Gosnell, Jonie
Gosnell, Levi
Gosnell, Marlys
Gosnell, Shane
Griffiths, Frank
Groseth, Brett
Grubb, Lee
Gutherless, Russell
Harder, Daniel
Harkness, Ben
Hasenauer, Becky
Hasenauer, Erin
Henslee, Austin
Huebner, Becky
Hunter, Chris
Janssen, Matt
Janssen, Sara
Jersak, Erin
Johnson, Darlene
Johnson, Jordan
Johnson, Justina
Johnson, Remmington
Jones, David
Kaiser, Mitch
Kaiser, Zach
Kautz, Tara
Kenny, Joe
Kihlthau, Ben
Kihlthau, Dina
Kihlthau, Rod
Knott, Caleb
Koop, Kristi
Kramer, Laura
Krehbiel, Annie
Krehbiel, Tad
Kroeker, Tyler
Laboso, Mary
Laboso, Winnie
Larsen, Abby
Leibhart, Melissa
Lorenz, Rebekah
Luecke, Jason
Lyon, Savannah
Mai, Jessica

Mares, Courtney
Martinson, Robert
Mayo, Kristin
Mayo, Paul
McCormick, Jonna
McDade, Jamie
McIntosh, Angela
Meyer, Amber
Meyer, Ashley
Miller, Stephen
Moog, Erika
Moog, Sue
Most, Levi
Nelson, Bethany
Nickerson, Kyle
Nielson, Hannah
Okoye, Amanda
Okoye, Brian
Okoye, Cynthia
Olsen, Alice
Petersen, David
Petersen, Nathaniel
Prentice, Jennifer
Prohaska, Adam
Prohaska, Amanda
Prohaska, Bonnie
Prohaska, Ron
Purcell, David
Quaney, Amy
Quaney, Lindy
Ragan, Jacob
Ravenscroft, Laura
Rodgers, Ruth Ann
Roesch, Tim
Rosane, Nate
Rundback, Brad
Schmidt, Jacob
Schmitt, LeAnne
Serlet, Danielle
Serlet, Rachelle
Shamburg, Erica
Shamburg, Richard
Shearer, Karli
Shouldice, Russ
Slack, Amy
Smith, Becky
Smith, Naomi
Sprague, Kathy
Steele, Todd
Street, Sydney
Stryker, Abby
Stryker, Jake
Stryker, Jean
Stryker, Micah

Stryker, Tad
Stuart-Walker, Adam
Stucky, Bruce
Stucky, Esther
Stucky, Rachel
Swedberg, Brady
Swesey, Mark
Tallman, Pauline
Terpsma, Ryan
Teters, Carey
Teters, Jeff
Thaxton, Nikki
Thiessen, Braedon
Thiessen, Christian
Thiessen, Emily
Thiessen, Leila
Thiessen, Rodney
Throssell, Rose
Tickle, Andy
Tickle, Linda
Turnbull, Chelsea
Van Mark, Jean
Van Mark, Jim
Vogt, Robert
Vohs, Saige
Walker, Abbie
Walker, Esther
Walker, Hannah
Wambolt, Evelyn
Wambolt, Hank
Wamsley, Justine
Watson, Seth
Welch, Amber
Welch, Eric
Wentworth, Maira
Willems, Jacob
Winn, Michaela
Winn, Rebekah
Wyckoff, Cody

2003

Anderson, Kacy
Ashcraft, Jack
Ashcraft, Virginia
Beetem, JoAnn
Berry, Angela
Boldt, Kevin
Boldt, Tracy
Boldt, Daniel
Boldt, Micah
Boyle, Brian
Castor, Faith
Castor, Jake

Cheek, George
Cheek, Jan
Cheek, Kris
Cheek, Merle
Cheek, Natalie
Cheek, Stella
Cockson, Andrew
Cockson, Carla
Cockson, Daniel
Cockson, David
Cockson, Paul
Cockson, Scot
Davis, Tobias
Driscoll, Hannah
Driscoll, Tabitha
Dyck, Carol
Dyck, Kendi
Dyck, Vanessa
Fasse, Eleanor
Feay, Bonnie
Feay, Dick
Frudd, Shannon
Gagnon, Ashley
Geist, Alexis
Geist, Derek
Geist, John Mark
Geist, Mark
Geist, Suzanne
Gentile, Andrew
Gosnell, Ivan
Gosnell, Levi
Gosnell, Marlys
Gosnell, Shane
Harder, Daniel
Harris, Steven
Hartung, Jodi
Hasenauer, Erin
Herrick, Chelsea
Hunt, Joselyn
Janssen, Matt
Janssen, Sara
Jersak, Erin
Jones, David
Kihlthau, Benjamin
Kihlthau, Dina
Kihlthau, Rod
Knott, Tiffanie
Kramer, Laura
Leibhart, Melissa
Lorenz, Josh
Lorenz, Rebekah
Mace, Esther
Martinson, Robert
McRae, James

McRae, Daphne
McRae, Natalie Jean
McRae, Kieran
McRae, Vanessa
Miller, Jacqulyn
Miller, Shane
Okoye, Amanda
Okoye, Brian
Olney, Kristen
Olsen, Alice
Phelps, Josh
Prohaska, Adam
Prohaska, Amanda
Prohaska, Bonnie
Prohaska, Ron
Ravenscroft, Laura
Reynders, Jen
Robinson, LaKira
Rodgers, Ruth Ann
Roesch, Tim
Shouldice, Russ
Shumake, Nathaniel
Sprague, Kathy
Sprague, Roger
Stryker, Abigail
Stryker, Jake
Stryker, Jean
Stryker, Micah
Stryker, Tad
Stuart-Walker, Adam
Stucky, Bruce
Stucky, Esther
Stucky, Rachel
Swesey, Mark
Tallman, Pauline
Thiessen, Braedon
Thiessen, Emily
Thiessen, Christian
Thiessen, Leila
Thiessen, Rodney
Throssell, Rose
Turbull, Briana
Vohs, Saige
Walker, Esther
Walker, Hannah
Wambolt, Evelyn
Wambolt, Hank
Whistler, Christine
Whistler, James
Willems, Jake
Wilson, Brandon
Wolf, Chris

Summer Staff, 2002

Fulltime Staff, 2004

Bill Summers Ford Sees Camp as Vital

Bill & Kathy Summers have seen the benefits of Maranatha Bible Camp in their own family. Their grandson, Zack, enjoyed his week at summer camp tremendously, and his parents saw a big change in his attitude. "The spiritual development that took place in his life after just one week of camp is what means the most to me … and what kind of price tag are you going to put on that?" says Bill. "Maranatha is one of the best investments you could ever make in a kid." The Summers family became enthusiastic supporters of Maranatha, and their involvement is ongoing.

Since Bill & Kathy bought the dealership in 1998, it has become well-known for its honesty, integrity, knowledgeable sales staff and excellent service after the sale. They see their business as part of the community, and take pride in earning repeat business from customers.

North Platte north lot,
12th & Jeffers,
Phone: 308-696-1888

North Platte south lot,
I-80 & Highway 83,
Phone: 308-532-2500

Ogalla lot,
602 W. 1st St.,
Phone: 308-284-2001

BILL FORD SUMMERS

"Where Quality and Integrity Shine Through"

KJLT Radio – A Story of God's Providence

KJLT's beautiful studio building was dedicated on March 5, 1977. KJLT-FM was started in 1990 with 100,000 wats of power 24 hours per day. The listeners have been thrilled with the beautiful music and teaching broadcasts. KJLT-AM airs more teaching programs and a more conservative music style, while the FM station features contemporary music and some Bible teaching programs. Both stations are non-commercial, supported by its listeners.

What is now KJLT began because of the vision and dream of primarily one man – Mr. John G. Townsend, who operated an electronics firm in Sutherland, Nebraska, for several years. After he found Christ as his Savior in 1945, God laid on his heart a desire to reach his fellow men with the good news of salvation. Then came the idea of Christian radio. After much research, planning and prayer, he began broadcasting on December 26, 1952, from a studio/transmitter building located just west of North Platte on U.S. Highway 30. It was a 1,000-watt commercial station known as KNBR.

In 1955, the decision was made to form a non-profit religious corporation and change the method of support. Mr. Townsend decided to transfer the license and the assets of the station to the corporation as a gift. Instead of selling advertising as a means of revenue, the need was taken directly to God's people. At that time, the station started promoting Maranatha Bible Camp on the air, a tradition that continues to this day.

On July 1, 1957, the call letters were changed to KJLT and the power increased to 5,000 watts. Now KJLT can be heard in western Nebraska, northeast Colorado and northwest Kansas. In 1990, KJLT added a non-commercial FM station and started broadcasting 24 hours a day.

Through more than 50 years of operation, God has supplied the needs through His people who believe in and are being blessed by Christian radio. We thank God for the many friends who continually give to help spread the message of hope in Christ for a hopeless world.

TierOne Bank Has Been a Fixture in the Region

Historically, the connection between Maranatha Bible Camp and TierOne Bank goes back to the days when the North Platte financial institution was know as McDonald State Bank and located at 5th & Dewey Streets. The bank, later known as United Nebraska Bank, was acquired by Nebraska-based TierOne Bank in 2004 and is the oldest continuously-operating business in North Platte.

McDonald State Bank was founded in 1878 by Charles McDonald, a pioneer who traveled by steamboat from Chattanooga, Tennessee, to Richardson County, Nebraska, in 1855. McDonald served in the second and third Nebraska Territorial Legislatures.

From there, he moved west and in 1860, purchased the Cottonwood Springs Ranch and Trading Post before the start of the Civil War. The ranch was the site of the best source of fresh water in the area, and soon (in 1863) a U.S. Army base, Fort McPherson, was located near there. William F. "Buffalo Bill" Cody was a frequent visitor at McDonald's ranch. Eventually, the permanent site of Maranatha Bible Camp would be established just a few miles from the ranch.

Charles McDonald's son, W.H. McDonald, succeeded his father as bank president in 1919 and did business with Maranatha's founder, Rev. Ivan E. Olsen.

In 1990, the bank moved to its current location at 111 S. Dewey St., where it continues to serve Maranatha Bible Camp's banking needs into the 21st century.

The current TierOne Bank building was constructed in 1990.

Left: For years, Bible Supplies was located at 317 N. Dewey Street, then moved a few doors north to 309 N. Dewey in the mid-1980s. Below: In 1995, the busines moved to the Westfield Shopping Center at 1923 West A Street.

Bible Supplies Owners Have Maranatha Ties

Bible Supplies, a non-denominational Christian bookstore in North Platte, started in 1949 as a small literature room in the basement of the Berean Fundamental Church. It moved to a store of its own in the 800 block of North Jeffers Street, where it stayed for many years, until it moved downtown to the 300 block of North Dewey. Since the beginning, Bible Supplies has stocked Bibles, Sunday school literature, educational resources and Christian books. It has expanded into many other lines of merchandise, including Christian greeting cards and music, family videos, t-shirts and novelty items. They serve churches throughout western and central Nebraska, and their customers represent many different religious denominations.

Craig & Nancy Fabik started managing Bible Supplies in 1986 and bought the business in 1990. They view their business as a ministry, providing a warm heart and a listening ear to those who have questions, concerns or heartaches. Craig & Nancy are former Summer Missionaries at Maranatha, having been on staff in 1986. They spent that summer running the Gift Shop and Sweet Shop, and still volunteer in the Sweet Shop during the summer.

Space was at a premium inside the store at 309 N. Dewey Street.

Scrappin' With Style

Unique North Platte Business Has Family Ties to Camp

Rosemary Johnson, the owner of Scrappin' With Style in North Plate, has been involved with Maranatha Bible Camp all her life. In fact, three generations of her family have experienced Maranatha, both as campers and as workers. Rosemary was instrumental in launching the Making Memories Scrapbooking Retreat at Maranatha, and loves to promote and support this event.

Scrappin' With Style, located in the Red Roof Plaza near North Platte I-80 exit #177, has a well-stocked work area and is a favorite gathering place for scrapping and rubber stamping enthusiasts in west central Nebraska.

Since it was established in April 2000, the business has expanded enough to force a move from its original downtown location to more spacious quarters in the Red Roof Plaza. Rosemary and her family are praising God for blessing their business beyond imagination!

Now to him who is able to do immeasurably more than all we ask or imagine, according to his power that is at work within us, to him be the glory!
Ephesians 3:20-21a

Scrappin' With Style has a wide variety of supplies and a spacious work area, including many tables for patrons to work on projects during its business hours.

See us online at www.scrappinwithstyle.net or call us at 308-534-6867

T.C. Engineering Helps Maranatha Prepare for Future

Maranatha Bible Camp began to develop its master site plan in the late 1980s, and T.C. Engineering, owned by Tom and Sandee Werblow of North Platte, has partnered with Maranatha to help make that plan a reality. Maranatha has benefited from the solid advice and excellent workmanship provided by Tom and his staff.

T.C. ENGINEERING'S HISTORY WITH CAMP

Year	Project
2001	Contact with Lincoln County for impact of new 3" water line along County Road.
2000	Analysis of foundation and hiring of pile driver for Cheek "tree" house.
1998	Electric service for new cabins/flood elevations.
1997	Re-organization of camp into Maranatha Bible Camp and Maranatha Foundation.
	Segregation of water systems to lessen regulatory demands.
	Contact with Lincoln County for flood impact of new 4-plex cabins.
1996	Analysis of flood near Dining Hall and impact on lake.
	Setting of flood plain elevations with Lincoln County.
1995	Review of Long Range Plan for Facilities Development including Conference Center.
	Lengthy submittal of flood plain elevations to Lincoln County and State.
1994	Initial review of flood plain elevations for Camp.
1993	Inquiry from camp about enzymes and grease traps for kitchen.
1992	Review of Soil Investigation for new gymnasium.
1991	General drawings of Camp produced including edge of lake for determining road location.
1989	Assist with well registrations to protect water rights for Camp.
1988	Arrange ground control and flight over Camp for contour elevations.
1987	Submittal of motel information to State for review and approval.
	Review of property boundarys and assist negotiating lines with neighbors.

CHEEK HOUSE PILING LAYOUT & LOADS

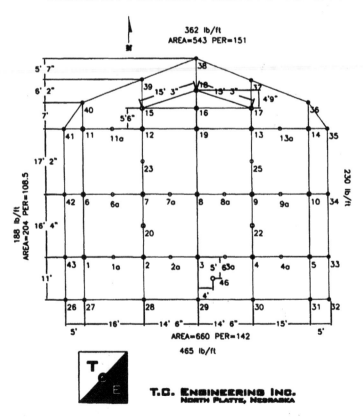

NATIVE AMERICAN INTERPRETATIONS

See Karen's work online at
www.nativeinterpretations.com

'Maranatha Camp'
by Karen Kramer

A cross glows near the highway
Portal of a byway.

Refuge from life's worldly trials
Haven of peace and friendly smiles.
Heart of faith through open door.
Sanctuary … with Christ, our Lord.

In laughing spirit with friends we love
On wooded path with our Lord above.
At one with nature, removed from strife
to find the genuine reason … for life.

For at Maranatha … we can open a door
and say … yes … to Christ, forevermore.
And if we listen – while alone we trod …

His whisper …
Be still –
and know …
I am God.

© Karen Kramer 2004

Artist Enjoyed Warrior Leadership Summit Involvement

Though I an a relative newcomer to the Camp, I have enjoyed the time spent there. The family and friends open roller skating has been so enjoyable and the Fourth of July celebration is just a wonderful experience for all who attend. Seeing Pastor Walker coming down the waterslide "feet to heaven" gave everyone a laugh, and as an artist, I got such a kick out of working the Sweet Shop. If you ask Jean Stryker, she will attest to my "modern art" asymmetrical ice cream cones.

I was honored to be invited by George Cheek to attend Warrior Leadership Summit – a great experience, as that is the core of my artistic vision. The hunting weekend at Camp gave me opportunity to use a part of my art for the greater good. A specialty painting, "Partners," was created and reproduced on canvas print for the benefit of Maranatha Camp's scholarship fund. This was accompanied by a framed piece of my original poetry, "Partners," which exemplified the print. Maranatha Camp has something for everyone – and an open door to Christ.

– Karen Kramer

ORIGINAL PAINTINGS • PRINTS FROM ORIGINALS • HANDCRAFTED JEWELRY & HANDBAGS
ORIGINAL-DESIGN LOGO T-SHIRTS AND CAPS

To contact the artist about current paintings, or for other inquiries, call 308-534-3523.

Top row, from left: The panoramic view from the top of Sioux Lookout was a great place for Bible devotional talks; A bus load of campers is ready to head home.

Second row, from left: The old cellar behind the kitchen along with a slab cabin in the background before the lake; Solid discipleship teaching was at the heart of the Navigator program.

Third row, from left: This slab cabin is well-worn after years of use; This vintage truck was a familiar sight around Camp in it's day; An early dormitory, this building is now renovated as Clark Hall.

9 781681 625850